50 Algorithms Every Programmer Should Know

Second Edition

Tackle computer science challenges with classic to modern algorithms in machine learning, software design, data systems, and cryptography

Imran Ahmad, PhD

<packt>

BIRMINGHAM—MUMBAI

50 Algorithms Every Programmer Should Know

Second Edition

Copyright © 2023 Packt Publishing

Senior Publishing Product Manager: Denim Pinto

Acquisition Editor – Peer Reviews: Tejas Mhasvekar

Project Editor: Rianna Rodrigues

Content Development Editors: Rebecca Robinson and Matthew Davies

Copy Editor: SafisE diting

Technical Editor: Karan Sonawane

Proofreader: SafisE diting

Indexer: Pratik Shirodkar

Presentation Designer: Rajesh Shirsath

Developer Relations Marketing Executive: Vipanshu Parashar

First published: June 2020

Second edition: September 2023

Production reference: 2191023

Published by Packt Publishing Ltd.

Grosvenor House

11 St Paul's Square

Birmingham

B3 1RB, UK.

ISBN 978-1-83702-583-1

www.packt.com

Foreword

In 2014, I enthusiastically embraced my new role as a data scientist, despite having a Ph.D in economics. Some might see this as a stark shift, but to me, it was a natural progression. However, traditional views of economics might suggest that econometricians and data scientists are on separate tracks.

At the outset of my data science adventure, I waded through a sea of online materials. The sheer volume made pinpointing the right resources akin to finding a diamond in the rough. Too often, content lacked practical insights relevant to my position, causing occasional bouts of disillusionment.

One beacon of clarity in my journey was my senior colleague, Imran. His consistent guidance and mentorship were transformative. He pointed me to resources that elevated my understanding, always generously sharing his deep knowledge. He had a gift for making complex topics understandable.

Beyond his expertise as a data scientist, Imran stands out as a visionary, leader, and adept engineer. He thrives on identifying innovative solutions, especially when faced with adversity. Challenges seem to invigorate him. With natural leadership ability, he navigates intricate projects with ease. His remarkable contributions to AI and machine learning are commendable. What's more, his talent for connecting with audiences, often laced with humor, sets him apart.

This expertise shines brightly in *50 Algorithms Every Programmer Should Know*. The book goes beyond listing algorithms; it reflects Imran's ability to make intricate subjects relatable. Real-life applications range from predicting the weather to building movie recommendation engines.

The book stands out for its holistic approach to algorithms—not just the methodology but the reasoning behind them. It's a treasure trove for those who champion responsible AI, emphasizing the importance of data transparency and bias awareness.

50 Algorithms Every Programmer Should Know is a must-have in a data scientist's arsenal. If you're venturing into data science or aiming to enhance your skill set, this book is a solid stepping stone.

Somaieh Nikpoor, PhD
Lead – Data Science and AI, Government of Canada.
Adjunct Professor, Sprott School of Business, Carleton University

Contributors

About the author

Imran Ahmad, PhD currently lends his expertise as a data scientist for the **Advanced Analytics Solution Center (A2SC)** within the Canadian Federal Government, where he harnesses machine learning algorithms for mission-critical applications.

In his 2010 doctoral thesis, he introduced a linear programming-based algorithm tailored for optimal resource assignment in expansive cloud computing landscapes. Later, in 2017, Dr. Ahmad pioneered the development of a real-time analytics framework, StreamSensing. This tool has become the cornerstone of several of his research papers, leveraging it to process multimedia data within various machine learning paradigms.

Outside of his governmental role, Dr. Ahmad holds a visiting professorship at Carleton University in Ottawa. Over the past several years, he has been also recognized as an authorized instructor for both Google Cloud and AWS.

I'm deeply grateful to my wife, Naheed, my son, Omar, and my daughter, Anum, for their unwavering support. A special nod to my parents, notably my father, Inayatuallah, for his relentless encouragement to continue learning. Further appreciation goes to Karan Sonawane, Rianna Rodrigues, and Denim from Packt for their invaluable contributions.

About the reviewers

Aishwarya Srinivasan previously worked as a data scientist on the Google Cloud AI Services team where she worked to build machine learning solutions for customer use cases. She holds a post-graduate degree in data science from Columbia University and has over 450,000 followers on LinkedIn. She was spotlighted as a *LinkedIn Top Voice for data science influencers (2020)* and has been recognized as a *Women in AI Trailblazer* of the Year.

Tarek Ziadé is a programmer based in Burgundy, France. He has worked at several major software companies, including Mozilla and Elastic, where he has built web services and tools for developers. Tarek founded the French Python user group, *Afpy*, and has written several best-selling books about Python and web services.

I would like to thank my family: Freya, Suki, Milo, Amina, and Martine. They have always supported me.

Brian Spiering started his coding career in his elementary school computer lab, hacking BASIC to make programs that entertained his peers and annoyed authority figures. Much later, Brian earned a PhD in cognitive psychology from the University of California, Santa Barbara. Brian currently teaches programming and artificial intelligence.

Learn more on Discord

To join the Discord community for this book – where you can share feedback, ask questions to the author, and learn about new releases – follow the QR code below:

https://packt.link/WHLel

Table of Contents

Section II: Machine Learning Algorithms 141

Chapter 6: Unsupervised Machine Learning Algorithms 143

Chapter 10: Understanding Sequential Models   311

Preface

In the realm of computing, from foundational theories to hands-on applications, algorithms are the driving force. In this updated edition, we delve even further into the dynamic world of algorithms, broadening our scope to tackle pressing, real-world issues. Starting with the rudiments of algorithms, we journey through a myriad of design techniques, leading to intricate areas like linear programming, page ranking, graphs, and a more profound exploration of machine learning. To ensure we're at the forefront of technological advancements, we've incorporated substantial discussions on sequential networks, LLMs, LSTM, GRUs, and now, cryptography and the deployment of large-scale algorithms in cloud computing environments.

The significance of algorithms in recommendation systems, a pivotal element in today's digital age, is also meticulously detailed. To effectively wield these algorithms, understanding their underlying math and logic is paramount. Our hands-on case studies, ranging from weather forecasts and tweet analyses to film recommendations and delving into the nuances of LLMs, exemplify their practical applications.

Equipped with the insights from this book, our goal is to bolster your confidence in deploying algorithms to tackle modern computational challenges. Step into this expanded journey of deciphering and leveraging algorithms in today's evolving digital landscape.

Who this book is for

If you're a programmer or developer keen on harnessing algorithms to solve problems and craft efficient code, this book is for you. From classic, widely-used algorithms to the latest in data science, machine learning, and cryptography, this guide covers a comprehensive spectrum. While familiarity with Python programming is beneficial, it's not mandatory.

A foundation in any programming language will serve you well. Moreover, even if you're not a programmer but have some technical inclination, you'll gain insights into the expansive world of problem-solving algorithms from this book.

What this book covers

Section 1: Fundamentals and Core Algorithms

Chapter 1, Overview of Algorithms, provides insight into the fundamentals of algorithms. It starts with the basic concepts of algorithms, how people started using algorithms to formulate problems, and the limitations of different algorithms. As Python is used in this book to write the algorithms, how to set up a Python environment to run the examples is explained. We will then look at how an algorithm's performance can be quantified and compared against other algorithms.

Chapter 2, Data Structures Used in Algorithms, discusses data structures in the context of algorithms. As we are using Python in this book, this chapter focuses on Python data structures, but the concepts presented can be used in other languages such as Java and C++. This chapter will show you how Python handles complex data structures and which structures should be used for certain types of data.

Chapter 3, Sorting and Searching Algorithms, starts by presenting different types of sorting algorithms and various approaches for designing them. Then, following practical examples, searching algorithms are also discussed.

Chapter 4, Designing Algorithms, covers the choices available to us when designing algorithms, discussing the importance of characterizing the problem that we are trying to solve. Next, it uses the famous **Traveling Salesperson Problem (TSP)** as a use case and applies the design techniques that we will be presenting. It also introduces linear programming and discusses its applications.

Chapter 5, Graph Algorithms, covers the ways we can capture graphs to represent data structures. It covers some foundational theories, techniques, and methods relating to graph algorithms, such as network theory analysis and graph traversals. We will investigate a case study using graph algorithms to delve into fraud analytics.

Section 2: Machine Learning Algorithms

Chapter 6, Unsupervised Machine Learning Algorithms, explains how unsupervised learning can be applied to real-world problems. We will learn about its basic algorithms and methodologies, such as clustering algorithms, dimensionality reduction, and association rule mining.

Chapter 7, Traditional Supervised Learning Algorithms, delves into the essentials of supervised machine learning, featuring classifiers and regressors. We will explore their capabilities using real-world problems as case studies. Six distinct classification algorithms are presented, followed by three regression techniques. Lastly, we'll compare their results to encapsulate the key takeaways from this discussion.

Chapter 8, Neural Network Algorithms, introduces the main concepts and components of a typical neural network. It then presents the various types of neural networks and the activation functions used in them. The backpropagation algorithm is discussed in detail, which is the most widely used algorithm for training a neural network. Finally, we will learn how to use deep learning to flag fraudulent documents by way of a real-world example application.

Chapter 9, Algorithms for Natural Language Processing, introduces algorithms for **natural language processing (NLP)**. It introduces the fundamentals of NLP and how to prepare data for NLP tasks. After that, it explains the concepts of vectorizing textual data and word embeddings. Finally, we present a detailed use case.

Chapter 10, Understanding Sequential Models, looks into training neural networks for sequential data. It covers the core principles of sequential models, providing an introductory overview of their techniques and methodologies. It will then consider how deep learning can improve NLP techniques.

Chapter 11, Advanced Sequential Modeling Algorithms, considers the limitations of sequential models and how sequential modeling has evolved to overcome these limitations. It delves deeper into the advanced aspects of sequential models to understand the creation of complex configurations. It starts by breaking down key elements, such as autoencoders and **Sequence-to-Sequence (Seq2Seq)** models. Next, it looks into attention mechanism and transformers, which are pivotal in the development of **Large Language Models (LLMs)**, which we will then study.

Section 3: Advanced Topics

Chapter 12, Recommendation Engines, covers the main types of recommendation engines and the inner workings of each. These systems are adept at suggesting tailored items or products to users, but they're not without their challenges. We'll discuss both their strengths and the limitations they present. Finally, we will learn how to use recommendation engines to solve a real-world problem.

Chapter 13, Algorithmic Strategies for Data Handling, introduces data algorithms and the basic concepts behind the classification of data. We will look at the data storage and data compression algorithms used to efficiently manage data, helping us to understand the trade-offs involved in designing and implementing data-centric algorithms.

Chapter 14, Cryptography, introduces you to algorithms related to cryptography. We will start by presenting the background of cryptography before discussing symmetric encryption algorithms. We will learn about the **Message-Digest 5 (MD5)** algorithm and the **Secure Hash Algorithm (SHA)**, presenting the limitations and weaknesses of each. Then, we will discuss asymmetric encryption algorithms and how they are used to create digital certificates. Finally, we will present a practical example that summarizes all of these techniques.

Chapter 15, Large-Scale Algorithms, starts by introducing large-scale algorithms and the efficient infrastructure required to support them. We will explore various strategies for managing multi-resource processing. We will examine the limitations of parallel processing, as outlined by Amdahl's law, and investigate the use of **Graphics Processing Units (GPUs)**. Upon completing this chapter, you will have gained a solid foundation in the fundamental strategies essential for designing large-scale algorithms.

Chapter 16, Practical Considerations, presents the issues around the explainability of an algorithm, which is the degree to which the internal mechanics of an algorithm can be explained in understandable terms. Then, we will present the ethics of using an algorithm and the possibility of creating biases when implementing them. Next, the techniques for handling NP-hard problems will be discussed. Finally, we will investigate factors that should be considered before choosing an algorithm.

Download the example code files

The code bundle for the book is also hosted on GitHub at `https://github.com/cloudanum/50Algorithms`. We also have other code bundles from our rich catalog of books and videos available at `https://github.com/PacktPublishing/`. Check them out! You can also find the same code bundle on Google Drive at `http://code.50algo.com`.

Download the color images

We also provide a PDF file that has color images of the screenshots and diagrams used in this book. You can download it here: https://packt.link/UBw6g.

Conventions used

There are a number of text conventions used throughout this book.

`Code in text`: Indicates code words in text, database table names, folder names, filenames, file extensions, pathnames and dummy URLs. Here is an example: "Let's try to create a simple graph using the `networtx` package in Python."

Bold: Indicates a new term, an important word, or words that you see onscreen. For example, new terms appear in text like this: "Python is also one of the languages that you can use in various cloud computing infrastructures, such as **Amazon Web Services (AWS)** and **Google Cloud Platform (GCP)**."

> Warnings or important notes appear like this.

> Tips and tricks appear like this

Get in touch

Feedback from our readers is always welcome.

General feedback: Email feedback@packtpub.com and mention the book's title in the subject of your message. If you have questions about any aspect of this book, please email us at questions@packtpub.com.

Errata: Although we have taken every care to ensure the accuracy of our content, mistakes do happen. If you have found a mistake in this book, we would be grateful if you reported this to us. Please visit http://www.packtpub.com/submit-errata, click **Submit Errata**, and fill in the form.

Piracy: If you come across any illegal copies of our works in any form on the internet, we would be grateful if you would provide us with the location address or website name. Please contact us at copyright@packtpub.com with a link to the material.

If you are interested in becoming an author: If there is a topic that you have expertise in and you are interested in either writing or contributing to a book, please visit http://authors.packtpub.com.

Share your thoughts

Once you've read *50 Algorithms Every Programmer Should Know - Second Edition*, we'd love to hear your thoughts! Scan the QR code below to go straight to the Amazon review page for this book and share your feedback.

https://packt.link/r/1803247762

Your review is important to us and the tech community and will help us make sure we're delivering excellent quality content.

Download a free PDF copy of this book

Thanks for purchasing this book!

Do you like to read on the go but are unable to carry your print books everywhere? Is your eBook purchase not compatible with the device of your choice?

Don't worry, now with every Packt book you get a DRM-free PDF version of that book at no cost.

Read anywhere, any place, on any device. Search, copy, and paste code from your favorite technical books directly into your application.

The perks don't stop there, you can get exclusive access to discounts, newsletters, and great free content in your inbox daily

Follow these simple steps to get the benefits:

1. Scan the QR code or visit the link below

https://packt.link/free-ebook/9781803247762

2. Submit your proof of purchase
3. That's it! We'll send your free PDF and other benefits to your email directly

Section 1

Fundamentals and Core Algorithms

This section introduces the core aspects of algorithms. We will explore what an algorithm is and how to design one. We will also learn about the data structures used in algorithms. This section also introduces sorting and searching algorithms along with algorithms to solve graphical problems. The chapters included in this section are:

- *Chapter 1, Overview of Algorithms*
- *Chapter 2, Data Structures Used in Algorithms*
- *Chapter 3, Sorting and Searching Algorithms*
- *Chapter 4, Designing Algorithms*
- *Chapter 5, Graph Algorithms*

1

Overview of Algorithms

An algorithm must be seen to be believed.

– Donald Knuth

This book covers the information needed to understand, classify, select, and implement important algorithms. In addition to explaining their logic, this book also discusses data structures, development environments, and production environments that are suitable for different classes of algorithms. This is the second edition of this book. In this edition, we especially focus on modern machine learning algorithms that are becoming more and more important. Along with the logic, practical examples of the use of algorithms to solve actual everyday problems are also presented.

This chapter provides an insight into the fundamentals of algorithms. It starts with a section on the basic concepts needed to understand the workings of different algorithms. To provide a historical perspective, this section summarizes how people started using algorithms to mathematically formulate a certain class of problems. It also mentions the limitations of different algorithms. The next section explains the various ways to specify the logic of an algorithm. As Python is used in this book to write the algorithms, how to set up a Python environment to run the examples is explained. Then, the various ways that an algorithm's performance can be quantified and compared against other algorithms are discussed. Finally, this chapter discusses various ways a particular implementation of an algorithm can be validated.

To sum up, this chapter covers the following main points:

- What is an algorithm?
- The phases of an algorithm
- Development environment
- Algorithm design techniques
- Performance analysis
- Validating an algorithm

What is an algorithm?

In the simplest terms, an algorithm is a set of rules for carrying out some calculations to solve a problem. It is designed to yield results for any valid input according to precisely defined instructions. If you look up the word algorithm in a dictionary (such as American Heritage), it defines the concept as follows:

> *An algorithm is a finite set of unambiguous instructions that, given some set of initial conditions, can be performed in a prescribed sequence to achieve a certain goal and that has a recognizable set of end conditions.*

Designing an algorithm is an effort to create a mathematical recipe in the most efficient way that can effectively be used to solve a real-world problem. This recipe may be used as the basis for developing a more reusable and generic mathematical solution that can be applied to a wider set of similar problems.

The phases of an algorithm

The different phases of developing, deploying, and finally, using an algorithm are illustrated in *Figure 1.1*:

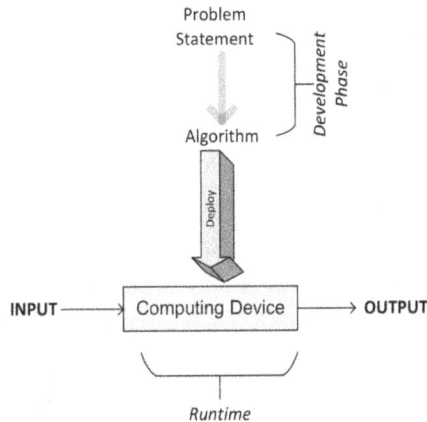

Figure 1.1: The different phases of developing, deploying, and using an algorithm

As we can see, the process starts with understanding the requirements from the problem statement that details what needs to be done. Once the problem is clearly stated, it leads us to the development phase.

The development phase consists of two phases:

1. **The design phase:** In the design phase, the architecture, logic, and implementation details of the algorithm are envisioned and documented. While designing an algorithm, we keep both accuracy and performance in mind. While searching for the best solution to a given problem, in many cases, we will end up having more than one candidate algorithm. The design phase of an algorithm is an iterative process that involves comparing different candidate algorithms. Some algorithms may provide simple and fast solutions but may compromise accuracy. Other algorithms may be very accurate but may take considerable time to run due to their complexity. Some of these complex algorithms may be more efficient than others. Before making a choice, all the inherent tradeoffs of the candidate algorithms should be carefully studied. Particularly for a complex problem, designing an efficient algorithm is important. A correctly designed algorithm will result in an efficient solution that will be capable of providing both satisfactory performance and reasonable accuracy at the same time.

2.   **The coding phase:** In the coding phase, the designed algorithm is converted into a computer program. It is important that the computer program implements all the logic and architecture suggested in the design phase.

The requirements of the business problem can be divided into functional and non-functional requirements. The requirements that directly specify the expected features of the solutions are called the functional requirements. Functional requirements detail the expected behavior of the solution. On the other hand, the non-functional requirements are about the performance, scalability, usability, and accuracy of the algorithm. Non-functional requirements also establish the expectations about the security of the data. For example, let us consider that we are required to design an algorithm for a credit card company that can identify and flag fraudulent transactions. Function requirements in this example will specify the expected behavior of a valid solution by providing the details of the expected output given a certain set of input data. In this case, the input data may be the details of the transaction, and the output may be a binary flag that labels a transaction as fraudulent or non-fraudulent. In this example, the non-functional requirements may specify the response time of each of the predictions. Non-functional requirements will also set the allowable thresholds for accuracy. As we are dealing with financial data in this example, the security requirements related to user authentication, authorization, and data confidentiality are also expected to be part of non-functional requirements.

Note that functional and non-functional requirements aim to precisely define *what* needs to be done. Designing the solution is about figuring out *how* it will be done. And implementing the design is developing the actual solution in the programming language of your choice. Coming up with a design that fully meets both functional and non-functional requirements may take lots of time and effort. The choice of the right programming language and development/production environment may depend on the requirements of the problem. For example, as C/C++ is a lower-level language than Python, it may be a better choice for algorithms needing compiled code and lower-level optimization.

Once the design phase is completed and the coding is complete, the algorithm is ready to be deployed. Deploying an algorithm involves the design of the actual production environment in which the code will run. The production environment needs to be designed according to the data and processing needs of the algorithm. For example, for parallelizable algorithms, a cluster with an appropriate number of computer nodes will be needed for the efficient execution of the algorithm. For data-intensive algorithms, a data ingress pipeline and the strategy to cache and store data may need to be designed. Designing a production environment is discussed in more detail in *Chapter 15, Large-Scale Algorithms*, and *Chapter 16, Practical Considerations*.

Once the production environment is designed and implemented, the algorithm is deployed, which takes the input data, processes it, and generates the output as per the requirements.

Development environment

Once designed, algorithms need to be implemented in a programming language as per the design. For this book, we have chosen the programming language Python. We chose it because Python is flexible and is an open-source programming language. Python is also one of the languages that you can use in various cloud computing infrastructures, such as **Amazon Web Services (AWS)**, Microsoft Azure, and **Google Cloud Platform (GCP)**.

The official Python home page is available at https://www.python.org/, which also has instructions for installation and a useful beginner's guide.

A basic understanding of Python is required to better understand the concepts presented in this book.

For this book, we expect you to use the most recent version of Python 3. At the time of writing, the most recent version is 3.12, which is what we will use to run the exercises in this book.

We will be using Python throughout this book. We will also be using Jupyter Notebook to run the code. The rest of the chapters in this book assume that Python is installed and Jupyter Notebook has been properly configured and is running.

Python packages

Python is a general-purpose language. It follows the philosophy of "batteries included," which means that there is a standard library that is available, without making the user download separate packages. However, the standard library modules only provide the bare minimum functionality. Based on the specific use case you are working on, additional packages may need to be installed. The official third-party repository for Python packages is called PyPI, which stands for **Python Package Index**. It hosts Python packages both as source distribution and pre-compiled code. Currently, there are more than 113,000 Python packages hosted at PyPI. The easiest way to install additional packages is through the pip package management system. pip is a nerdy recursive acronym, which are abundant in Python culture. pip stands for **Pip Installs Python**. The good news is that starting from version 3.4 of Python, pip is installed by default. To check the version of pip, you can type on the command line:

```
pip --version
```

This `pip` command can be used to install additional packages:

```
pip install PackageName
```

The packages that have already been installed need to be periodically updated to get the latest functionality. This is achieved by using the `upgrade` flag:

```
pip install PackageName --upgrade
```

And to install a specific version of a Python package:

```
pip install PackageName==2.1
```

> Adding the right libraries and versions has become part of setting up the Python programming environment. One feature that helps with maintaining these libraries is the ability to create a requirements file that lists all the packages that are needed. The requirements file is a simple text file that contains the name of the libraries and their associated versions. A sample of the requirements file looks as follows:
>
> ```
> scikit-learn==0.24.1
> tensorflow==2.5.0
> tensorboard==2.5.0
> ```
>
> By convention, the `requirements.txt` is placed in the project's top-level directory.
>
> Once created, the requirements file can be used to set up the development environment by installing all the Python libraries and their associated versions by using the following command:
>
> ```
> pip install -r requirements.txt
> ```

Now let us look into the main packages that we will be using in this book.

The SciPy ecosystem

Scientific Python (SciPy)—pronounced sigh pie—is a group of Python packages created for the scientific community. It contains many functions, including a wide range of random number generators, linear algebra routines, and optimizers.

SciPy is a comprehensive package and, over time, people have developed many extensions to customize and extend the package according to their needs. SciPy is performant as it acts as a thin wrapper around optimized code written in C/C++ or Fortran.

The following are the main packages that are part of this ecosystem:

- **NumPy**: For algorithms, the ability to create multi-dimensional data structures, such as arrays and matrices, is really important. NumPy offers a set of array and matrix data types that are important for statistics and data analysis. Details about NumPy can be found at `http://www.numpy.org/`.

- **scikit-learn**: This machine learning extension is one of the most popular extensions of SciPy. Scikit-learn provides a wide range of important machine learning algorithms, including classification, regression, clustering, and model validation. You can find more details about scikit-learn at `http://scikit-learn.org/`.

- **pandas**: pandas contains the tabular complex data structure that is used widely to input, output, and process tabular data in various algorithms. The pandas library contains many useful functions and it also offers highly optimized performance. More details about pandas can be found at `http://pandas.pydata.org/`.

- **Matplotlib**: Matplotlib provides tools to create powerful visualizations. Data can be presented as line plots, scatter plots, bar charts, histograms, pie charts, and so on. More information can be found at `https://matplotlib.org/`.

Using Jupyter Notebook

We will be using Jupyter Notebook and Google's Colaboratory as the IDE. More details about the setup and the use of Jupyter Notebook and Colab can be found in *Appendix A* and *B*.

Algorithm design techniques

An algorithm is a mathematical solution to a real-world problem. When designing an algorithm, we keep the following three design concerns in mind as we work on designing and fine-tuning the algorithms:

- **Concern 1**: Is this algorithm producing the result we expected?
- **Concern 2**: Is this the most optimal way to get these results?
- **Concern 3**: How is the algorithm going to perform on larger datasets?

It is important to understand the complexity of the problem itself before designing a solution for it. For example, it helps us to design an appropriate solution if we characterize the problem in terms of its needs and complexity.

Generally, the algorithms can be divided into the following types based on the characteristics of the problem:

- **Data-intensive algorithms**: Data-intensive algorithms are designed to deal with a large amount of data. They are expected to have relatively simplistic processing requirements. A compression algorithm applied to a huge file is a good example of data-intensive algorithms. For such algorithms, the size of the data is expected to be much larger than the memory of the processing engine (a single node or cluster), and an iterative processing design may need to be developed to efficiently process the data according to the requirements.

- **Compute-intensive algorithms**: Compute-intensive algorithms have considerable processing requirements but do not involve large amounts of data. A simple example is the algorithm to find a very large prime number. Finding a strategy to divide the algorithm into different phases so that at least some of the phases are parallelized is key to maximizing the performance of the algorithm.

- **Both data and compute-intensive algorithms**: There are certain algorithms that deal with a large amount of data and also have considerable computing requirements. Algorithms used to perform sentiment analysis on live video feeds are a good example of where both the data and the processing requirements are huge in accomplishing the task. Such algorithms are the most resource-intensive algorithms and require careful design of the algorithm and intelligent allocation of available resources.

To characterize the problem in terms of its complexity and needs, it helps if we study its data and compute dimensions in more depth, which we will do in the following section.

The data dimension

To categorize the data dimension of the problem, we look at its **volume**, **velocity**, and **variety** (the **3Vs**), which are defined as follows:

- **Volume**: The volume is the expected size of the data that the algorithm will process.

- **Velocity**: The velocity is the expected rate of new data generation when the algorithm is used. It can be zero.

- **Variety**: The variety quantifies how many different types of data the designed algorithm is expected to deal with.

Figure 1.2 shows the 3Vs of the data in more detail. The center of this diagram shows the simplest possible data, with a small volume and low variety and velocity. As we move away from the center, the complexity of the data increases. It can increase in one or more of the three dimensions.

For example, in the dimension of velocity, we have the batch process as the simplest, followed by the periodic process, and then the near real-time process. Finally, we have the real-time process, which is the most complex to handle in the context of data velocity. For example, a collection of live video feeds gathered by a group of monitoring cameras will have a high volume, high velocity, and high variety and may need an appropriate design to have the ability to store and process data effectively:

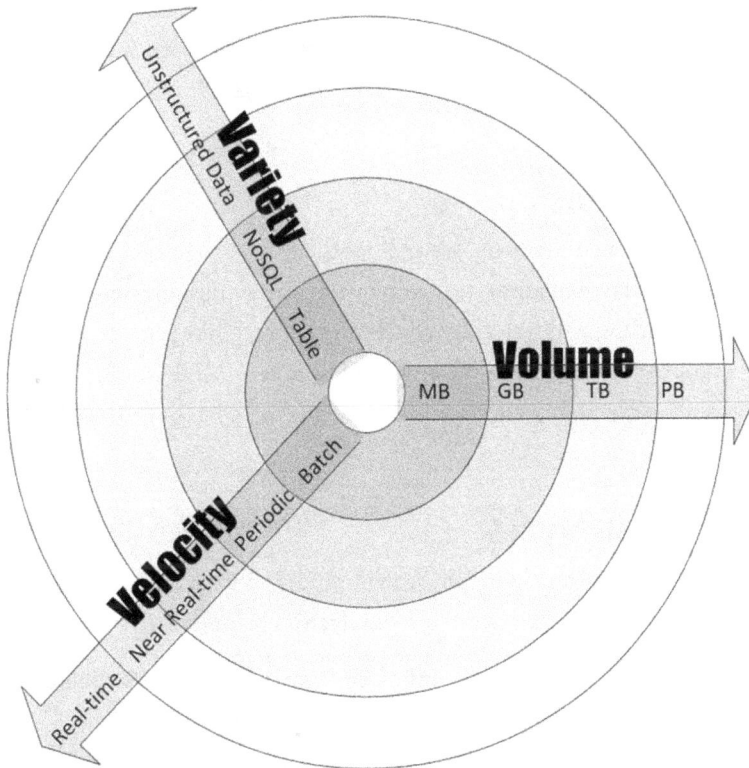

Figure 1.2: 3Vs of Data: Volume, Velocity, and Variety

Let us consider three examples of use cases having three different types of data:

- First, consider a simple data-processing use case where the input data is a .csv file. In this case, the volume, velocity, and variety of the data will be low.

- Second, consider the use case where the input data is the live stream of a security video camera. Now the volume, velocity, and variety of the data will be quite high and should be kept in mind while designing an algorithm for it.

- Third, consider the use case of a typical sensor network. Let us assume that the data source of the sensor network is a mesh of temperature sensors installed in a large building. Although the velocity of the data being generated is typically very high (as new data is being generated very quickly), the volume is expected to be quite low (as each data element is typically only 16-bits long consisting of an 8-bit measurement plus 8-bit metadata such as a timestamp and the geo-coordinates.

The processing requirements, storage needs, and suitable software stack selection will be different for all the above three examples and, in general, are dependent on the volume, velocity, and variety of the data sources. It is important to first characterize data as the first step of designing an algorithm.

The compute dimension

To characterize the compute dimension, we analyze the processing needs of the problem at hand. The processing needs of an algorithm determine what sort of design is most efficient for it. For example, complex algorithms, in general, require lots of processing power. For such algorithms, it may be important to have multi-node parallel architecture. Modern deep algorithms usually involve considerable numeric processing and may need the power of GPUs or TUPs as discussed in *Chapter 16, Practical Considerations*.

Performance analysis

Analyzing the performance of an algorithm is an important part of its design. One of the ways to estimate the performance of an algorithm is to analyze its complexity.

Complexity theory is the study of how complicated algorithms are. To be useful, any algorithm should have three key features:

- **Should be correct**: A good algorithm should produce the correct result. To confirm that an algorithm is working correctly, it needs to be extensively tested, especially testing edge cases.

- **Should be understandable**: A good algorithm should be understandable. The best algorithm in the world is not very useful if it's too complicated for us to implement on a computer.

- **Should be efficient**: A good algorithm should be efficient. Even if an algorithm produces the correct result, it won't help us much if it takes a thousand years or if it requires 1 billion terabytes of memory.

There are two possible types of analysis to quantify the complexity of an algorithm:

- **Space complexity analysis**: Estimates the runtime memory requirements needed to execute the algorithm.
- **Time complexity analysis**: Estimates the time the algorithm will take to run.

Let us study them one by one:

Space complexity analysis

Space complexity analysis estimates the amount of memory required by the algorithm to process input data. While processing the input data, the algorithm needs to store the transient temporary data structures in memory. The way the algorithm is designed affects the number, type, and size of these data structures. In an age of distributed computing and with increasingly large amounts of data that needs to be processed, space complexity analysis is becoming more and more important. The size, type, and number of these data structures will dictate the memory requirements for the underlying hardware. Modern in-memory data structures used in distributed computing need to have efficient resource allocation mechanisms that are aware of the memory requirements at different execution phases of the algorithm. Complex algorithms tend to be iterative in nature. Instead of bringing all the information into the memory at once, such algorithms iteratively populate the data structures. To calculate the space complexity, it is important to first classify the type of iterative algorithm we plan to use. An iterative algorithm can use one of the following three types of iterations:

- **Converging Iterations**: As the algorithm proceeds through iterations, the amount of data it processes in each individual iteration decreases. In other words, space complexity decreases as the algorithm proceeds through its iterations. The main challenge is to tackle the space complexity of the initial iterations. Modern scalable cloud infrastructures such as AWS and Google Cloud are best suited to run such algorithms.
- **Diverging Iterations**: As the algorithm proceeds through iterations, the amount of data it processes in each individual iteration increases. As the space complexity increases with the algorithm's progress through iterations, it is important to set constraints to prevent the system from becoming unstable. The constraints can be set by limiting the number of iterations and/or by setting a limit on the size of initial data.
- **Flat Iterations**: As the algorithm proceeds through iterations, the amount of data it processes in each individual iteration remains constant. As space complexity does not change, elasticity in infrastructure is not needed.

To calculate the space complexity, we need to focus on one of the most complex iterations. In many algorithms, as we converge towards the solution, the resource needs are gradually reduced. In such cases, initial iterations are the most complex and give us a better estimate of space complexity. Once chosen, we estimate the total amount of memory used by the algorithm, including the memory used by its transient data structures, execution, and input values. This will give us a good estimate of the space complexity of an algorithm.

The following are guidelines to minimize the space complexity:

- Whenever possible, try to design an algorithm as iterative.
- While designing an iterative algorithm, whenever there is a choice, prefer a larger number of iterations over a smaller number of iterations. A fine-grained larger number of iterations is expected to have less space complexity.
- Algorithms should bring only the information needed for current processing into memory. Whatever is not needed should be flushed out from the memory.

Space complexity analysis is a must for the efficient design of algorithms. If proper space complexity analysis is not conducted while designing a particular algorithm, insufficient memory availability for the transient temporary data structures may trigger unnecessary disk spillovers, which could potentially considerably affect the performance and efficiency of the algorithm.

In this chapter, we will look deeper into time complexity. Space complexity will be discussed in *Chapter 15, Large-Scale Algorithms*, in more detail, where we will deal with large-scale distributed algorithms with complex runtime memory requirements.

Time complexity analysis

Time complexity analysis estimates how long it will take for an algorithm to complete its assigned job based on its structure. In contrast to space complexity, time complexity is not dependent on any hardware that the algorithm will run on. Time complexity analysis solely depends on the structure of the algorithm itself. The overall goal of time complexity analysis is to try to answer these important two questions:

- Will this algorithm scale? A well-designed algorithm should be fully capable of taking advantage of the modern elastic infrastructure available in cloud computing environments. An algorithm should be designed in a way such that it can utilize the availability of more CPUs, processing cores, GPUs, and memory. For example, an algorithm used for training a model in a machine learning problem should be able to use distributed training as more CPUs are available.

Such algorithms should also take advantage of GPUs and additional memory if made available during the execution of the algorithm.

- How well will this algorithm handle larger datasets?

To answer these questions, we need to determine the effect on the performance of an algorithm as the size of the data is increased and make sure that the algorithm is designed in a way that not only makes it accurate but also scales well. The performance of an algorithm is becoming more and more important for larger datasets in today's world of "big data."

In many cases, we may have more than one approach available to design the algorithm. The goal of conducting time complexity analysis, in this case, will be as follows:

"Given a certain problem and more than one algorithm, which one is the most efficient to use in terms of time efficiency?"

There can be two basic approaches to calculating the time complexity of an algorithm:

- **A post-implementation profiling approach**: In this approach, different candidate algorithms are implemented, and their performance is compared.
- **A pre-implementation theoretical approach**: In this approach, the performance of each algorithm is approximated mathematically before running an algorithm.

The advantage of the theoretical approach is that it only depends on the structure of the algorithm itself. It does not depend on the actual hardware that will be used to run the algorithm, the choice of the software stack chosen at runtime, or the programming language used to implement the algorithm.

Estimating the performance

The performance of a typical algorithm will depend on the type of data given to it as an input. For example, if the data is already sorted according to the context of the problem we are trying to solve, the algorithm may perform blazingly fast. If the sorted input is used to benchmark this particular algorithm, then it will give an unrealistically good performance number, which will not be a true reflection of its real performance in most scenarios. To handle this dependency of algorithms on the input data, we have different types of cases to consider when conducting a performance analysis.

The best case

In the best case, the data given as input is organized in a way that the algorithm will give its best performance. Best-case analysis gives the upper bound of the performance.

The worst case

The second way to estimate the performance of an algorithm is to try to find the maximum possible time it will take to get the job done under a given set of conditions. This worst-case analysis of an algorithm is quite useful as we are guaranteeing that regardless of the conditions, the performance of the algorithm will always be better than the numbers that come out of our analysis. Worst-case analysis is especially useful for estimating the performance when dealing with complex problems with larger datasets. Worst-case analysis gives the lower bound of the performance of the algorithm.

The average case

This starts by dividing the various possible inputs into various groups. Then, it conducts the performance analysis from one of the representative inputs from each group. Finally, it calculates the average of the performance of each of the groups.

Average-case analysis is not always accurate as it needs to consider all the different combinations and possibilities of input to the algorithm, which is not always easy to do.

Big O notation

Big O notation was first introduced by Bachmann in 1894 in a research paper to approximate an algorithm's growth. He wrote:

"... with the symbol $O(n)$ we express a magnitude whose order in respect to n does not exceed the order of n" (Bachmann 1894, p. 401).

Big-O notation provides a way to describe the long-term growth rate of an algorithm's performance. In simpler terms, it tells us how the runtime of an algorithm increases as the input size grows. Let's break it down with the help of two functions, $f(n)$ and $g(n)$. If we say $f = O(g)$, what we mean is that as n approaches infinity, the ratio $\frac{f(n)}{g(n)}$ stays limited or bounded. In other words, no matter how large our input gets, $f(n)$ will not grow disproportionately faster than $g(n)$.

Let's look at particular functions:

$$f(n) = 1000n^2 + 100n + 10$$

and

$$g(n) = n^2$$

Note that both functions will approach infinity as n approaches infinity. Let's find out if $f = O(g)$ by applying the definition.

First, let us calculate $\frac{f(n)}{g(n)}$,

which will be equal to $\frac{f(n)}{g(n)} = \frac{1000n^2+100n+10}{n^2} = (1000 + \frac{100}{n} + \frac{10}{n^2})$.

It is clear that $\frac{f(n)}{g(n)}$ is bounded and will not approach infinity as n approaches infinity.

Thus $f(n) = O(g) = O(n^2)$.

(n^2) represents that the complexity of this function increases as the square of input n. If we double the number of input elements, the complexity is expected to increase by 4.

Note the following 4 rules when dealing with Big-O notation.

Rule 1:

When an algorithm operates with a sequential structure, executing one function $f(n)$ followed by another function $g(n)$, the overall complexity of the tasks becomes a sum of the two. Therefore, it's represented as $O(f(n)+g(n))$.

Rule 2:

For algorithms that have a divided structure, where one task splits into multiple sub-tasks, if each sub-task has a complexity of $f(n)$, the algorithm's overall complexity remains $O(f(n))$, assuming the sub-tasks are processed simultaneously or don't depend on each other.

Rule 3:

Considering recursive algorithms, if an algorithm calls itself with a fraction of the input size, say $f(n/2)$ or $f(n/3)$, and performs other operations taking $g(n)$ steps, the combined complexity can be denoted as $O(f(n/2)+g(n))$ or $O(f(n/3)+g(n))$, depending on the fraction.

Rule 4:

For nested recursive structures, if an algorithm divides its input into smaller chunks and processes each recursively, and each chunk is further divided and processed similarly, the overall complexity would be a cumulative representation of these nested operations. For instance, if a problem of size 'n' divides into sub-problems of size n/2, and these sub-problems are similarly processed, the complexity might be expressed as $O(f(n) \times g(n/2))$.

Rule 5:

When calculating the complexity of an algorithm, ignore constant multiples. If k is a constant, $O(kf(n))$ is the same as $O(f(n))$.

Also, $O(f(k \times n))$ is the same as $O(f(n))$.

Thus $O(5n^2) = O(n^2)$.

And $O((3n^2)) = O(n^2)$.

Note that:

- The complexity quantified by Big O notation is only an estimate.
- For smaller datasets, the time complexity might not be a significant concern. This is because, with limited data, even less-efficient algorithms can execute rapidly.
- $T(n)$ time complexity is more than the original function. A good choice of $T(n)$ will try to create a tight upper bound for $F(n)$.

The following table summarizes the different kinds of Big O notation types discussed in this section:

Complexity Class	Name	Example Operations
O(1)	Constant	Append, get item, set item.
O(logn)	Logarithmic	Finding an element in a sorted array.
O(n)	Linear	Copy, insert, delete, iteration
O(n^2)	Quadratic	Nested loops

Constant time (O(1)) complexity

If an algorithm takes the same amount of time to run, independent of the size of the input data, it is said to run in constant time. It is represented by $O(1)$. Let's take the example of accessing the nth element of an array. Regardless of the size of the array, it will take constant time to get the results. For example, the following function will return the first element of the array and has a complexity of $O(1)$:

```python
def get_first(my_list):
    return my_list[0]


get_first([1, 2, 3])
```

```
1
```

```python
get_first([1, 2, 3, 4, 5, 6, 7, 8, 9, 10])
```

```
1
```

Note that:

- The addition of a new element to a stack is done by using push and removing an element from a stack is done by using pop. Regardless of the size of the stack, it will take the same time to add or remove an element.

- When accessing the element of the hashtable, note that it is a data structure that stores data in an associative format, usually as key-value pairs.

Linear time (O(n)) complexity

An algorithm is said to have a complexity of linear time, represented by $O(n)$, if the execution time is directly proportional to the size of the input. A simple example is to add the elements in a single-dimensional data structure:

```python
def get_sum(my_list):
    sum = 0
    for item in my_list:
        sum = sum + item
    return sum
```

Note the main loop of the algorithm. The number of iterations in the main loop increases linearly with an increasing value of n, producing an $O(n)$ complexity in the following figure:

```python
get_sum([1, 2, 3])
```

```
6
```

```python
get_sum([1, 2, 3, 4])
```

```
10
```

Some other examples of array operations are as follows:

- Searching an element
- Finding the minimum value among all the elements of an array

Quadratic time (O(n2)) complexity

An algorithm is said to run in quadratic time if the execution time of an algorithm is proportional to the square of the input size; for example, a simple function that sums up a two-dimensional array, as follows:

```python
def get_sum(my_list):
    sum = 0
```

```
    for row in my_list:
        for item in row:
            sum += item
    return sum
```

Note the nested inner loop within the other main loop. This nested loop gives the preceding code the complexity of $O(n^2)$:

```
get_sum([[1, 2], [3, 4]])
```

```
10
```

```
get_sum([[1, 2, 3], [4, 5, 6]])
```

```
21
```

Another example is the *bubble sort algorithm* (which will be discussed in *Chapter 2, Data Structures Used in Algorithms*).

Logarithmic time (O(logn)) complexity

An algorithm is said to run in logarithmic time if the execution time of the algorithm is proportional to the logarithm of the input size. With each iteration, the input size decreases by constant multiple factors. An example of a logarithmic algorithm is binary search. The binary search algorithm is used to find a particular element in a one-dimensional data structure, such as a Python list. The elements within the data structure need to be sorted in descending order. The binary search algorithm is implemented in a function named search_binary, as follows:

```
def search_binary(my_list, item):
    first = 0
    last = len(my_list)-1
    found_flag = False
    while(first <= last and not found_flag):
        mid = (first + last)//2
        if my_list[mid] == item:
            found_flag = True
        else:
            if item < my_list[mid]:
                last = mid - 1
            else:
                first = mid + 1
    return found_flag
```

```
searchBinary([8,9,10,100,1000,2000,3000], 10)
```

```
True
```

```
searchBinary([8,9,10,100,1000,2000,3000], 5)
```

```
False
```

The main loop takes advantage of the fact that the list is ordered. It divides the list in half with each iteration until it gets to the result.

After defining the function, it is tested to search a particular element. The binary search algorithm is further discussed in *Chapter 3, Sorting and Searching Algorithms*.

Note that among the four types of Big O notation types presented, $O(n^2)$ has the worst performance and $O(logn)$ has the best performance. On the other hand, $O(n^2)$ is not as bad as $O(n^3)$, but still, algorithms that fall in this class cannot be used on big data as the time complexity puts limitations on how much data they can realistically process. The performance of four types of Big O notations is shown in *Figure 1.3*:

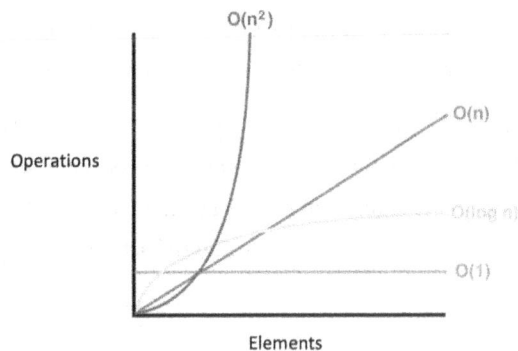

Figure 1.3: Big O complexity chart

One way to reduce the complexity of an algorithm is to compromise on its accuracy, producing a type of algorithm called an **approximate algorithm**.

Selecting an algorithm

How do you know which one is a better solution? How do you know which algorithm runs faster? Analyzing the time complexity of an algorithm may answer these types of questions.

To see where it can be useful, let's take a simple example where the objective is to sort a list of numbers. There are a bunch of algorithms readily available that can do the job. The issue is how to choose the right one.

First, an observation that can be made is that if there are not too many numbers in the list, then it does not matter which algorithm we choose to sort the list of numbers. So, if there are only 10 numbers in the list (*n=10*), then it does not matter which algorithm we choose as it would probably not take more than a few microseconds, even with a very simple algorithm. But as *n* increases, the choice of the right algorithm starts to make a difference. A poorly designed algorithm may take a couple of hours to run, while a well-designed algorithm may finish sorting the list in a couple of seconds. So, for larger input datasets, it makes a lot of sense to invest time and effort, perform a performance analysis, and choose the correctly designed algorithm that will do the job required in an efficient manner.

Validating an algorithm

Validating an algorithm confirms that it is actually providing a mathematical solution to the problem we are trying to solve. A validation process should check the results for as many possible values and types of input values as possible.

Exact, approximate, and randomized algorithms

Validating an algorithm also depends on the type of the algorithm as the testing techniques are different. Let's first differentiate between deterministic and randomized algorithms.

For deterministic algorithms, a particular input always generates exactly the same output. But for certain classes of algorithms, a sequence of random numbers is also taken as input, which makes the output different each time the algorithm is run. The k-means clustering algorithm, which is detailed in *Chapter 6, Unsupervised Machine Learning Algorithms*, is an example of such an algorithm:

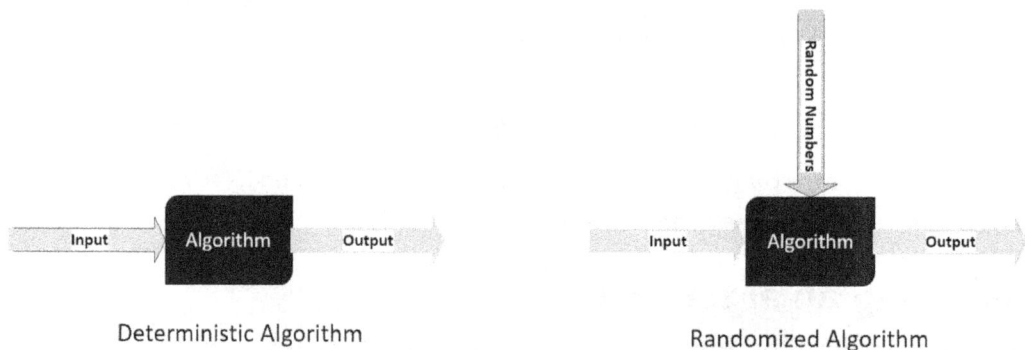

Figure 1.4: Deterministic and Randomized Algorithms

Algorithms can also be divided into the following two types based on assumptions or approximation used to simplify the logic to make them run faster:

- **An exact algorithm**: Exact algorithms are expected to produce a precise solution without introducing any assumptions or approximations.

- **An approximate algorithm**: When the problem complexity is too much to handle for the given resources, we simplify our problem by making some assumptions. The algorithms based on these simplifications or assumptions are called approximate algorithms, which don't quite give us the precise solution.

Let's look at an example to understand the difference between exact and approximate algorithms—the famous traveling salesman problem, which was presented in 1930. Traveling salesman challenges you to find the shortest route for a particular salesman that visits each city (from a list of cities) and then returns to the origin, which is why he is named the traveling salesman. The first attempt to provide the solution will include generating all the permutations of cities and choosing the combination of cities that is cheapest. It is obvious that time complexity starts to become unmanageable beyond 30 cities.

If the number of cities is more than 30, one way of reducing the complexity is to introduce some approximations and assumptions.

For approximate algorithms, it is important to set the expectations for accuracy when gathering the requirements. Validating an approximation algorithm is about verifying that the error of the results is within an acceptable range.

Explainability

When algorithms are used for critical cases, it becomes important to have the ability to explain the reason behind each and every result whenever needed. This is necessary to make sure that decisions based on the results of the algorithms do not introduce bias.

The ability to exactly identify the features that are used directly or indirectly to come up with a particular decision is called the **explainability** of an algorithm. Algorithms, when used for critical use cases, need to be evaluated for bias and prejudice. The ethical analysis of algorithms has become a standard part of the validation process for those algorithms that can affect decision-making that relates to the lives of people.

For algorithms that deal with deep learning, explainability is difficult to achieve. For example, if an algorithm is used to refuse the mortgage application of a person, it is important to have the transparency and ability to explain the reason.

Algorithmic explainability is an active area of research. One of the effective techniques that have been recently developed is **Local Interpretable Model-Agnostic Explanations (LIME)**, as proposed in the proceedings of the 22nd **Association for Computing Machinery (ACM)** at the **Special Interest Group on Knowledge Discovery and Data Mining (SIGKDD)** international conference on knowledge discovery and data mining in 2016. LIME is based on a concept where small changes are introduced to the input for each instance and then an effort to map the local decision boundary for that instance is made. It can then quantify the influence of each variable for that instance.

Summary

This chapter was about learning the basics of algorithms. First, we learned about the different phases of developing an algorithm. We discussed the different ways of specifying the logic of an algorithm that are necessary for designing it. Then, we looked at how to design an algorithm. We learned two different ways of analyzing the performance of an algorithm. Finally, we studied different aspects of validating an algorithm.

After going through this chapter, we should understand the different phases in developing and deploying an algorithm. We also learned how to use Big O notation to evaluate the performance of an algorithm.

The next chapter is about the data structures used in algorithms. We will start by looking at the data structures available in Python. We will then look at how we can use these data structures to create more sophisticated data structures, such as stacks, queues, and trees, which are needed to develop complex algorithms.

Learn more on Discord

To join the Discord community for this book – where you can share feedback, ask questions to the author, and learn about new releases – follow the QR code below:

```
https://packt.link/WHLel
```

2

Data Structures Used in Algorithms

Algorithms need in-memory data structures that can hold temporary data while executing. Choosing the right data structures is essential for their efficient implementation. Certain classes of algorithms are recursive or iterative in logic and need data structures that are specially designed for them. For example, a recursive algorithm may be more easily implemented, exhibiting better performance, if nested data structures are used. In this chapter, data structures are discussed in the context of algorithms. As we are using Python in this book, this chapter focuses on Python data structures, but the concepts presented in this chapter can be used in other languages such as Java and C++.

By the end of this chapter, you should be able to understand how Python handles complex data structures and which one should be used for a certain type of data.

Here are the main points discussed in this chapter:

- Exploring Python built-in data types
- Using Series and DataFrames
- Exploring matrices and matrix operations
- Understanding abstract data types

Exploring Python built-in data types

In any language, data structures are used to store and manipulate complex data. In Python, data structures are storage containers for managing, organizing, and searching data in an efficient way. They are used to store a group of data elements called collections that need to be stored and processed together. In Python, the important data structures that can be used to store collections are summarized in *Table 2.1*:

Data Structure	Brief Explanation	Example
List	An ordered, possibly nested, mutable sequence of elements	`["John", 33,"Toronto", True]`
Tuple	An ordered immutable sequence of elements	`('Red','Green','Blue','Yellow')`
Dictionary	An unordered collection of key-value pairs	`{'brand': 'Apple', 'color': 'black'}`
Set	An unordered collection of elements	`{'a', 'b', 'c'}`

Table 2.1: Python Data Structures

Let us look into them in more detail in the upcoming subsections.

Lists

In Python, a list is the main data type used to store a mutable sequence of elements. The sequence of elements stored in the list need not be of the same type.

A list can be defined by enclosing the elements in [ ] and they need to be separated by a comma. For example, the following code creates four data elements together that are of different types:

```python
list_a = ["John", 33,"Toronto", True]
print(list_a)
```

```
['John', 33, 'Toronto', True]
```

In Python, a list is a handy way of creating one-dimensional writable data structures, which are especially needed at different internal stages of algorithms.

Using lists

Utility functions in data structures make them very useful as they can be used to manage data in lists.

Let's look into how we can use them:

- **List indexing**: As the position of an element is deterministic in a list, the index can be used to get an element at a particular position. The following code demonstrates the concept:

  ```
  bin_colors=['Red','Green','Blue','Yellow']
  ```

  The four-element list created by this code is shown in *Figure 2.1*:

  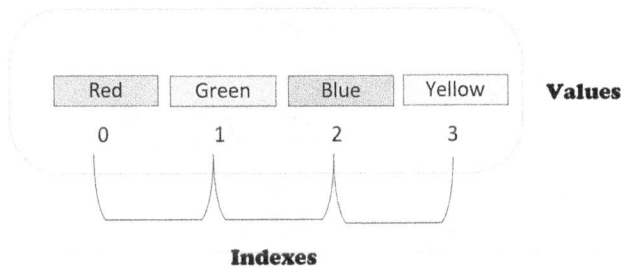

  Figure 2.1: A four-element list in Python

  Now, we will run the code:

  ```
  bin_colors[1]
  ```
  ```
  'Green'
  ```

  Note that Python is a zero-indexing language. This means that the initial index of any data structure, including lists, will be 0. Green, which is the second element, is retrieved by index 1 – that is, bin_colors[1].

- **List slicing**: Retrieving a subset of the elements of a list by specifying a range of indexes is called **slicing**. The following code can be used to create a slice of the list:

  ```
  bin_colors[0:2]
  ```
  ```
  ['Red', 'Green']
  ```

Note that lists are one of the most popular single-dimensional data structures in Python.

> While slicing a list, the range is indicated as follows: the first number (inclusive) and the second number (exclusive). For example, `bin_colors[0:2]` will include `bin_color[0]` and `bin_color[1]` but not `bin_color[2]`. While using lists, this should be kept in mind, as some users of the Python language complain that this is not very intuitive.

Let's have a look at the following code snippet:

```python
bin_colors=['Red','Green','Blue','Yellow']
bin_colors[2:]
```

```
['Blue', 'Yellow']
```

```python
bin_colors[:2]
```

```
['Red', 'Green']
```

If the starting index is not specified, it means the beginning of the list, and if the ending index is not specified, it means the end of the list, as demonstrated by the preceding code.

- **Negative indexing**: In Python, we also have negative indices, which count from the end of the list. This is demonstrated in the following code:

```python
bin_colors=['Red','Green','Blue','Yellow']
bin_colors[:-1]
```

```
['Red', 'Green', 'Blue']
```

```python
bin_colors[:-2]
```

```
['Red', 'Green']
```

```python
bin_colors[-2:-1]
```

```
['Blue']
```

Note that negative indices are especially useful when we want to use the last element as a reference point instead of the first one.

- **Nesting**: An element of a list can be of any data type. This allows nesting in lists. For iterative and recursive algorithms, this provides important capabilities.

Let's have a look at the following code, which is an example of a list within a list (nesting):

```python
a = [1,2,[100,200,300],6]
max(a[2])
```

```
300
```

```python
a[2][1]
```

```
200
```

- **Iteration:** Python allows iterating over each element on a list by using a for loop. This is demonstrated in the following example:

```python
for color_a in bin_colors:
    print(color_a + " Square")
```

```
Red Square
Green Square
Blue Square
Yellow Square
```

Note that the preceding code iterates through the list and prints each element. Now let us remove the last element from the stack using pop() function.

Modifying lists: append and pop operations

Let's take a look at modifying some lists, including the append and pop operations.

Adding elements with append()

When you want to insert a new item at the end of a list, you employ the append() method. It works by adding the new element to the nearest available memory slot. If the list is already at full capacity, Python extends the memory allocation, replicates the previous items in this newly carved out space, and then slots in the new addition:

```python
bin_colors = ['Red', 'Green', 'Blue', 'Yellow']
bin_colors.append('Purple')
print(bin_colors)
```

```
['Red', 'Green', 'Blue', 'Yellow', 'Purple']
```

Removing elements with pop()

To extract an element from the list, particularly the last one, the pop() method is a handy tool. When invoked, this method extracts the specified item (or the last item if no index is given). The elements situated after the popped item get repositioned to maintain memory continuity:

```
bin_colors.pop()
print(bin_colors)
```

```
['Red', 'Green', 'Blue', 'Yellow']
```

> Note that we didn't specify an index, so pop() removed the last element from the array, which was the color 'Purple' we added in the above example.

The range() function

The range() function can be used to easily generate a large list of numbers. It is used to auto-populate sequences of numbers in a list.

The range() function is simple to use. We can use it by just specifying the number of elements we want in the list. By default, it starts from zero and increments by one:

```
x = range(4)
for n in x:
  print(n)
```

```
0 1 2 3
```

We can also specify the end number and the step:

```
odd_num = range(3,30,2)
for n in odd_num:
  print(n)
```

```
3 5 7 9 11 13 15 17 19 21 23 25 27 29
```

The preceding range function will give us odd numbers from 3 to 29.

To iterate through a list, we can use the for function:

```
for i in odd_num:
    print(i*100)
```

```
300 500 700 900 1100 1300 1500 1700 1900 2100 2300 2500 2700 2900
```

We can use the range() function to generate a list of random numbers. For example, to simulate ten trials of a dice, we can use the following code:

```
import random
dice_output = [random.randint(1, 6) for x in range(10)]
print(dice_output)
```

```
[6, 6, 6, 6, 2, 4, 6, 5, 1, 4]
```

The time complexity of lists

The time complexity of various functions of a list can be summarized as follows using the Big O notation:

- **Inserting an element**: The insertion of an element at the end of a list typically has a constant time complexity, denoted as $O(1)$. This means the time taken for this operation remains fairly consistent, irrespective of the list's size.

- **Deleting an element**: Deleting an element from a list can have a time complexity of $O(n)$ in its worst-case scenario. This is because, in the least favorable situation, the program might need to traverse the entire list before removing the desired element.

- **Slicing**: When we slice a list or extract a portion of it, the operation can take time proportional to the size of the slice; hence, its time complexity is $O(n)$.

- **Element retrieval**: Finding an element within a list, without any indexing, can require scanning through all its elements in the worst case. Thus, its time complexity is also $O(n)$.

- **Copying**: Creating a copy of the list necessitates visiting every element once, leading to a time complexity of $O(n)$.

Tuples

The second data structure that can be used to store a collection is a tuple. In contrast to lists, tuples are immutable (read-only) data structures. Tuples consist of several elements surrounded by ( ).

Like lists, elements within a tuple can be of different types. They also allow their elements to be complex data types. So, there can be a tuple within a tuple providing a way to create a nested data structure. The capability to create nested data structures is especially useful in iterative and recursive algorithms.

The following code demonstrates how to create tuples:

```
bin_colors=('Red','Green','Blue','Yellow')
print(f"The second element of the tuple is {bin_colors[1]}")
```

```
The second element of the tuple is Green
```

```
print(f"The elements after third element onwards are {bin_colors[2:]}")
```

```
The elements after third element onwards are ('Blue', 'Yellow')
```

```
# Nested Tuple Data structure
nested_tuple = (1,2,(100,200,300),6)
print(f"The maximum value of the inner tuple {max(nested_tuple[2])}")
```

```
The maximum value of the inner tuple 300
```

> Wherever possible, immutable data structures (such as tuples) should be preferred over mutable data structures (such as lists) due to performance. Especially when dealing with big data, immutable data structures are considerably faster than mutable ones. When a data structure is passed to a function as immutable, its copy does not need to be created as the function cannot change it. So, the output can refer to the input data structure. This is called referential transparency and improves the performance. There is a price we pay for the ability to change data elements in lists and we should carefully analyze whether it is really needed so we can implement the code as read-only tuples, which will be much faster.

Note that, as Python is a zero-index-based language, a[2] refers to the third element, which is a tuple, (100,200,300), and a[2][1] refers to the second element within this tuple, which is 200.

The time complexity of tuples

The time complexity of various functions of tuples can be summarized as follows (using Big O notation):

- **Accessing an element**: Tuples allow direct access to their elements via indexing. This operation is constant time, *O(1)*, meaning the time taken remains consistent regardless of the tuple's size.

- **Slicing**: When a portion of a tuple is extracted or sliced, the operation's efficiency is proportional to the size of the slice, resulting in a time complexity of *O(n)*.

- **Element retrieval**: Searching for an element in a tuple, in the absence of any indexing aid, might require traversing all its elements in the worst-case scenario. Hence, its time complexity is *O(n)*.

- **Copying**: Duplicating a tuple, or creating its copy, requires iterating through each element once, giving it a time complexity of *O(n)*.

Dictionaries and sets

In this section, we will discuss sets and dictionaries, which are used to store data in which there is no explicit or implicit ordering. Both dictionaries and sets are quite similar. The difference is that a dictionary has a key-value pair. A set can be thought of as a collection of unique keys.

Let us look into them one by one.

Dictionaries

Holding data as key-value pairs is important, especially in distributed algorithms. In Python, a collection of these key-value pairs is stored as a data structure called a dictionary. To create a dictionary, a key should be chosen as an attribute that is best suited to identify data throughout data processing. The limitation on the value of keys is that they must be hashable types. A hashable is the type of object on which we can run the hash function, generating a hash code that never changes during its lifetime. This ensures that the keys are unique and searching for a key is fast. Numeric types and flat immutable types are all hashable and are good choices for the dictionary keys. The value can be an element of any type, for example, a number or string. Python also always uses complex data types such as lists as values. Nested dictionaries can be created by using a dictionary as the data type of a value.

To create a simple dictionary that assigns colors to various variables, the key-value pairs need to be enclosed in { }. For example, the following code creates a simple dictionary consisting of three key-value pairs:

```
bin_colors ={
  "manual_color": "Yellow",
  "approved_color": "Green",
  "refused_color": "Red"
}

print(bin_colors)
```

```
{'manual_color': 'Yellow', 'approved_color': 'Green', 'refused_color':
'Red'}
```

The three key-value pairs created by the preceding piece of code are also illustrated in the following screenshot:

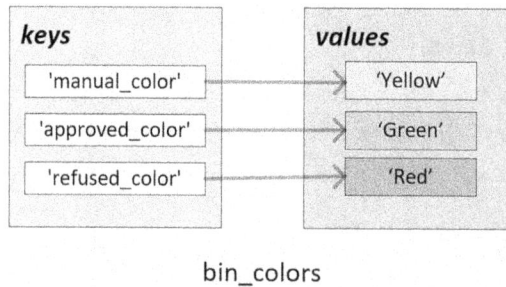

bin_colors

Figure 2.2: Key-value pairs in a simple dictionary

Now, let's see how to retrieve and update a value associated with a key:

1. To retrieve a value associated with a key, either the get function can be used or the key can be used as the index:

    ```
    bin_colors.get('approved_color')
    ```

    ```
    'Green'
    ```

    ```
    bin_colors['approved_color']
    ```

    ```
    'Green'
    ```

2. To update a value associated with a key, use the following code:

    ```
    bin_colors['approved_color']="Purple"
    print(bin_colors)
    ```

    ```
    {'manual_color': 'Yellow', 'approved_color': 'Purple', 'refused_
    color': 'Red'}
    ```

Note that the preceding code shows how we can update a value related to a particular key in a dictionary.

When iterating through a dictionary, usually, we will need both the keys and the values. We can iterate through a dictionary in Python by using .items():

```
for k,v in bin_colors.items():
    print(k,'->',v+' color')
```

```
manual_color -> Yellow color
```

```
approved_color -> Purple color
refused_color -> Red color
```

To delete an element from a dictionary, we will use the del function:

```
del bin_colors['approved_color']
print(bin_colors)
```

```
{'manual_color': 'Yellow', 'refused_color': 'Red'}
```

The time complexity of a dictionary

For Python dictionaries, the time complexities for various operations are listed here:

- **Accessing a value by key**: Dictionaries are designed for fast look-ups. When you have the key, accessing the corresponding value is, on average, a constant time operation, *O(1)*. This holds true unless there's a hash collision, which is a rare scenario.

- **Inserting a key-value pair**: Adding a new key-value pair is generally a swift operation with a time complexity of *O(1)*.

- **Deleting a key-value pair**: Removing an entry from a dictionary, when the key is known, is also an *O(1)* operation on average.

- **Searching for a key**: Verifying the presence of a key, thanks to hashing mechanisms, is usually a constant time, *O(1)*, operation. However, worst-case scenarios could elevate this to *O(n)*, especially with many hash collisions.

- **Copying**: Creating a duplicate of a dictionary necessitates going through each key-value pair, resulting in a linear time complexity, *O(n)*.

Sets

Closely related to a dictionary is a set, which is defined as an unordered collection of distinct elements that can be of different types. One of the ways to define a set is to enclose the values in { }. For example, have a look at the following code block:

```
green = {'grass', 'leaves'}
print(green)
```

```
{'leaves', 'grass'}
```

The defining characteristic of a set is that it only stores the distinct value of each element. If we try to add another redundant element, it will ignore that, as illustrated in the following:

```
green = {'grass', 'leaves','leaves'}
```

```
print(green)
```

```
{'leaves', 'grass'}
```

To demonstrate what sort of operations can be done on sets, let's define two sets:

- A set named `yellow`, which has things that are yellow
- A set named `red`, which has things that are red

Note that some things are common between these two sets. The two sets and their relationship can be represented with the help of the following Venn diagram:

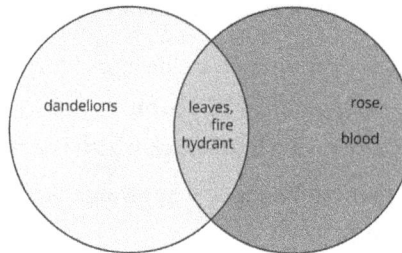

Figure 2.3: Venn diagram showing how elements are stored in sets

If we want to implement these two sets in Python, the code will look like this:

```
yellow = {'dandelions', 'fire hydrant', 'leaves'}
red = {'fire hydrant', 'blood', 'rose', 'leaves'}
```

Now, let's consider the following code, which demonstrates set operations using Python:

```
print(f"The union of yellow and red sets is {yellow|red}")
```

```
The union of yellow and red sets is {leaves, blood, dandelions, fire
hydrant, rose}
```

```
print(f"The intersection of yellow and red is {yellow&red}")
```

```
The intersection of yellow and red is {'fire hydrant', 'leaves'}
```

As shown in the preceding code snippet, sets in Python can have operations such as unions and intersections. As we know, a union operation combines all of the elements of both sets, and the intersection operation will give a set of common elements between the two sets. Note the following:

- `yellow|red` is used to get the union of the preceding two defined sets.
- `yellow&red` is used to get the overlap between yellow and red.

As sets are unordered, the items of a set have no index. That means that we cannot access the items by referring to an index.

We can loop through the set items using a for loop:

```
for x in yellow:
    print(x)
```

```
fire hydrant
leaves
dandelions
```

We can also check if a specified value is present in a set by using the in keyword.

```
print("leaves" in yellow)
```

```
True
```

Time complexity analysis for sets

The following is the time complexity analysis for sets:

Sets	Complexity
Add an element	O(1)
Remove an element	O(1)
Copy	O(n)

Table 2.2: Time complexity for sets

When to use a dictionary and when to use a set

Let us assume that we are looking for a data structure for our phone book. We want to store the phone numbers of the employees of a company. For this purpose, a dictionary is the right data structure. The name of each employee will be the key and the value will be the phone number:

```
employees_dict = {
    "Ikrema Hamza": "555-555-5555",
    "Joyce Doston" : "212-555-5555",
}
```

But if we want to store only the unique value of the employees, then that should be done using sets:

```
employees_set = {
    "Ikrema Hamza",
```

```
        "Joyce Doston"
    }
```

Using Series and DataFrames

Processing data is one of the core things that need to be done while implementing most of the algorithms. In Python, data processing is usually done by using various functions and data structures of the pandas library.

In this section, we will look into the following two important data structures of the pandas library, which will be used to implement various algorithms later in this book:

- **Series**: A one-dimensional array of values
- **DataFrame**: A two-dimensional data structure used to store tabular data

Let us look into the Series data structure first.

Series

In the pandas library, a Series is a one-dimensional array of values for homogenous data. We can think of a Series as a single column in a spreadsheet. We can think of Series as holding various values of a particular variable.

A Series can be defined as follows:

```
import pandas as pd
person_1 = pd.Series(['John',"Male",33,True])
print(person_1)
```

```
0       John
1       Male
2       33
3       True
dtype:      object
```

Note that in pandas Series-based data structures, there is a term called "axis," which is used to represent a sequence of values in a particular dimension. *Series* has only "axis 0" because it has only one dimension. We will see how this axis concept is applied to a DataFrame in the next section.

DataFrame

A DataFrame is built upon the Series data structure. It is stored as two-dimensional tabular data. It is used to process traditional structured data. Let's consider the following table:

id	name	age	decision
1	Fares	32	True
2	Elena	23	False
3	Doug	40	True

Now, let's represent this using a DataFrame.

A simple DataFrame can be created by using the following code:

```
employees_df = pd.DataFrame([
    ['1', 'Fares', 32, True],
    ['2', 'Elena', 23, False],
    ['3', 'Doug', 40, True]])
employees_df.columns = ['id', 'name', 'age', 'decision']
print(employees_df)
```

```
   id   name   age   decision
0   1   Fares   32   True
1   2   Elena   23   False
2   3   Doug    40   True
```

Note that, in the preceding code, df.column is a list that specifies the names of the columns. In DataFrame, a single column or row is called an axis.

> DataFrames are also used in other popular languages and frameworks to implement a tabular data structure. Examples are R and the Apache Spark framework.

Creating a subset of a DataFrame

Fundamentally, there are two main ways of creating the subset of a DataFrame:

- Column selection
- Row selection

Let's look at them one by one.

Column selection

In machine learning algorithms, selecting the right set of features is an important task. Out of all of the features that we may have, not all of them may be needed at a particular stage of the algorithm. In Python, feature selection is achieved by column selection, which is explained in this section.

A column may be retrieved by name, as in the following:

```
df[['name','age']]
```

```
     name    age
0    Fares   32
1    Elena   23
2    Doug    40
```

The positioning of a column is deterministic in a DataFrame. A column can be retrieved by its position, as follows:

```
df.iloc[:,3]
```

```
0    True
1    False
2    True
Name: decision, dtype: bool
```

Note that, in this code, we are retrieving all rows of the DataFrame.

Row selection

Each row in a DataFrame corresponds to a data point in our problem space. We need to perform row selection if we want to create a subset of the data elements that we have in our problem space. This subset can be created by using one of the two following methods:

- By specifying their position
- By specifying a filter

A subset of rows can be retrieved by its position, as follows:

```
df.iloc[1:3,:]
```

```
     id   name    age    decision
1    2    Elena   23     False
```

Note that the preceding code will return the second and third rows plus all columns. It uses the iloc method, which allows us to access the elements by their numerical index.

To create a subset by specifying the filter, we need to use one or more columns to define the selection criterion. For example, a subset of data elements can be selected by this method, as follows:

```
df[df.age>30]
```

	id	name	age	decision
0	1	Fares	32	True
2	3	Doug	40	True

```
df[(df.age<35)&(df.decision==True)]
```

	id	name	age	decision
0	1	Fares	32	True

Note that this code creates a subset of rows that satisfies the condition stipulated in the filter.

Time complexity analysis for sets

Let's unveil the time complexities of some fundamental DataFrame operations.

- Selection operations

  - **Column selection**: Accessing a DataFrame column, often done using the bracket notation or dot notation (for column names without spaces), is an $O(1)$ operation. It offers a quick reference to the data without copying.

  - **Row selection**: Using methods like .loc[] or .iloc[] to select rows, especially with slicing, has a time complexity of $O(n)$, where "n" represents the number of rows you're accessing.

- Insertion operations

  - **Column insertion**: Appending a new column to a DataFrame is typically an $O(1)$ operation. However, the actual time can vary depending on the data type and size of the data being added.

  - **Row insertion**: Adding rows using methods like .append() or .concat() can result in an $O(n)$ complexity since it often requires rearranging and reallocation.

- Deletion operations

    - **Column deletion**: Dropping a column from a DataFrame, facilitated by the .drop() method, is an *O(1)* operation. It marks the column for garbage collection rather than immediate deletion.

    - **Row deletion**: Similar to row insertion, row deletion can lead to an *O(n)* time complexity, as the DataFrame has to rearrange its structure.

Matrices

A matrix is a two-dimensional data structure with a fixed number of columns and rows. Each element of a matrix can be referred to by its column and the row.

In Python, a matrix can be created by using a numpy array or a list. But numpy arrays are much faster than lists because they are collections of homogenous data elements located in a contiguous memory location. The following code can be used to create a matrix from a numpy array:

```python
import numpy as np
matrix_1 = np.array([[11, 12, 13], [21, 22, 23], [31, 32, 33]])
print(matrix_1)
```

```
[[11 12 13]
 [21 22 23]
 [31 32 33]]
```

```python
print(type(matrix_1))
```

```
<class 'numpy.ndarray'>
```

Note that the preceding code will create a matrix that has three rows and three columns.

Matrix operations

There are many operations available for matrix data manipulation. For example, let's try to transpose the preceding matrix. We will use the transpose() function, which will convert columns into rows and rows into columns:

```python
print(matrix_1.transpose())
```

```
array([[11, 21, 31],
       [12, 22, 32],
       [13, 23, 33]])
```

Note that matrix operations are used a lot in multimedia data manipulation.

Big O notation and matrices

When discussing the efficiency of operations, the Big O notation provides a high-level understanding of its impact as data scales:

- **Access**: Accessing an element, whether in a Python list or a numpy array, is a constant time operation, $O(1)$. This is because, with the index of the element, you can directly access it.

- **Appending**: Appending an element at the end of a Python list is an average-case $O(1)$ operation. However, for a numpy array, the operation can be $O(n)$ in the worst case, as the entire array might need to be copied to a new memory location if there's no contiguous space available.

- **Matrix multiplication**: This is where numpy shines. Matrix multiplication can be computationally intensive. Traditional methods can have a time complexity of $O(n^3)$ for $n \times n$ matrices. However, numpy uses optimized algorithms, like the Strassen algorithm, which reduces this significantly.

Now that we have learned about data structures in Python, let's move on to abstract data types in the next section.

Exploring abstract data types

Abstract data types (ADTs) are high-level abstractions whose behavior is defined by a set of variables and a set of related operations. ADTs define the implementation guidance of "what" needs to be expected but give the programmer freedom in "how" it will be exactly implemented. Examples are vectors, queues, and stacks. This means that two different programmers can take two different approaches to implementing an ADT, like a stack. By hiding the implementation level details and giving the user a generic, implementation-independent data structure, the use of ADTs creates algorithms that result in simpler and cleaner code. ADTs can be implemented in any programming language, such as C++, Java, and Scala. In this section, we shall implement ADTs using Python. Let's start with vectors first.

Vector

A vector is a single-dimension structure for storing data. They are one of the most popular data structures in Python. There are two ways of creating vectors in Python, as follows:

- **Using a Python list**: The simplest way to create a vector is by using a Python list, as follows:

```
vector_1 = [22,33,44,55]
```

```
print(vector_1)
```

```
[22, 33, 44, 55]
```

```
print(type(vector_1))
```

```
<class 'list'>
```

Note that this code will create a list with four elements.

- **Using a numpy array:** Another popular way to create a vector is to use numpy arrays. numpy arrays are generally faster and more memory-efficient than Python lists, especially for operations that involve large amounts of data. This is because numpy is designed to work with homogenous data and can take advantage of low-level optimizations. A numpy array can be implemented as follows:

```
vector_2 = np.array([22,33,44,55])
print(vector_2)
```

```
[22 33 44 55]
```

```
print(type(vector_2))
```

```
<class 'numpy.ndarray'>
```

Note that we created vector_2 using np.array in this code.

> In Python, we can represent integers using underscores to separate parts. This makes them more readable and less error-prone. This is especially useful when dealing with large numbers. So, one billion can be represented as 1000_000_000.

```
large_number=1000_000_000
print(large_number)
```

```
1000000000
```

Time complexity of vectors

When discussing the efficiency of vector operations, it's vital to understand the time complexity:

- **Access:** Accessing an element in both a Python list and a numpy array (vector) takes constant time, $O(1)$. This ensures rapid data retrieval.

- **Appending**: Appending an element to a Python list has an average time complexity of *O(1)*. However, for a numpy array, appending could take up to *O(n)* in the worst case since numpy arrays require contiguous memory locations.

- **Searching**: Finding an element in a vector has a time complexity of *O(n)* because, in the worst case, you might have to scan through all elements.

Stacks

A stack is a linear data structure to store a one-dimensional list. It can store items either in a **Last-In, First-Out (LIFO)** or **First-In, Last-Out (FILO)** manner. The defining characteristic of a stack is the way elements are added to and removed from it. A new element is added at one end and an element is removed from that end only.

The following are the operations related to stacks:

- **isEmpty**: Returns true if the stack is empty
- **push**: Adds a new element
- **pop**: Returns the element added most recently and removes it

Figure 2.4 shows how push and pop operations can be used to add and remove data from a stack:

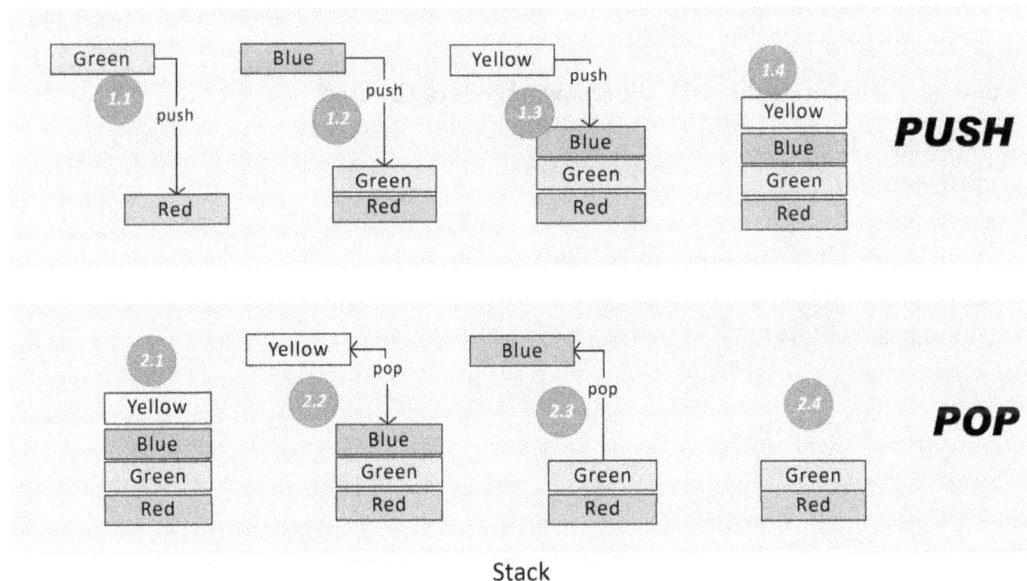

Stack

Figure 2.4: Push and pop operations

The top portion of *Figure 2.4* shows the use of push operations to add items to the stack. In *steps 1.1, 1.2*, and *1.3*, push operations are used three times to add three elements to the stack. The bottom portion of the preceding diagram is used to retrieve the stored values from the stack. In *steps 2.2* and *2.3*, pop operations are used to retrieve two elements from the stack in LIFO format.

Let's create a class named Stack in Python, where we will define all of the operations related to the Stack class. The code of this class will be as follows:

```python
class Stack:
    def __init__(self):
        self.items = []
    def isEmpty(self):
        return self.items == []
    def push(self, item):
        self.items.append(item)
    def pop(self):
        return self.items.pop()
    def peek(self):
        return self.items[len(self.items)-1]
    def size(self):
        return len(self.items)
```

To push four elements to the stack, the following code can be used:

```python
# Populate the stack
stack=Stack()
stack.push('Red')
stack.push('Green')
stack.push("Blue")
stack.push("Yellow")
```

Note that the preceding code creates a stack with four data elements:

```
# Pop
stack.pop()

stack.isEmpty()
```

Time complexity of stack operations

Let us look into the time complexity of stack operations:

- **Push:** This operation adds an element to the top of the stack. Since it doesn't involve any iteration or checking, the time complexity of the push operation is *O(1)*, or constant time. The element is placed on top regardless of the stack's size.

- **Pop:** Popping refers to removing the top element from the stack. Given that there's no need to interact with the rest of the stack, the pop operation also has a time complexity of *O(1)*. It's a direct action on the top element.

Practical example

A stack is used as the data structure in many use cases. For example, when a user wants to browse the history in a web browser, it is a LIFO data access pattern, and a stack can be used to store the history. Another example is when a user wants to perform an undo operation in word processing software.

Queues

Like stacks, a queue stores *n* elements in a single-dimensional structure. The elements are added and removed in FIFO format. One end of the queue is called the rear and the other is called the front. When elements are removed from the front, the operation is called dequeue. When elements are added at the rear, the operation is called enqueue.

In the following diagram, the top portion shows the enqueue operation. *Steps 1.1, 1.2,* and *1.3* add three elements to the queue and the resultant queue is shown in *1.4*. Note that **Yellow** is the rear and **Red** is the front.

The bottom portion of the following diagram shows a dequeue operation. *Steps 2.2, 2.3, and 2.4* remove elements from the queue one by one from the front of the queue:

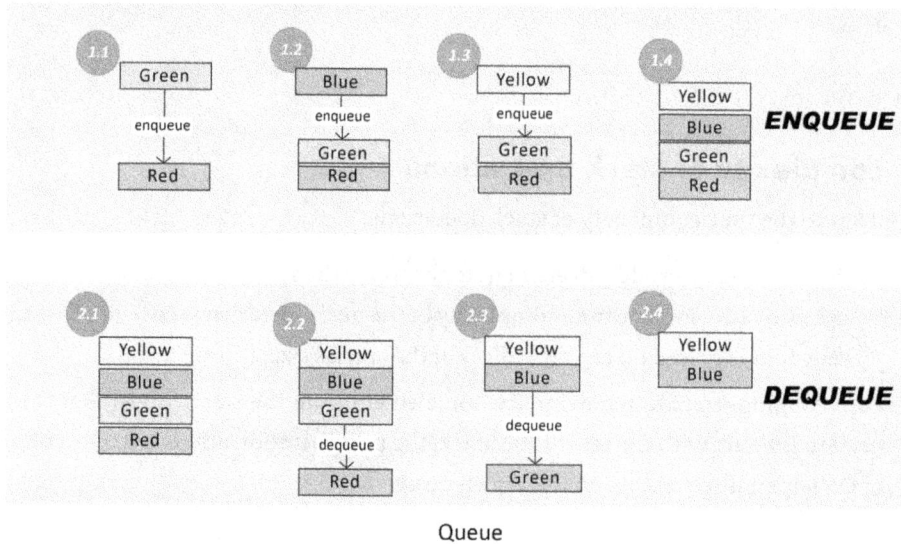

Figure 2.5: Enqueue and dequeue operations

The queue shown in the preceding diagram can be implemented by using the following code:

```python
class Queue(object):
    def __init__(self):
        self.items = []
    def isEmpty(self):
        return self.items == []
    def enqueue(self, item):
        self.items.insert(0,item)
    def dequeue(self):
        return self.items.pop()
    def size(self):
        return len(self.items)
```

Let's enqueue and dequeue elements as shown in the preceding diagramm with the help of the following code:

```python
# Using Queue
queue = Queue()
queue.enqueue("Red")
```

```
queue.enqueue('Green')
queue.enqueue('Blue')
queue.enqueue('Yellow')
print(f"Size of queue is {queue.size()}")
```

```
Size of queue is 4
```

```
print(queue.dequeue())
```

```
Red
```

Note that the preceding code creates a queue first and then enqueues four items into it.

Time complexity analysis for queues

Let us look into the time complexity for queues:

- **Enqueue**: This operation inserts an element t the end of the queue. Given its straightforward nature, without any need for iterating or traversing, the enqueue operation bears a time complexity of $O(1)$ – a constant time.

- **Dequeue**: Dequeueing means removing the front element from the queue. As the operation only involves the first element without any checks or iterations through the queue, its time complexity remains constant at $O(1)$.

The basic idea behind the use of stacks and queues

Let's look into the basic idea behind the use of stacks and queues using an analogy. Let's assume that we have a table where we put our incoming mail from our postal service, for example, Canada Mail. We stack them until we have some time to open and look at the letters, one by one. There are two possible ways of doing this:

- We put the letters in a stack and, whenever we get a new letter, we put it on the top of the stack. When we want to read a letter, we start with the one that is on top. This is what we call a **stack**. Note that the latest letter to arrive will be on the top and will be processed first. Picking up a letter from the top of the list is called a pop operation. Whenever a new letter arrives, putting it on the top is called a push operation. If we end up having a sizable stack and lots of letters are continuously arriving, there is a chance that we never get a chance to reach a very important letter waiting for us at the lower end of the stack.

- We prop up and arrange the letters horizontally like books on a bookshelf. As new letters come in, we add them to the collection on the left side. When we want to open the letters, we pull them from the right side. In this way we always open the oldest letters first. First in, first out. This is what we call a **queue**. Adding a letter to the stack is called an enqueue operation. Removing the letter from the stack is called a dequeue operation.

Tree

In the context of algorithms, a tree is one of the most useful data structures due to its hierarchical data storage capabilities. While designing algorithms, we use trees wherever we need to represent hierarchical relationships among the data elements that we need to store or process.

Let's look deeper into this interesting and quite important data structure.

Each tree has a finite set of nodes so that it has a starting data element called a **root** and a set of nodes joined together by links called **branches**.

Terminology

Let's look into some of the terminology related to the tree data structure:

Root node	A node with no parent is called the root node. For example, in the following diagram (*Figure 2.6*), the root node is A. In algorithms, usually, the root node holds the most important value in the tree structure.
Level of a node	The distance from the root node is the level of a node. For example, in the following diagram, the level of nodes D, E, and F is two.
Siblings nodes	Two nodes in a tree are called siblings if they are at the same level. For example, if we check the following diagram, nodes B and C are siblings.
Child and parent node	Node F is a child of node C if both are directly connected and the level of node C is less than node F. Conversely, node C is a parent of node F. Nodes C and F in the following diagram show this parent-child relationship.
Degree of a node	The degree of a node is the number of children it has. For example, in the following diagram, node B has a degree of two.
Degree of a tree	The degree of a tree is equal to the maximum degree that can be found among the constituent nodes of a tree. For example, the tree presented in the following diagram has a degree of two.

Subtree	A subtree of a tree is a portion of the tree with the chosen node as the root node of the subtree and all of the children as the nodes of the tree. For example, a subtree at node E of the tree presented in the following diagram consists of node E as the root node and nodes G and H as the two children.
Leaf node	A node in a tree with no children is called a leaf node. For example, in the following figure, nodes D, G, H, and F are the four leaf nodes.
Internal node	Any node that is neither a root nor a leaf node is an internal node. An internal node will have at least one parent and at least one child node.

Note that trees are a kind of network or graph that we will study in *Chapter 6, Unsupervised Machine Learning Algorithms*. For graphs and network analysis, we use the terms **link** or **edge** instead of branches. Most of the other terminology remains unchanged.

Types of trees

There are different types of trees, which are explained as follows:

- **Binary tree:** If the degree of a tree is two, that tree is called a *binary tree*. For example, the tree shown in the following diagram is a binary tree as it has a degree of two:

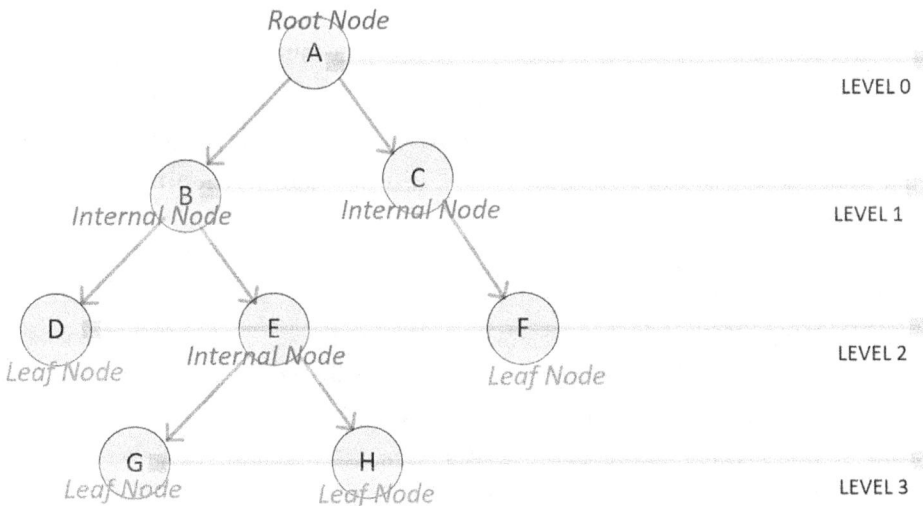

Figure 2.6: A binary tree

Note that the preceding diagram (*Figure 2.6*) shows a tree that has four levels with eight nodes.

- **Full tree**: A full tree is one in which all of the nodes are of the same degree, which will be equal to the degree of the tree. The following diagram (*Figure 2.7*) shows the kinds of trees discussed earlier:

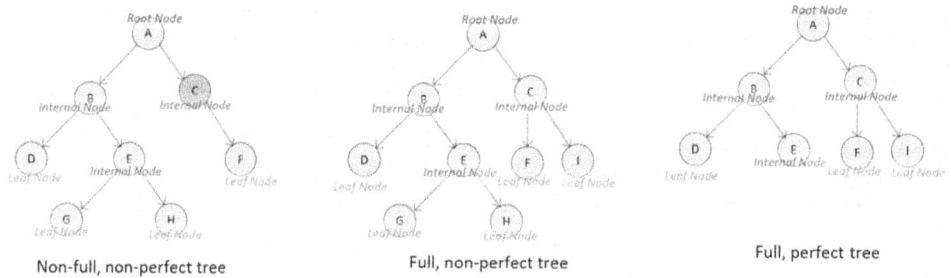

Non-full, non-perfect tree   Full, non-perfect tree   Full, perfect tree

Figure 2.7: A full tree

Note that the binary tree on the left is not a full tree, as node C has a degree of one and all other nodes have a degree of two. The tree in the middle and the one on the right are both full trees.

- **Perfect tree**: A perfect tree is a special type of full tree in which all the leaf nodes are at the same level. For example, the binary tree on the right as shown in the preceding diagram is a perfect, full tree as all the leaf nodes are at the same level – that is, **level 2**.

- **Ordered tree**: If the children of a node are organized in some order according to particular criteria, the tree is called an **ordered tree**. A tree, for example, can be ordered from left to right in ascending order in which the nodes at the same level will increase in value while traversing from left to right.

Practical examples

An ADT tree is one of the main data structures that is used in developing decision trees, as will be discussed in *Chapter 7, Traditional Supervised Learning Algorithms*. Due to its hierarchical structure, it is also popular in algorithms related to network analysis, as will be discussed in detail in *Chapter 6, Unsupervised Machine Learning Algorithms*. Trees are also used in various search and sort algorithms in which divide and conquer strategies need to be implemented.

Summary

In this chapter, we discussed data structures that can be used to implement various types of algorithms. After going through this chapter, you should now be able to select the right data structure to be used to store and process data with an algorithm. You should also be able to understand the implications of your choice on the performance of the algorithm.

The next chapter is about sorting and searching algorithms, in which we will use some of the data structures presented in this chapter in the implementation of the algorithms.

Learn more on Discord

To join the Discord community for this book – where you can share feedback, ask questions to the author, and learn about new releases – follow the QR code below:

`https://packt.link/WHLel`

3

Sorting and Searching Algorithms

In this chapter, we will look at the algorithms that are used for sorting and searching. This is an important class of algorithms that can be used on their own or can become the foundation for more complex algorithms. These include **Natural Language Processing (NLP)** and pattern-extracting algorithms. This chapter starts by presenting different types of sorting algorithms. It compares the performance of various approaches to designing a sorting algorithm. Then, some searching algorithms are presented in detail. Finally, a practical example of the sorting and searching algorithms presented in this chapter is studied.

By the end of this chapter, we should be able to understand the various algorithms that are used for sorting and searching, and we will be able to comprehend their strengths and weaknesses. As searching and sorting algorithms are the building blocks for many complex algorithms, understanding them in detail will help us better understand modern complex algorithms as well, as presented in the later chapters.

The following are the main concepts discussed in this chapter:

- Introducing sorting algorithms
- Introducing searching algorithms
- Performance analysis of sorting and searching algorithms
- Practical applications of sorting and searching

Let's first look at some sorting algorithms.

Introducing sorting algorithms

The ability to efficiently sort and search items in a complex data structure is important as it is needed by many modern algorithms. The right strategy to sort and search data will depend on the size and type of the data, as discussed in this chapter. While the end result is exactly the same, the right sorting and searching algorithm will be needed for an efficient solution to a real-world problem. Thus, carefully analyzing the performance of these algorithms is important.

Sorting algorithms are used extensively in distributed data storage systems such as modern NoSQL databases that enable cluster and cloud computing architectures. In such data storage systems, data elements need to be regularly sorted and stored so that they can be retrieved efficiently.

The following sorting algorithms are presented in this chapter:

- Bubble sort
- Merge sort
- Insertion sort
- Shell sort
- Selection sort

But before we look into these algorithms, let us first discuss the variable-swapping technique in Python that we will be using in the code presented in this chapter.

Swapping variables in Python

When implementing sorting and searching algorithms, we need to swap the values of two variables. In Python, there is a standard way to swap two variables, which is as follows:

```python
var_1 = 1
var_2 = 2
var_1, var_2 = var_2, var_1
print(var_1,var_2)
```

```
2, 1
```

This simple way of swapping values is used throughout the sorting and searching algorithms in this chapter.

Let's start by looking at the bubble sort algorithm in the next section.

Bubble sort

Bubble sort is one of the simplest and slowest algorithms used for sorting. It is designed in such a way that the highest value in a list of data *bubbles* makes its way to the top as the algorithm loops through iterations. Bubble sort requires little runtime memory to run because all the ordering occurs within the original data structure. No new data structures are needed as temporary buffers. But its worst-case performance is $O(N2)$, which is quadratic time complexity (where N is the number of elements being sorted). As discussed in the following section, it is recommended to be used only for smaller datasets. Actual recommended limits for the size of the data for the use of bubble sort for sorting will depend on the memory and the processing resources available but keeping the number of elements (N) below 1000 can be considered as a general recommendation.

Understanding the logic behind bubble sort

Bubble sort is based on various iterations, called passes. For a list of size N, bubble sort will have *N-1* passes. To understand its working, let's focus on the first iteration: pass one.

The goal of pass one is to push the highest value to the highest index (top of the list). In other words, we will see the highest value of the list *bubbling* its way to the top as pass one progresses.

Bubble sort's logic is based on comparing adjacent neighbor values. If the value at a higher index is higher in value than the value at a lower index, we exchange the values. This iteration continues until we reach the end of the list. This is shown in *Figure 3.1*:

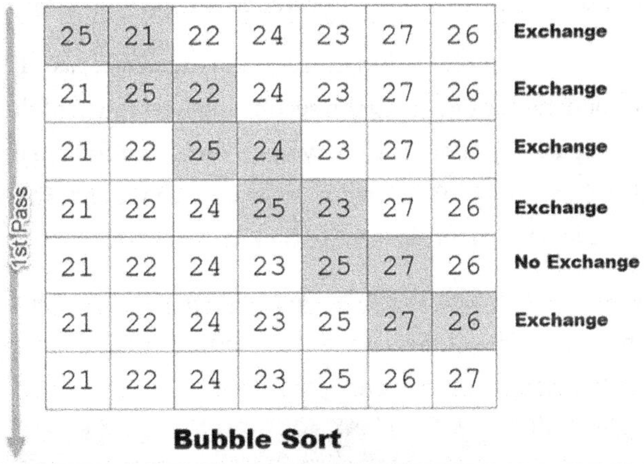

Figure 3.1: Bubble sort algorithm

Let's now see how bubble sort can be implemented using Python. If we implement pass one of bubble sort in Python, it will look as follows:

```python
list = [25,21,22,24,23,27,26]
last_element_index = len(list)-1
print(0,list)
for idx in range(last_element_index):
        if list[idx]>list[idx+1]:
                list[idx],list[idx+1]=list[idx+1],list[idx]
        print(idx+1,list)
```

```
0 [25, 21, 22, 24, 23, 27, 26]
1 [21, 25, 22, 24, 23, 27, 26]
2 [21, 22, 25, 24, 23, 27, 26]
3 [21, 22, 24, 25, 23, 27, 26]
4 [21, 22, 24, 23, 25, 27, 26]
5 [21, 22, 24, 23, 25, 27, 26]
6 [21, 22, 24, 23, 25, 26, 27]
```

Note that after the *first pass*:

- The highest value is at the top of the list, stored at idx+1.
- While executing the first pass, the algorithm has to compare each of the elements of the list individually to *bubble* the maximum value to the top.

After completing the first pass, the algorithm moves on to the *second pass*. The goal of the second pass is to move the second-highest value to the second-highest index of the list. To do that, the algorithm will again compare adjacent neighbor values, exchanging them if they are not in order. The second pass will exclude the value at the top index, which was put in the right place by the first pass. So, it will have one less data element to tackle.

After completing the second pass, the algorithm keeps on performing the third pass and subsequent ones until all the data points of the list are in ascending order. The algorithm will need *N-1* passes for a list of size *N* to completely sort it.

```
[21, 22, 24, 23, 25, 26, 27]
```

We mentioned that performance is one of the limitations of the bubble sort algorithm. Let's quantify the performance of bubble sort through the performance analysis of the bubble sort algorithm:

```python
def bubble_sort(list):
# Exchange the elements to arrange in order
    last_element_index = len(list)-1
    for pass_no in range(last_element_index,0,-1):
        for idx in range(pass_no):
            if list[idx]>list[idx+1]:
                list[idx],list[idx+1]=list[idx+1],list[idx]
    return list

list = [25,21,22,24,23,27,26]
bubble_sort(list)
```

```
[21, 22, 23, 24, 25, 26, 27]
```

Optimizing bubble sort

The above implementation of bubble sort implemented with the bubble_sort function is a straightforward sorting method where adjacent elements are repeatedly compared and swapped if they are out of order. The algorithm consistently requires $O(N2)$ comparisons and swaps in the worst-case scenario, where N is the number of elements in the list. This is because, for a list of N elements, the algorithm invariably goes through *N-1* passes, regardless of the initial order of the list.

The following is an optimized version of bubble sort:

```python
def optimized_bubble_sort(list):
    last_element_index = len(list)-1
    for pass_no in range(last_element_index, 0, -1):
        swapped = False
        for idx in range(pass_no):
            if list[idx] > list[idx+1]:
                list[idx], list[idx+1] = list[idx+1], list[idx]
                swapped = True
        if not swapped:
            break
    return list
list = [25,21,22,24,23,27,26]
```

```
optimized_bubble_sort(list)
```

```
[21, 22, 23, 24, 25, 26, 27]
```

The `optimized_bubble_sort` function introduces a notable enhancement to the bubble sort algorithm's performance. By adding a `swapped` flag, this optimization permits the algorithm to detect early if the list is already sorted before making all *N-1* passes. When a pass completes without any swaps, it's a clear indicator that the list has been sorted, and the algorithm can exit prematurely. Therefore, while the worst-case time complexity remains $O(N2)$ for completely unsorted or reverse-sorted lists, the best-case complexity improves to $O(N)$ for already sorted lists due to this optimization.

In essence, while both functions have a worst-case time complexity of $O(N2)$, the `optimized_bubble_sort` has the potential to perform significantly faster in real-world scenarios where data might be partially sorted, making it a more efficient version of the conventional bubble sort algorithm.

Performance analysis of the bubble sort algorithm

It is easy to see that bubble sort involves two levels of loops:

- **An outer loop:** These are also called **passes**. For example, pass one is the first iteration of the outer loop.

- **An inner loop:** This is when the remaining unsorted elements in the list are sorted until the highest value is bubbled to the right. The first pass will have *N-1* comparisons, the second pass will have *N-2* comparisons, and each subsequent pass will reduce the number of comparisons by one.

The time complexity of the bubble sort algorithm is as follows:

- **Best case:** If the list is already sorted (or almost all elements are sorted), then the runtime complexity is $O(1)$.

- **Worst case:** If none or very few elements are sorted, then the worst-case runtime complexity is $O(n2)$ as the algorithm will have to completely run through both the inner and outer loops.

Now let us look into the insertion sort algorithm.

Insertion sort

The basic idea of insertion sort is that in each iteration, we remove a data point from the data structure we have and then insert it into its right position. That is why we call this the insertion sort algorithm.

In the first iteration, we select the two data points and sort them. Then, we expand our selection and select the third data point and find its correct position, based on its value. The algorithm progresses until all the data points are moved to their correct positions.

This process is shown in the following diagram:

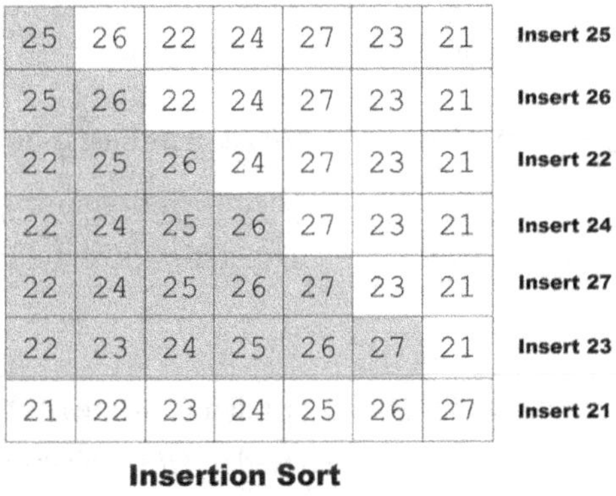

Insertion Sort

Figure 3.2: Insertion sort algorithm

The insertion sort algorithm can be coded in Python as follows:

```python
def insertion_sort(elements):
    for i in range(1, len(elements)):
        j = i - 1
        next_element = elements[i]

        # Iterate backward through the sorted portion,
        # looking for the appropriate position for 'next_element'
        while j >= 0 and elements[j] > next_element:
            elements[j + 1] = elements[j]
            j -= 1

        elements[j + 1] = next_element
    return elements
```

```
list = [25,21,22,24,23,27,26]
insertion_sort(list)
```

```
[21, 22, 23, 24, 25, 26, 27]
```

In the core loop of the algorithm, we traverse through each element of the list starting from the second element (indexed at *1*). For each element, the algorithm checks the preceding elements to find their correct position in the sorted sublist. This check is performed in the condition `elements[j] > next_element`, ensuring that we're placing our current 'next_element' in the appropriate position in the sorted portion of the list.

Let's look at the performance of the insertion sort algorithm.

Performance analysis of the insertion sort algorithm

Understanding the efficiency of an algorithm is crucial in determining its suitability for different applications. Let's delve into the performance characteristics of the insertion sort.

Best case scenario

When the input data is already sorted, insertion sort demonstrates its best behavior. In such cases, the algorithm efficiently runs in linear time, denoted as $O(n)$, where n represents the number of elements in the data structure.

Worst case scenario

The efficiency takes a hit when the input is in reverse order, meaning the largest element is at the beginning. Here, for every element i (where i stands for the current element's index in the loop), the inner loop might need to shift almost all preceding elements. The performance of insertion sort in this scenario can be represented mathematically by a quadratic function of the form:

$$(w \times i^2) + (N \times i) + \epsilon$$

where:

- w is a weighting factor, adjusting the effect of i^2.
- N represents a coefficient that scales with the size of the input.
- ϵ is a constant, typically representing minor overheads not covered by the other terms.

Average case scenario

Generally, the average performance of insertion sort tends to be quadratic, which can be problematic for larger datasets.

Use cases and recommendations

Insertion sort is exceptionally efficient for:

- Small datasets.
- Nearly sorted datasets, where only a few elements are out of order.

However, for larger, more random datasets, algorithms with better average and worst-case performances, like merge sort or quick sort, are more suitable. Insertion sort's quadratic time complexity makes it less scalable for substantial amounts of data.

Merge sort

Merge sort stands distinctively among sorting algorithms, like bubble sort and insertion sort, for its unique approach. Historically, it's noteworthy that John von Neumann introduced this technique in 1940. While many sorting algorithms perform better on partially sorted data, merge sort remains unfazed; its performance remains consistent irrespective of the initial arrangement of the data. This resilience makes it the preferred choice for sorting large datasets.

Divide and conquer: the core of merge sort

Merge sort employs a divide-and-conquer strategy comprising two key phases – splitting and merging:

1. **Splitting phase**: Unlike directly iterating over the list, this phase recursively divides the dataset into halves. This division continues until each section reaches a minimal size (for illustrative purposes, let's say a single element). While it might seem counterintuitive to split data to such granular levels, this granularity facilitates the organized merging in the next phase.
2. **Merging phase**: Here, the previously divided parts are systematically merged. The algorithm continually processes and combines these sections until the entire list is sorted.

Refer to *Figure 3.3* for a visual representation of the merge sort algorithm.

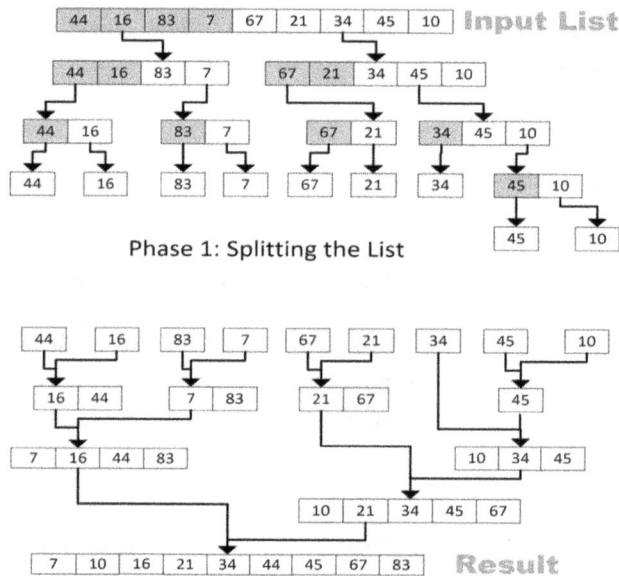

Figure 3.3: Merge sort algorithm

Pseudocode overview

Before delving into the actual code, let's understand its logic with some pseudocode:

```
merge_sort (elements, start, end)
    if(start < end)
        midPoint = (end - start) / 2 + start
        merge_sort (elements, start, midPoint)
        merge_sort (elements, midPoint + 1, end)
        merge(elements, start, midPoint, end)
```

The pseudocode gives a snapshot of the algorithm's steps:

1. Divide the list around a central midPoint.

2. Recursively split until each section has just one element.

3. Systematically merge the sorted sections into a comprehensive sorted list.

Python implementation

Here's the Python rendition of merge sort:

```
def merge_sort(elements):
```

```python
    # Base condition to break the recursion
    if len(elements) <= 1:
        return elements

    mid = len(elements) // 2   # Split the list in half
    left = elements[:mid]
    right = elements[mid:]

    merge_sort(left)    # Sort the left half
    merge_sort(right)   # Sort the right half

    a, b, c = 0, 0, 0
    # Merge the two halves
    while a < len(left) and b < len(right):
        if left[a] < right[b]:
            elements[c] = left[a]
            a += 1
        else:
            elements[c] = right[b]
            b += 1
        c += 1

    # If there are remaining elements in the left half
    while a < len(left):
        elements[c] = left[a]
        a += 1
        c += 1
    # If there are remaining elements in the right half
    while b < len(right):
        elements[c] = right[b]
        b += 1
        c += 1
    return elements

list = [21, 22, 23, 24, 25, 26, 27]
merge_sort(list)
```

```
[21, 22, 23, 24, 25, 26, 27]
```

Shell sort

The bubble sort algorithm compares immediate neighbors and exchanges them if they are out of order. On the other hand, insertion sort creates the sorted list by transferring one element at a time. If we have a partially sorted list, insertion sort should give reasonable performance.

But for a totally unsorted list, sized *N*, you can argue that bubble sort will have to fully iterate through *N-1* passes in order to get it fully sorted.

Donald Shell proposed Shell sort (named after him), which questions the importance of selecting immediate neighbors for comparison and swapping.

Now, let's understand this concept.

In pass one, instead of selecting immediate neighbors, we use elements that are at a fixed gap, eventually sorting a sublist consisting of a pair of data points. This is shown in the following diagram. In pass two, it sorts sublists containing four data points (see the following diagram). In subsequent passes, the number of data points per sublist keeps on increasing and the number of sublists keeps on decreasing until we reach a situation where there is just one sublist that consists of all the data points.

At this point, we can assume that the list is sorted:

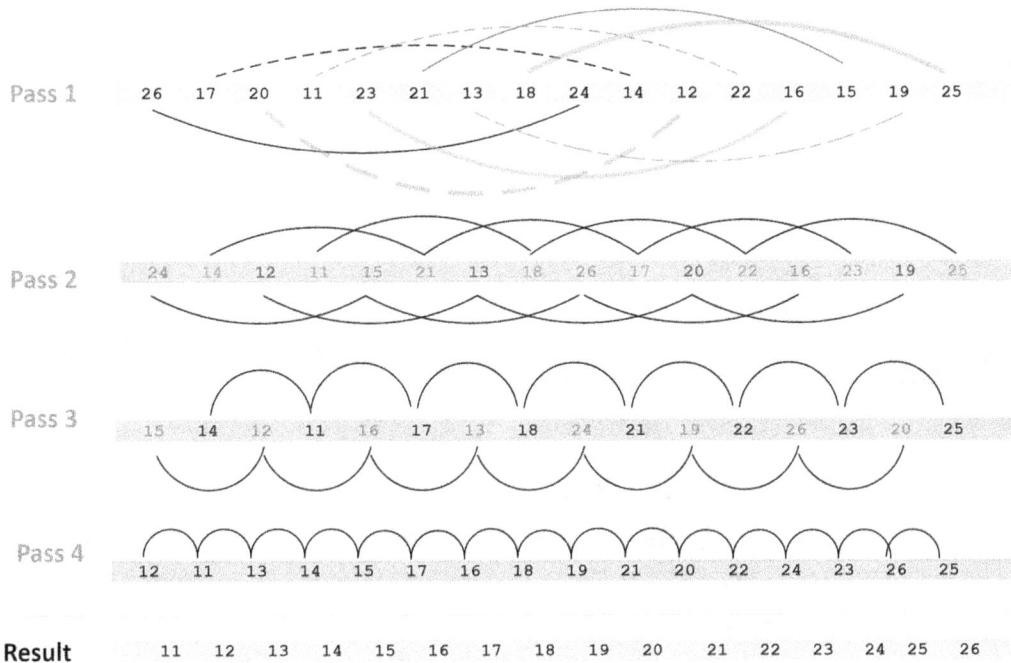

Passes of Shell Sort Algorithm

Figure 3.4: Passes in the Shell sort algorithm

In Python, the code for implementing the Shell sort algorithm is as follows:

```python
def shell_sort(elements):
    distance = len(elements) // 2
    while distance > 0:
        for i in range(distance, len(elements)):
            temp = elements[i]
            j = i
```

```
# Sort the sub list for this distance
            while j >= distance and elements[j - distance] > temp:
                list[j] = elements[j - distance]
                j = j-distance
            list[j] = temp
    # Reduce the distance for the next element
        distance = distance//2
    return elements
list = [21, 22, 23, 24, 25, 26, 27]
shell_sort(list)
```

```
[21, 22, 23, 24, 25, 26, 27]
```

Note that calling the ShellSort function has resulted in sorting the input array.

Performance analysis of the Shell sort algorithm

It can be observed that, in the worst case, the Shell sort algorithm will have to run through both loops giving it a complexity of *O(n2)*. Shell sort is not for big data. It is used for medium-sized datasets. Roughly speaking, it has a reasonably good performance on a list with up to 6,000 elements. If the data is partially in the correct order, the performance will be better. In a best-case scenario, if a list is already sorted, it will only need one pass through *N* elements to validate the order, producing a best-case performance of *O(N)*.

Selection sort

As we saw earlier in this chapter, bubble sort is one of the simplest sorting algorithms. Selection sort is an improvement on bubble sort, where we try to minimize the total number of swaps required with the algorithm. It is designed to make one swap for each pass, compared to *N-1* passes with the bubble sort algorithm. Instead of bubbling the largest value toward the top in baby steps (as done in bubble sort, resulting in *N-1* swaps), we look for the largest value in each pass and move it toward the top. So, after the first pass, the largest value will be at the top. After the second pass, the second largest value will be next to the top value. As the algorithm progresses, the subsequent values will move to their correct place based on their values.

The last value will be moved after the *(N-1)*th pass. So, selection sort takes *N-1* passes to sort *N* items:

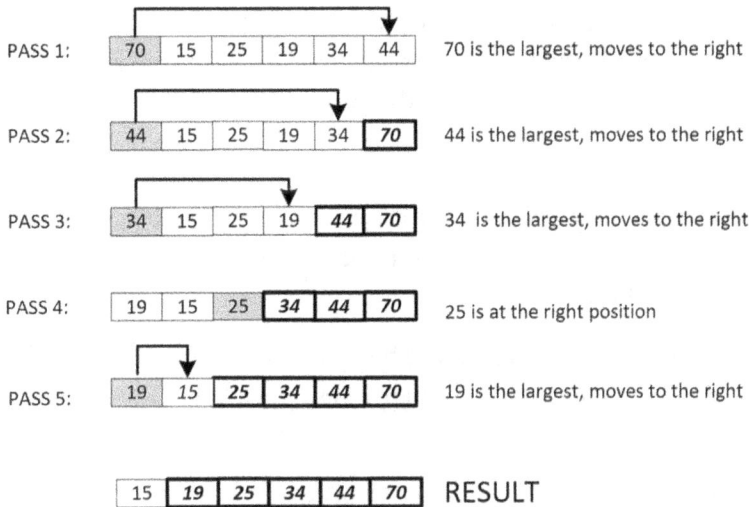

PASS 1: | 70 | 15 | 25 | 19 | 34 | 44 | 70 is the largest, moves to the right

PASS 2: | 44 | 15 | 25 | 19 | 34 | **70** | 44 is the largest, moves to the right

PASS 3: | 34 | 15 | 25 | 19 | *44* | **70** | 34 is the largest, moves to the right

PASS 4: | 19 | 15 | 25 | *34* | *44* | **70** | 25 is at the right position

PASS 5: | 19 | *15* | *25* | *34* | *44* | **70** | 19 is the largest, moves to the right

| 15 | *19* | *25* | *34* | *44* | *70* | RESULT

Figure 3.5: Selection sort algorithm

The implementation of selection sort in Python is shown here:

```python
def selection_sort(list):
    for fill_slot in range(len(list) - 1, 0, -1):
        max_index = 0
        for location in range(1, fill_slot + 1):
            if list[location] > list[max_index]:
                max_index = location
        list[fill_slot],list[max_index] = list[max_index],list[fill_slot]
    return list


list = [21, 22, 23, 24, 25, 26, 27]
selection_sort(list)
```

```
[21, 22, 23, 24, 25, 26, 27]
```

Performance analysis of the selection sort algorithm

Selection sort's worst-case performance is $O(N2)$. Note that its worst performance is similar to bubble sort, and it should not be used for sorting larger datasets. Still, selection sort is a better-designed algorithm than bubble sort and its average performance is better than bubble sort due to the reduction in the number of exchanges.

Choosing a sorting algorithm

When it comes to sorting algorithms, there isn't a one-size-fits-all solution. The optimal choice often hinges on the specific circumstances surrounding your data, such as its size and current state. Here, we'll delve into how to make an informed decision and highlight some real-world examples.

Small and already sorted lists

For petite datasets, especially those already in order, it's usually overkill to deploy a sophisticated algorithm. While an algorithm like merge sort is undeniably powerful, its complexities might overshadow its benefits for small data.

Real-life example: Imagine sorting a handful of books on a shelf by their authors' last names. It's simpler and quicker to just scan through and rearrange them manually (akin to a bubble sort) than to employ a detailed sorting method.

Partially sorted data

When dealing with data that's already somewhat organized, algorithms like insertion sort shine. They capitalize on the existing order, enhancing efficiency.

Real-life example: Consider a classroom scenario. If students line up by height but a few are slightly out of place, the teacher can easily spot and adjust these minor discrepancies (mimicking insertion sort), rather than reordering the entire line.

Large datasets

For extensive data, where the sheer volume can be overwhelming, merge sort proves to be a reliable ally. Its divide-and-conquer strategy efficiently tackles big lists, making it an industry favorite.

Real-life example: Think about a massive library that receives thousands of books. Sorting these by publication date or author necessitates a systematic approach. Here, a method like merge sort, which breaks down the task into manageable chunks, is invaluable.

Introduction to searching algorithms

At the heart of many computational tasks lies a fundamental need: locating specific data within complex structures. On the surface, the most straightforward approach might be to scan every single data point until you find your target. But, as we can imagine, this method loses its sheen as the volume of data swells.

Why is searching so critical? Whether it's a user querying a database, a system accessing files, or an application fetching specific data, efficient searching determines the speed and responsiveness of these operations. Without adept searching techniques, systems can become sluggish, especially with burgeoning datasets.

As the need for fast data retrieval rises, the role of sophisticated search algorithms becomes undeniable. They provide the agility and efficiency needed to wade through vast amounts of data, ensuring that systems remain nimble and users are satisfied. Thus, search algorithms act as the navigators of the digital realm, guiding us to the precise data we seek amid a sea of information.

The following searching algorithms are presented in this section:

- Linear search
- Binary search
- Interpolation search

Let's look at each of them in more detail.

Linear search

One of the simplest strategies for searching data is to simply loop through each element looking for the target. Each data point is searched for a match and, when a match is found, the results are returned and the algorithm exits the loop. Otherwise, the algorithm keeps on searching until it reaches the end of the data. The obvious disadvantage of linear search is that it is very slow due to the inherent exhaustive search. The advantage is that the data does not need to be sorted, as required by the other algorithms presented in this chapter.

Let's look at the code for linear search:

```python
def linear_search(elements, item):
    index = 0
    found = False

    # Match the value with each data element
    while index < len(elements) and found is False:
        if elements[index] == item:
            found = True
        else:
            index = index + 1
    return found
```

Let's now look at the output of the preceding code:

```
list = [12, 33, 11, 99, 22, 55, 90]
print(linear_search(list, 12))
print(linear_search(list, 91))
```

```
True
False
```

Note that running the LinearSearch function returns a True value if it can successfully find the data.

Performance analysis of the linear search algorithm

As discussed, linear search is a simple algorithm that performs an exhaustive search. Its worst-case behavior is O(N). More info can be found at https://wiki.python.org/moin/TimeComplexity.

Binary search

The prerequisite of the binary search algorithm is sorted data. The algorithm iteratively divides a list into two parts and keeps track of the lowest and highest indices until it finds the value it is looking for:

```
def binary_search(elements, item):
    first = 0
    last = len(elements) - 1

    while first<=last:
        midpoint = (first + last) // 2
        if elements[midpoint] == item:
            return True
        else:
            if item < elements[midpoint]:
                last = midpoint - 1
            else:
                first = midpoint + 1
    return False
```

The output is as follows:

```
list = [12, 33, 11, 99, 22, 55, 90]
sorted_list = bubble_sort(list)
```

```
print(binary_search(list, 12))
print(binary_search(list, 91))
```

```
True
False
```

Note that calling the BinarySearch function will return True if the value is found in the input list.

Performance analysis of the binary search algorithm

Binary search is so named because, at each iteration, the algorithm divides the data into two parts. If the data has N items, it will take a maximum of O(logN) steps to iterate. This means that the algorithm has an O(logN) runtime.

Interpolation search

Binary search is based on the logic that it focuses on the middle section of the data. Interpolation search is more sophisticated. It uses the target value to estimate the position of the element in the sorted array. Let's try to understand it by using an example. Let's assume we want to search for a word in an English dictionary, such as the word *river*. We will use this information to interpolate and start searching for words starting with *r*. A more generalized interpolation search can be programmed as follows:

```
def int_polsearch(list,x ):
    idx0 = 0
    idxn = (len(list) - 1)
    while idx0 <= idxn and x >= list[idx0] and x <= list[idxn]:

# Find the mid point
        mid = idx0 +int(((float(idxn - idx0)/(list[idxn] - list[idx0])) *
(x - list[idx0])))

# Compare the value at mid point with search value
        if list[mid] == x:
            return True
        if list[mid] < x:
            idx0 = mid + 1
    return False
```

The output is as follows:

```
list = [12, 33, 11, 99, 22, 55, 90]
sorted_list = bubble_sort(list)
print(int_polsearch(list, 12))
print(int_polsearch(list, 91))
```

```
True
False
```

Note that before using `IntPolsearch`, the array first needs to be sorted using a sorting algorithm.

Performance analysis of the interpolation search algorithm

If the data is unevenly distributed, the performance of the interpolation search algorithm will be poor. The worst-case performance of this algorithm is $O(N)$, and if the data is somewhat reasonably uniform, the best performance is `O(log(log N))`.

Practical applications

The ability to efficiently and accurately search data in a given data repository is critical to many real-life applications. Depending on your choice of searching algorithm, you may need to sort the data first as well. The choice of the right sorting and searching algorithms will depend on the type and the size of the data, as well as the nature of the problem you are trying to solve.

Let's try to use the algorithms presented in this chapter to solve the problem of matching a new applicant at the immigration department of a certain country with historical records. When someone applies for a visa to enter the country, the system tries to match the applicant with the existing historical records. If at least one match is found, then the system further calculates the number of times that the individual has been approved or refused in the past. On the other hand, if no match is found, the system classes the applicant as a new applicant and issues them a new identifier.

The ability to search, locate, and identify a person in the historical data is critical for the system. This information is important because if someone has applied in the past and the application is known to have been refused, then this may affect that individual's current application in a negative way. Similarly, if someone's application is known to have been approved in the past, this approval may increase the chances of that individual getting approval for their current application. Typically, the historical database will have millions of rows, and we will need a well-designed solution to match new applicants in the historical database.

Let's assume that the historical table in the database looks like the following:

Personal ID	Application ID	First name	Surname	DOB	Decision	Decision date
45583	677862	John	Doe	2000-09-19	Approved	2018-08-07
54543	877653	Xman	Xsir	1970-03-10	Rejected	2018-06-07
34332	344565	Agro	Waka	1973-02-15	Rejected	2018-05-05
45583	677864	John	Doe	2000-09-19	Approved	2018-03-02
22331	344553	Kal	Sorts	1975-01-02	Approved	2018-04-15

In this table, the first column, `Personal ID`, is associated with each of the unique applicants in the historical database. If there are 30 million unique applicants in the historical database, then there will be 30 million unique personal IDs. Each personal ID identifies an applicant in the historical database system.

The second column we have is `Application ID`. Each application ID identifies a unique application in the system. A person may have applied more than once in the past. So, this means that, in the historical database, we will have more unique application IDs than personal IDs. John Doe will only have one personal ID but has two application IDs, as shown in the preceding table.

The preceding table only shows a sample of the historical dataset. Let's assume that we have close to 1 million rows in our historical dataset, which contains the records of the last 10 years of applicants. New applicants are continuously arriving at the average rate of around 2 applicants per minute. For each applicant, we need to do the following:

- Issue a new application ID for the applicant.
- See if there is a match with an applicant in the historical database.
- If a match is found, use the personal ID for that applicant, as found in the historical database. We also need to determine how many times the application has been approved or refused in the historical database.
- If no match is found, then we need to issue a new personal ID for that individual.

Suppose a new person arrives with the following credentials:

- `First Name: John`
- `Surname: Doe`
- `DOB: 2000-09-19`

Now, how can we design an application that can perform an efficient and cost-effective search?

One strategy for searching the new application in the database can be devised as follows:

1. Sort the historical database by DOB.
2. Each time a new person arrives, issue a new application ID to the applicant.
3. Fetch all the records that match that date of birth. This will be the primary search.
4. Out of the records that have come up as matches, perform a secondary search using the first and last name.
5. If a match is found, use `Personal ID` to refer to the applicants. Calculate the number of approvals and refusals.
6. If no match is found, issue a new personal ID to the applicant.

Let's try choosing the right algorithm to sort the historical database. We can safely rule out bubble sort as the size of the data is huge. Shell sort will perform better, but only if we have partially sorted lists. So, merge sort may be the best option for sorting the historical database.

When a new person arrives, we need to search for and locate that person in the historical database. As the data is already sorted, either interpolation search or binary search can be used. Because applicants are likely to be equally spread out, as per DOB, we can safely use binary search.

Initially, we search based on DOB, which returns a set of applicants sharing the same date of birth. Now, we need to find the required person within the small subset of people who share the same date of birth. As we have successfully reduced the data to a small subset, any of the search algorithms, including bubble sort, can be used to search for the applicant. Note that we have simplified the secondary search problem here a bit. We also need to calculate the total number of approvals and refusals by aggregating the search results, if more than one match is found.

In a real-world scenario, each individual needs to be identified in the secondary search using some fuzzy search algorithm, as the first and last names may be spelled slightly differently. The search may need to use some kind of distance algorithm to implement the fuzzy search, where the data points whose similarity is above a defined threshold are considered the same.

Summary

In this chapter, we presented a set of sorting and searching algorithms. We also discussed the strengths and weaknesses of different sorting and searching algorithms. We quantified the performance of these algorithms and learned when to use each algorithm.

In the next chapter, we will study dynamic algorithms. We will also look at a practical example of designing an algorithm and the details of the page ranking algorithm. Finally, we will study the linear programming algorithm.

Learn more on Discord

To join the Discord community for this book – where you can share feedback, ask questions to the author, and learn about new releases – follow the QR code below:

`https://packt.link/WHLel`

4

Designing Algorithms

This chapter presents the core design concepts of various algorithms. It discusses the strengths and weaknesses of various techniques for designing algorithms. By understanding these concepts, we will learn how to design efficient algorithms.

This chapter starts by discussing the different choices available to us when designing algorithms. Then, it discusses the importance of characterizing the particular problem that we are trying to solve. Next, it uses the famous **Traveling Salesperson Problem (TSP)** as a use case and applies the different design techniques that we will be presenting. Then, it introduces linear programming and discusses its applications. Finally, it presents how linear programming can be used to solve a real-world problem.

By the end of this chapter, you should be able to understand the basic concepts of designing an efficient algorithm.

The following concepts are discussed in this chapter:

- The various approaches to designing an algorithm
- Understanding the trade-offs involved in choosing the correct design for an algorithm
- Best practices for formulating a real-world problem
- Solving a real-world optimization problem

Let's first look at the basic concepts of designing an algorithm.

Introducing the basic concepts of designing an algorithm

An algorithm, according to the American Heritage Dictionary, is defined as follows:

> *A finite set of unambiguous instructions that given some set of initial conditions can be performed in a prescribed sequence to achieve a certain goal and that has a recognizable set of end conditions.*

Designing an algorithm is about coming up with this *"finite set of unambiguous instructions"* in the most efficient way to *"achieve a certain goal."* For a complex real-world problem, designing an algorithm is a tedious task. To come up with a good design, we first need to fully understand the problem we are trying to solve. We start by figuring out what needs to be done (that is, understanding the requirements) before looking into how it will be done (that is, designing the algorithm). Understanding the problem includes addressing both the functional and non-functional requirements of the problem. Let's look at what these are:

- Functional requirements formally specify the input and output interfaces of the problem that we want to solve and the functions associated with them. Functional requirements help us understand data processing, data manipulation, and the calculations that need to be implemented to generate the result.

- Non-functional requirements set the expectations about the performance and security aspects of the algorithm.

Note that designing an algorithm is about addressing both the functional and non-functional requirements in the best possible way under the given set of circumstances and keeping in mind the set of resources available to run the designed algorithm.

To come up with a good response that can meet the functional and non-functional requirements, our design should respect the following three concerns, as discussed in *Chapter 1, Overview of Algorithms*:

- **Correctness**: Will the designed algorithm produce the result we expect?
- **Performance**: Is this the optimal way to get these results?
- **Scalability**: How is the algorithm going to perform on larger datasets?

In this section, let's look at these concerns one by one.

Concern 1: correctness: will the designed algorithm produce the result we expect?

An algorithm is a mathematical solution to a real-world problem. To be useful, it should produce accurate results. How to verify the correctness of an algorithm should not be an afterthought; instead, it should be baked into the design of the algorithm. Before strategizing how to verify an algorithm, we need to think about the following two aspects:

- **Defining the truth**: To verify the algorithm, we need some known correct results for a given set of inputs. These known correct results are called the truths, in the context of the problem we are trying to solve. The truth is important as it is used as a reference when we iteratively work on evolving our algorithm toward a better solution.

- **Choosing metrics**: We also need to think about how we are going to quantify the deviation from the defined truth. Choosing the correct metrics will help us to accurately quantify the quality of our algorithm.

  For example, for supervised machine learning algorithms, we can use existing labeled data as the truth. We can choose one or more metrics, such as accuracy, recall, or precision, to quantify deviation from the truth. It is important to note that, in some use cases, the correct output is not a single value. Instead, the correct output is defined as the range for a given set of inputs. As we work on the design and development of our algorithm, the objective will be to iteratively improve the algorithm until it is within the range specified in the requirements.

- **Consideration of edge cases**: An edge case happens when our designed algorithm is operating at the extremes of operating parameters. An edge case is usually a scenario that is rare but needs to be well tested, as it can cause our algorithm to fail. The non-edge cases are called the "happy path" covering all the scenarios that usually happen when the operating parameters are within the normal range. The vast majority of the time, the algorithm will remain on the "happy path." Unfortunately, there is no way to come up with all possible edge cases for a given algorithm, but we should consider as many edge cases as possible. But without consideration and thinking about the edge cases, problems may arise.

Concern 2: performance: is this the optimal way to get these results?

The second concern is about finding the answer to the following question:

Is this the optimal solution and can we verify that no other solution exists for this problem that is better than our solution?

At first glance, this question looks quite simple to answer. However, for a certain class of algorithms, researchers have unsuccessfully spent decades verifying whether a particular solution generated by an algorithm is also the best and that no other solution exists that can give better performance. So, it becomes important that we first understand the problem, its requirements, and the resources available to run the algorithm.

To provide the best solution to a certain complex problem, we need to answer the fundamental question of whether we should even aim to find the optimal solution for this problem. If finding and verifying the optimal solution is a hugely time-consuming and complex task, then a workable solution may be our best bet. These approximate workable solutions are *heuristics*.

So, understanding the problem and its complexities is important and helps us estimate the resource requirements.

Before we start looking deeper into this, first, let's define a couple of terms here:

- **Polynomial algorithm**: If an algorithm has a time complexity of $O(n^k)$, we call it a polynomial algorithm, where k is a constant.

- **Certificate**: A proposed candidate solution produced at the end of an iteration is called a certificate. As we progress iteratively in solving a particular problem, we typically generate a series of certificates. If the solution is moving toward convergence, each generated certificate will be better than the previous one. At some point, when our certificate meets the requirements, we will choose that certificate as the final solution.

In *Chapter 1, Overview of Algorithms*, we introduced Big O notation, which can be used to analyze the time complexity of an algorithm. In the context of analyzing time complexity, we are looking at the following different time intervals:

- **Candidate solution generation time**, t_r: It is the time it takes for an algorithm to produce a candidate solution.

- **Candidate solution verification time**, t_s: It is the time it takes to verify the candidate solution (certificate).

Characterizing the complexity of the problem

Over the years, the research community has divided problems into various categories according to their complexity.

Before we attempt to design the solution to a problem, it makes sense to first try to characterize it. Generally, there are three types of problems:

- Problems for which we can guarantee that a polynomial algorithm exists that can be used to solve them

- Problems for which we can prove that they cannot be solved by a polynomial algorithm

- Problems for which we are unable to find a polynomial algorithm to solve them, but we are also unable to prove that a polynomial solution for those problems is impossible to find

Let's look at the various classes of problems according to their complexity:

- **Non-Deterministic Polynomial (NP)**: Problems that can be solved in polynomial time by a non-deterministic computer. Broadly, it means that a reasonable solution to a problem can be found and verified in polynomial times by making a reasonable guess at every step without an effort to find the optimal solution. Formally, for a problem to be an **NP** problem, it must meet the following condition, named Condition A:

    - **Condition A**: It is guaranteed that there is a polynomial algorithm that can be used to verify that the candidate solution (certificate) is optimal.

- **Polynominal (P)**: Problems that can be solved in polynomial time by a deterministic computer. These problems can be solved by some algorithm with runtime $O(N^k)$ for some power k, no matter how large. These are types of problems that can be thought of as a subset of **NP**. In addition to meeting the condition of an NP problem, Condition A, P problems need to meet another condition, named Condition B:

    - **Condition A**: It is guaranteed that there is a polynomial algorithm that can be used to verify that the candidate solution (certificate) is optimal.

    - **Condition B**: It is guaranteed that there is at least one polynomial algorithm that can be used to solve them.

Exploring the relationship between P and NP

Understanding the relationship between P and NP is still a work in progress. What we know for sure is that P is a subset of NP, i.e., $P \subseteq NP$. That is obvious from the above discussion where NP needs to meet only the first of the two conditions that P needs to meet.

The relationship between P and NP problems is shown in *Figure 4.1*:

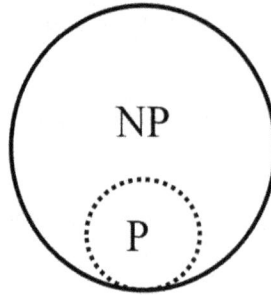

Figure 4.1: Relationship between P and NP problems

What we do not know for sure is that if a problem is NP, is it P as well? This is one of the greatest problems in computer science that remains unresolved. Millennium Prize Problems, selected by the Clay Mathematics Institute, has announced a 1-million-dollar prize for the solution to this problem as it will have a major impact on fields such as AI, cryptography, and theoretical computer sciences. There are certain problems, such as sorting, that are known to be in P. Others, such as the knapsack and TSP, are known to be in NP.

There is a lot of ongoing research effort to answer this question. As yet, no researcher has discovered a polynomial-time-deterministic algorithm to solve the knapsack or TSP. It is still a work in progress and no one has been able to prove that no such algorithm is possible.

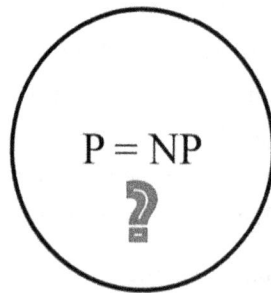

Figure 4.2: DoesP = NP? We do not know as yet

Introducing NP-complete and NP-hard

Let's continue the list of various classes of problems:

- **NP-complete:** The NP-complete category contains the hardest problems of all NP problems. An NP-complete problem meets the following two conditions:

- There are no known polynomial algorithms to generate a certificate.
- There are known polynomial algorithms to verify that the proposed certificate is optimal.

- **NP-hard**: The NP-hard category contains problems that are at least as hard as any problem in the NP category, but that do not themselves need to be in the NP category.

Now, let's try to draw a diagram to illustrate these different classes of problems:

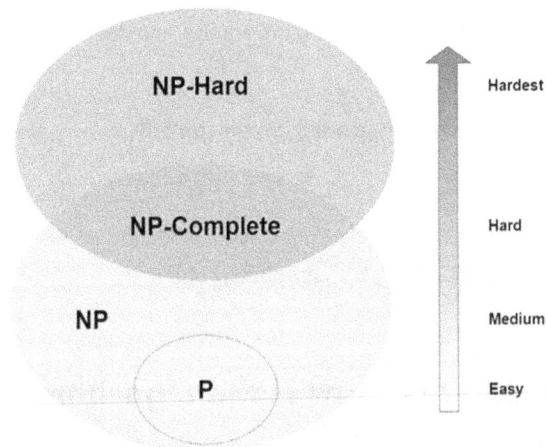

Figure 4.3: Relationship between P, NP, NP-complete, and NP-hard

Note that it is still to be proven by the research community whether P = NP. Although this has not yet been proven, it is extremely likely that P ≠ NP. In that case, no polynomial solution exists for NP-complete problems. Note that the preceding diagram is based on this assumption.

The distinction between P, NP, NP-complete, and NP-hard

Unfortunately, the distinction between P, NP, NP-compete, and NP-hard is not clear-cut. Let us summarize and study some examples to make better sense of the concepts discussed in this section:

- **P**: It is the class of problems solvable in polynomial time. For example:
    - Hashtable lookup
    - Shortest path algorithms like Djikstra's algorithms
    - Linear and binary search algorithms

- **NP-problem**: The problems are not solvable in polynomial time, but their solution can be verified in polynomial time. For example:

  - RSA encryption algorithm

- **NP-hard**: These are complex problems that no one has come up with a solution for as yet, but if solved, would have a polynomial time solution. For example:

  - Optimal clustering using the *K*-means algorithm

- **NP-complete**: The NP-complete problems are the "hardest" in NP. They are both NP-hard and NP. For example:

  - Calculation of an optimal solution for the TSP

> Finding a solution for one of either classes (NP-hard or NP-complete) would imply a solution for all NP-hard/NP-complete problems.

Concern 3 – scalability: how is the algorithm going to perform on larger datasets?

An algorithm processes data in a defined way to produce a result. Generally, as the size of the data increases, it takes more and more time to process the data and calculate the required results. The term **big data** is sometimes used to roughly identify datasets that are expected to be challenging for the infrastructure and algorithms to work with due to their volume, variety, and velocity. A well-designed algorithm should be scalable, which means that it should be designed in a way that means, wherever possible, it should be able to run efficiently, making use of the available resources and generating the correct results in a reasonable timeframe. The design of the algorithm becomes even more important when dealing with big data. To quantify the scalability of an algorithm, we need to keep the following two aspects in mind:

- **The increase in resource requirements as the input data is increased**: Estimating a requirement such as this is called space complexity analysis.

- **The increase in the time taken to run as the input data is increased**: Estimating this is called time complexity analysis.

Note that we are living in an era that is defined by data explosion. The term big data has become mainstream, as it captures the size and complexity of the data that is typically required to be processed by modern algorithms.

While in the development and testing phase, many algorithms use only a small sample of data. When designing an algorithm, it is important to look into the scalability aspect of the algorithms. In particular, it is important to carefully analyze (that is, test or predict) the effect of an algorithm's performance as datasets increase in size.

The elasticity of the cloud and algorithmic scalability

Cloud computing has made new options available to deal with the resource requirements of an algorithm. Cloud computing infrastructures are capable of provisioning more resources as the processing requirements increase. The ability of cloud computing is called the elasticity of the infrastructure and has now provided us with more options for designing an algorithm. When deployed on the cloud, an algorithm may demand additional CPUs or VMs based on the size of the data to be processed.

Typical deep learning algorithms are a good example. To train a good deep learning model, lots of labeled data is needed. For a well-designed deep learning algorithm, the processing required to train a deep learning model is directly proportional to the number of examples or close to it. When training a deep learning model in the cloud, as the size of data increases, we try to provision more resources to keep training time within manageable limits.

Understanding algorithmic strategies

A well-designed algorithm tries to optimize the use of the available resources most efficiently by dividing the problem into smaller subproblems wherever possible. There are different algorithmic strategies for designing algorithms. An algorithmic strategy deals with the following three aspects of an algorithm list containing aspects of the missing algorithm.

We will present the following three strategies in this section:

- The divide-and-conquer strategy
- The dynamic programming strategy
- The greedy algorithm strategy

Understanding the divide-and-conquer strategy

One of the strategies is to find a way to divide a larger problem into smaller problems that can be solved independently of each other. The subsolutions produced by these subproblems are then combined to generate the overall solution to the problem. This is called the divide-and-conquer strategy.

Mathematically, if we are designing a solution for a problem (P) with n inputs that needs to process dataset d, we split the problem into k subproblems, $P1$ to Pk. Each of the subproblems will process a partition of the dataset, d. Typically, we will have $P1$ to Pk processing $d1$ to dk respectively.

Let's look at a practical example.

A practical example – divide-and-conquer applied to Apache Spark

Apache Spark (https://spark.apache.org/) is an open-source framework that is used to solve complex distributed problems. It implements a divide-and-conquer strategy to solve problems. To process a problem, it divides the problem into various subproblems and processes them independently of each other. These subproblems can run on separate machines enabling horizontal scaling. We will demonstrate this by using a simple example of counting words from a list.

Let's assume that we have the following list of words:

```
words_list = ["python", "java", "ottawa", "news", "java", "ottawa"]
```

We want to calculate the frequency of each word in this list. For that, we will apply the divide-and-conquer strategy to solve this problem in an efficient way.

The implementation of divide-and-conquer is shown in the following diagram:

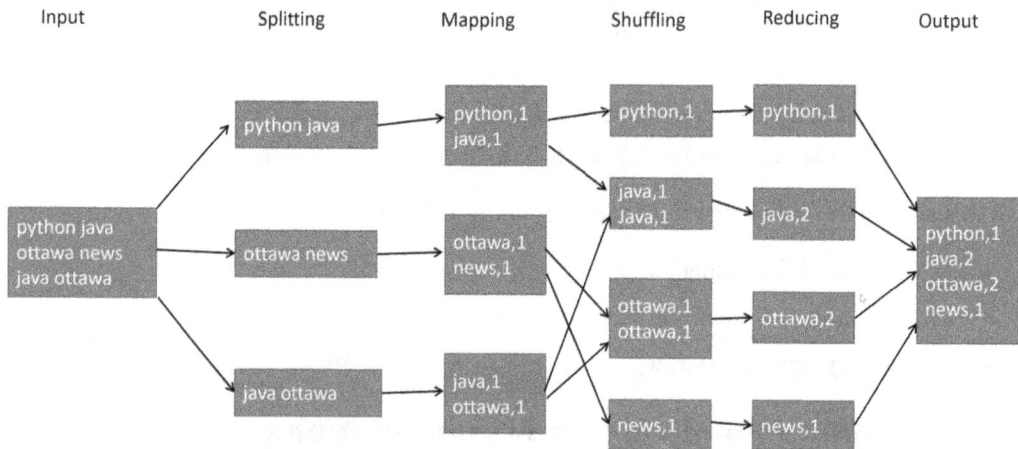

Figure 4.4: Divide and conquer

The preceding diagram shows the following phases into which a problem is divided:

1. **Splitting:** The input data is divided into partitions that can be processed independently of each other. This is called splitting. We have three splits in the preceding figure.

2. **Mapping**: Any operation that can run independently on a split is called a map. In the preceding diagram, the map operation converts each of the words in the partition in to key-value pairs. Corresponding to the three splits, there are three mappers that are run in parallel.

3. **Shuffling**: Shuffling is the process of bringing similar keys together. Once similar keys are brought together, aggregation functions can be run on their values. Note that shuffling is a performance-intensive operation, as similar keys need to be brought together that can be originally distributed across the network.

4. **Reducing**: Running an aggregation function on the values of similar keys is called reducing. In the preceding diagram, we have to count the number of words.

Let's see how we can write the code to implement this. To demonstrate the divide-and-conquer strategy, we need a distributed computing framework. We will run Python running on Apache Spark for this:

1. First, in order to use Apache Spark, we will create a runtime context of Apache Spark:

```
import findspark
findspark.init()
from pyspark.sql import SparkSession
spark = SparkSession.builder.master("local[*]").getOrCreate()
sc = spark.sparkContext
```

2. Now, let's create a sample list containing some words. We will convert this list into Spark's native distributed data structure, called a **Resilient Distributed Dataset (RDD)**:

```
wordsList = ['python', 'java', 'ottawa', 'ottawa', 'java','news']
wordsRDD = sc.parallelize(wordsList, 4)
# Print out the type of wordsRDD
print (wordsRDD.collect())
```

3. It will print:

```
['python', 'java', 'ottawa', 'ottawa', 'java', 'news']
```

4. Now, let's use a map function to convert the words into a key-value pair:

```
wordPairs = wordsRDD.map(lambda w: (w, 1))
print (wordPairs.collect())
```

5. It will print:

```
[('python', 1), ('java', 1), ('ottawa', 1), ('ottawa', 1), ('java',
1), ('news', 1)]
```

6. Let's use the reduce function to aggregate and get the result:

```
wordCountsCollected = wordPairs.reduceByKey(lambda x,y: x+y)
print(wordCountsCollected.collect())
```

7. It prints:

```
[('python', 1), ('java', 2), ('ottawa', 2), ('news', 1)]
```

This shows how we can use the divide-and-conquer strategy to count the number of words. Note that divide-and-conquer is useful when a problem can be divided into subproblems and each subproblem can at least be partially solved independently of other subproblems. It is not the best choice for algorithms that require intensive iterative processing, such as optimization algorithms. For such algorithms, dynamic programming is suitable, which is presented in the next section.

> Modern cloud computing infrastructures, such as Microsoft Azure, Amazon Web Services, and Google Cloud, achieve scalability in a distributed infrastructure that uses several CPUs/GPUs in parallel by implementing a divide-and-conquer strategy either directly or indirectly behind the scenes.

Understanding the dynamic programming strategy

In the previous section, we studied divide and conquer, which is a top-down method. In contrast, dynamic programming is a bottom-up strategy. We start with the smallest subproblem and keep on combining the solutions. We keep on combining until we reach the final solution. Dynamic programming, like the divide-and-conquer method, solves problems by combining the solutions with subproblems.

Dynamic programming is a strategy proposed in the 1950s by Richard Bellman to optimize certain classes of algorithms. Note that in dynamic programming, the word "programming" refers to the use of a tabular method and has nothing to do with writing code. In contrast to the divide and conquer strategy, dynamic programming is applicable when the subproblems are not independent. It is typically applied to optimization problems in which each subproblem's solution has a value.

Our objective is to find a solution with optimal value. A dynamic programming algorithm solves every subproblem just once and then saves its answer in a table, thereby avoiding the work of recomputing the answer every time the subproblem is encountered.

Components of dynamic programming

Dynamic programming is based on two major components:

- **Recursion:** It solves subproblems recursively.
- **Memoization:** Memoization or caching. It is based on an intelligent caching mechanism that tries to reuse the results of heavy computations. This intelligent caching mechanism is called memoization. The subproblems partly involve a calculation that is repeated in those subproblems. The idea is to perform that calculation once (which is the time-consuming step) and then reuse it on the other subproblems. This is achieved using memoization, which is especially useful in solving recursive problems that may evaluate the same inputs multiple times.

Conditions for using dynamic programming

The problem we are trying to solve with dynamic programming should have two characteristics.

- **Optimal structure:** Dynamic programming gives good performance benefits when the problem we are trying to solve can be divided into subproblems.
- **Overlapping subproblems:** Dynamic programming uses a **recursive** function that solves a particular problem by calling a copy of itself and solving smaller subproblems of the original problems. The computed solutions of the subproblems are stored in a table, so that these don't have to be re-computed. Hence, this technique is needed where an overlapping sub-problem exists.

Dynamic programming is a perfect fit for combinatorial optimization problems, which are problems that needs providing optimal combinations of input elements as a solution.

Examples include:

- Finding the optimal way to deliver packages for a company like FedEx or UPS
- Finding the optimal airline routes and airports
- Deciding how to assign drivers for an online food delivery system like Uber Eats

Understanding greedy algorithms

As the name indicates, a greedy algorithm relatively quickly produces a good solution, but it cannot be the optimal solution. Like dynamic programming, greedy algorithms are mainly used to solve optimization problems where a divide-and-conquer strategy cannot be used. In the greedy algorithm, the solution is calculated following a sequence of steps. At each step, a locally optimal choice is made.

Conditions for using greedy programming

Greedy is a strategy that works well on problems with the following two characteristics:

- **Global from local**: A global optimum can be arrived at by selecting a local optimum.
- **Optimal substructure**: An optimal solution to the problem is made from optimal solutions to subproblems.

To understand the greedy algorithm, let's first define two terms:

- **Algorithmic overheads**: Whenever we try to find the optimal solution to a certain problem, it takes some time. As the problems that we are trying to optimize become more and more complex, the time it takes to find the optimal solution also increases. We represent algorithmic overheads with Ωi.
- **Delta from optimal**: For a given optimization problem, there exists an optimal solution. Typically, we iteratively optimize the solution using our chosen algorithm. For a given problem, there always exists a perfect solution, called the optimal solution, to the current problem. As discussed, based on the classification of the problem we are trying to solve, it's possible for the optimal solution to be unknown or for it to take an unreasonable amount of time to calculate and verify it. Assuming that the optimal solution is known, the difference from optimal for the current solution in the ith iteration is called delta from optimal and is represented by Δi.

For complex problems, we have two possible strategies:

- Spend more time finding a solution nearest to optimal so that Δi is as small as possible.
- Minimize the algorithmic overhead, Ωi. Use the quick-and-dirty approach and just use a workable solution.

Greedy algorithms are based on the second strategy, where we do not make an effort to find a global optimal and choose to minimize the algorithm overheads instead.

Using a greedy algorithm is a quick and simple strategy for finding the global optimal value for multistage problems. It is based on selecting the local optimal values without making an effort to verify whether local optimal values are globally optimal as well. Generally, unless we are lucky, a greedy algorithm will not result in a value that can be considered globally optimal. However, finding a global optimal value is a time-consuming task. Hence, the greedy algorithm is fast compared to the divide-and-conquer and dynamic programming algorithms.

Generally, a greedy algorithm is defined as follows:

1. Let's assume that we have a dataset, *D*. In this dataset, choose an element, *k*.

2. Let's assume the candidate solution or certificate is *S*. Consider including *k* in the solution, *S*. If it can be included, then the solution is *Union(S, e)*.

3. Repeat the process until *S* is filled up or *D* is exhausted.

Example:

The **Classification And Regression Tree (CART)** algorithm is a greedy algorithm, which searches for an optimum split at the top level. It repeats the process at each subsequent level. Note that the CART algorithm does not calculate and check whether the split will lead to the lowest possible impurity several levels down. CART uses a greedy algorithm because finding the optimal tree is known to be an NP-complete problem. It has an algorithmic complexity of $O(exp(m))$ time.

A practical application – solving the TSP

Let's first look at the problem statement for the TSP, which is a well-known problem that was coined as a challenge in the 1930s. The TSP is an NP-hard problem. To start with, we can randomly generate a tour that meets the condition of visiting all of the cities without caring about the optimal solution. Then, we can work to improve the solution with each iteration. Each tour generated in an iteration is called a candidate solution (also called a certificate). Proving that a certificate is optimal requires an exponentially increasing amount of time. Instead, different heuristics-based solutions are used that generate tours that are near to optimal but are not optimal.

A traveling salesperson needs to visit a given list of cities to get their job done:

INPUT	A list of *n* cities (denoted as *V*) and the distances between each pair of cities, d_{ij} $(1 \leq i, j \leq n)$
OUTPUT	The shortest tour that visits each city exactly once and returns to the initial city

Note the following:

- The distances between the cities on the list are known
- Each city in the given list needs to be visited *exactly* once

Can we generate the travel plan for the salesperson? What will be the optimal solution that can minimize the total distance traveled by the traveling salesperson?

The following are the distances between five Canadian cities that we can use for the TSP:

	Ottawa	Montreal	Kingston	Toronto	Sudbury
Ottawa	-	199	196	450	484
Montreal	199	-	287	542	680
Kingston	196	287	-	263	634
Toronto	450	542	263	-	400
Sudbury	484	680	634	400	-

Note that the objective is to get a tour that starts and ends in the initial city. For example, a typical tour can be Ottawa–Sudbury–Montreal–Kingston–Toronto–Ottawa with a cost of *484 + 680 + 287 + 263 + 450 = 2,164*. Is this the tour in which the salesperson has to travel the minimum distance? What will be the optimal solution that can minimize the total distance traveled by the traveling salesperson? I will leave this up to you to think about and calculate.

Using a brute-force strategy

The first solution that comes to mind to solve the TSP is using brute force to come up with the shortest path in which the salesperson visits every city exactly once and returns to the initial city. So, the brute-force strategy works as follows:

- Evaluate all possible tours.
- Choose the one for which we get the shortest distance.

The problem is that for n number of cities, there are *(n-1)!* possible tours. That means that five cities will produce *4! = 24* tours, and we will select the one that corresponds to the lowest distance. It is obvious that this method will only work when we do not have too many cities. As the number of cities increases, the brute-force strategy becomes unsolvable due to the large number of permutations generated by using this approach.

Let's see how we can implement the brute-force strategy in Python.

First, note that a tour, {*1,2,3*}, represents a tour of the city from city 1 to city 2 and city 3. The total distance in a tour is the total distance covered in a tour. We will assume that the distance between the cities is the shortest distance between them (which is the Euclidean distance).

Let's first define three utility functions:

- distance_points: Calculates the absolute distance between two points
- distance_tour: Calculates the total distance the salesperson has to cover in a given tour
- generate_cities: Randomly generates a set of *n* cities located in a rectangle of width 500 and height 300

Let's look at the following code:

```python
import random
from itertools import permutations
```

In the preceding code, we implemented alltours from the permutations function of the itertools package. We have also represented the distance with a complex number. This means the following:

Calculating the distance between two cities, *a* and *b*, is as simple as distance (a,b).

We can create *n* number of cities just by calling generate_cities(n):

```python
def distance_tour(aTour):
    return sum(distance_points(aTour[i - 1], aTour[i])
                for i in range(len(aTour))
    )
aCity = complex


def distance_points(first, second):
    return abs(first - second)


def generate_cities (number_of_cities):
    seed=111
    width=500
    height=300
    random.seed((number_of_cities, seed))
    return frozenset(aCity(random.randint(1, width),
                        random.randint(1, height))
                    for c in range(number_of_cities))
```

Now let's define a function, brute_force, that generates all the possible tours of the cities. Once it has generated all possible tours, it will choose the one with the shortest distance:

```python
def brute_force(cities):
    return shortest_tour(alltours(cities))

def shortest_tour(tours):
    return min(tours, key=distance_tour)
```

Now let's define the utility functions that can help us plot the cities. We will define the following functions:

- visualize_tour: Plots all the cities and links in a particular tour. It also highlights the city from which the tour started.
- visualize_segment: Used by visualize_tour to plot cities and links in a segment.

Look at the following code:

```python
import matplotlib.pyplot as plt
def visualize_tour(tour, style='bo-'):
if len(tour) > 1000:
        plt.figure(figsize=(15, 10))
    start = tour[0:1]
    visualize_segment(tour + start, style)
    visualize_segment(start, 'rD')

def visualize_segment (segment, style='bo-'):
    plt.plot([X(c) for c in segment], [Y(c) for c in segment], style,
clip_on=False)
    plt.axis('scaled')
    plt.axis('off')

def X(city):
    "X axis";
    return city.real
def Y(city):
    "Y axis";
    return city.imag
```

Let's implement a function, tsp(), that does the following:

1. Generates the tour based on the algorithm and number of cities requested.
2. Calculates the time it took for the algorithm to run.
3. Generates a plot.

Once tsp() is defined, we can use it to create a tour:

```python
from time import time
from collections import Counter
def tsp(algorithm, cities):
    t0 = time()
    tour = algorithm(cities)
    t1 = time()
    # Every city appears exactly once in tour
    assert Counter(tour) == Counter(cities)
    visalize_tour(tour)
    print("{}:{} cities => tour length {;.0f} (in {:.3f} sec".format(
        name(algorithm), len(tour), distance_tour(tour), t1-t0))
def name(algorithm):
    return algorithm.__name__.replace('_tsp','')


tps(brute_force, generate_cities(10))
```

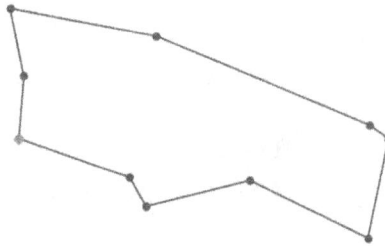

Figure 4.5: Solution of TSP

Note that we have used it to generate the tour for 10 cities. As *n = 10*, it will generate *(10-1)! =* *362,880* possible permutations. If n increases, the number of permutations sharply increases and the brute-force method cannot be used.

Using a greedy algorithm

If we use a greedy algorithm to solve the TSP, then, at each step, we can choose a city that seems reasonable, instead of finding a city to visit that will result in the best overall path. So, whenever we need to select a city, we just select the nearest city without bothering to verify that this choice will result in the globally optimal path.

The approach of the greedy algorithm is simple:

1. Start from any city.

2. At each step, keep building the tour by moving to the next city where the nearest neighborhood has not been visited before.

3. Repeat *step 2*.

Let's define a function named greedy_algorithm that can implement this logic:

```python
def greedy_algorithm(cities, start=None):
    city_ = start or first(cities)
    tour = [city_]
    unvisited = set(cities - {city_})
    while unvisited:
        city_ = nearest_neighbor(city_, unvisited)
        tour.append(city_)
        unvisited.remove(city_)
    return tour


def first(collection): return next(iter(collection))


def nearest_neighbor(city_a, cities):
    return min(cities, key=lambda city_: distance_points(city_, city_a))
```

Now, let's use greedy_algorithm to create a tour for 2,000 cities:

```python
tsp(greedy_algorithm, generate_cities(2000))
```

```
nn: 1991 cities ⇒ tour length 15846 (in 0.514 sec)
```

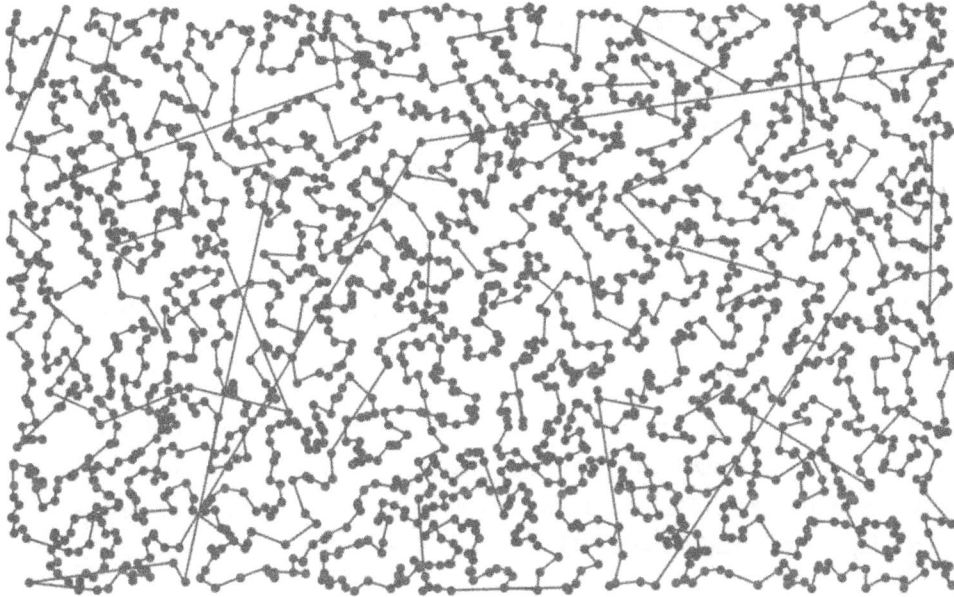

Figure 4.6: Cities displayed in Jupyter Notebook

Note that it took only 0.514 seconds to generate the tour for 2,000 cities. If we had used the brute-force method, it would have generated *(2000-1)!* = $1.65e^{5732}$ permutations, which is almost infinite.

Note that the greedy algorithm is based on heuristics and there is no proof that the solution will be optimal.

Comparison of Three Strategies

To summarize, the outcome of the greedy algorithm is more efficient in terms of calculation time whereas the brute-force method provides the combination with the global optimum. This means the calculation time as well as the quality of the outcome differ. The proposed greedy algorithm may reach nearly as high outcomes as brute force does, with significantly less calculation time, but as it does not search for an optimal solution, it is based on a effort-based strategy and there are no guarantees.

Now, let's look at the design of the **PageRank** algorithm.

Presenting the PageRank algorithm

As a practical example, let's look at the PageRank algorithm, which is used by Google to rank the search results of a user query. It generates a number that quantifies the importance of search results in the context of the query the user has executed. This was designed by two Ph.D. students, Larry Page and Sergey Brin, at Stanford in the late 1990s, who also went on to start Google. *The PageRank algorithm* was named after Larry Page.

Let's first formally define the problem for which PageRank was initially designed.

Problem definition

Whenever a user enters a query on a search engine on the web, it typically results in a large number of results. To make the results useful for the end user, it is important to rank the web pages using some criteria. The results that are displayed use this ranking to summarize the results for the user and are dependent on the criteria defined by the underlying algorithm being used.

Implementing the PageRank algorithm

First, while using the PageRank algorithm, the following representation is used:

- Web pages are represented by nodes in a directed graph.
- The graph edges correspond to hyperlinks.

The most important part of the PageRank algorithm is to come up with the best way to calculate the importance of each page that is returned by the query results. The rank of a particular web page in the network is calculated as the probability that a person randomly traversing the edges (i.e., clicking on links) will arrive at that page. Also, this algorithm is parametrized by the damping factor alpha, which has a default value of 0.85. This damping factor is the probability that the user will continue clicking. Note that the page with the highest PageRank is the most attractive: regardless of where the person starts, this page has the highest probability of being the final destination.

The algorithm requires many iterations or passes through the collection of web pages to determine the right importance (or PageRank value) of each web page.

To calculate a number from 0 to 1 that can quantify the importance of a particular page, the algorithm incorporates information from the following two components:

- **Information that was specific to the query entered by the user**: This component estimates, in the context of the query entered by the user, how relevant the content of the web page is. The content of the page is directly dependent on the author of the page.

- **Information that was not relevant to the query entered by the user**: This component tries to quantify the importance of each web page in the context of its links, views, and neighborhood. The neighborhood of a web page is the group of web pages directly connected to a certain page. This component is difficult to calculate as web pages are heterogeneous, and coming up with criteria that can be applied across the web is difficult to develop.

In order to implement the PageRank algorithm in Python, first, let's import the necessary libraries:

```python
import numpy as np
import networkx as nx
import matplotlib.pyplot as plt
```

Note that the network is from https://networkx.org/. For the purpose of this demonstration, let's assume that we are analyzing only five web pages in the network. Let's call this set of pages my_pages and together they are in a network named my_web:

```python
my_web = nx.DiGraph()
my_pages = range(1,6)
```

Now, let's connect them randomly to simulate an actual network:

```python
connections = [(1,3),(2,1),(2,3),(3,1),(3,2),(3,4),(4,5),(5,1),(5,4)]
my_web.add_nodes_from(my_pages)
my_web.add_edges_from(connections)
```

Now, let's plot this graph:

```python
pos = nx.shell_layout(my_web)
nx.draw(my_web, pos, arrows=True, with_labels=True)
plt.show()
```

It creates the visual representation of our network, as follows:

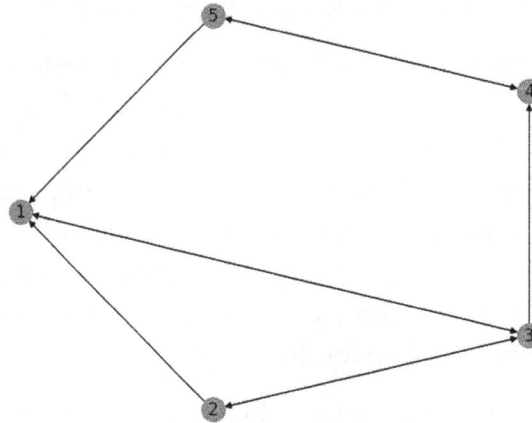

Figure 4.7: Visual representation of the network

In the PageRank algorithm, the patterns of a web page are contained in a matrix called the transition matrix. There are algorithms that constantly update the transition matrix to capture the constantly changing state of the web. The size of the transition matrix is n x n, where n is the number of nodes. The numbers in the matrix are the probability that a visitor will next go to that link due to the outbound link.

In our case, the preceding graph shows the static web that we have. Let's define a function that can be used to create the transition matrix:

```
def create_page_rank(a_graph):
    nodes_set = len(a_graph)
    M = nx.to numpy_matrix(a_graph)
    outwards = np.squeeze(np.asarray (np. sum (M, axis=1)))
    prob outwards = np.array([
        1.0 / count if count>0
        else 0.0
        for count in outwards
    ])
    G = np.asarray(np.multiply (M.T, prob_outwards))
    p = np.ones(nodes_set) / float (nodes_set)
    return G, p
```

Note that this function will return G, which represents the transition matrix for our graph.

Let's generate the transition matrix for our graph:

```
G,p = create_page_rank(my_web)
print (G)
```

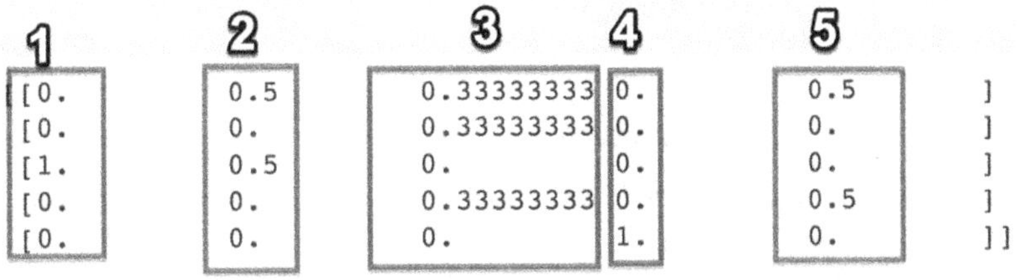

Figure 4.8: Transition matrix

Note that the transition matrix is 5 x 5 for our graph. Each column corresponds to each node in the graph. For example, column 2 is about the second node. There is a 0.5 probability that the visitor will navigate from node 2 to node 1 or node 3. Note that the diagonal of the transition matrix is 0 as in our graph, there is no outbound link from a node to itself. In an actual network, it may be possible.

Note that the transition matrix is a sparse matrix. As the number of nodes increases, most of its values will be 0. Thus, the structure of a graph is extracted as a *transition matrix*. In a transaction matrix, nodes are represented in columns and rows:

- **Columns:** Indicates to the node that a web surfer is online
- **Rows:** Indicates the probability that the surfer will visit other nodes because of outbound links

In the real web, the transition matrix that feeds the PageRank algorithm is built by spiders' continuous exploration of links.

Understanding linear programming

Many real-world problems involve maximizing or minimizing an objective, with some given constraints. One approach is to specify the objective as a linear function of some variables. We also formulate the constraints on resources as equalities or inequalities on those variables. This approach is called the linear programming problem. The basic algorithm behind linear programming was developed by George Dantzig at the University of California at Berkeley in the early 1940s. Dantzig used this concept to experiment with logistical supply-and-capacity planning for troops while working for the US Air Force.

At the end of the Second World War, Dantzig started working for the Pentagon and matured his algorithm into a technique that he named linear programming. It was used for military combat planning.

Today, it is used to solve important real-world problems that relate to minimizing or maximizing a variable based on certain constraints. Some examples of these problems are as follows:

- Minimizing the time to repair a car at a mechanic shop based on the resources
- Allocating available distributed resources in a distributed computing environment to minimize response times
- Maximizing the profit of a company based on the optimal assignment of resources within the company

Formulating a linear programming problem

The conditions for using linear programming are as follows:

- We should be able to formulate the problem through a set of equations.
- The variables used in the equation must be linear.

Defining the objective function

Note that the objective of each of the preceding three examples is about minimizing or maximizing a variable. This objective is mathematically formulated as a linear function of other variables and is called the objective function. The aim of a linear programming problem is to minimize or maximize the objective function while remaining within the specified constraints.

Specifying constraints

When trying to minimize or maximize something, there are certain constraints in real-world problems that need to be respected. For example, when trying to minimize the time it takes to repair a car, we also need to consider that there is a limited number of mechanics available. Specifying each constraint through a linear equation is an important part of formulating a linear programming problem.

A practical application – capacity planning with linear programming

Let's look at a practical use case where linear programming can be used to solve a real-world problem.

Let's assume that we want to maximize the profits of a state-of-the-art factory that manufactures two different types of robots:

- **Advanced model (A):** This provides full functionality. Manufacturing each unit of the advanced model results in a profit of $4,200.

- **Basic model (B):** This only provides basic functionality. Manufacturing each unit of the basic model results in a profit of $2,800.

There are three different types of people needed to manufacture a robot. The exact number of days needed to manufacture a robot of each type is as follows:

Type of Robot	Technician	AI Specialist	Engineer
Robot A: advanced model	3 days	4 days	4 days
Robot B: basic model	2 days	3 days	3 days

The factory runs on 30-day cycles. A single AI specialist is available for 30 days in a cycle. Each of the two engineers will take 8 days off in 30 days. So, an engineer is available only for 22 days in a cycle. There is a single technician available for 20 days in a 30-day cycle.

The following table shows the number of people we have in the factory:

	Technician	AI Specialist	Engineer
Number of people	1	1	2
Total number of days in a cycle	1 x 20 = 20 days	1 x 30 = 30 days	2 x 22 = 44 days

This can be modeled as follows:

- Maximum profit = 4200A + 2800B

- This is subject to the following:

    - $A \geq 0$: The number of advanced robots produced can be 0 or more.
    - $B \geq 0$: The number of basic robots produced can be 0 or more.
    - $3A + 2B \leq 20$: These are the constraints of the technician's availability.
    - $4A+3B \leq 30$: These are the constraints of the AI specialist's availability.
    - $4A+ 3B \leq 44$: These are the constraints of the engineers' availability.

First, we import the Python package named pulp, which is used to implement linear programming:

```
import pulp
```

Then, we call the `LpProblem` function in this package to instantiate the problem class. We name the instance `Profit maximising problem`:

```python
# Instantiate our problem class
model = pulp.LpProblem("Profit_maximising_problem", pulp.LpMaximize)
```

Then, we define two linear variables, `A` and `B`. Variable `A` represents the number of advanced robots that are produced and variable `B` represents the number of basic robots that are produced:

```python
A = pulp.LpVariable('A', lowBound=0,  cat='Integer')
B = pulp.LpVariable('B', lowBound=0, cat='Integer')
```

We define the objective function and constraints as follows:

```python
# Objective function
model += 5000 * A + 2500 * B, "Profit"


# Constraints
model += 3 * A + 2 * B <= 20
model += 4 * A + 3 * B <= 30
model += 4 * A + 3 * B <= 44
```

We use the solve function to generate a solution:

```python
# Solve our problem
model.solve()
pulp.LpStatus[model.status]
```

Then, we print the values of A and B and the value of the objective function:

```python
# Print our decision variable values
print (A.varValue)
print (B.varValue)
```

The output is:

```
6.0
1.0
```

```python
# Print our objective function value
print (pulp.value(model.objective))
```

It prints:

```
32500.0
```

> Linear programming is extensively used in the manufacturing industry to find the optimal number of products that should be used to optimize the use of available resources.

And here we come to the end of this chapter! Let's summarize what we have learned.

Summary

In this chapter, we studied various approaches to designing an algorithm. We looked at the trade-offs involved in choosing the correct design of an algorithm. We looked at the best practices for formulating a real-world problem. We also learned how to solve a real-world optimization problem. The lessons learned from this chapter can be used to implement well-designed algorithms.

In the next chapter, we will focus on graph-based algorithms. We will start by looking at different ways of representing graphs. Then, we will study the techniques to establish a neighborhood around various data points to conduct a particular investigation. Finally, we will study the optimal ways to search for information in graphs.

Learn more on Discord

To join the Discord community for this book – where you can share feedback, ask questions to the author, and learn about new releases – follow the QR code below:

https://packt.link/WHLel

5

Graph Algorithms

Graphs offer a distinct way to represent data structures, especially when compared to structured or tabular data. While structured data, such as databases, excel at storing and querying static, uniform information, graphs shine in capturing intricate relationships and patterns that exist among entities. Think of Facebook, where every user is a node, and each friendship or interaction becomes a connecting edge; this web of connections can be best represented and analyzed using graph structures.

In the computational realm, certain problems, often those involving relationships and connections, are more naturally addressed using graph algorithms. At their core, these algorithms aim to understand the structure of the graph. This understanding involves figuring out how data points (or nodes) connect via links (or edges) and how to effectively navigate these connections to retrieve or analyze the desired data.

In this chapter, we'll embark on a journey through the following territories:

- **Graph representations**: Various ways to capture graphs.
- **Network theory analysis**: The foundational theory behind network structures.
- **Graph traversals**: Techniques to efficiently navigate through a graph.
- **Case study**: Delving into fraud analytics using graph algorithms.
- **Neighborhood techniques**: Methods to ascertain and analyze localized regions within larger graphs.

Upon completion, we will have a robust grasp of graphs as data structures. We should be able to formulate complex relationships—both direct and indirect—and will be equipped to tackle complex, real-world problems using graph algorithms.

Understanding graphs: a brief introduction

In the vast interconnected landscapes of modern data, beyond the confines of tabular models, graph structures emerge as powerful tools to encapsulate intricate relationships. Their rise isn't merely a trend but a response to challenges posed by the digital world's interwoven fabric. Historical strides in graph theory, like Leonhard Euler's pioneering solution to the Seven Bridges of Königsberg problem, laid the foundation for understanding complex relationships. Euler's method of translating real-world issues into graphical representations revolutionized how we perceive and navigate graphs.

Graphs: the backbone of modern data networks

Graphs not only provide the backbone for platforms such as social media networks and recommendation engines but also serve as the key to unlocking patterns in seemingly unrelated sectors, like road networks, electrical circuits, organic molecules, ecosystems, and even the flow of logic in computer programs. What's pivotal to graphs is their intrinsic capability to express both tangible and intangible interactions.

But why is this structure, with its nodes and edges, so central to modern computing? The answer lies in graph algorithms. Tailored for understanding and interpreting relationships, these mathematical algorithms are precisely designed to process connections. They establish clear steps to decode a graph, revealing both its overarching characteristics and intricate details.

Before delving into representations of graphs, it's crucial to establish a foundational understanding of the mechanics behind them. Graphs, rooted in the rich soil of mathematics and computer science, offer an illustrative method to depict relationships among entities.

Real-world applications

The increasingly intricate patterns and connections observed in modern data find clarity in graph theory. Beyond the simple nodes and edges lie the solutions to some of the world's most complex problems. When the mathematical precision of graph algorithms meets real-world challenges, the outcomes can be astonishingly transformative:

- **Fraud detection:** In the world of digital finance, fraudulent transactions can be deeply interconnected, often weaving a subtle web meant to deceive conventional detection systems. Graph theory is deployed to spot these patterns. For instance, a sudden spike in interconnected small transactions from a singular source to multiple accounts might be a hint at money laundering.

By charting out these transactions on a graph, analysts can identify unusual patterns, isolate suspicious nodes, and trace the origin of potential fraud, ensuring that digital economies remain secure.

- **Air traffic control**: The skies are bustling with movement. Every aircraft must navigate a maze of routes while ensuring safe distances from others. Graph algorithms map the skies, treating each aircraft as a node and their flight paths as edges. The 2010 US air travel congestion events are a testament to the power of graph analytics. Scientists used graph theory to decipher systemic cascading delays, offering insights to optimize flight schedules and reduce the chances of such occurrences in the future.

- **Disease spread modeling**: The proliferation of diseases, especially contagious ones, doesn't happen randomly; they follow the invisible lines of human interaction and movement. Graph theory creates intricate models that mimic these patterns. By treating individuals as nodes and their interactions as edges, epidemiologists have successfully projected disease spread, identifying potential hotspots and enabling timely interventions. For instance, during the early days of the COVID-19 pandemic, graph algorithms played a pivotal role in predicting potential outbreak clusters, helping to guide lockdowns and other preventive measures.

- **Social media recommendations**: Ever wondered how platforms like Facebook or Twitter suggest friends or content? Underlying these suggestions are vast graphs representing user interactions, interests, and behaviors. For example, if two users have multiple mutual friends or similar engagement patterns, there's a high likelihood they might know each other or have aligned interests. Graph algorithms help decode these connections, enabling platforms to enhance user experience through relevant recommendations.

The basics of a graph: vertices (or nodes)

These are the individual entities or data points in the graph. Imagine each friend on your Facebook list as a separate vertex:

- **Edges (or links)**: The connections or relationships between the vertices. When you become friends with someone on Facebook, an edge is formed between your vertex and theirs.

- **Network**: A larger structure formed by the interconnected web of vertices and edges. For example, the entirety of Facebook, with all its users and their friendships, can be viewed as a colossal network.

In *Figure 5.1*, **A, B,** and **C** represent vertices, while the lines connecting them are edges. It's a simple representation of a graph, laying the groundwork for the more intricate structures and operations we'll explore.

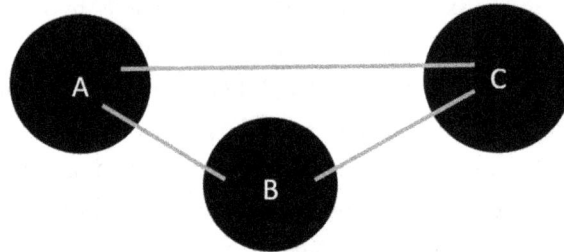

Figure 5.1: Graphic representation of a simple graph

Graph theory and network analysis

Graph theory and network analysis, although intertwined, serve different functions in understanding complex systems. While graph theory is a branch of discrete mathematics that provides the foundational concepts of nodes (entities) and edges (relationships), network analysis is the application of these principles to study and interpret real-world networks. For instance, graph theory might define the structure of a social media platform where individuals are nodes and their friendships are edges; conversely, network analysis would delve into this structure to uncover patterns, like influencer hubs or isolated communities, thereby providing actionable insights into user behavior and platform dynamics.

We will first start by looking into how we can mathematically and visually represent the graphs. Then we'll harness the power of network analysis on these representations using a pivotal set of tools known as "graph algorithms."

Representations of graphs

A graph is a structure that represents data in terms of vertices and edges. A graph is represented as $a_{Graph} = (\mathcal{V}, \mathcal{E})$, where $\mathcal{V}$ represents a set of vertices and $\mathcal{E}$ represents a set of edges. Note that a_{Graph} has $|\mathcal{V}|$ vertices and $|\mathcal{E}|$ edges. It's important to note that unless specified otherwise, an edge can be bidirectional, implying a two-way relationship between the connected vertices.

A vertex, $v \in \mathcal{V}$, represents a real-world object, such as a person, a computer, or an activity. An edge, $v \in \mathcal{E}$, connects two vertices in a network:

$$e(v1, v2) \mid e \in \mathcal{E} \,\&\, vi \in \mathcal{V}$$

The preceding equation indicates that in a graph, all edges belong to a set, ε, and all vertices belong to a set, γ. Note that the notation '|' used here is a symbolic representation indicating that an element belongs to a particular set, ensuring clarity in the relationship between edges, vertices, and their respective sets.

A vertex symbolizes tangible entities like individuals or computers, whereas an edge, connecting two vertices, denotes a relationship. Such relationships can be friendships between individuals, online connections, physical links between devices, or participatory connections such as attending a conference.

Graph mechanics and types

There are multiple types of graphs, each with its unique attributes:

- **Simple graph**: A graph with no parallel edges or loops.
- **Directed graph (DiGraph)**: A graph where each edge has a direction, indicating a one-way relationship.
- **Undirected graph**: A graph where edges don't have a specific direction, suggesting a mutual relationship.
- **Weighted graph**: A graph where each edge carries a weight, often representing distances, costs, etc.

In this chapter, we will use the networkx Python package to represent graphs. It can be downloaded from https://networkx.org/. Let's try to create a simple graph using the networtx package in Python. A "simple graph," as alluded to in graph theory, is a graph that has no parallel edges or loops. To begin with, let's try to create an empty graph, aGraph, with no vertex or node:

```python
import networkx as nx
graph = nx.Graph()
```

Let's add a single vertex:

```python
graph.add_node("Mike")
```

We can also add a series of vertices using a list:

```python
graph.add_nodes_from(["Amine", "Wassim", "Nick"])
```

We can also add one edge between the existing vertices, as shown here:

```python
graph.add_edge("Mike", "Amine")
```

Let's now print the edges and avertices:

```
print(graph.nodes())
print(graph.edges())
```

```
['Mike', 'Amine', 'Wassim', 'Nick']
[('Mike', 'Amine')]
```

Please note that if we add an edge, this also leads to adding the associated vertices, if they do not already exist, as shown here:

```
G.add_edge("Amine", "Imran")
```

If we print the list of nodes, the following is the output that we observe:

```
print(graph.edges())
```

```
[('Mike', 'Amine'), ('Amine', 'Imran')]
```

Note that the request to add a vertex that already exists is silently ignored. The request is ignored or considered based on the type of graph we have created.

Ego-centered networks

At the heart of many network analyses lies a concept called the ego-centered network, or simply, the egonet. Imagine wanting to study not just an individual node but also its immediate surroundings. This is where the egonet comes into play.

Basics of egonets

For a given vertex—let's call it m—the surrounding nodes that are directly connected to m from its direct neighborhood. This neighborhood, combined with m itself, constitutes the egonet of m. In this context:

- m is referred to as the *ego*.
- The directly connected nodes are termed *one-hop neighbors* or simply *alters*.

One-hop, two-hop, and beyond

When we say "one-hop neighbors," we refer to nodes that are directly connected to our node of interest. Think of it as a single step or "hop" from one node to the next. If we were to consider nodes that are two steps away, they'd be termed "two-hop neighbors," and so on. This nomenclature can extend to any number of hops, paving the way to understanding n-degree neighborhoods.

The ego network of a particular node, **3**, is shown in the following graph:

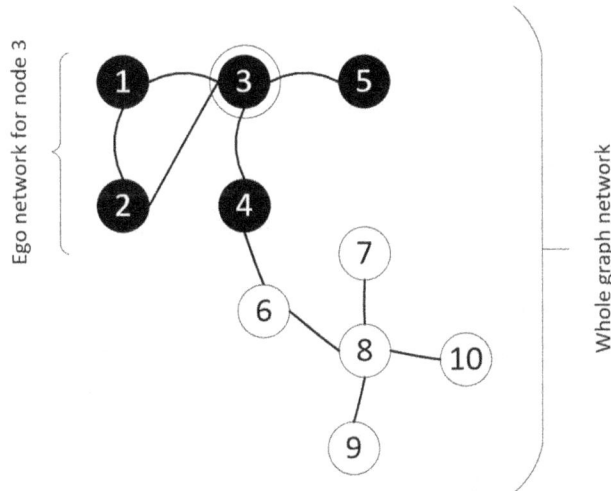

Figure 5.2: Egonet of node 3, showcasing the ego and its one-hop neighbors

Applications of egonets

Egonets are widely utilized in social network analysis. They are pivotal in understanding local structures in large networks and can offer insights into individual behaviors, based on their immediate network surroundings.

For instance, in online social platforms, egonets can help detect influential nodes or understand information dissemination patterns within localized network regions.

Introducing network analysis theory

Network analysis allows us to delve into data that's interconnected, presenting it in the form of a network. It involves studying and employing methodologies to examine data that's arranged in this network format. Here, we'll break down the core elements and concepts related to network analysis.

At the heart of a network lies the "vertex," serving as the fundamental unit. Picture a network as a web; vertices are the points of this web, while the links connecting them represent relationships between different entities under study. Notably, different relationships can exist between two vertices, implying that edges can be labeled to denote various kinds of relationships. Imagine two people being connected as "friends" and "colleagues"; both are different relationships but link the same individuals.

To fully harness the potential of network analysis, it's vital to gauge the significance of a vertex within a network, especially concerning the problem at hand. Multiple techniques exist to aid us in ascertaining this significance.

Let's look at some of the important concepts used in network analysis theory.

Understanding the shortest path

In graph theory, a "path" is defined as a sequence of nodes, connecting a starting node to an ending node, without revisiting any node in between. Essentially, a path outlines the route between two chosen vertices. The "length" of this path is determined by counting the number of edges it contains. Among the various paths possible between two nodes, the one with the least number of edges is termed the "shortest path."

Identifying the shortest path is a fundamental task in many graph algorithms. However, its determination isn't always straightforward. Over time, multiple algorithms have been developed to tackle this problem, with Dijkstra's algorithm, introduced in the late 1950s, being one of the most renowned. This algorithm is designed to pinpoint the shortest distance in a graph and has found its way into applications like GPS devices, which rely on it to deduce the minimal distance between two points. In the realm of network routing, Dijkstra's method again proves invaluable.

Big tech companies like Google and Apple are in a continuous race, especially when it comes to enhancing their map services. The goal is not just to identify the shortest route but to do so swiftly, often in mere seconds.

Later in this chapter, we'll explore the **breadth-first search** (**BFS**) algorithm, a method that can serve as a foundation for Dijkstra's algorithm. The standard BFS assumes equal costs to traverse any path in a graph. However, Dijkstra's takes into account varying traversal costs. To adapt BFS into Dijkstra's, we need to integrate these varying traversal costs.

Lastly, while Dijkstra's algorithm focuses on identifying the shortest path from a single source to all other vertices, if one aims to determine the shortest paths between every pair of vertices in a graph, the Floyd-Warshall algorithm is more suitable.

Creating a neighborhood

When diving into graph algorithms, the term "neighborhood" frequently emerges. So, what do we imply by a neighborhood in this setting? Think of it as a close-knit community centered around a specific node. This "community" comprises nodes that either have a direct connection or are closely associated with the focal node.

As an analogy, envision a city map where landmarks represent nodes. The landmarks in the immediate vicinity of a notable place form its "neighborhood."

A widely adopted approach to demarcate these neighborhoods is through the k-order strategy. Here, we determine a node's neighborhood by pinpointing vertices that lie k hops away. For a hands-on understanding, at $k=1$, the neighborhood houses all nodes linked directly to the focal node. For $k=2$, it broadens to include nodes connected to these immediate neighbors, and the pattern continues.

Imagine a central dot within a circle as our target vertex. At $k=1$, any dot connected directly to this central figure is its neighbor. As we increment k the circle's radius grows, encapsulating dots situated further away.

Harnessing and interpreting neighborhoods is important for graph algorithms, as it identifies key analysis zones.

Let's look at the various criteria to create neighborhoods:

1. Triangles
2. Density

Let us look into them in more detail.

Triangles

In the expansive world of graph theory, pinpointing vertices that share robust interconnections can unveil critical insights. A classic approach is to spot triangles— subgraphs where three nodes maintain direct connections among themselves.

Let's explore this through a tangible use case, fraud detection, which we'll dissect in more detail in this chapter's case study. Imagine a scenario where there's an interconnected web – an "egonet" – revolving around a central person—let's name him Max. In this egonet, apart from Max, there are two individuals, Alice and Bob. Now, this trio forms a "triangle" - Max is our primary figure (or "ego"), while Alice and Bob are the secondary figures (or "alters").

Here's where it gets interesting: if Alice and Bob have past records of fraudulent activities, it raises red flags about Max's credibility. It's like discovering two of your close friends have been involved in dubious deeds - it naturally puts you under scrutiny. However, if only one of them has a questionable past, then Max's situation becomes ambiguous. We can't label him outright but would need deeper investigation.

To visualize, picture Max at the center of a triangle, with Alice and Bob at the other vertices. Their interrelationships, especially if they carry negative connotations, can influence the perception of Max's integrity.

Density

In the realm of graph theory, density is a metric that quantifies how closely knit a network is. Specifically, it's the ratio of the number of edges present in the graph to the maximum possible number of edges. Mathematically, for a simple undirected graph, density is defined as:

$$Density = \frac{2 \times Number\ of\ Edges}{Number\ of\ Vertices\ x\ (Number\ of\ Vertices - 1\ )}$$

To put this into perspective, let's consider an example:

Suppose we are part of a book club with five members: Alice, Bob, Charlie, Dave, and Eve. If every member knows and has interacted with every other member, there would be a total of 10 connections (or edges) among them (Alice-Bob, Alice-Charlie, Alice-Dave, Alice-Eve, Bob-Charlie, and so on). In this case, the maximum number of possible connections or edges is 10. If all these connections exist, then the density is:

$$Density = \frac{2 \times 10}{5 \times 4} = 1$$

This indicates a perfectly dense or fully connected network.

However, let's assume Alice knows only Bob and Charlie, Bob knows Alice and Dave, and Charlie knows only Alice. Dave and Eve, although members, haven't interacted with anyone yet. In this scenario, there are only three actual connections: Alice-Bob, Alice-Charlie, and Bob-Dave. Let's calculate the density:

$$Density = \frac{2 \times 3}{5 \times 4} = 0.3$$

This value, being less than 1, shows that the book club's interaction network isn't fully connected; many potential interactions (edges) haven't occurred yet.

In essence, a density close to 1 indicates a tightly connected network, while a value closer to 0 suggests sparse interactions. Understanding density can help in various scenarios, from analyzing social networks to optimizing infrastructure planning, by gauging how interconnected the elements of the system are.

Understanding centrality measures

Centrality measures offer a window into understanding the significance of individual nodes within a graph. Think of centrality to identify key players or hubs in a network. For instance, in a social setting, it can help pinpoint influencers or central figures that hold sway. In urban planning, centrality might indicate pivotal buildings or junctions that play a critical role in traffic flow or accessibility. Understanding centrality is essential because it reveals nodes that are crucial for the functioning, cohesion, or influence within a network.

The most employed centrality metrics in graph analysis encompass:

- **Degree:** Reflects the direct connections a node has.
- **Betweenness:** Indicates how often a node acts as a bridge along the shortest path between two other nodes.
- **Closeness:** Represents how close a node is to all other nodes in the network.
- **Eigenvector:** Measures a node's influence based on the quality of its connections, not just the quantity.

Note that centrality measures apply to all graphs. As we know, graphs are a general representation of objects (vertices or nodes) and their relationships (edges), and centrality measures help identify the importance or influence of these nodes within the graph. Recall that networks are specific realizations or applications of graphs, often representing real-world systems like social networks, transportation systems, or communication networks. So, while the centrality measures discussed can be applied universally across all types of graphs, they are often highlighted in the context of networks due to their practical implications in understanding and optimizing real-world systems.

Let's delve deeper into these metrics to better appreciate their utility and nuances.

Degree

The number of edges connected to a particular vertex is called its **degree**. It can indicate how well connected a particular vertex is and its ability to quickly spread a message across a network.

Let's consider $a_{Graph} = (\mathcal{V}, \mathcal{E})$, where $\mathcal{V}$ represents a set of vertices and $\mathcal{E}$ represents a set of edges. Recall that a_{Graph} has $|\mathcal{V}|$ vertices and $|\mathcal{E}|$ edges. If we divide the degree of a node by $(|\mathcal{V}| - 1)$, it is called degree centrality:

$$C_{DC_a} = \frac{deg\,(a)}{|\mathcal{V}| - 1}$$

Now, let's look at a specific example. Consider the following graph:

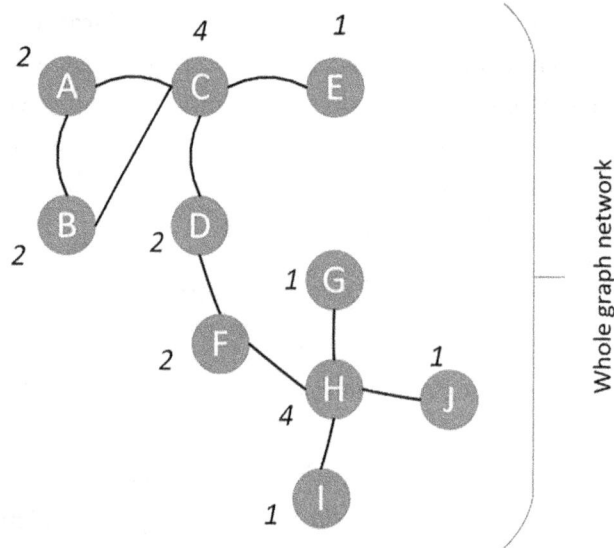

Figure 5.3: A sample graph illustrating the concept of degree and degree centrality

Now, in the preceding graph, vertex C has a degree of 4. Its degree centrality can be calculated as follows:

$$C_{DC_c} = \frac{deg\ (c)}{|V| - 1} = \frac{4}{10 - 1} = 0.44$$

Betweenness

Betweenness centrality is a key measure that gauges the significance of a vertex within a graph. When applied to social media contexts, it assesses the likelihood that an individual plays a crucial role in communications within a specific subgroup. In terms of computer networks, where a vertex symbolizes a computer, betweenness offers insights into the potential impact on communications between nodes if a particular computer (or vertex) were to fail.

To calculate the betweenness of vertex a in a certain $a_{Graph} = (\mathcal{V}, \mathcal{E})$, follow these steps:

1. Compute the shortest paths between each pair of vertices in a_{Graph}. Let's represent this with $^n shortest_{Total}$

2. From $^n shortest_{Total}$, count the number of shortest paths that pass through vertex a. Let's represent this with $^n shortest_a$

3.   Calculate the betweenness with:

$$^c betweenness_a = \frac{^n shortest_a}{^n shortest_{Total}}$$

Fairness and closeness

In graph theory, we often want to determine how central or how distant a specific vertex is in relation to other vertices. One way to quantify this is by calculating a metric known as "fairness." For a given vertex, say "a," in a graph "g," the fairness is determined by adding up the distances from vertex "a" to every other vertex in the graph. Essentially, it gives us a sense of how "spread out" or "far" a vertex is from its neighbors. This concept ties in closely with the idea of centrality, where the centrality of a vertex measures its overall distance from all other vertices.

Conversely, "closeness" can be thought of as the opposite of fairness. While it might be intuitive to think of closeness as the negative sum of a vertex's distances from other vertices, that's not technically accurate. Instead, closeness measures how near a vertex is to all other vertices in a graph, often calculated by taking the reciprocal of the sum of its distances to others.

Both fairness and closeness are essential metrics in network analysis. They provide insight into how information might flow within a network or how influential a particular node might be. By understanding these metrics, one can derive a deeper comprehension of network structures and their underlying dynamics.

Eigenvector centrality

Eigenvector centrality is a metric that evaluates the significance of nodes within a graph. Rather than just considering the number of direct connections a node has, it takes into account the quality of those connections. In simple terms, a node is considered important if it is connected to other nodes that are themselves significant within the network.

To give this a bit more mathematical context, imagine each node v has a centrality score $x(v)$. For every node v, its eigenvector centrality is calculated based on the sum of the centrality scores of its neighbors, scaled by a factor λ (eigenvector's associated eigenvalue):

$$x(v) = \frac{1}{\lambda} \sum_{u \varepsilon M(v)} x(u)$$

where $M(v)$ denotes the neighbors of v.

This idea of weighing the importance of a node based on its neighbors was foundational for Google when they developed the PageRank algorithm. The algorithm assigns a rank to every web page on the internet, signifying its importance, and is heavily influenced by the concept of eigenvector centrality.

For readers interested in our upcoming watchtower example, understanding the essence of eigenvector centrality will provide deeper insights into the workings of sophisticated network analysis techniques.

Calculating centrality metrics using Python

Let's create a network and then try to calculate its centrality metrics.

1. Setting the foundation: libraries and data

This includes importing necessary libraries and defining our data:

```
import networkx as nx
import matplotlib.pyplot as plt
```

For our sample, we've considered a set of vertices and edges:

```
vertices = range(1, 10)
edges = [(7, 2), (2, 3), (7, 4), (4, 5), (7, 3), (7, 5), (1, 6), (1, 7),
(2, 8), (2, 9)]
```

In this setup, vertices represent individual points or nodes in our network. The edges signify the relationships or links between these nodes.

2. Crafting the graph

With the foundation set, we proceed to craft our graph. This involves feeding our data (vertices and edges) into the graph structure:

```
graph = nx.Graph()
graph.add_nodes_from(vertices)
graph.add_edges_from(edges)
```

Here, the Graph() function initiates an empty graph. The subsequent methods, add_nodes_from and add_edges_from, populate this graph with our defined nodes and edges.

3. Painting a picture: visualizing the graph

A graphical representation often speaks louder than raw data. Visualization not only aids comprehension but also offers a snapshot of the graph's overall structure:

```
nx.draw(graph, with_labels=True, node_color='y', node_size=800)
plt.show()
```

This code paints the graph for us. The with_labels=True method ensures each node is labeled, node_color provides a distinct color, and node_size adjusts the node's size for clarity.

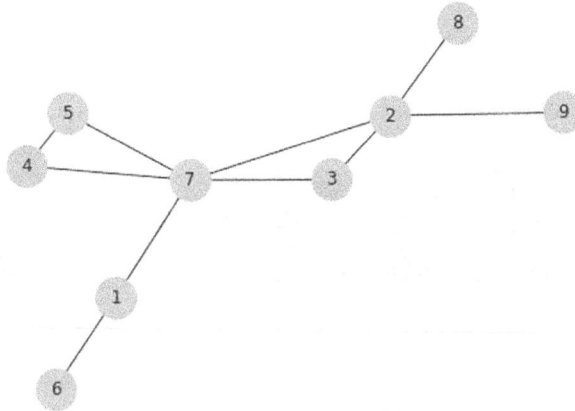

Figure 5.4: A schematic representation of the graph, showcasing nodes and their inter-relationships

Once our graph is established, the next pivotal step is to compute and understand the centrality measures of each node. Centrality measures, as previously discussed, gauge the importance of nodes in the network.

- **Degree centrality**: This measure gives the fraction of nodes that a particular node is connected to. In simpler terms, if a node has a high degree centrality, it's connected to many other nodes in a graph. The function nx.degree_centrality(graph) returns a dictionary with nodes as keys and their respective degree centrality as values:

```
print("Degree Centrality:", nx.degree_centrality(graph))
```

```
Degree Centrality: {1: 0.25, 2: 0.5, 3: 0.25, 4: 0.25, 5: 0.25, 6: 0.125, 7: 0.625, 8: 0.125, 9: 0.125}
```

- **Betweenness centrality**: This metric indicates the number of shortest paths passing through a particular node. Nodes with high betweenness centrality can be seen as "bridges" or "bottlenecks" between different parts of a graph. The function nx.betweenness_centrality(graph) computes this for each node:

```
print("Betweenness Centrality:", nx.betweenness_centrality(graph))
```

```
Betweenness Centrality: {1: 0.25, 2: 0.46428571428571425, 3: 0.0, 4:
0.0, 5: 0.0, 6: 0.0, 7: 0.7142857142857142, 8: 0.0, 9: 0.0}
```

- **Closeness centrality**: This represents how close a node is to all other nodes in a graph. A node with high closeness centrality can quickly interact with all other nodes, making it centrally located. This measure is calculated with nx.closeness_centrality(graph):

```
print("Closeness Centrality:", nx.closeness_centrality(graph))
```

```
Closeness Centrality: {1: 0.5, 2: 0.6153846153846154, 3:
0.5333333333333333, 4: 0.47058823529411764, 5: 0.47058823529411764,
6: 0.34782608695652173, 7: 0.7272727272727273, 8: 0.4, 9: 0.4}
```

- **Eigenvector centrality**: Unlike the degree centrality, which counts direct connections, the eigenvector centrality considers the quality or strength of these connections. Nodes connected to other high-scoring nodes get a boost, making it a measure of influential nodes. We further sort these centrality values for ease of interpretation:

```
eigenvector_centrality = nx.eigenvector_centrality(graph)
sorted_centrality = sorted((vertex, '{:0.2f}'.format(centrality_
val))
                            for vertex, centrality_val in
eigenvector_centrality.items())
print("Eigenvector Centrality:", sorted_centrality)
```

```
Eigenvector Centrality: [(1, '0.24'), (2, '0.45'), (3, '0.36'), (4,
'0.32'), (5, '0.32'), (6, '0.08'), (7, '0.59'), (8, '0.16'), (9,
'0.16')]
```

Note that the metrics of centrality are expected to give the centrality measure of a particular vertex in a graph or subgraph. Looking at the graph, the vertex labeled 7 seems to have the most central location. Vertex 7 has the highest values in all four metrics of centrality, thus reflecting its importance in this context.

Now let's look into how we can retrieve information from the graphs. Graphs are complex data structures with lots of information stored both in vertices and edges. Let's look at some strategies that can be used to navigate through graphs efficiently, in order to gather information from them to answer queries.

Social network analysis

Social Network Analysis (SNA) stands out as a significant application within graph theory. At its core, an analysis qualifies as SNA when it adheres to the following criteria:

- Vertices in a graph symbolize individuals.

- Edges signify social connections between these individuals, which include friendships, shared interests, familial ties, differences in opinions, and more.

- The primary objective of graph analysis leans toward understanding a pronounced social context.

One intriguing facet of SNA is its capacity to shed light on patterns linked to criminal behavior. By mapping out relationships and interactions, it's feasible to pinpoint patterns or anomalies that might indicate fraudulent activities or behaviors. For instance, analyzing the connectivity patterns might reveal unusual connections or frequent interactions in specific locations, hinting at potential criminal hotspots or networks.

> LinkedIn has contributed a lot to the research and development of new techniques related to SNA. In fact, LinkedIn can be thought of as a pioneer of many algorithms in this area.

Thus, SNA—due to its inherent distributed and interconnected architecture of social networks— is one of the most powerful use cases for graph theory. Another way to abstract a graph is by considering it as a network and applying an algorithm designed for networks. This whole area is called network analysis theory, which we will discuss next.

Understanding graph traversals

To make use of graphs, information needs to be mined from them. Graph traversal is defined as the strategy used to make sure that every vertex and edge is visited in an orderly manner. An effort is made to make sure that each vertex and edge is visited exactly once—no more and no less. Broadly, there can be two different ways of traveling a graph to search the data in it.

Earlier in this chapter we learned that going by breadth is called **breadth-first search (BFS)** –
going by depth is called **depth-first search (DFS)**. Let's look at them one by one.

BFS

BFS works best when there is a concept of layers or levels of neighborhoods in the a_{Graph} we deal
with. For example, when the connections of a person on LinkedIn are expressed as a graph, there
are first-level connections and then there are second-level connections, which directly translate
to the layers.

The BFS algorithm starts from a root vertex and explores the vertices in the neighborhood vertices.
It then moves to the next neighborhood level and repeats the process.

Let's look at a BFS algorithm. For that, let's first consider the following undirected graph:

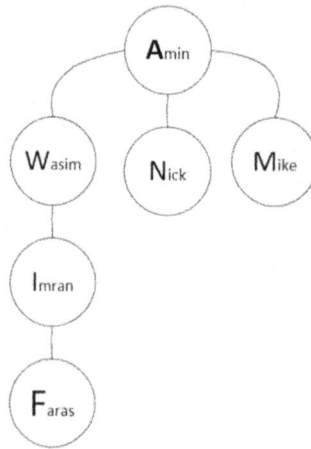

Figure 5.5: An undirected graph demonstrating personal connections

Constructing the adjacency list

In Python, the dictionary data structure lends itself conveniently to representing the adjacency
list of a graph. Here's how we can define an undirected graph:

```python
graph={ 'Amin'   : {'Wasim', 'Nick', 'Mike'},
        'Wasim' : {'Imran', 'Amin'},
        'Imran' : {'Wasim','Faras'},
        'Faras' : {'Imran'},
        'Mike'  : {'Amin'},
        'Nick'  : {'Amin'}}
```

To implement it in Python, we will proceed as follows.

We will first explain the initialization and then the main loop.

BFS algorithm implementation

The algorithm implementation will involve two main phases: the initialization and the main loop.

Initialization

Our traversal through the graph relies on two key data structures:

- **visited**: A set that will hold all the vertices we've explored. It starts empty.
- **queue**: A list used to hold vertices pending exploration. Initially, it will contain just our starting vertex.

Main loop

The primary logic of BFS revolves around exploring nodes layer by layer:

1. Remove the first node from the queue and consider it as the current node for the iteration:

   ```python
   node = queue.pop(0)
   ```

2. If the node hasn't been visited, mark it as visited and fetch its neighbors:

   ```python
   if node not in visited:
       visited.add(node)
       neighbours = graph[node]
   ```

3. Append unvisited neighbors to the queue:

   ```python
   for neighbour in neighbours:
       if neighbour not in visited:
           queue.append(neighbour)
   ```

4. Once the main loop is complete, the `visited` data structure is returned, which contains all the nodes traversed.

Complete BFS code implementation

The complete code, with both initialization and the main loop, will be as follows:

```python
def bfs(graph, start):
    visited = set()
    queue = [start]
```

```
    while queue:
        node = queue.pop(0)
        if node not in visited:
            visited.add(node)
            neighbours = graph[node]
            unvisited_neighbours = [neighbour for neighbour in neighbours
                                    if neighbour not in visited]
            queue.extend(unvisited_neighbours)
    return visited
```

The BFS traversal mechanism is as follows:

1. The process starts at level one, represented by the node "Amin."

2. It then expands to level two, visiting "Wasim'," "Nick," and "Mike."

3. Subsequently, BFS delves into levels three and four, visiting "Imran" and "Faras," respectively.

By the time BFS completes its traversal, all nodes have been accounted for in the visited set, and the queue is empty.

Using BFS for specific searches

To practically understand BFS in action, let's use our implemented function to find a path to a specific person in our graph:

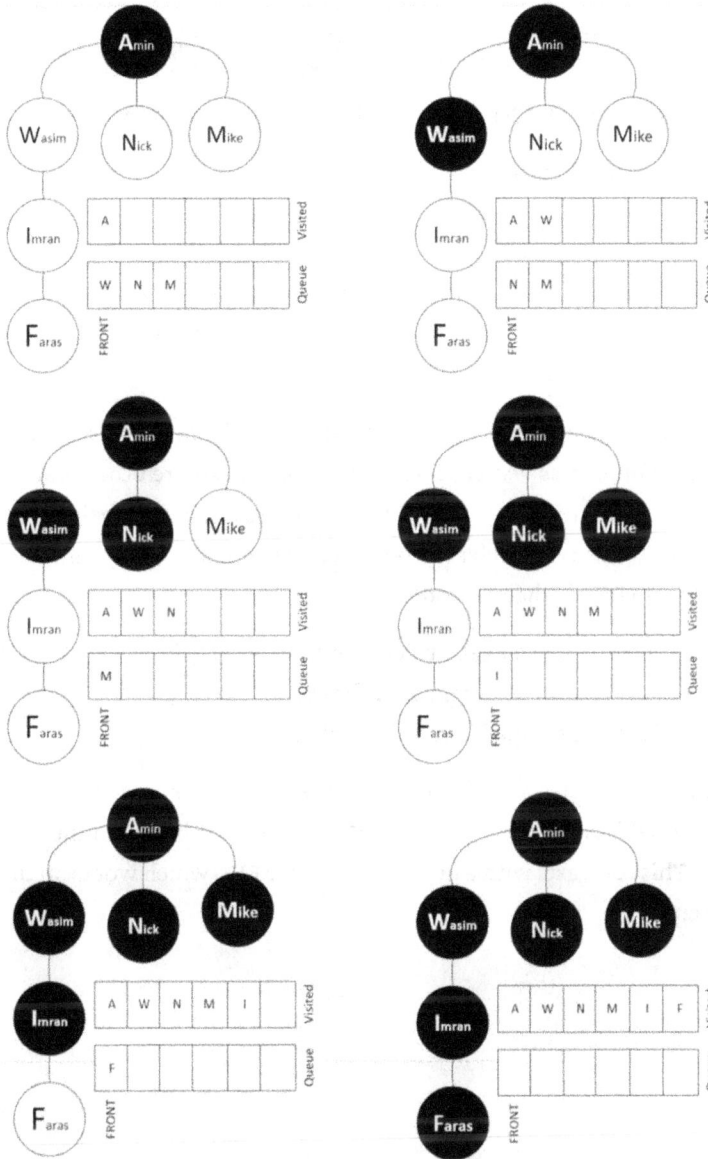

Figure 5.6: Layered traversal of a graph using BFS

Now, let's try to find a specific person from this graph using BFS. Let's specify the data that we are searching for and observe the results:

```
start_node = 'Amin'
print(bfs(graph, start_node))
```

```
{'Faras', 'Nick', 'Wasim', 'Imran', 'Amin', 'Mike'}
```

This signifies the sequence of nodes accessed when BFS starts from Amin.

Now let's look into the DFS algorithm.

DFS

DFS offers an alternative approach to graph traversal than **BFS**. While BFS seeks to explore the graph level by level, focusing on immediate neighbors first, DFS ventures as deep as possible down a path before backtracking.

Imagine a tree. Starting from the root, DFS dives down to the furthest leaf on a branch, marks all nodes along that branch as visited, then backtracks to explore other branches in a similar manner. The idea is to reach the furthest leaf node on a given branch before considering other branches. "Leaf" is a term used to refer to nodes in a tree that don't have any child nodes or, in a graph context, any unvisited adjacent nodes.

To ensure that the traversal doesn't get stuck in a loop, especially in cyclic graphs, DFS employs a Boolean flag. This flag indicates whether a node has been visited, preventing the algorithm from revisiting nodes and getting trapped in infinite cycles.

To implement DFS, we will use a stack data structure, which was discussed in detail in *Chapter 2, Data Structures Used in Algorithms*. Remember that a stack is based on the **Last In, First Out (LIFO)** principle. This contrasts with a queue, as used for BFS, which works on the **First In, First Out (FIFO)** principle:

The following code is used for DFS:

```python
def dfs(graph, start, visited=None):
    if visited is None:
        visited = set()
    visited.add(start)
    print(start)
    for next in graph[start] - visited:
        dfs(graph, next, visited)
    return visited
```

Let's again use the following code to test the `dfs` function defined previously:

```python
graph={ 'Amin' : {'Wasim', 'Nick', 'Mike'},
        'Wasim' : {'Imran', 'Amin'},
        'Imran' : {'Wasim','Faras'},
        'Faras' : {'Imran'},
        'Mike'  :{'Amin'},
        'Nick'  :{'Amin'}}
```

If we run this algorithm, the output will look like the following:

```
Amin
Wasim
Imran
Faras
Nick
Mike
```

Let's look at the exhaustive traversal pattern of this graph using the DFS methodology:

1. The iteration starts from the top node, Amin.

2. Then, it moves to level two, Wasim. From there, it moves toward the lower levels until it reaches the end, which is the Imran and Fares nodes.

3. After completing the first full branch, it backtracks and then goes to level two to visit Nick and Mike.

The traversal pattern is shown in *Figure 5.7*:

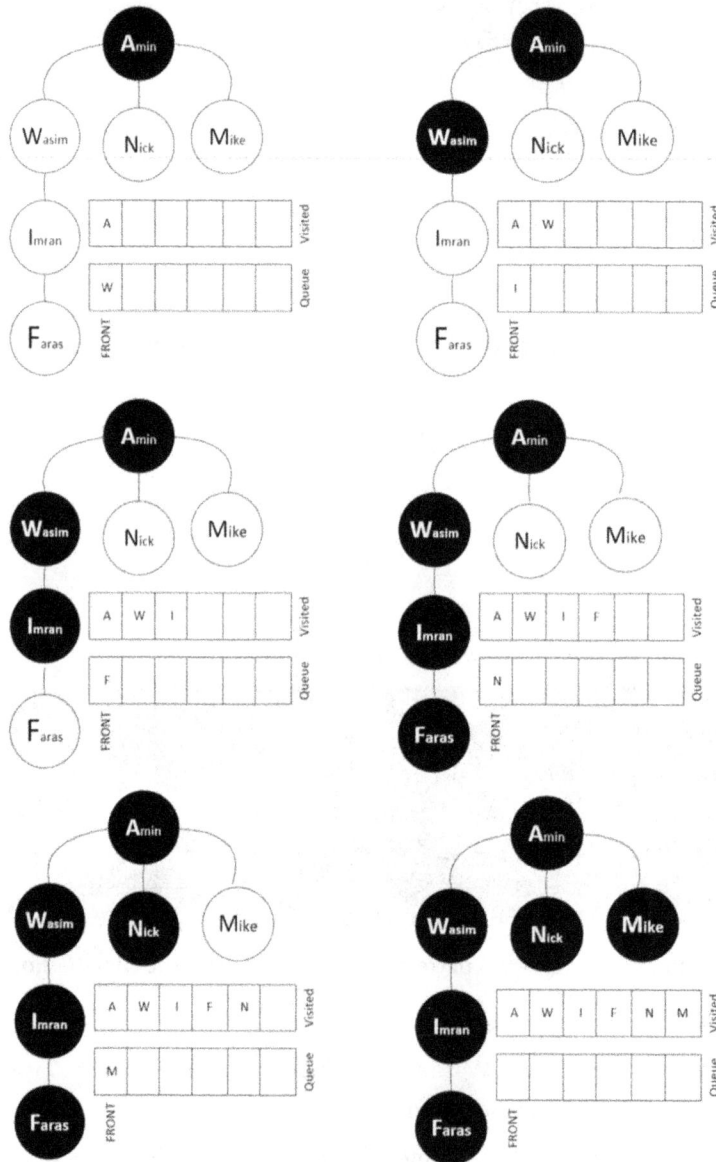

Figure 5.7: A visual representation of DFS traversal

Note that DFS can be used in trees as well.

Let's now look at a case study, which explains how the concepts we have discussed so far in this chapter can be used to solve a real-world problem.

Case study: fraud detection using SNA

Introduction

Humans are inherently social, and their behavior often reflects the company they keep. In the realm of fraud analytics, a principle called "homophily" signifies the likelihood of individuals having associations based on shared attributes or behaviors. A homophilic network, for instance, might comprise people from the same hometown, university, or with shared hobbies. The underlying principle is that individuals' behavior, including fraudulent activity, might be influenced by their immediate connections. This is also sometimes referred to as "guilt by association."

What is fraud in this context?

In the context of this case study, fraud refers to deceptive activities that may include impersonation, credit card theft, fake check submission, or any other illicit activities that can be represented and analyzed in a network of relationships. In an effort to understand the process, let's first look at a simple case. For that, let's use a network with nine vertices and eight edges. In this network, four of the vertices are known fraud cases and are classified as **fraud (F)**. Five of the remaining people have no fraud-related history and are classified as **non-fraud (NF)**.

We will write code with the following steps to generate this graph:

1. Let's import the packages that we need:

    ```
    import networkx as nx
    import matplotlib.pyplot as plt
    ```

2. Define the data structures of vertices and edges:

    ```
    vertices = range(1,10)
    edges= [(7,2), (2,3), (7,4), (4,5), (7,3), (7,5),
    (1,6),(1,7),(2,8),(2,9)]
    ```

3. Instantiate the graph:

    ```
    graph = nx.Graph()
    ```

4. Now, draw the graph:

    ```
    graph.add_nodes_from(vertices)
    graph.add_edges_from(edges)
    positions = nx.spring_layout(graph)
    ```

5. Let's define the NF nodes:

```
nx.draw_networkx_nodes(graph, positions,
                       nodelist=[1, 4, 3, 8, 9],
                       with_labels=True,
                       node_color='g',
                       node_size=1300)
```

6. Now, let's create the nodes that are known to be involved in fraud:

```
nx.draw_networkx_nodes(graph, positions,
                       nodelist=[1, 4, 3, 8, 9],
                       with_labels=True,
                       node_color='g',
                       node_size=1300)
```

7. Finally, create labels for the nodes:

```
labels = {1: '1 NF', 2: '2 F', 3: '3 NF', 4: '4 NF', 5: '5 F', 6: '6
F', 7: '7 F', 8: '8 NF', 9: '9 NF'}

nx.draw_networkx_labels(graph, positions, labels, font_size=16)

nx.draw_networkx_edges(graph, positions, edges, width=3, alpha=0.5,
edge_color='b')
plt.show()
```

Once the preceding code runs, it will show us a graph like this:

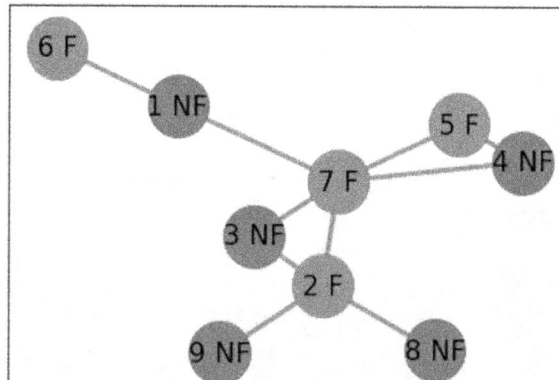

Figure 5.8: Initial network representation showing both fraudulent and non-fraudulent nodes

Note that we have already conducted a detailed analysis to classify each node as a graph or non-graph. Let's assume that we add another vertex, named *q*, to the network, as shown in the following figure. We have no prior information about this person and whether this person is involved in fraud or not. We want to classify this person as NF or F based on their links to the existing members of the social network:

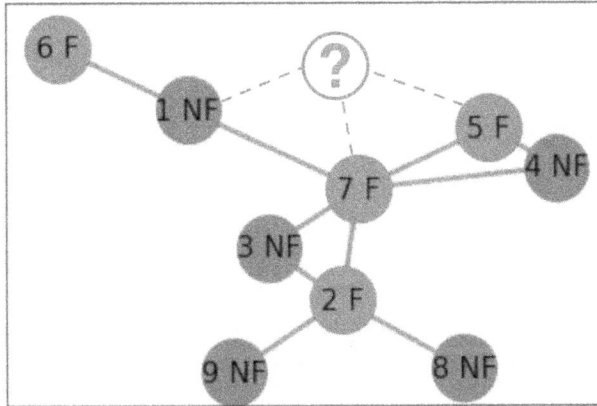

Figure 5.9: Introduction of a new node to the existing network

We have devised two ways to classify this new person, represented by node *q*, as F or NF:

- Using a simple method that does not use centrality metrics and additional information about the type of fraud
- Using a watchtower methodology, which is an advanced technique that uses the centrality metrics of the existing nodes, as well as additional information about the type of fraud

We will discuss each method in detail.

Conducting simple fraud analytics

The simple technique of fraud analytics is based on the assumption that in a network, the behavior of a person is affected by the people they are connected to. In a network, two vertices are more likely to have similar behavior if they are associated with each other.

Based on this assumption, we will devise a simple technique. If we want to find the probability that a certain node, *a*, belongs to F, the probability is represented by *P(F/q)* and is calculated as follows:

$$P(F|q) = \frac{1}{degree_q} \sum_{n_j \in Neighborhood_n | class(n_j)=F} w(n, n_j) DOS_{normalized_j}$$

Let's apply this to the preceding figure, where $Neighborhood_n$ represents the neighborhood of vertex n and $w(n, n_j)$ represents the weight of the connection between n and n_j. Also, $DOS_{normalized}$ is the value of the *degree* of suspicion normalized between 0 and 1. Finally, $degree_q$ is the degree of node q.

The probability is calculated as follows:

$$P(F|q) = \frac{1+1}{3} = \frac{2}{3} = 0.67$$

Based on this analysis, the likelihood of this person being involved in fraud is 67%. We need to set a threshold. If the threshold is 30%, then this person is above the threshold value, and we can safely flag them as *F*.

Note that this process needs to be repeated for each of the new nodes in the network.

Now, let's look at an advanced way of conducting fraud analytics.

Presenting the watchtower fraud analytics methodology

The previous simple fraud analytics technique has the following two limitations:

- It does not evaluate the importance of each vertex in the social network. A connection to a hub that is involved in fraud may have different implications than a relationship with a remote, isolated person.

- When labeling someone as a known case of fraud in an existing network, we do not consider the severity of the crime.

The watchtower fraud analytics methodology addresses these two limitations. First, let's look at a couple of concepts.

Scoring negative outcomes

If a person is known to be involved in fraud, we say that there is a negative outcome associated with this individual. Not every negative outcome is of the same severity or seriousness. A person known to be impersonating another person will have a more serious type of negative outcome associated with them, compared to someone who is just trying to use an expired $20 gift card in a creative way to make it valid.

From a score of 1 to 10, we will rate various negative outcomes as follows:

Negative outcome	Negative outcome score
Impersonation	10
Involvement in credit card theft	8
Fake check submission	7
Criminal record	6
No record	0

Note that these scores will be based on our analysis of fraud cases and their impact from historical data.

Degree of suspicion

The **degree of suspicion (DOS)** quantifies our level of suspicion that a person may be involved in fraud. A DOS value of 0 means that this is a low-risk person, and a DOS value of 9 means that this is a high-risk person.

Analysis of historical data shows that professional fraudsters have important positions in their social networks. To incorporate this, we first calculate all of the four centrality metrics of each vertex in our network. We then take the average of these vertices. This translates to the importance of that particular person in the network.

If a person associated with a vertex is involved in fraud, we illustrate this negative outcome by scoring the person using the pre-determined values shown in the preceding table. This is done so that the severity of the crime is reflected in the value of each individual DOS.

Finally, we multiply the average of the centrality metrics and the negative outcome score to get the value of the DOS. We normalize the DOS by dividing it by the maximum value of the DOS in the network.

Let's calculate the DOS for each of the nine nodes in the previous network:

	Node 1	Node 2	Node 3	Node 4	Node 5	Node 6	Node 7	Node 8	Node 9
Degree of centrality	0.25	0.5	0.25	0.25	0.25	0.13	0.63	0.13	0.13
Betweenness	0.25	0.47	0	0	0	0	0.71	0	0
Closeness	0.5	0.61	0.53	0.47	0.47	0.34	0.72	0.4	0.4
Eigenvector	0.24	0.45	0.36	0.32	0.32	0.08	0.59	0.16	0.16

Average of centrality Metrics	0.31	0.51	0.29	0.26	0.26	0.14	0.66	0.17	0.17
Negative outcome score	0	6	0	0	7	8	10	0	0
DOS	0	3	0	0	1.82	1.1	6.625	0	0
Normalized DOS	0	0.47	0	0	0.27	0.17	1	0	0

Each of the nodes and their normalized DOS is shown in the following figure:

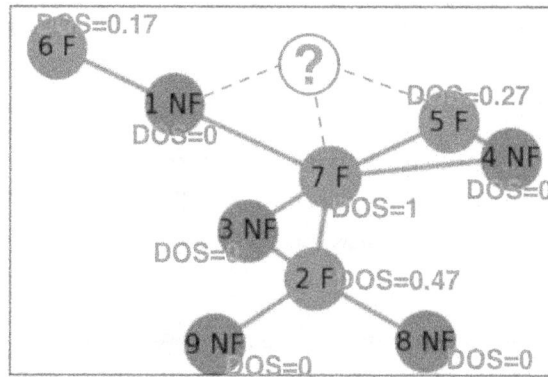

Figure 5.10: Visualization of nodes with their calculated DOS values

In order to calculate the DOS of the new node that has been added, we will use the following formula:

$$DOS_k = \frac{1}{degree_k} \sum_{n_j \in Neighborhood_n} w(n, n_j)DOS_{normalized_j}$$

Using the relevant values, we will calculate the DOS as follows:

$$DOS_k = \frac{(0 + 1 + 0.27)}{3} = 0.42$$

This will indicate the risk of fraud associated with this new node added to the system. It means that on a scale of 0 to 1, this person has a DOS value of 0.42. We can create different risk bins for the DOS, as follows:

Value of the DOS	Risk classification
DOS = 0	No risk
0<DOS<=0.10	Low risk
0.10<DOS<=0.3	Medium risk
DOS>0.3	High risk

Based on these criteria, it can be seen that the new individual is a high-risk person and should be flagged.

Usually, a time dimension is not involved when conducting such an analysis. But now, there are some advanced techniques that look at the growth of a graph as time progresses. This allows researchers to look at the relationship between vertices as the network evolves. Although such time-series analysis on graphs will increase the complexity of the problem many times over, it may give additional insight into the evidence of fraud that was not possible otherwise.

Summary

In this chapter, we learned about graph-based algorithms. This chapter used different techniques of representing, searching, and processing data represented as graphs. We also developed skills to be able to calculate the shortest distance between two vertices, and we built neighborhoods in our problem space. This knowledge should help us use graph theory to address problems such as fraud detection.

In the next chapter, we will focus on different unsupervised machine learning algorithms. Many of the use-case techniques discussed in this chapter complement unsupervised learning algorithms, which will be discussed in detail in the next chapter. Finding evidence of fraud in a dataset is an example of such use cases.

Learn more on Discord

To join the Discord community for this book – where you can share feedback, ask questions to the author, and learn about new releases – follow the QR code below:

`https://packt.link/WHLel`

Section 2

Machine Learning Algorithms

This section explains the different kinds of machine learning algorithms, such as unsupervised machine learning algorithms and traditional supervised learning algorithms, in detail and also introduces algorithms for natural language processing. The chapters included in this section are:

- *Chapter 6, Unsupervised Machine Learning Algorithms*
- *Chapter 7, Traditional Supervised Learning Algorithms*
- *Chapter 8, Neural Network Algorithms*
- *Chapter 9, Algorithms for Natural Language Processing*
- *Chapter 10, Understanding Sequential Models*
- *Chapter 11, Advanced Sequential Modeling Algorithms*

6

Unsupervised Machine Learning Algorithms

This chapter is about unsupervised machine learning algorithms. We aim, by the end of this chapter, to be able to understand how unsupervised learning, with its basic algorithms and methodologies, can be effectively applied to solve real-world problems.

We will cover the following topics:

- Introducing unsupervised learning
- Understanding clustering algorithms
- Dimensionality reduction
- Association rules mining

Introducing unsupervised learning

If the data is not generated randomly, it tends to exhibit certain patterns or relationships among its elements within a multi-dimensional space. Unsupervised learning involves the process of detecting and utilizing these patterns within a dataset to structure and comprehend it more effectively. Unsupervised learning algorithms uncover these patterns and use them as a foundation for imparting a certain structure to the dataset. The identification of these patterns contributes to a deeper understanding and representation of the data. Extracting patterns from raw data leads to a better understanding of the raw data.

This concept is shown in *Figure 6.1*:

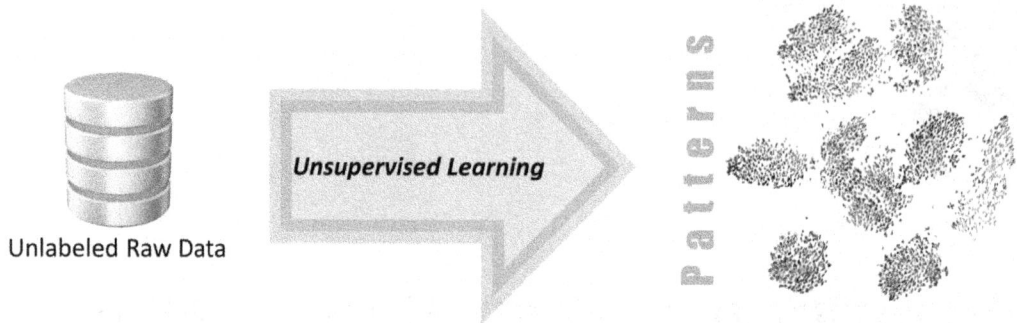

Figure 6.1: Using unsupervised machine learning to extract patterns from unlabeled raw data

In the upcoming discussion, we will navigate through the CRISP-DM lifecycle, a popular model for the machine learning process. Within this context, we'll pinpoint where unsupervised learning fits in. To illustrate, think of unsupervised learning like a detective piecing together clues to form patterns or groups, without having any predefined knowledge of what the end result might be. Just as a detective's insights can be crucial in solving a case, unsupervised learning plays a pivotal role in the machine learning lifecycle.

Unsupervised learning in the data-mining lifecycle

Let us first look into the different phases of a typical machine learning process. To understand the different phases of the machine learning lifecycle, we will study the example of using machine learning for a data mining process. Data mining is the process of discovering meaningful correlations, patterns, and trends in a given dataset. To discuss the different phases of data mining using machine learning, this book utilizes the **Cross-Industry Standard Process for Data Mining (CRISP-DM)**. CRISP-DM was conceived and brought to life by a group of data miners from different organizations, including notable names like Chrysler and IBM. More details can be found at https://www.ibm.com/docs/en/spss-modeler/saas?topic=dm-crisp-help-overview.

The CRISP-DM lifecycle consists of six distinct phases, which are shown in the following figure:

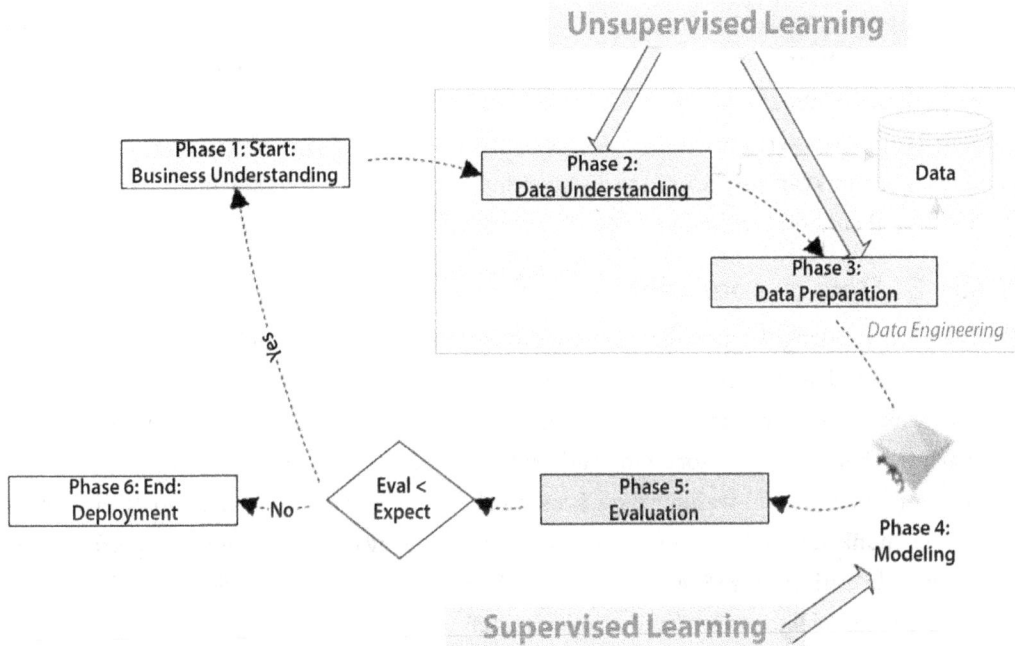

Figure 6.2: Different phases of the CRISP-DM lifecycle

Let's break down and explore each phase, one by one.

Phase 1: Business understanding

This phase is about gathering the requirements and involves trying to fully understand the problem in depth from a business point of view. Defining the scope of the problem and properly rephrasing it according to machine learning is an important part of this phase. This phase involves identifying the goals, defining the scope of the project, and understanding the requirements of the stakeholders.

> It is important to note that Phase 1 of the CRISP-DM lifecycle is about business understanding. It focuses on what needs to be done, not on how it will be done.

Phase 2: Data understanding

This phase is about understanding the data that is available for data mining. In this phase, we will find out whether we have all information needed to solve the problem defined in Phase 1 in the given datasets. We can use tools like data visualization, dashboards, and summary reports to understand the patterns in the data. As explained later in this chapter, unsupervised machine learning algorithms can also be used to discover the patterns in the data and to understand them by analyzing their structure in detail.

Phase 3: Data preparation

This is about preparing the data for the ML model that we will later train in Phase 4. Depending on the use case and requirements, data preparation may include removing outliers, normalization, taking out null values, and reducing the dimensionality of the data. This is discussed in more detail in later chapters. After processing and preparing the data, it is usually split in a 70-30 ratio. The larger chunk, called the training data, is used to educate the model on various patterns, while the smaller chunk, referred to as the testing data, is saved for evaluating the model's performance on unseen data during Phase 5. An optional set of data can also be kept aside for validating and fine-tuning the model to prevent it from overfitting.

Phase 4: Modeling

This is the phase where we formulate the patterns in the data by training the model. For model training, we will use the training data partition prepared in Phase 3. Model training involves feeding our prepared data into the machine learning algorithm. Through iterative learning, the algorithm identifies and learns the inherent patterns within the data. The objective is to formulate patterns representing the relationships and dependencies among different variables in the dataset. We will discuss in later chapters how the complexity and nature of these mathematical formulations depend heavily on our chosen algorithm – for instance, a linear regression model will generate a linear equation, while a decision tree model will construct a tree-like model of decisions.

In addition to model training, model tuning is another component of this phase of the CRISP-DM lifecycle. This process includes optimizing the parameters of the learning algorithm to enhance its performance, thus making predictions more accurate. It involves fine-tuning the model using an optional validation set, which assists in adjusting the model's complexity to find the right balance between learning from the data and generalizing to unseen data. A validation set, in machine learning terms, is a subset of your dataset that is used for the fine adjustment of a predictive model.

It assists in modulating the model's complexity, aiming to find an optimal balance between learning from known data and generalizing to unseen data. This balance is important in preventing overfitting, which is a scenario where the model learns the training data too well but performs poorly on new, unseen data. Hence, model tuning not only refines the model's predictive power but also ensures its robustness and reliability.

Phase 5: Evaluation

This stage involves evaluating the recently trained model by using the test data derived from Phase 3. We measure the model's performance against the established baseline, which is set during Phase 1. Setting a baseline in machine learning serves as a reference point, which can be determined using various methods. It could be established through basic rule-based systems, simple statistical models, random chance, or even based on the performance of human experts. The purpose of this baseline is to offer a minimal performance threshold that our machine learning models should surpass. The baseline acts as a benchmark for comparison, giving us a reference point for our expectations. If the model's evaluation aligns with the expectations originally defined in Phase 1, we proceed further. If not, we must revisit and iterate through all the previous phases, starting again with Phase 1.

Phase 6: Deployment

Once the evaluation phase, Phase 5, concludes, we examine whether the performance of the trained model meets or surpasses the established expectations. It's vital to remember that a successful evaluation doesn't automatically imply readiness for deployment. The model has performed well on our test data, but that is not the only criterion for determining whether the model is ready to solve real-world problems, as defined in Phase 1. We must consider factors such as how the model will perform with new data it has never seen before, how it will integrate with existing systems, and how it will handle unforeseen edge cases. Therefore, it's only when these extensive evaluations have been met satisfactorily that we can confidently proceed to deploy the model into a production environment, where it begins to provide a usable solution to our predefined problem.

> Phase 2 (Data understanding) and Phase 3 (Data preparation) of the CRISP-DM lifecycle are all about understanding the data and preparing it for training the model. These phases involve data processing. Some organizations employ specialists for this data engineering phase.

It is obvious that the process of suggesting a solution to a problem is fully data-driven. A combination of supervised and unsupervised machine learning is used to formulate a workable solution. This chapter focuses on the unsupervised learning part of the solution.

> Data engineering comprises Phase 2 and Phase 3 and is the most time-consuming part of machine learning. It can take as much as 70% of the time and resources of a typical **Machine Learning** (**ML**) project (*Data Management in Machine Learning: Challenges, Techniques, and Systems*, Cody et al, SIGMOD '17: Proceedings of the 2017 ACM International Conference on Management of Data, May 2017). Unsupervised learning algorithms can play an important role in data engineering.

The following sections provide more details regarding unsupervised algorithms.

Current research trends in unsupervised learning

The field of machine learning research has undergone a considerable transformation. In earlier times, the focus was primarily centered on supervised learning techniques. These methods are immediately useful for inference tasks, offering clear advantages such as time savings, cost reductions, and discernible improvements in prediction accuracy.

Conversely, the intrinsic capabilities of unsupervised machine learning algorithms have only gained attention more recently. Unlike their supervised counterparts, unsupervised techniques function without direct instructions or preconceived assumptions. They are adept at exploring broader "dimensions" or facets in data, thus enabling a more comprehensive examination of a dataset.

To clarify, in machine learning terminology, "features" are the individual measurable properties or characteristics of the phenomena being observed. For example, in a dataset concerning customer information, features could be aspects like the customer's age, purchase history, or browsing behavior. "Labels," on the other hand, represent the outcomes we want the model to predict based on these features.

While supervised learning focuses primarily on establishing relationships between these features and a specific label, unsupervised learning does not restrict itself to a pre-determined label. Instead, it can delve deeper, unearthing intricate patterns among various features that might be overlooked when using supervised methods. This makes unsupervised learning potentially more expansive and versatile in its applications.

This inherent flexibility of unsupervised learning, however, brings with it a challenge. Since the exploration space is larger, it can often result in **increased computational** requirements, leading to greater costs and longer processing times. Furthermore, managing the scale or "scope" of unsupervised learning tasks can be more complex due to their exploratory nature. Yet, the ability to unearth hidden patterns or correlations within the data makes unsupervised learning a powerful tool for data-driven insights.

Today, research trends are moving toward the integration of supervised and unsupervised learning methods. This combined strategy aims to exploit the advantages of both methods.

Now let us look into some practical examples.

Practical examples

Currently, unsupervised learning is used to get a better sense of the data and provide it with more structure—for example, it is used in marketing segmentation, data categorization, fraud detection, and market basket analysis (which is discussed later in this chapter). Let us look at the example of the use of unsupervised learning for marketing segmentation.

Marketing segmentation using unsupervised learning

Unsupervised learning serves as a powerful tool for marketing segmentation. Marketing segmentation refers to the process of dividing a target market into distinct groups based on shared characteristics, enabling companies to tailor their marketing strategies and messages to effectively reach and engage specific customer segments. The characteristics used for grouping the target market could include demographics, behaviors, or geographic similarities. By leveraging algorithms and statistical techniques, it enables businesses to extract meaningful insights from their customer data, identify hidden patterns, and group customers into distinct segments based on similarities in their behavior, preferences, or characteristics. This data-driven approach empowers marketers to develop tailored strategies, improve customer targeting, and enhance overall marketing effectiveness.

Understanding clustering algorithms

One of the simplest and most powerful techniques used in unsupervised learning is based on grouping similar patterns together through clustering algorithms. It is used to understand a particular aspect of the data that is related to the problem we are trying to solve. Clustering algorithms look for natural grouping in data items. As the group is not based on any target or assumptions, it is classified as an unsupervised learning technique.

Consider a vast library full of books as an example. Each book represents a data point – containing a multitude of attributes like genre, author, publication year, and so forth. Now, imagine a librarian (the clustering algorithm) who is tasked with organizing these books. With no pre-existing categories or instructions, the librarian starts sorting the books based on their attributes – all the mysteries together, the classics together, books by the same author together, and so on. This is what we mean by "natural groups" in data items, where items that share similar characteristics are grouped together.

Groupings created by various clustering algorithms are based on finding the similarities between various data points in the problem space. Note that, in the context of machine learning, a data point is a set of measurements or observations that exist in a multi-dimensional space. In simpler terms, it's a single piece of information that helps the machine learn about the task it is trying to accomplish. The best way to determine the similarities between data points will vary from problem to problem and will depend on the nature of the problem we are dealing with. Let's look at the various methods that can be used to calculate the similarities between various data points.

Quantifying similarities

Unsupervised learning techniques, such as clustering algorithms, work effectively by determining similarities between various data points within a given problem space. The effectiveness of these algorithms largely depends on our ability to correctly measure these similarities, and in machine learning terminology, these are often referred to as "distance measures." But what exactly is a distance measure?

In essence, a distance measure is a mathematical formula or method that calculates the "distance" or similarity between two data points. It's crucial to understand that, in this context, the term "distance" doesn't refer to physical distance, but rather to the similarity or dissimilarity between data points based on their features or characteristics.

In clustering, we can talk about two main types of distances: intercluster and intracluster. The intercluster distance refers to the distance between different clusters, or groups of data points. In contrast, intracluster distance refers to the distance within the same cluster, or, in other words, the distance between data points within the same group. The objective of a good clustering algorithm is to maximize intercluster distance (making sure each cluster is distinct from the others) while minimizing intracluster distance (ensuring data points within the same cluster are as similar as possible). The following are three of the most popular methods that are used to quantify similarities:

- Euclidean distance measure

- Manhattan distance measure
- Cosine distance measure

Let's look at these distance measures in more detail.

Euclidean distance

The distance between different points can quantify the similarity between two data points and is extensively used in unsupervised machine learning techniques, such as clustering. Euclidean distance is the most common and simplest distance measure used. The term "distance," in this context, quantifies how similar or different two data points are in a multi-dimensional space, which is crucial in understanding the grouping of data points. One of the simplest and most widely used measures of this distance is the Euclidean distance.

The Euclidean distance can be thought of as the straight-line distance between two points in a three-dimensional space, similar to how we might measure distance in the real world. For example, consider two cities on a map; the Euclidean distance would be the "as-the-crow-flies" distance between these two cities, a straight line from city A to city B, ignoring any potential obstacles such as mountains or rivers.

In a similar manner, in the multi-dimensional space of our data, the Euclidean distance calculates the shortest possible "straight line" distance between two data points. By doing so, it provides a quantitative measure of how close or far apart the data points are, based on their features or attributes. For example, let's consider two points, $A(1,1)$ and $B(4,4)$, in a two-dimensional space, as shown in the following plot:

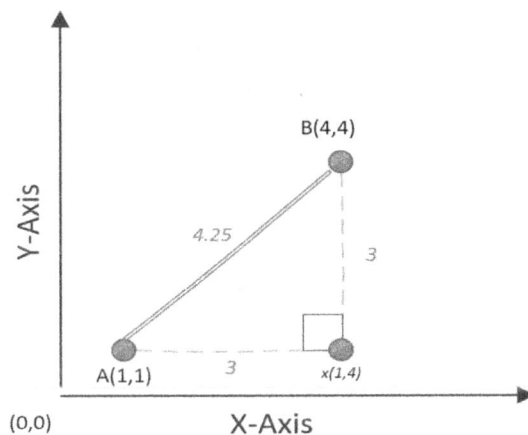

Figure 6.3: Calculating the Euclidean distance between two given points

To calculate the distance between A and B—that is d(A,B), we can use the following Pythagorean formula:

$$d(A, B) = \sqrt{(a_2 - b_2)^2 + (a_1 - b_1)^2} = \sqrt{(4-1)^2 + (4-1)^2} = \sqrt{9+9} = 4.25$$

Note that this calculation is for a two-dimensional problem space. For an *n*-dimensional problem space, we can calculate the distance between two points, **A** and **B**, as follows:

$$d(A, B) = \sqrt{\sum_{i=1}^{n}(a_i - b_i)^2}$$

Manhattan distance

In many situations, measuring the shortest distance between two points using the Euclidean distance measure will not truly represent the similarity or closeness between two points—for example, if two data points represent locations on a map, then the actual distance from point A to point B using ground transportation, such as a car or taxi, will be more than the distance calculated by the Euclidean distance. Let's think of a bustling city grid, where you can't cut straight through buildings to get from one point to another (like in the case of Euclidean distance), but rather, you must navigate through the grid of streets. Manhattan distance mirrors this real-world navigation – it calculates the total distance traveled along these grid lines from point A to point B.

For situations such as these, we use Manhattan distance, which estimates the distance between two points, traveled when moving along grid-like city streets from a starting point to a destination. In contrast to straight-line distance measures like the Euclidean distance, the Manhattan distance provides a more accurate reflection of the practical distance between two locations in such contexts. The comparison between the Manhattan and Euclidean distance measures is shown in the following plot:

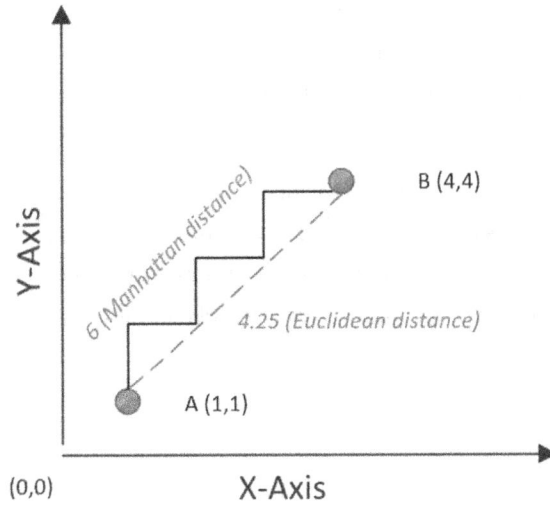

Figure 6.4: Calculating the Manhattan distance between two points

Note that, in the figure, the Manhattan distance between these points is represented as a zigzag path that moves strictly along the grid lines of this plot. In contrast, the Euclidean distance is shown as a direct, straight line from point A to point B. It is obvious that the Manhattan distance will always be equal to or larger than the corresponding Euclidean distance calculated.

Cosine distance

While Euclidean and Manhattan distance measures serve us well in simpler, lower-dimensional spaces, their effectiveness diminishes as we venture into more complex, "high-dimensional" settings. A "high-dimensional" space refers to a dataset that contains a large number of features or variables. As the number of dimensions (features) increases, the calculation of distance becomes less meaningful and more computationally intensive with Euclidean and Manhattan distances.

To tackle this issue, we use the "cosine distance" measure in high-dimensional contexts. This measure works by assessing the cosine of the angle formed by two data points connected to an origin point. It's not the physical distance between the points that matters here, but the angle they create.

If the data points are close in the multi-dimensional space, they'll form a smaller angle, regardless of the number of dimensions involved. Conversely, if the data points are far apart, the resulting angle will be larger. Hence, cosine distance provides a more nuanced measure of similarity in high-dimensional data, helping us make better sense of complex data patterns:

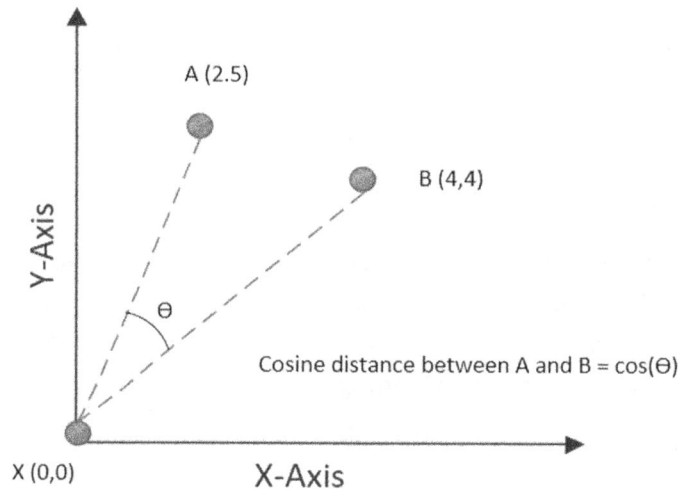

Figure 6.5: Calculating the cosine distance

Textual data can almost be considered a highly dimensional space. It stems from the unique nature of text data, where each unique word can be considered a distinct dimension or feature. As the cosine distance measure works very well with h-dimensional spaces, it is a good choice when dealing with textual data.

Note that, in the preceding figure, the cosine of the angle between A(2,5) and B(4.4) is the cosine distance represented by θ in *Figure 6.5*. The reference between these points is the origin—that is, X(0,0). But in reality, any point in the problem space can act as the reference data point, and it does not have to be the origin.

Let us now look into one of the most popular unsupervised machine learning techniques – that is, the k-means clustering algorithm.

k-means clustering algorithm

The k-means clustering algorithm gets its name from the procedure of creating "k" clusters and using means or averages to ascertain the "closeness" between data points. The term "means" refers to the method of calculating the centroid or the "center point" of each cluster, which is essentially the average of all the data points within the cluster. In other words, the algorithm calculates the mean value for each feature within the cluster, which results in a new data point – the centroid. This centroid then acts as the reference point for measuring the "closeness" of other data points.

The popularity of k-means stems from its scalability and speed. The algorithm is computationally efficient because it uses a straightforward iterative process where the centroids of clusters are repeatedly adjusted until they become representative of the cluster members. This simplicity makes the algorithm particularly fast and scalable for large datasets.

However, a notable limitation of the k-means algorithm is its inability to determine the optimal number of clusters, "k," independently. The ideal "k" depends on the natural groupings within a given dataset. The design philosophy behind this constraint is to keep the algorithm straightforward and fast, hence assuming an external mechanism to calculate "k." Depending on the context of the problem, "k" could be directly determined. For instance, if the task involves segregating a class of data science students into two clusters, one focusing on data science skills and the other on programming skills, "k" would naturally be two. However, for problems where the value of "k" is not readily apparent, an iterative process involving trial and error, or a heuristic-based method, might be required to estimate the most suitable number of clusters for a dataset.

The logic of k-means clustering

In this part, we'll dive into the workings of the k-means clustering algorithm. We'll break down how it operates, step by step, to give you a clear understanding of its mechanisms and uses. This section describes the logic of the k-means clustering algorithm.

Initialization

In order to group them, the k-means algorithm uses a distance measure to find the similarity or closeness between data points. Before using the k-means algorithm, the most appropriate distance measure needs to be selected. By default, the Euclidean distance measure will be used. However, depending on the nature and requirement of your data, you might find another distance measure, such as Manhattan or cosine, more suitable. Also, if the dataset has outliers, then a mechanism needs to be devised to determine the criteria that are to be identified and remove the outliers of the dataset.

Various statistical methods are available for outlier detection, such as the Z-score method or the **Interquartile Range (IQR)** method. Now let's look at the different steps involved in the k-means algorithm.

The steps of the k-means algorithm

The steps involved in the k-means clustering algorithm are as follows:

Step 1	We choose the number of clusters, k.
Step 2	Among the data points, we randomly choose k points as cluster centers.
Step 3	Based on the selected distance measure, we iteratively compute the distance from each point in the problem space to each of the k cluster centers. Based on the size of the dataset, this may be a time-consuming step—for example, if there are 10,000 points in the cluster and $k = 3$, this means that 30,000 distances need to be calculated.
Step 4	We assign each data point in the problem space to the nearest cluster center.
Step 5	Now each data point in our problem space has an assigned cluster center. But we are not done, as the selection of the initial cluster centers was based on random selection. We need to verify that the current randomly selected cluster centers are actually the center of gravity of each cluster. We recalculate the cluster centers by computing the mean of the constituent data points of each of the k clusters. This step explains why this algorithm is called k-means.
Step 6	If the cluster centers have shifted in step 5, this means that we need to recompute the cluster assignment for each data point. For this, we will go back to step 3 to repeat that compute-intensive step. If the cluster centers have not shifted or if our predetermined stop condition (for example, the number of maximum iterations) has been satisfied, then we are done.

The following figure shows the result of running the k-means algorithm in a two-dimensional problem space:

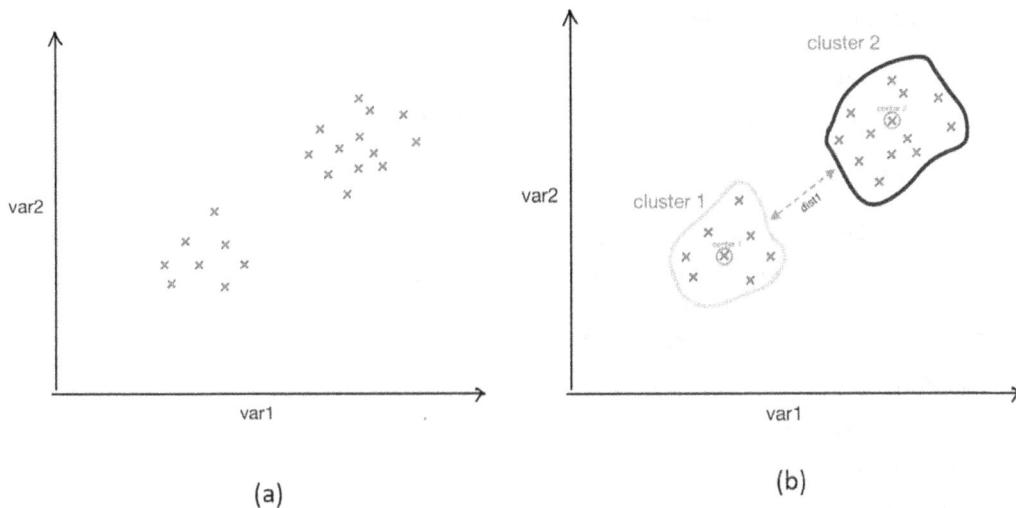

Figure 6.6: Results of k-means clustering (a) Data points before clustering; (b) resultant clusters after running the k-means clustering algorithm

Note that the two resulting clusters created after running k-means are well differentiated in this case. Now let us look into the stop condition of the k-means algorithm.

Stop condition

In unsupervised learning algorithms like k-means, the stop condition plays a crucial role in determining when the algorithm should cease its iterative process. For the k-means algorithm, the default stop condition is when there is no more shifting of cluster centers in step 5. But as with many other algorithms, k-means algorithms may take a lot of time to converge, especially while processing large datasets in a high-dimensional problem space.

Instead of waiting for the algorithm to converge, we can also explicitly define the stop condition as follows:

- By specifying the maximum execution time:

  - **Stop condition:** $t > t_{max}$, where t is the current execution time and t_{max} is the maximum execution time we have set for the algorithm.

- By specifying the maximum iterations:

  - **Stop condition:** if $m > m_{max}$, where m is the current iteration and m_{max} is the maximum number of iterations we have set for the algorithm.

Coding the k-means algorithm

We'll perform k-means clustering on a simple two-dimensional dataset you've provided, with two features, x and y. Imagine a swarm of fireflies scattered across a garden at night. Your task is to group these fireflies based on their proximity to each other. This is the essence of k-means clustering, a popular unsupervised learning algorithm.

We're given a dataset, much like our garden, with data points plotted in a two-dimensional space. Our data points are represented by x and y coordinates:

```
import pandas as pd
dataset = pd.DataFrame({
    'x': [11, 21, 28, 17, 29, 33, 24, 45, 45, 52, 51, 52, 55, 53, 55, 61,
62, 70, 72, 10],
    'y': [39, 36, 30, 52, 53, 46, 55, 59, 63, 70, 66, 63, 58, 23, 14, 8,
18, 7, 24, 10]
})
```

Our task is to cluster these data points using the k-means algorithm.

Firstly, we import the required libraries:

```
from sklearn import cluster
import matplotlib.pyplot as plt
```

Next, we'll initiate the KMeans class by specifying the number of clusters (k). For this example, let's assume we want to divide our data into 3 clusters:

```
kmeans = cluster.KMeans(n_clusters=2)
```

Now, we train our KMeans model with our dataset. It is worth mentioning that this model only needs the feature matrix (x) and not the target vector (y) because it's an unsupervised learning algorithm:

```
kmeans.fit(dataset)
```

Let us now look into the labels and the cluster centers:

```
labels = labels = kmeans.labels_
centers = kmeans.cluster_centers_
print(labels)
```

```
[0 0 0 0 0 0 0 0 1 1 1 1 1 1 1 1 1 1 0]
```

```
print(centers)
```

```
[[16.77777778 48.88888889]
 [57.09090909 15.09090909]]
```

Finally, to visualize our clusters, we plot our data points, coloring them according to their assigned cluster. The centers of clusters, also known as centroids, are also plotted:

```
plt.scatter(dataset['x'], dataset['y'], c=labels)
plt.scatter(kmeans.cluster_centers_[:, 0], kmeans.cluster_centers_[:, 1],
s=300, c='red')
plt.show()
```

In the plot, the colored points represent our data points and their respective clusters, while the red points denote the centroids of each cluster.

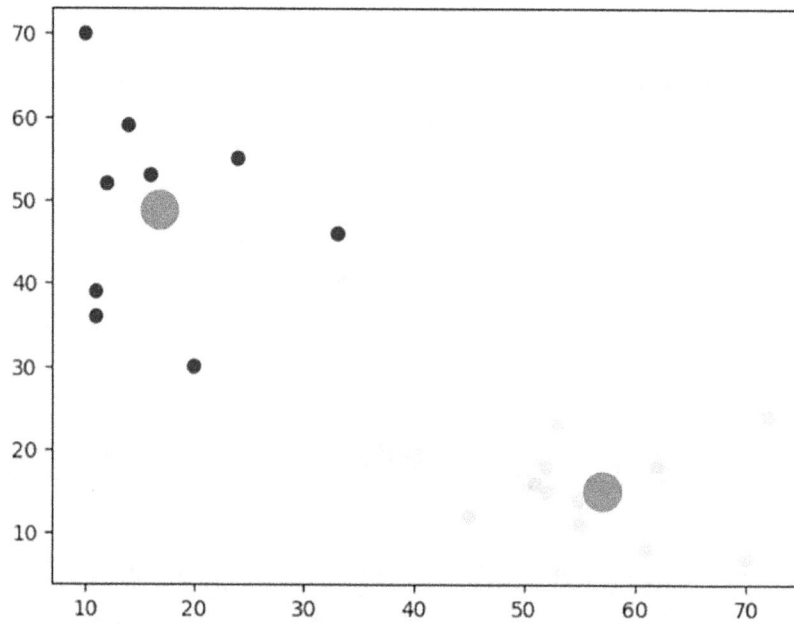

Figure 6.7: Results of k-means clustering

Note that the bigger dots in the plot are the centroids as determined by the k-means algorithm.

Limitation of k-means clustering

The k-means algorithm is designed to be a simple and fast algorithm. Because of the intentional simplicity of its design, it comes with the following limitations:

- The biggest limitation of k-means clustering is that the initial number of clusters has to be predetermined.
- The initial assignment of cluster centers is random. This means that each time the algorithm is run, it may give slightly different clusters.
- Each data point is assigned to only one cluster.
- k-means clustering is sensitive to outliers.

Now let us look into another unsupervised machine learning technique, hierarchical clustering.

Hierarchical clustering

K-means clustering uses a top-down approach because we start the algorithm from the most important data points, which are the cluster centers. There is an alternative approach of clustering where, instead of starting from the top, we start the algorithm from the bottom. The bottom, in this context, is each of the individual data points in the problem space. The solution is to keep on grouping similar data points together as it progresses up toward the cluster centers. This alternative bottom-up approach is used by hierarchical clustering algorithms and is discussed in this section.

Steps of hierarchical clustering

The following steps are involved in hierarchical clustering:

1. We create a separate cluster for each data point in our problem space. If our problem space consists of 100 data points, then it will start with 100 clusters.

2. We group only those points that are closest to each other.

3. We check for the stop condition; if the stop condition is not yet satisfied, then we repeat step 2.

The resulting clustered structure is called a **dendrogram.**

In a dendrogram, the height of the vertical lines determines how close the items are, as shown in the following diagram:

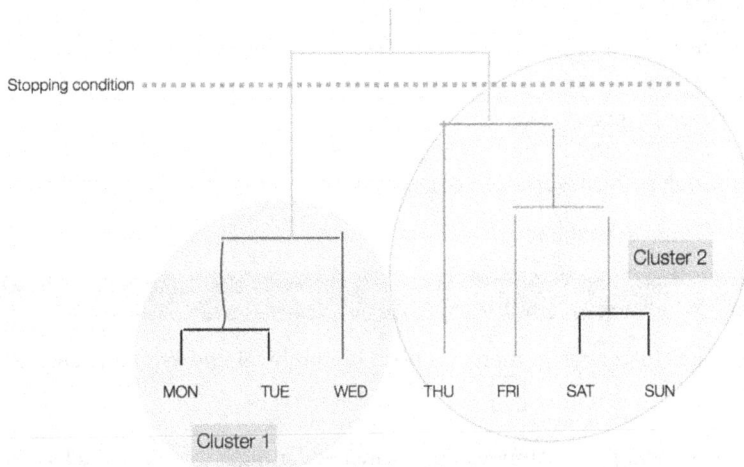

Figure 6.8: Hierarchical clustering

Note that the stop condition is shown as a dotted line in *Figure 6.8*.

Coding a hierarchical clustering algorithm

Let's learn how we can code a hierarchical algorithm in Python:

1. We will first import AgglomerativeClustering from the sklearn.cluster library, along with the pandas and numpy packages:

    ```
    from sklearn.cluster import AgglomerativeClustering
    import pandas as pd
    import numpy as np
    ```

2. Then we will create 20 data points in a two-dimensional problem space:

    ```
    dataset = pd.DataFrame({
        'x': [11, 11, 20, 12, 16, 33, 24, 14, 45, 52, 51, 52, 55, 53,
    55, 61, 62, 70, 72, 10],
        'y': [39, 36, 30, 52, 53, 46, 55, 59, 12, 15, 16, 18, 11, 23,
    14, 8, 18, 7, 24, 70]
    })
    ```

3. Then we create the hierarchical cluster by specifying the hyperparameters. Note that a hyperparameter refers to a configuration parameter of a machine learning model that is set before the training process and influences the model's behavior and performance. We use the fit_predict function to actually process the algorithm:

    ```
    cluster = AgglomerativeClustering(n_clusters=2,
    affinity='euclidean', linkage='ward')
    cluster.fit_predict(dataset)
    ```

4. Now let's look at the association of each data point to the two clusters that were created:

    ```
    print(cluster.labels_)
    ```

    ```
    [0 0 0 0 0 0 0 0 1 1 1 1 1 1 1 1 1 1 1 0]
    ```

You can see that the cluster assignment for both hierarchical and *k*-means algorithms are very similar.

The hierarchical clustering algorithm has its distinct advantages and drawbacks when compared to the *k*-means clustering algorithm. One key advantage is that hierarchical clustering doesn't require the number of clusters to be specified beforehand, unlike *k*-means.

This feature can be incredibly useful when the data doesn't clearly suggest an optimal number of clusters. Hierarchical clustering also provides a dendrogram, a tree-like diagram that can be very insightful for visualizing the nested grouping of data and understanding the hierarchical structure.

However, hierarchical clustering has its drawbacks. It is computationally more intensive than *k*-means, making it less suitable for large datasets.

Understanding DBSCAN

Density-based spatial clustering of applications with noise (DBSCAN) is an unsupervised learning technique that performs clustering based on the density of the points. The basic idea is based on the assumption that if we group the data points in a crowded or high-density space together, we can achieve meaningful clustering.

This approach to clustering has two important implications:

- Using this idea, the algorithm is likely to cluster together the points that exist together regardless of their shape or pattern. This methodology helps in creating clusters of arbitrary shapes. By "shape," we refer to the pattern or distribution of data points in a multi-dimensional space. This capability is advantageous because real-world data is often complex and non-linear, and the ability to create clusters of arbitrary shapes enables more accurate representation and understanding of such data.
- Unlike the k-means algorithm, we do not need to specify the number of clusters and the algorithm can detect the appropriate number of groupings in the data.

The following steps involve the DBSCAN algorithm:

1. The algorithm establishes a neighborhood around each data point. The term "neighborhood," in this context, refers to an area wherein other data points are examined for proximity to the point of interest. This is accomplished by counting the number of data points within a distance usually represented by a variable, *eps*. The *eps* variable, in this setting, specifies the maximum distance between two data points for them to be considered as being in the same neighborhood. The distance is by default determined by the Euclidean distance measure.

2. Next, the algorithm quantifies the density of each data point. It uses a variable named `min_samples`, which represents the minimum number of other data points that should be in the *eps* distance for a data point to be regarded as a "core instance." In simpler terms, a core instance is a data point that is densely surrounded by other data points. Logically, regions with a high density of data points will have a greater number of these core instances.

3. Each of the identified neighborhoods identifies a cluster. It is crucial to note that the neighborhood surrounding one core instance (a data point that has a minimum number of other data points within its "eps" distance) may encompass additional core instances. This means that core instances are not exclusive to a single cluster but can contribute to the formation of multiple clusters due to their proximity to several data points. Consequently, the borders of these clusters may overlap, leading to a complex, interconnected cluster structure.

4. Any data point that is not a core instance or does not lie in the neighborhood of a core instance is considered an outlier.

Let us see how we can create clusters using DBSCAN in Python.

Creating clusters using DBSCAN in Python

First, we will import the necessary functions from the `sklearn` library:

```
from sklearn.cluster import DBSCAN
from sklearn.datasets import make_moons
```

Let's employ DBSCAN to tackle a slightly more complex clustering problem, one that involves structures known as "half-moons." In this context, "half-moons" refer to two sets of data points that are shaped like crescents, with each moon representing a unique cluster. Such datasets pose a challenge because the clusters are not linearly separable, meaning a straight line cannot easily divide the different groups.

This is where the concept of "nonlinear class boundaries" comes into play. In contrast to linear class boundaries, which can be represented by a straight line, nonlinear class boundaries are more complex, often necessitating curved lines or multidimensional surfaces to accurately segregate different classes or clusters.

To generate this half-moon dataset, we can leverage the `make_moons()` function. This function creates a swirl pattern resembling two moons. The "noisiness" of the moon shapes and the number of samples to generate can be adjusted according to our needs.

Here's what the generated dataset looks like:

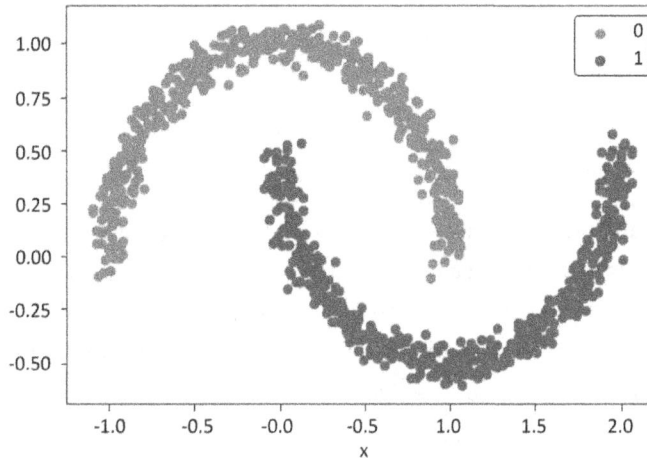

Figure 6.9: Data used for DBSCAN

In order to use DBSCAN, we need to provide the eps and `min_samples` parameters as discussed:

```python
from matplotlib import pyplot
from pandas import DataFrame
# generate 2d classification dataset
X, y = make_moons (n_samples=1000, noise=0.05)
# scatter plot, dots colored by class value
df = DataFrame (dict (x=X[,0], y=X[,1], label=y))
colors = {0: 'red', 1:'blue'}
fig, ax = pyplot.subplots()
grouped = df.groupby('label')
for key, group in grouped:
    group.plot(ax=ax, kind='scatter', x='x', y='y', label=key, color-
colors[key])
pyplot.show()
```

Evaluating the clusters

The objective of good quality clustering is that the data points that belong to the separate clusters should be differentiable. This implies the following:

- The data points that belong to the same cluster should be as similar as possible.
- Data points that belong to separate clusters should be as different as possible.

Human intuition can be used to evaluate the clustering results by visualizing the clusters, but there are mathematical methods that can quantify the quality of the clusters. They not only measure the tightness of each cluster (cohesion) and the separation between different clusters but also offer a numerical, hence objective, way to assess the quality of clustering. Silhouette analysis is one such technique that compares the tightness and separation in the clusters created by the k-means algorithm. It's a metric that quantifies the degree of cohesion and separation in clusters. While this technique has been mentioned in the context of k-means, it is in fact generalizable and can be applied to evaluate the results of any clustering algorithm, not just k-means.

Silhouette analysis assigns a score, known as the Silhouette coefficient, to each data point in the range of 0 to 1. It essentially measures how close each data point in one cluster is to the points in the neighboring clusters.

Application of clustering

Clustering is used wherever we need to discover the underlying patterns in datasets.

In government use cases, clustering can be used for the following:

- **Crime-hotspot analysis**: Clustering is applied to geolocation data, incident reports, and other related features. It aids in identifying areas with high incidences of crime, enabling law enforcement agencies to optimize patrol routes and deploy resources more effectively.
- **Demographic social analysis**: Clustering can analyze demographic data such as age, income, education, and occupation. This aids in understanding the socioeconomic composition of different regions, informing public policy and social service provision.

In market research, clustering can be used for the following:

- **Market segmentation**: By clustering consumer data including spending habits, product preferences, and lifestyle indicators, businesses can identify distinct market segments. This allows for tailored product development and marketing approaches.

- **Targeted advertisements**: Clustering helps analyze customer online behavior, including browsing patterns, click-through rates, and purchase history. This enables companies to create personalized advertisements for each customer cluster, enhancing engagement and conversion rates.

- **Customer categorization**: Through clustering, businesses can categorize customers based on their interaction with products or services, their feedback, and their loyalty. This aids in understanding customer behavior, predicting trends, and developing retention strategies.

Principal component analysis (PCA) is also used for generally exploring the data and removing noise from real-time data, such as stock-market trading. In this context, "noise" refers to random or irregular fluctuations that may obscure underlying patterns or trends in the data. PCA helps in filtering out these erratic fluctuations, allowing for clearer data analysis and interpretation.

Dimensionality reduction

Each feature in our data corresponds to a dimension in our problem space. Minimizing the number of features to make our problem space simpler is called **dimensionality reduction**. It can be done in one of the following two ways:

- **Feature selection**: Selecting a set of features that are important in the context of the problem we are trying to solve

- **Feature aggregation**: Combining two or more features to reduce dimensions using one of the following algorithms:

    - **PCA**: A linear unsupervised ML algorithm
    - **Linear discriminant analysis (LDA)**: A linear supervised ML algorithm
    - **KPCA**: A nonlinear algorithm

Let's look deeper at one of the popular dimensionality reduction algorithms, namely PCA, in more detail.

Principal component analysis

PCA is a method in unsupervised machine learning that is typically employed to reduce the dimensionality of datasets through a process known as linear transformation. In simpler terms, it's a way of simplifying data by focusing on its most important parts, which are identified based on their variance.

Consider a graphical representation of a dataset, where each data point is plotted on a multi-dimensional space. PCA helps identify the principal components, which are the directions where the data varies the most. In *Figure 6.10*, we see two of these, PC1 and PC2. These principal components illustrate the overall "shape" of the distribution of data points.

Each principal component corresponds to a new, lesser dimension that captures as much information as possible. In a practical sense, these principal components can be viewed as summary indicators of the original data, making the data more manageable and easier to analyze. For instance, in a large dataset concerning customer behavior, PCA can help us identify the key driving factors (principal components) that define the majority of customer behaviors.

Determining the coefficients for these principal components involves calculating the eigenvectors and eigenvalues of the data covariance matrix, which is a topic we'll delve into more deeply in a later section. These coefficients serve as weights for each original feature in the new component space, defining how each feature contributes to the principal component.

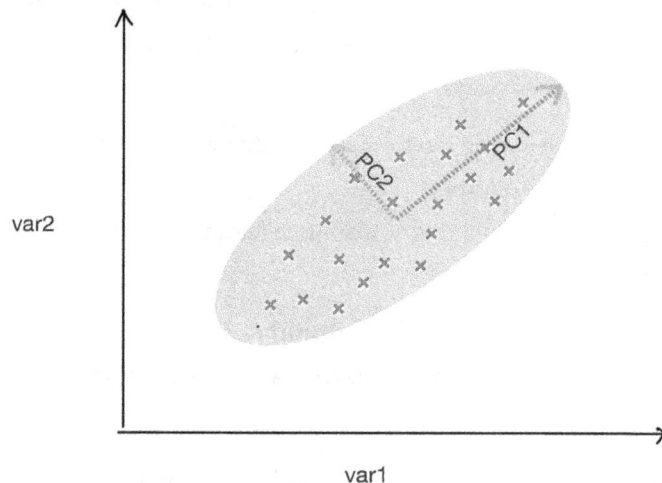

Figure 6.10: Principle component analysis

To elaborate further, imagine you have a dataset containing various aspects of a country's economy, such as GDP, employment rates, inflation, and more. The data is vast and multi-dimensional. Here, PCA would allow you to reduce these multiple dimensions into two principal components, PC1 and PC2. These components would encapsulate the most crucial information while discarding noise or less important details.

The resulting graph, with PC1 and PC2 as axes, would give you an easier-to-interpret visual representation of the economic data, with each point representing an economy's status based on its combination of GDP, employment rates, and other factors.

This makes PCA an invaluable tool for simplifying and interpreting high-dimensional data.

Let's consider the following code:

```python
from sklearn.decomposition import PCA
import pandas as pd
url = "https://storage.googleapis.com/neurals/data/iris.csv"
iris = pd.read_csv(url)

iris
X = iris.drop('Species', axis=1)
pca = PCA(n_components=4)
pca.fit(X)
```

	Sepal.Length	Sepal.Width	Petal.Length	Petal.Width	Species
0	5.1	3.5	1.4	0.2	setosa
1	4.9	3.0	1.4	0.2	setosa
2	4.7	3.2	1.3	0.2	setosa
3	4.6	3.1	1.5	0.2	setosa
4	5.0	3.6	1.4	0.2	setosa
...	...	...	...	...	...
145	6.7	3.0	5.2	2.3	virginica
146	6.3	2.5	5.0	1.9	virginica
147	6.5	3.0	5.2	2.0	virginica
148	6.2	3.4	5.4	2.3	virginica
149	5.9	3.0	5.1	1.8	virginica

```python
X = iris.drop('Species', axis=1)
pca = PCA(n_components=4)
pca.fit(X)
```

```
PCA(n_components=4)
```

Now let's print the coefficients of our PCA model:

```
pca_df=(pd.DataFrame(pca.components_,columns=X.columns))
pca_df
```

	Sepal.Length	Sepal.Width	Petal.Length	Petal.Width	
0	0.361387	-0.084523	0.856671	0.358289	Coefficients for PC1
1	0.656589	0.730161	-0.173373	-0.075481	Coefficients for PC2
2	-0.582030	0.597911	0.076236	0.545831	Coefficients for PC3
3	-0.315487	0.319723	0.479839	-0.753657	Coefficients for PC4

Figure 6.11: Diagram highlighting coefficients of the PCA model

Note that the original DataFrame has four features: Sepal.Length, Sepal.Width, Petal.Length, and Petal.Width. The preceding DataFrame specifies the coefficients of the four principal components, PC1, PC2, PC3, and PC4—for example, the first row specifies the coefficients of PC1 that can be used to replace the original four variables.

It is important to note here that the number of principal components (in this case, four: PC1, PC2, PC3, and PC4) does not necessarily need to be two as in our previous economy example. The number of principal components is a choice we make based on the level of complexity we are willing to handle in our data. The more principal components we choose, the more of the original data's variance we can retain, at the cost of increased complexity.

Based on these coefficients, we can calculate the PCA components for our input DataFrame X:

```
X['PC1'] = X['Sepal.Length']* pca_df['Sepal.Length'][0] + X['Sepal.
Width']* pca_df['Sepal.Width'][0]+ X['Petal.Length']* pca_df['Petal.
Length'][0]+X['Petal.Width']* pca_df['Petal.Width'][0]


X['PC2'] = X['Sepal.Length']* pca_df['Sepal.Length'][1] + X['Sepal.
Width']* pca_df['Sepal.Width'][1]+ X['Petal.Length']* pca_df['Petal.
Length'][1]+X['Petal.Width']* pca_df['Petal.Width'][1]


X['PC3'] = X['Sepal.Length']* pca_df['Sepal.Length'][2] + X['Sepal.
Width']* pca_df['Sepal.Width'][2]+ X['Petal.Length']* pca_df['Petal.
Length'][2]+X['Petal.Width']* pca_df['Petal.Width'][2]


X['PC4'] = X['Sepal.Length']* pca_df['Sepal.Length'][3] + X['Sepal.
Width']* pca_df['Sepal.Width'][3]+ X['Petal.Length']* pca_df['Petal.
Length'][3]+X['Petal.Width']* pca_df['Petal.Width'][3]


X
```

Now let's print X after the calculation of the PCA components:

	Sepal.Length	Sepal.Width	Petal.Length	Petal.Width	PC1	PC2	PC3	PC4
0	5.1	3.5	1.4	0.2	2.818240	5.646350	-0.659768	0.031089
1	4.9	3.0	1.4	0.2	2.788223	5.149951	-0.842317	-0.065675
2	4.7	3.2	1.3	0.2	2.613375	5.182003	-0.613952	0.013383
3	4.6	3.1	1.5	0.2	2.757022	5.008654	-0.600293	0.108928
4	5.0	3.6	1.4	0.2	2.773649	5.653707	-0.541773	0.094610
...	...	...	...	...	...	...	...	...
145	6.7	3.0	5.2	2.3	7.446475	5.514485	-0.454028	-0.392844
146	6.3	2.5	5.0	1.9	7.029532	4.951636	-0.753751	-0.221016
147	6.5	3.0	5.2	2.0	7.266711	5.405811	-0.501371	-0.103650
148	6.2	3.4	5.4	2.3	7.403307	5.443581	0.091399	-0.011244
149	5.9	3.0	5.1	1.8	6.892554	5.044292	-0.268943	0.188390

Figure 6.12: Printed calculation of the PCA components

Now let's print the variance ratio and try to understand the implications of using PCA:

```
print(pca.explained_variance_ratio_)
```

```
[0.92461872 0.05306648 0.01710261 0.00521218]
```

The variance ratio indicates the following:

- If we choose to replace the original four features with PC1, then we will be able to capture about 92.3% of the variance of the original variables. We will introduce some approximations by not capturing 100% of the variance of the original four features.

- If we choose to replace the original four features with PC1 and PC2, then we will capture an additional 5.3% of the variance of the original variables.

- If we choose to replace the original four features with PC1, PC2, and PC3, then we will now capture a further 0.017% of the variance of the original variables.

- If we choose to replace the original four features with four principal components, then we will capture 100% of the variance of the original variables (92.4 + 0.053 + 0.017 + 0.005), but replacing four original features with four principal components is meaningless as we did not reduce the dimensions at all and achieved nothing. Next, let us look into the limitations of PCA.

Limitations of PCA

Despite its many benefits, PCA is not without its limitations, as outlined below:

- First, PCA is most effective when dealing with continuous variables, as its underlying mathematical principles are designed to handle numerical data. It struggles with categorical variables, which are common in datasets that include attributes like gender, nationality, or product type. For instance, if you were analyzing a survey dataset with a mixture of numerical responses (such as age or income) and categorical responses (such as preferences or options selected), PCA wouldn't be suitable for the categorical data.

- Furthermore, PCA operates by creating an approximation of the original high-dimensional data in a lower-dimensional space. While this reduction simplifies data handling and processing, it comes with a cost: a loss of some information. This is a trade-off that needs to be carefully evaluated in each use case. For instance, if you're dealing with a biomedical dataset where each feature represents a specific genetic marker, using PCA could risk losing critical information that might be relevant for a particular disease's diagnosis or treatment.

So, while PCA is a powerful tool for dimensionality reduction, particularly when dealing with large datasets with many interrelated numerical variables, its limitations need to be considered carefully to ensure it is the right choice for a given application.

Association rules mining

Patterns in a particular dataset are the treasure that needs to be discovered, understood, and mined for the information they contain. There is an important set of algorithms that tries to focus on pattern analysis in a given dataset. One of the more popular algorithms in this class of algorithm is called the **association rules mining** algorithm, which provides us with the following capabilities:

- The ability to measure the frequency of a pattern
- The ability to establish *cause-and-effect* relationships among the patterns
- The ability to quantify the usefulness of patterns by comparing their accuracy to random guessing

Now we will look at some examples of association rules mining.

Examples of use

Association rules mining is used when we are trying to investigate the cause-and-effect relationships between different variables of a dataset. The following are example questions that it can help to answer:

- Which values of humidity, cloud cover, and temperature can lead to rain tomorrow?
- What type of insurance claim can indicate fraud?
- What combinations of medicine may lead to complications for patients?

As these examples illustrate, association rules mining has a broad array of applications spanning from business intelligence to healthcare and environmental studies. This algorithm is a potent instrument in the data scientist's toolkit, capable of translating complex patterns into actionable insights across diverse fields.

Market basket analysis

Recommendation engines, an important topic extensively discussed in *Chapter 12, Recommendation Engines* of this book, are powerful tools for personalizing user experiences. However, there's a simpler, yet effective method for generating recommendations known as market basket analysis. Market basket analysis operates based on information about which items are frequently bought together. Unlike more sophisticated recommendation engines, this method does not take into account additional user-specific data or individual item preferences expressed by the user. It's essential to draw a distinction here. Recommendation engines typically create personalized suggestions based on the user's past behavior, preferences, and a wealth of other user-specific information. In contrast, market basket analysis solely focuses on the combinations of items purchased, regardless of who bought them or their individual preferences.

One of the key advantages of market basket analysis is the relative ease of data collection. Gathering comprehensive user preference data can be complex and time-consuming. However, data regarding items bought together can often be simply extracted from transaction records, making market basket analysis a convenient starting point for businesses venturing into the domain of recommendations. For example, this kind of data is generated when we shop at Walmart, and no special technique is required to get the data.

By "special techniques," we refer to additional steps such as conducting user surveys, employing tracking cookies, or building complex data pipelines. Instead, the data is readily available as a byproduct of the sales process. This data, when collected over a period of time, is called **transnational data**.

When association rules analysis is applied to transnational datasets of the shopping carts being used in convenience stores, supermarkets, and fast-food chains, it is called **market basket analysis**. It measures the conditional probability of buying a set of items together, which helps to answer the following questions:

- What is the optimal placement of items on the shelf?
- How should the items appear in the marketing catalog?
- What should be recommended, based on a user's buying patterns?

As market basket analysis can estimate how items are related to each other, it is often used for mass-market retail, such as supermarkets, convenience stores, drug stores, and fast-food chains. The advantage of market basket analysis is that the results are almost self-explanatory, which means that they are easily understood by business users.

Let's look at a typical superstore. All the unique items that are available in the store can be represented by a set, $\pi = \{item_1, item_2, \ldots, item_m\}$. So, if that superstore is selling 500 distinct items, then π will be a set of size 500.

People will buy items from this store. Each time someone buys an item and pays at the counter, it is added to a set of the items in a particular transaction, called an **itemset**. In a given period of time, the transactions are grouped together in a set represented by Δ, where $\Delta = \{t_1, t_2, \ldots, t_n\}$.

Let's look at the following simple transaction data consisting of only four transactions. These transactions are summarized in the following table:

t_1	Wickets, pads
t_2	Bats, wickets, pads, helmets
t_3	Helmets, balls
t_4	Bats, pads, helmets

Let's look at this example in more detail:

$\pi = \{bat, wickets, pads, helmets, balls\}$, which represents all the unique items available at the store.

Let's consider one of the transactions, t_3, from Δ. Note that items bought in t_3 can be represented in the itemset $t_3 = \{helmets, balls\}$, signifying that a customer bought two items. This set is termed an itemset because it encompasses all items purchased in a single transaction. Given that there are two items in this itemset, the size of itemset t_3 is said to be two. This terminology allows us to classify and analyze purchasing patterns more effectively.

Association rules mining

An association rule mathematically describes the relationship items involved in various transactions. It does this by investigating the relationship between two item sets in the form $X \Rightarrow Y$, where $X \subset \pi$, $Y \subset \pi$. In addition, X and Y are non overlapping item sets; which means that $X \cap Y = \emptyset$.

An association rule could be described in the following form:

$$\{helmets, balls\} \Rightarrow \{bike\}$$

Here, *{helmets, balls}* is *X*, and *{bike}* is *Y*.

Let us look into the different types of association rules.

Types of rules

Running associative analysis algorithms will typically result in the generation of a large number of rules from a transaction dataset. Most of them are useless. To pick rules that can result in useful information, we can classify them as one of the following three types:

- Trivial
- Inexplicable
- Actionable

Let's look at each of these types in more detail.

Trivial rules

Among the large numbers of rules generated, many that are derived will be useless as they summarize common knowledge about the business. They are called trivial rules. Even if confidence in the trivial rules is high, they remain useless and cannot be used for any data-driven decision-making. Note that, here, "confidence" refers to a metric used in association analysis that quantifies the probability of occurrence of a particular event (let's say B), given that another event (A) has already occurred. We can safely ignore all trivial rules.

The following are examples of trivial rules:

- Anyone who jumps from a high-rise building is likely to die.
- Working harder leads to better scores in exams.
- The sales of heaters increase as the temperature drops.
- Driving a car over the speed limit on a highway leads to a higher chance of an accident.

Inexplicable rules

Among the rules that are generated after running the association rules algorithm, the ones that have no obvious explanation are the trickiest to use. Note that a rule can only be useful if it can help us discover and understand a new pattern that is expected to eventually lead toward a certain course of action. If that is not the case, and we cannot explain why event X led to event Y, then it is an inexplicable rule, because it's just a mathematical formula that ends up exploring the pointless relationship between two events that are unrelated and independent.

The following are examples of inexplicable rules:

- People who wear red shirts tend to score better in exams.
- Green bicycles are more likely to be stolen.
- People who buy pickles end up buying diapers as well.

Actionable rules

Actionable rules are the golden rules we are looking for. They are understood by the business and lead to insights. They can help us to discover the possible causes of an event when presented to an audience familiar with the business domain—for example, actionable rules may suggest the best placement in a store for a particular product based on current buying patterns. They may also suggest which items to place together to maximize their chances of selling as users tend to buy them together.

The following are examples of actionable rules and their corresponding actions:

- **Rule 1**: Displaying ads to users' social media accounts results in a higher likelihood of sales.
- **Actionable item**: Suggests alternative ways of advertising a product.
- **Rule 2**: Creating more price points increases the likelihood of sales.
- **Actionable item**: One item may be advertised in a sale, while the price of another item is raised.

Let us now look into how to rank the rules.

Ranking rules

Association rules are measured in three ways:

- Support (frequency) of items
- Confidence
- Lift

Let's look at them in more detail.

Support

The support measure is a number that quantifies how frequent the pattern we are looking for is in our dataset. It is calculated by first counting the number of occurrences of our pattern of interest and then dividing it by the total number of all the transactions.

Let's look at the following formula for a particular *itemset$_a$*:

$$numItemset_a = Number\ of\ transactions\ that\ contain\ itemset_a$$

$$num_{total} = Total\ number\ of\ transactions$$

$$support(itemset_a) = \frac{numItemset_a}{num_{total}}$$

By just looking at the support, we can get an idea of how rare the occurrence of a pattern is. Low support means that we are looking for a rare event. In a business context, these rare events could be exceptional cases or outliers, which might carry significant implications. For instance, they may denote unusual customer behavior or a unique sales trend, potentially marking opportunities or threats that require strategic attention.

For example, if *itemset$_a$* = *{helmet, ball}* appears in two transactions out of six, then support *(itemset$_a$) = 2/6 = 0.33*.

Confidence

The confidence is a number that quantifies how strongly we can associate the left side (*X*) with the right side (*Y*) by calculating the conditional probability. It calculates the probability that event *X* will lead toward event *Y*, given that event *X* occurred.

Mathematically, consider the rule $X \Rightarrow Y$.

The confidence of this rule is represented as confidence$(X \Rightarrow Y)$ and is measured as follows:

$$confidence(X \Rightarrow Y) = \frac{support(X \cup Y)}{support(X)}$$

Let's look at an example. Consider the following rule:

$$\{helmet, ball\} \Rightarrow \{wickets\}$$

The confidence of this rule is calculated by the following formula:

$$confidence(helmet, ball \Rightarrow wickets) = \frac{support(helmet, ball \cup wickets)}{support(helmet, ball)} = \frac{\frac{1}{6}}{\frac{2}{6}} = 0.5$$

This means that if someone has {helmet, balls} in the basket, then there is a 0.5 or 50% probability that they will also have wickets to go with it.

Lift

Another way to estimate the quality of a rule is by calculating the lift. The lift returns a number that quantifies how much improvement has been achieved by a rule at predicting the result compared to just assuming the result at the right-hand side of the equation. "Improvement" refers to the degree of enhancement or betterment achieved by a rule in its ability to predict an outcome compared to a baseline or default approach. It represents the extent to which the rule provides more accurate or insightful predictions than what would be obtained by making assumptions solely based on the right-hand side of the equation. If the X and Y itemsets are independent, then the lift is calculated as follows:

$$Lift(X \Rightarrow Y) = \frac{support(X \cup Y)}{support(X) \times support(Y)}$$

Algorithms for association analysis

In this section, we will explore the following two algorithms that can be used for association analysis:

- **Apriori algorithm**: Proposed by Agrawal, R. and Srikant in 1994.
- **FP-growth algorithm**: An improvement suggested by Han et al. in 2001.

Let's look at each of these algorithms.

Apriori algorithm

The apriori algorithm is an iterative and multiphase algorithm used to generate association rules. It is based on a generation-and-test approach.

Before executing the apriori algorithm, we need to define two variables: $support_{threshold}$ and $Confidence_{threshold}$.

The algorithm consists of the following two phases:

- **Candidate-generation phase**: It generates the candidate itemsets, which contain sets of all itemsets above support$_{threshold}$.
- **Filter phase**: It filters out all rules below the expected confidence$_{threshold}$.

After filtering, the resulting rules are the answer.

Limitations of the apriori algorithm

The major bottleneck in the apriori algorithm is the generation of candidate rules in Phase 1—for example, $\pi = \{item_1, item_2, \ldots, item_m\}$ can produce 2^m possible itemsets. Because of its multiphase design, it first generates these itemsets and then works toward finding the frequent itemsets. This limitation is a huge performance bottleneck and makes the apriori algorithm unsuitable for larger items because it generates too many itemsets before it can find frequent items, which will have an effect on the time taken.

Let us now look into the FP-growth algorithm.

FP-growth algorithm

The **frequent pattern growth (FP-growth)** algorithm is an improvement on the apriori algorithm. It starts by showing the frequent transaction FP-tree, which is an ordered tree. It consists of two steps:

- Populating the FP-tree
- Mining frequent patterns

Let's look at these steps one by one.

Populating the FP-tree

Let's consider the transaction data shown in the following table. Let's first represent it as a sparse matrix:

ID	Bat	Wickets	Pads	Helmet	Ball
1	0	1	1	0	0
2	1	1	1	1	0
3	0	0	0	1	1
4	1	0	1	1	0

Let's calculate the frequency of each item and sort them in descending order by frequency:

Item	Frequency
pads	3
helmets	3
bats	2
wickets	2
balls	1

Now let's rearrange the transaction-based data based on the frequency:

ID	Original Items	Reordered Items
t1	Wickets, pads	Pads, wickets
t2	Bat, wickets, pads, helmets	Helmets, pads, wickets, bats
t3	Helmets, balls	Helmets, balls
t4	Bats, pads, helmets	Helmets, pads, bats

To build the FP-tree, let's start with the first branch of the FP-tree. The FP-tree starts with a **Null** as the root. To build the tree, we can represent each item with a node, as shown in the following diagram (the tree representation of t_1 is shown here).

Note that the label of each node is the name of the item and its frequency is appended after the colon. Also, note that the **pads** item has a frequency of 1:

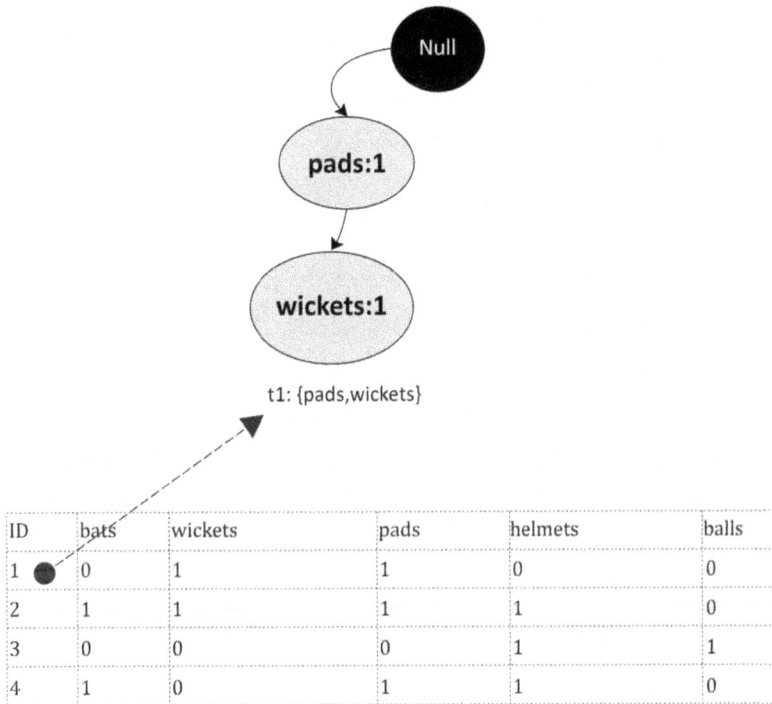

Figure 6.13: FP-tree representation first transaction

Using the same pattern, let's draw all four transactions, resulting in the full FP-tree. The FP-tree has four leaf nodes, each representing the itemset associated with the four transactions. Note that we need to count the frequencies of each item and need to increase it when used multiple times—for example, when adding t_2 to the FP-tree, the frequency of **helmets** was increased to two. Similarly, while adding t_4, it was increased again to three.

The resulting tree is shown in the following diagram:

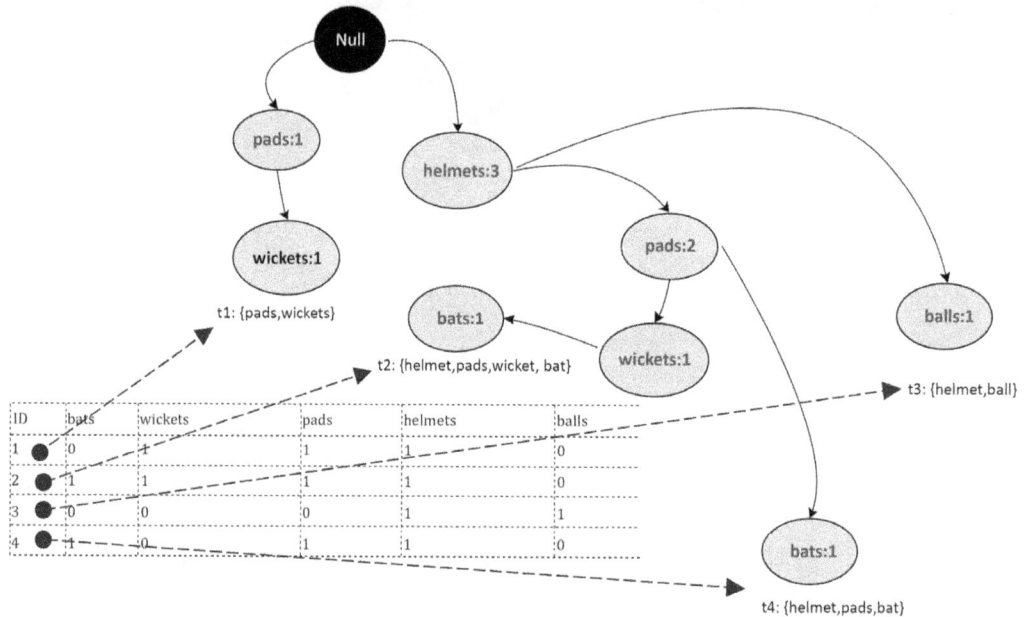

Figure 6.14: FP-tree representing all transactions

Note that the FP-tree generated in the preceding diagram is an ordered tree. This leads us to the second phase of the FP-growth tree: mining frequent patterns.

Mining frequent patterns

The second phase of the FP-growth process is focused on mining the frequent patterns from the FP-tree. Creating an ordered tree is a deliberate move, aimed at producing a data structure that facilitates effortless navigation when hunting for these frequent patterns.

We start this journey from a leaf node, which is an end node, and traverse upward. As an example, let's begin from one of the leaf node items, "bats." Our next task is to figure out the conditional pattern base for "bat." The term "conditional pattern base" might sound complex, but it's merely a collection of all paths that lead from a specific leaf node item to the root of the tree. For our item "bat," the conditional pattern base will comprise all paths from the "bat" node to the top of the tree. At this point, understanding the difference between ordered and unordered trees becomes critical. In an ordered tree such as the FP-tree, the items adhere to a fixed order, simplifying the pattern mining process. An unordered tree doesn't provide this structured setup, which could make discovering frequent patterns more challenging.

When computing the conditional pattern base for "bats," we are essentially mapping out all paths from the "bats" node to the root. These paths reveal the items that often co-occur with "bat" in transactions. In essence, we're following the "branch" of the tree associated with "bat" to understand its relationships with other items. This visual illustration clarifies where we get this information from and how the FP-tree assists in illuminating frequent patterns in transaction data. The conditional pattern base for **bat** will be as follows:

Wicket: 1	Pads: 1	Helmet: 1
Pad: 1	Helmet: 1	

The **frequent pattern** for **bat** will be as follows:

$$\{wicket, pads, helmet\}: bat$$

$$\{pad, helmet\}: bat$$

Code for using FP-growth

Let's see how we can generate association rules using the FP-growth algorithm in Python. For this, we will be using the pyfpgrowth package. First, if we have never used pyfpgrowth before, let's install it first:

```
!pip install pyfpgrowth
```

Then, let's import the packages that we need to use to implement this algorithm:

```
import pandas as pd
import numpy as np
import pyfpgrowth as fp
```

Now we will create the input data in the form of transactionSet:

```
dict1 = {
    'id':[0,1,2,3],
    'items':[["wickets","pads"],
    ["bat","wickets","pads","helmet"],
    ["helmet","pad"],
    ["bat","pads","helmet"]]
}
transactionSet = pd.DataFrame(dict1)
```

```
       id     items
 0     0     [wickets, pads]
```

```
1     1      [bat, wickets, pads, helmet]
2     2      [helmet, pad]
3     3      [bat, pads, helmet]
```

Once the input data is generated, we will generate patterns that will be based on the parameters that we passed in `find_frequent_patterns()`. Note that the second parameter passed to this function is the minimum support, which is 1 in this case:

```
patterns = fp.find_frequent_patterns(transactionSet['items'],1)
```

The patterns have been generated. Now let's print the patterns. The patterns list the combinations of items with their supports:

```
patterns
```

```
{('pad',): 1,
 ('helmet', 'pad'): 1,
 ('wickets',): 2,
 ('pads', 'wickets'): 2,
 ('bat', 'wickets'): 1,
 ('helmet', 'wickets'): 1,
 ('bat', 'pads', 'wickets'): 1,
 ('helmet', 'pads', 'wickets'): 1,
 ('bat', 'helmet', 'wickets'): 1,
 ('bat', 'helmet', 'pads', 'wickets'): 1,
 ('bat',): 2,
 ('bat', 'helmet'): 2,
 ('bat', 'pads'): 2,
 ('bat', 'helmet', 'pads'): 2,
 ('pads',): 3,
 ('helmet',): 3,
 ('helmet', 'pads'): 2}
```

Now let's generate the rules:

```
rules = fp.generate_association_rules(patterns,0.3)
rules
```

```
{('helmet',): (('pads',), 0.6666666666666666),
 ('pad',): (('helmet',), 1.0),
 ('pads',): (('helmet',), 0.6666666666666666),
 ('wickets',): (('bat', 'helmet', 'pads'), 0.5),
 ('bat',): (('helmet', 'pads'), 1.0),
 ('bat', 'pads'): (('helmet',), 1.0),
 ('bat', 'wickets'): (('helmet', 'pads'), 1.0),
 ('pads', 'wickets'): (('bat', 'helmet'), 0.5),
 ('helmet', 'pads'): (('bat',), 1.0),
 ('helmet', 'wickets'): (('bat', 'pads'), 1.0),
 ('bat', 'helmet'): (('pads',), 1.0),
 ('bat', 'helmet', 'pads'): (('wickets',), 0.5),
 ('bat', 'helmet', 'wickets'): (('pads',), 1.0),
 ('bat', 'pads', 'wickets'): (('helmet',), 1.0),
 ('helmet', 'pads', 'wickets'): (('bat',), 1.0)}
```

Each rule has a left-hand side and a right-hand side, separated by a colon (:). It also gives us the support of each of the rules in our input dataset.

Summary

In this chapter, we looked at various unsupervised machine learning techniques. We looked at the circumstances in which it is a good idea to try to reduce the dimensionality of the problem we are trying to solve and the different methods of doing this. We also studied the practical examples where unsupervised machine learning techniques can be very helpful, including market basket analysis.

In the next chapter, we will look at the various supervised learning techniques. We will start with linear regression and then we will look at more sophisticated supervised machine learning techniques, such as decision-tree-based algorithms, SVM, and XGBoost. We will also study the Naive Bayes algorithm, which is best suited for unstructured textual data.

Learn more on Discord

To join the Discord community for this book – where you can share feedback, ask questions to the author, and learn about new releases – follow the QR code below:

`https://packt.link/WHLel`

7

Traditional Supervised Learning Algorithms

Artificial intelligence is the new electricity.

—*Andrew Ng*

In *Chapter 7*, we will turn our attention to supervised machine learning algorithms. These algorithms, characterized by their reliance on labeled data for model training, are multifaceted and versatile in nature. Let's consider some instances such as decision trees, **Support Vector Machines (SVMs)**, and linear regression, to name a few, which all fall under the umbrella of supervised learning.

As we delve deeper into this field, it's important to note that this chapter doesn't cover neural networks, a significant category within supervised machine learning. Given their complexity and the rapid advancements occurring in the field, neural networks merit an in-depth exploration, which we will embark on in the following three chapters. The vast expanse of neural networks necessitates more than a single chapter to fully discuss their complexities and potential.

In this chapter, we will delve into the essentials of supervised machine learning, featuring classifiers and regressors. We will explore their capabilities using real-world problems as case studies. Six distinct classification algorithms will be presented, followed by three regression techniques. Lastly, we'll compare their results to encapsulate the key takeaways from this discussion.

The overall objective of this chapter is for you to understand the different types of supervised machine learning techniques, and to know what the best supervised machine learning techniques are for certain classes of problems.

The following concepts are discussed in this chapter:

- Understanding supervised machine learning
- Understanding classification algorithms
- The methods to evaluate the performance of classifiers
- Understanding regression algorithms
- The methods to evaluate the performance of regression algorithms

Let's start by looking at the basic concepts behind supervised machine learning.

Understanding supervised machine learning

Machine learning focuses on using data-driven approaches to create autonomous systems that can help us to make decisions with or without human supervision. In order to create these autonomous systems, machine learning uses a group of algorithms and methodologies to discover and formulate repeatable patterns in data. One of the most popular and powerful methodologies used in machine learning is the supervised machine learning approach. In supervised machine learning, an algorithm is given a set of inputs, called **features**, and their corresponding outputs, called **labels**. These features often comprise structured data like user profiles, historical sales figures, or sensor measurements, while the labels usually represent specific outcomes we want to predict, such as customer purchasing habits or product quality ratings. Using a given dataset, a supervised machine learning algorithm is used to train a model that captures the complex relationship between the features and labels represented by a mathematical formula. This trained model is the basic vehicle that is used for predictions.

> The ability to learn from existing data in supervised learning is similar to the ability of the human brain to learn from experience. This learning ability in supervised learning uses one of the attributes of the human brain and is a fundamental way of opening the gates to bring decision-making power and intelligence to machines.

Let's consider an example where we want to use supervised machine learning techniques to train a model that can categorize a set of emails into legitimate ones (called **legit**) and unwanted ones (called **spam**). In order to get started, we need examples from the past so that the machine can learn what sort of content of emails should be classified as spam.

This content-based learning task using text data is a complex process and is achieved through one of the supervised machine learning algorithms. Some examples of supervised machine learning algorithms that can be used to train the model in this example include decision trees and Naive Bayes classifiers, which we will discuss later in this chapter.

For now, we will focus on how we can formulate supervised machine learning problems.

Formulating supervised machine learning problems

Before going deeper into the details of supervised machine learning algorithms, let's define some of the basic supervised machine learning terminology:

Terminology	Explanation
Label	A label is the variable that our model is tasked with predicting. There can be only one label in a supervised machine learning model.
Features	The set of input variables used to predict the label is called the features.
Feature engineering	Transforming features to prepare them for the chosen supervised machine learning algorithm is called feature engineering.
Feature vector	Before providing an input to a supervised machine learning algorithm, all the features are combined in to a data structure called a feature vector.
Historical data	The data from the past that is used to formulate the relationship between the label and the features is called historical data. Historical data comes with examples.
Training/testing data	Historical data with examples is divided into two parts—a larger dataset called the training data and a smaller dataset called the testing data.
Model	A mathematical formulation of the patterns that best capture the relationship between the label and the features.
Training	Creating a model using training data.
Testing	Evaluating the quality of the trained model using testing data.
Prediction	The act of utilizing our trained model to estimate the label. In this context, "prediction" is the definitive output of the model, specifying a precise outcome. It's crucial to distinguish this from "prediction probability," which rather than providing a concrete result gives a statistical likelihood of each potential outcome.

A trained supervised machine learning model is capable of making predictions by estimating the label based on the features.

Let's introduce the notation that we will use in this chapter to discuss the machine learning techniques:

Variable	Meaning
y	Actual label
ý	Predicted label
d	Total number of examples
b	Number of training examples
c	Number of testing examples
X_train	Training feature vector

Note that in this context, an "example" refers to a single instance in our dataset. Each example comprises a set of features (input data) and a corresponding label (the outcome we're predicting)

Let's delve into some practical applications of the terms we've introduced. Consider a feature vector, essentially a data structure encompassing all the features.

For instance, if we have "n" features and "b" training examples, we represent this training feature vector as X_train. Hence, if our training dataset consists of five examples and five variables or features, X_train will have five rows—one for each example, and a total of 25 elements (5 examples x 5 features).

In this context, X_train is a specific term representing our training dataset. Each example in this dataset is a combination of features and its associated label. We use superscripts to denote a specific example's row number. Thus, a single example in our dataset is given as $(X^{(1)}, y^{(1)})$ where $X^{(1)}$ refers to the features of the first example and $y^{(1)}$ is its corresponding label.

Our complete labeled dataset, D, can therefore be expressed as $D = \{(X^{(1)}, y^{(1)}), (y^{(2)}, y^{(2)}), \ldots, (X^{(d)}, y^{(d)})\}$, where D signifies the total number of examples.

We partition D into two subsets - the training set D_{train} and the testing set D_{test}. The training set, D_{train}, can be depicted as $D_{train} = \{(X^{(1)}, y^{(1)}), (X^{(2)}, y^{(2)}), \ldots, (X^{(b)}, y^{(b)})\}$, where '$b$' is the number of training examples.

The primary goal of training a model is to ensure that the predicted target value ('ý') for any i^{th} example in the training set aligns as closely as possible with the actual label ('y'). This ensures that the model's predictions reflect the true outcomes presented in the examples.

Now, let's see how some of these terminologies are formulated practically.

As we discussed, a feature vector is defined as a data structure that has all the features stored in it.

If the number of features is n and the number of training examples is b, then X_train represents the training feature vector.

For the training dataset, the feature vector is represented by X_train. If there are b examples in the training dataset, then X_train will have b rows. If there are n variables, then the training dataset will have a dimension of n x b.

We will use superscript to represent the row number of a training example.

This particular example in our labeled dataset is represented by $(Features^{(1)}, label^{(1)}) = (X^{(1)}, y^{(1)})$.

So, our labeled dataset is represented by $D = \{(X^{(1)}, y^{(1)}), (X^{(2)}, y^{(2)}), \ldots, (X^{(d)}, y^{(d)})\}$.

We divide that into two parts—D_{train} and D_{test}.

So, our training set can be represented by $D_{train} = \{(X^{(1)}, y^{(1)}), (X^{(2)}, y^{(2)}), \ldots, (X^{(b)}, y^{(b)})\}$.

The objective of training a model is that for any i^{th} example in the training set, the predicted value of the target value should be as close to the actual value in the examples as possible. In other words:

$$\hat{y}(i) \approx y(i); for \; 1 \leq i \leq b$$

So, our testing set can be represented by $D_{test} = \{X^{(1)}, y^{(1)}), (X^{(2)}, y^{(2)}), \ldots, (X^{(c)}, y^{(c)})\}$.

The values of the label are represented by a vector, Y:

$$Y = \{y^{(1)}, y^{(2)}, \ldots, y^{(m)}\}$$

Let's illustrate the concepts with an example.

Let's imagine we're working on a project to predict house prices based on various features, like the number of bedrooms, the size of the house in square feet, and its age. Here's how we'd apply our machine learning terminology to this real-world scenario.

In this context, our "features" would be the number of bedrooms, house size, and age. Let's say we have 50 examples (i.e., 50 different houses for which we have these details and the corresponding price). We can represent these in a training feature vector called X_train.

X_train becomes a table with 50 rows (one for each house) and 3 columns (one for each feature: bedrooms, size, and age). It's a 50 x 3 matrix holding all our feature data.

An individual house's feature set and price might be represented as $((X^{(i)}, y^{(i)}))$, where $X^{(i)}$ contains the features of the ith house and $y^{(i)}$ is its actual price.

Our entire dataset D can then be viewed as $D = \{(X^{(1)}, y^{(1)}), (X^{(2)}, y^{(2)})), ... , ((X^{(50)}, y^{(50)}))\}$.

Suppose we use 40 houses for training and the remaining 10 for testing. Our training set D_{train} would be the first 40 examples: $\{(X^{(1)}, y^{(1)}), (X^{(2)}, y^{(2)})), ... , ((X^{(40)}, y^{(40)}))\}$.

After training our model, the goal is to predict house prices $\acute{y}(i)$ that closely match the actual prices $y(i)$ for all houses in our training set.

Our testing set D_{test} consists of the remaining 10 examples: $\{(X^{(41)}, y^{(41)}), (X^{(42)}, y^{(42)}), ... , (X^{(50)}, y^{(50)}))\}$.

Lastly, we have the Y vector, comprising all our actual house prices: $Y = \{y^{(1)}, y^{(2)}, ..., y^{(50)}\}$.

With this concrete example, we can see how these concepts and equations translate into practice when predicting house prices with supervised machine learning.

Understanding enabling conditions

A supervised machine learning algorithm needs certain enabling conditions to be met in order to perform. Enabling conditions are certain prerequisites that ensure the efficacy of a supervised machine learning algorithm. These enabling conditions are as follows:

- **Enough examples**: Supervised machine learning algorithms need enough examples to train a model. We say that we have enough examples when we have conclusive evidence that the pattern of interest is fully represented in our dataset.

- **Patterns in historical data**: The examples used to train a model need to have patterns in them. The likelihood of the occurrence of our event of interest should be dependent on a combination of patterns, trends, and events. The label mathematically represents the event of interest in our model. Without these, we are dealing with random data that cannot be used to train a model.

- **Valid assumptions**: When we train a supervised machine learning model using examples, we expect that the assumptions that apply to the examples will also be valid in the future. Let's look at an actual example. If we want to train a machine learning model for the government that can predict the likelihood of whether a visa will be granted to a student, the understanding is that the laws and policies will not change when the model is used for predictions. If new policies or laws are enforced after training the model, the model may need to be retrained to incorporate this new information.

Let us look into how we can differentiate between a classifier and a regressor.

Differentiating between classifiers and regressors

In a machine learning model, the label can be a category variable or a continuous variable. Continuous variables are numeric variables that can have an infinite number of values between two values, while categorical variables are qualitative variables that are classified into distinct categories. The type of label determines what type of supervised machine learning model we have. Fundamentally, we have two types of supervised machine learning models:

- **Classifiers**: If the label is a category variable, the machine learning model is called a classifier. Classifiers can be used to answer the following type of business questions:

    - Is this abnormal tissue growth a malignant tumor?

    - Based on the current weather conditions, will it rain tomorrow?

    - Based on the profile of a particular applicant, should their mortgage application be approved?

- **Regressors**: If the label is a continuous variable, we train a regressor. Regressors can be used to answer the following types of business questions:

    - Based on the current weather condition, how much will it rain tomorrow?

    - What will the price of a particular home be with given characteristics?

Let's look at both classifiers and regressors in more detail.

Understanding classification algorithms

In supervised machine learning, if the label is a category variable, the model is categorized as a classifier. Recall that the model is essentially a mathematical representation learned from the training data:

- The historical data is called **labeled data**.
- The production data, which the label needs to be predicted for, is called **unlabeled data**.

> The ability to accurately label unlabeled data using a trained model is the real power of classification algorithms. Classifiers predict labels for unlabeled data to answer a particular business question.

Before we present the details of classification algorithms, let's first present a business problem that we will use as a challenge for classifiers. We will then use six different algorithms to answer the same challenge, which will help us compare their methodology, approach, and performance.

Presenting the classifiers challenge

We will first present a common problem, which we will use as a challenge to test six different classification algorithms. This common problem is referred to as the classifier challenge in this chapter. Using all six classifiers to solve the same problem will help us in two ways:

- All the input variables need to be processed and assembled as a complex data structure, called a feature vector. Using the same feature vector helps us avoid repeating data preparation for all six algorithms.

- We can accurately compare the performance of various algorithms as we use the same feature vector for input.

The classifiers challenge is about predicting the likelihood of a person making a purchase. In the retail industry, one of the things that can help maximize sales is understanding better the behavior of the customers. This can be done by analyzing the patterns found in historical data. Let's state the problem, first.

The problem statement

Given the historical data, can we train a binary classifier that can predict whether a particular user will eventually buy a product based on their profile?

First, let's explore the labeled dataset available to solve this problem:

$$x \in \Re b, y \in \{0, 1\}$$

Note that x is a member of a set of real numbers. $\Re b$ indicates that it is a vector with b real-time features. $y \in \{0, 1\}$ implies that is a binary variable, as we are dealing with a binary classification problem. The output can be 0 or 1, where each number represents a different class.

For this particular example, when y = 1, we call it a positive class, and when y = 0, we call it a negative class. To make it more tangible, when y equals 1, we're dealing with a positive class, meaning the user is likely to make a purchase. Conversely, when y equals 0, it represents the negative class, suggesting the user isn't likely to buy anything. This model will allow us to predict future user behavior based on their historical actions.

> Although the level of the positive and negative classes can be chosen arbitrarily, it is a good practice to define the positive class as the event of interest. If we try to flag the fraudulent transaction for a bank, then the positive class (that is, y = 1) should be the fraudulent transaction, not the other way around.

Now, let's look at the following:

- The actual label, denoted by y
- The predicted label, denoted by $\acute{y}$

Note that for our classifiers challenge, the actual value of the label found in this example is represented by y. If, in our example, someone has purchased an item, we say $y = 1$. The predicted values are represented by $\acute{y}$. The input feature vector, x, will have a dimension equal to the number of input variables. We want to determine what the probability is that a user will make a purchase, given a particular input.

So, we want to determine the probability that $y = 1$, given a particular value of feature vector x. Mathematically, we can represent this as follows:

$$\acute{y} = P(y = 1|x) : where; x \in \mathfrak{R}^{n_x}$$

Note that the expression $P(y = 1|x)$ represents the conditional probability of the event y being equal to 1, given the occurrence of event x. In other words, it represents the probability of the outcome y being true or positive, given the knowledge or presence of a specific condition x.

Now, let's look at how we can process and assemble different input variables in the feature vector, x. The methodology for assembling different parts of x using the processing pipeline is discussed in more detail in the following section.

Feature engineering using a data processing pipeline

Preparing data for a chosen machine learning algorithm is called **feature engineering** and is a crucial part of the machine learning life cycle. Feature engineering is done in different stages or phases. The multi-stage processing code used to process data is collectively known as a **data pipeline**. Making a data pipeline using standard processing steps, wherever possible, makes it reusable and decreases the effort needed to train the models. By using more well-tested software modules, the quality of the code is also enhanced.

In addition to feature engineering, it's important to note that data cleaning is a crucial part of this process as well. This involves addressing issues like outlier detection and missing value treatment. For instance, outlier detection allows you to identify and handle anomalous data points that could negatively impact your model's performance. Similarly, missing value treatment is a technique used to fill in or handle missing data points in your dataset, ensuring your model has a complete picture of the data. These are important steps to be included in the data pipeline, helping to improve the reliability and accuracy of your machine learning models.

Let's design a reusable processing pipeline for the classifiers challenge. As mentioned, we will prepare data once and then use it for all the classifiers.

Importing data

Let us start by importing the necessary libraries:

```
import numpy as np
import sklearn,sklearn.tree
import matplotlib.pyplot as plt
import pandas as pd
import sklearn.metrics as metrics
from sklearn.model_selection import train_test_split
from sklearn.preprocessing import OneHotEncoder, StandardScaler
```

Note that we will use the pandas library in Python, which is a powerful open-source data manipulation and analysis tool that provides high-performance data structures and data analysis tools. We will also use sklearn, which provides a comprehensive suite of tools and algorithms for various machine learning tasks.

Importing data

The labeled data for this problem containing the examples is stored in a file called Social_Network_ Ads.csv in the CSV format. Let us start by reading this file:

```
# Importing the dataset
dataset = pd.read_csv('https://storage.googleapis.com/neurals/data/Social_
Network_Ads.csv')
```

This file can be downloaded from https://storage.googleapis.com/neurals/data/Social_ Network_Ads.csv.

Feature selection

The process of selecting features that are relevant to the context of the problem that we want to solve is called **feature selection**. It is an essential part of feature engineering.

Once the file is imported, we drop the User ID column, which is used to identify a person and should be excluded when training a model. Generally, User ID is an identifying field that uniquely represents each person but holds no meaningful contribution to the patterns or trends we try to model.

For this reason, it's a common practice to drop such columns before training a machine learning model:

```
dataset = dataset.drop(columns=['User ID'])
```

Now, let's preview the dataset using the head command, which will print the first five rows of this dataset:

```
dataset.head(5)
```

The dataset looks like this:

	Gender	Age	EstimatedSalary	Purchased
0	Male	19	19000	0
1	Male	35	20000	0
2	Female	26	43000	0
3	Female	27	57000	0
4	Male	19	76000	0

Figure 7.1: Example dataset

Now, let's look at how we can further process the input dataset.

One-hot encoding

Several machine learning models operate best when all features are expressed as continuous variables. This stipulation implies that we need an approach to transforming categorical features into continuous ones. One common technique to achieve this is 'one-hot encoding.'

In our context, the Gender feature is categorical, and we aim to convert it into a continuous variable using one-hot encoding. But what is one-hot encoding, exactly?

One-hot encoding is a process that transforms a categorical variable into a format that machine learning algorithms can understand better. It does so by creating new binary features for each category in the original feature. For example, if we apply one-hot encoding to 'Gender, ' it would result in two new features: Male and Female. If the gender is Male, the 'Male' feature would be 1 (indicating true), and 'Female' would be 0 (indicating false), and vice versa.

Let's now apply this one-hot encoding process to our 'Gender' feature and continue our model preparation process:

```
enc = sklearn.preprocessing.OneHotEncoder()
```

The drop='first' parameter indicates that the first category in the 'Gender' feature should be dropped.

First, let us perform one-hot encoding on 'Gender':

```
enc.fit(dataset.iloc[:,[0]])
onehotlabels = enc.transform(dataset.iloc[:,[0]]).toarray()
```

Here, we use the fit_transform method to apply one-hot encoding to the 'Gender' column. The reshape(-1, 1) function is used to ensure that the data is in the correct 2D format expected by the encoder. The toarray() function is used to convert the output, which is a sparse matrix, into a dense numpy array for easier manipulation later on.

Next, let us add the encoded Gender back to the dataframe:

```
genders = pd.DataFrame({'Female': onehotlabels[:, 0], 'Male':
onehotlabels[:, 1]})
```

Note that this line of code adds the encoded 'Gender' data back to the DataFrame. Since we've set drop='first', and assuming that the 'Male' category is considered the first category, our new column, 'Female,' will have a value of 1 if the gender is female, and 0 if it is male.

Then, we drop the original Gender column from the DataFrame, as it has now been replaced with our new Female column:

```
result = pd.concat([genders,dataset.iloc[:,1:]], axis=1, sort=False)
```

Once it's converted, let's look at the dataset again:

```
result.head(5)
```

	Female	Male	Age	Estimated Salary	Purchased
0	0.0	1.0	19	19,000	0
1	0.0	1.0	35	20,000	0
2	1.0	0.0	26	43,000	0
3	1.0	0.0	27	57,000	0
4	0.0	1.0	19	76,000	0

Figure 7.2: Add a caption here....

Notice that in order to convert a variable from a category variable into a continuous variable, one-hot encoding has converted Gender into two separate columns—Male and Female.

Let us look into how we can specify the features and labels.

Specifying the features and label

Let's specify the features and labels. We will use y through out this book to represent the label and X to represent the feature set:

```
y=result['Purchased']
X=result.drop(columns=['Purchased'])
```

X represents the feature vector and contains all the input variables that we need to use to train the model.

Dividing the dataset into testing and training portions

Next, we will partition our dataset into two parts: 70% for training and 30% for testing. The rationale behind this particular division is that, as a rule of thumb in machine learning practice, we want a sizable portion of the dataset to train our model so that it can learn effectively from various examples. This is where the larger 70% comes into play. However, we also need to ensure that our model generalizes well to unseen data and doesn't just memorize the training set. To evaluate this, we will set aside 30% of the data for testing. This data is not used during the training process and acts as a benchmark for gauging the trained model's performance and its ability to make predictions on new, unseen data:

```
X_train, X_test, y_train, y_test = train_test_split(X, y,
test_size = 0.25, random_state = 0)
```

This has created the following four data structures:

- X_train: A data structure containing the features of the training data
- X_test: A data structure containing the features of the training test
- y_train: A vector containing the values of the label in the training dataset
- y_test: A vector containing the values of the label in the testing dataset

Let us now apply feature normalization to the dataset.

Scaling the features

As we proceed with the preparation of our dataset for our machine learning model, an important step is **feature normalization**, also known as scaling. In many machine learning algorithms, scaling the variables to a uniform range, typically from 0 to 1, can enhance the model's performance by ensuring that no individual feature can dominate others due to its scale.

This process can also help the algorithm converge more quickly to the solution. Now, let's apply this transformation to our dataset for optimal results.

First, we initialize an instance of the StandardScaler class, which will be used to conduct the scaling operation:

```
# Feature Scaling
sc = StandardScaler()
```

Then, we use the fit_transform method. This transformation scales the features such that they have a mean of 0 and a standard deviation of 1, which is the essence of standard scaling. The transformed data is stored in the X_train_scaled variable:

```
X_train = sc.fit_transform(X_train)
```

Next, we will apply the transform method, which applies the same transformation (as in the prior code) to the test dataset X_test:

```
X_test = sc.transform(X_test)
```

After we scale the data, it is ready to be used as input to the different classifiers that we will present in the subsequent sections.

Evaluating the classifiers

Once the model is trained, we need to evaluate its performance. To do that, we will use the following process:

1. We will divide the labeling dataset into two parts—a training partition and a testing partition. We will use the testing partition to evaluate the trained model.

2. We will use the features of our testing partition to generate labels for each row. This is our set of predicted labels.

3. We will compare the set of predicted labels with the actual labels to evaluate the model.

> Unless we try to solve something quite trivial, there will be some misclassifications when we evaluate the model. How we interpret these misclassifications to determine the quality of the model depends on which performance metrics we choose to use.

Once we have both the set of actual labels and the predicted labels, a bunch of performance metrics can be used to evaluate the models.

The best metric for quantifying the model will depend on the requirements of the business problem that we want to solve, as well as the characteristics of the training dataset.

Let us now look at the confusion matrix.

Confusion matrices

A confusion matrix is used to summarize the results of the evaluation of a classifier. The confusion matrix for a binary classifier looks as follows:

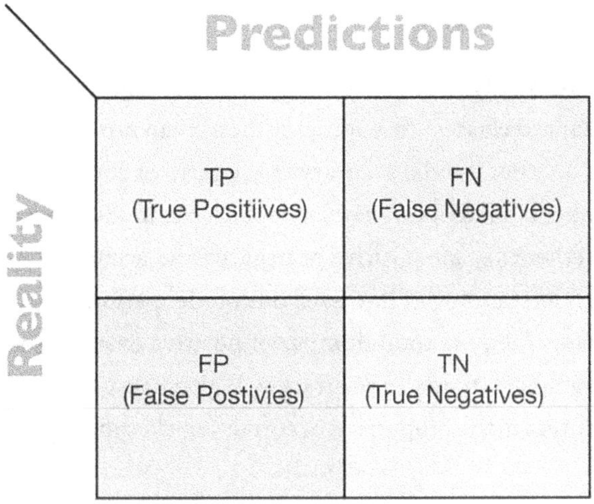

Figure 7.3: Confusion matrix

> If the label of the classifier we train has two levels, it is called a **binary classifier**. The first critical use case of supervised machine learning—specifically, a binary classifier—was during the First World War to differentiate between an aircraft and flying birds.

The classification can be divided into the following four categories:

- **True Positives (TPs)**: The positive classifications that were correctly classified
- **True Negatives (TNs)**: The negative classifications that were correctly classified
- **False Positives (FPs)**: The positive classifications that were actually negative
- **False Negatives (FNs)**: The negative classifications that were actually positive

Let's see how we can use these four categories to create various performance metrics.

A confusion matrix provides a comprehensive snapshot of a model's performance by detailing the number of correct and incorrect predictions. It enumerates TPs, TNs, FPs, and FNs. Among these, the correct classifications refer to the instances where our model correctly identified the class, i.e., TPs and TNs. The model's accuracy, which signifies the proportion of these correct classifications (TPs and TNs) out of all the predictions made, can then be calculated directly from this confusion matrix. A confusion matrix gives you the number of correct classifications and misclassifications through a count of TPs, TNs, FPs, and FNs. The model accuracy is defined as the proportion of correct classifications among all predictions and can be easily seen from the confusion matrix as follows.

When we have an approximately equal number of positive and negative examples in our data – a situation known as balanced classes – the accuracy metric can provide a valuable measure of our model's performance. In other words, accuracy is the ratio of correct predictions made by the model to the total number of predictions. For example, if our model correctly identifies 90 out of 100 test instances, whether they are positive or negative, its accuracy will be 90%. This metric can give us a general understanding of how well our model performs across both classes. If our data has balanced classes (i.e., the total number of positive examples is roughly equal to the number of negative examples), than the accuracy will give us a good insight into the quality of our trained model. Accuracy is the proportion of correction classifications among all predictions.

Mathematically:

$$Accuracy = \frac{Correct\ classifications}{Total\ number\ of\ classifications} = \frac{TP + FP}{TP + FP + FN + TN}$$

Understanding recall and precision

While calculating accuracy, we do not differentiate between TPs and TNs. Evaluating a model through accuracy is straightforward, but when the data has imbalanced classes, it will not accurately quantify the quality of the trained model. When the data has imbalanced classes, two additional metrics will better quantify the quality of the trained model, recall and precision. We will use an example of a popular diamond mining process to explain the concepts of these two additional metrics.

For centuries, alluvial diamond mining has been one of the most popular ways of extracting diamonds from the sand of riverbeds all over the world. Erosion over thousands of years is known to wash diamonds from their primary deposits to riverbeds in different parts of the world. To mine diamonds, people have collected sand from the banks of rivers in a large open pit. After going though extensive washing, a large number of rocks are left in the pit.

A vast majority of these washed rocks are just ordinary stones. Identifying one of the rocks as a diamond is rare but a very important event. In our scenario, the owners of a mine are experimenting with the use of computer vision to identify which of the washed rocks are just ordinary rocks and which of the washed rocks are diamonds. They are using shape, color, and reflection to classify the washed rocks using computer vision.

In the context of this example:

TP	A washed rock correctly identified as a diamond
TN	A washed rock correctly identified as a stone
FP	A stone incorrectly identified as a diamond
FN	A diamond incorrectly identified as a stone

Let us explain recall and precision while keeping this diamond extraction process from the mine in mind:

- **Recall**: This calculates the *hit rate*, which is the proportion of identified events of interest in a gigantic repository of events. In other words, this metric rates our ability to find or "hit" most of the events of interest and leaves as little as possible unidentified. In the context of identifying diamonds in a pit of a large number of washed stones, recall is about quantifying the success of the treasure hunt. For a certain pit filled up with washed stones, recall will be the ratio of the number of diamonds identified to the total number of diamonds in the pit:

$$Recall = \frac{No.\ of\ correctly\ identified\ diamonds}{Total\ number\ of\ diamonds\ in\ the\ pit} \frac{TP}{TP + FN}$$

  Let us assume there were 10 diamonds in the pit, each valued at $1,000. Our machine learning algorithm was able to identify nine of them. So, the recall will be *9/10 = 0.90*.

  So, we are able to retrieve 90% of our treasure. In dollar cost, we were able to identify $9,000 of treasure out of a total value of $10,000.

- **Precision**: In precision, we only focus on the data points flagged by the trained model as positive and discard everything else. If we filter only the events flagged as positive by our trained model (i.e., TPs and FPs) and then calculate the accuracy, this is called precision.

  Now, let us investigate precision in the context of the diamond mining example. Let us consider a scenario where we want to use computer vision to identify diamonds among a pit of washed rocks and send them to customers.

The process is supposed to be automated. The worst-case scenario is the algorithm misclassifying a stone as a diamond, resulting in the end customer receiving it in the mail and getting charged for it. So, it should be obvious that for this process to be feasible, precision should be high.

For the diamond mining example:

$$Precision = \frac{No.\ of\ correctly\ identified\ diamonds}{Total\ number\ of\ rocks\ flagged\ as\ diamonds} = \frac{TP}{TP + FP}$$

Understanding the recall and precision trade-off

Making decisions with a classifier involves a two-step process. Firstly, the classifier generates a decision score ranging from 0 to 1. Then, it applies a decision threshold to determine the class for each data point. Data points scoring above the threshold are assigned a positive class, while those scoring below are assigned a negative class. The two steps can be explained as follows:

1. The classifier generates a decision score, which is a number from 0 to 1.
2. The classifier uses the value of a parameter, called a decision threshold, to allocate one of the two classes to the current datapoint. Any decision (score > decision) threshold is predicted to be positive, and any data point having a decision (score < decision) threshold is predicted to be negative.

Envision a scenario where you operate a diamond mine. Your task is to identify precious diamonds in a heap of ordinary rocks. To facilitate this process, you've developed a machine learning classifier. The classifier reviews each rock, assigns it a decision score ranging from 0 to 1, and finally, classifies the rock based on this score and a predefined decision threshold.

The decision score essentially represents the classifier's confidence that a given rock is indeed a diamond, with rocks closer to 1 highly likely to be diamonds. The decision threshold, on the other hand, is a predefined cut-off point that decides the ultimate classification of a rock. Rocks scoring above the threshold are classified as diamonds (the positive class), while those scoring below are discarded as ordinary rocks (the negative class).

Now, imagine all the rocks are arranged in ascending order of their decision scores, as shown in *Figure 7.4*. The rocks on the far left have the lowest scores and are least likely to be diamonds, while those on the far right have the highest scores, making them most likely to be diamonds. In an ideal scenario, every rock to the right of the decision threshold would be a diamond, and every rock to the left would be an ordinary stone.

Consider a situation, as depicted in *Figure 7.4*, where the decision threshold is at the center. On the right side of the decision boundary, we find three actual diamonds (TPs) and one ordinary rock wrongly flagged as a diamond (FPs). On the left, we have two ordinary rocks correctly identified (TNs) and two diamonds wrongly classified as ordinary rocks (FNs).

Thus, on the left-hand side of the decision threshold, you will find two correct classifications and two misclassifications. They are 2TNs and 2FNs.

Let us calculate the recall and precision for *Figure 7.4*:

$$Recall = \frac{No.\ of\ correctly\ identified\ diamonds}{Total\ number\ of\ diamonds\ in\ the\ pit} = \frac{TP}{TP + FN} = \frac{3}{6} = 0.5$$

$$precision = \frac{No.\ of\ correctly\ identifed\ diamonds}{Total\ number\ of\ rocks\ flagged\ as\ diamonds} = \frac{TP}{TP + FP} = \frac{3}{4} = 0.75$$

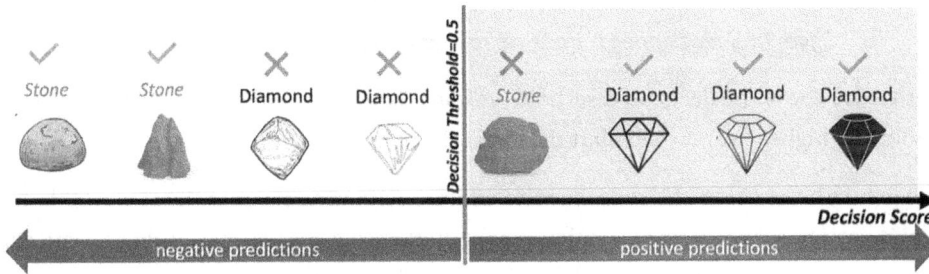

Figure 7.4: Precision/recall trade-off: rocks are ranked by their classifier score

Those that are above the decision threshold are considered diamonds.

Note that the higher the threshold, the higher the precision but the lower the recall.

Adjusting the decision threshold influences the trade-off between precision and recall. If we move the threshold to the right (as shown in *Figure 7.5*), we increase the criteria for a rock to be classified as a diamond, increasing precision but decreasing recall:

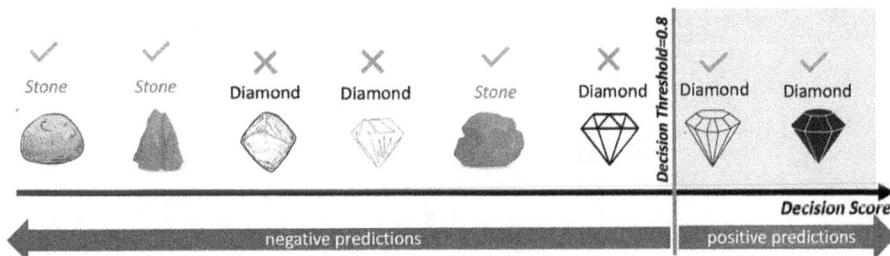

Figure 7.5: Precision/recall trade-off: rocks are ranked by their classifier score

Those that are above the decision threshold are considered diamonds. Note that the higher the threshold, the higher the precision but the lower the recall.

In *Figure 7.6*, we have decreased the decision threshold. In other words, we have decreased our criteria for a rock to be classified as a diamond. So, FNs (the treasure misses) will decrease, but FPs (the false signal) will increase as well. Thus, if we decrease the threshold (as shown in *Figure 7.6*), we loosen the criteria for diamond classification, increasing recall but decreasing precision:

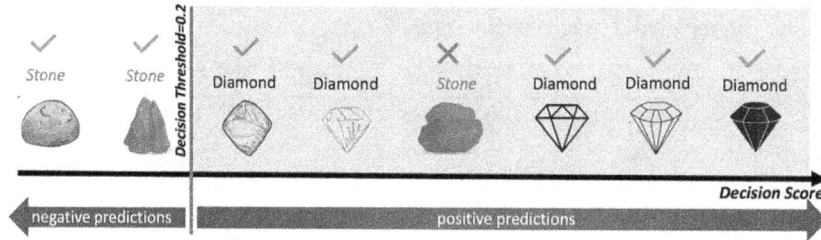

Figure 7.6: Precision/recall trade-off: rocks are ranked by their classifier score

Those that are above the decision threshold are considered diamonds. Note that the higher the threshold, the higher the precision but the lower the recall.

So, playing with the value of the decision boundary is about managing the trade-off between recall and precision. We increase the decision boundary to get better precision and can expect more recall, and we lower the decision boundary to get better recall and can expect less precision.

Let us draw a graph between precision and recall to better understand the trade-off:

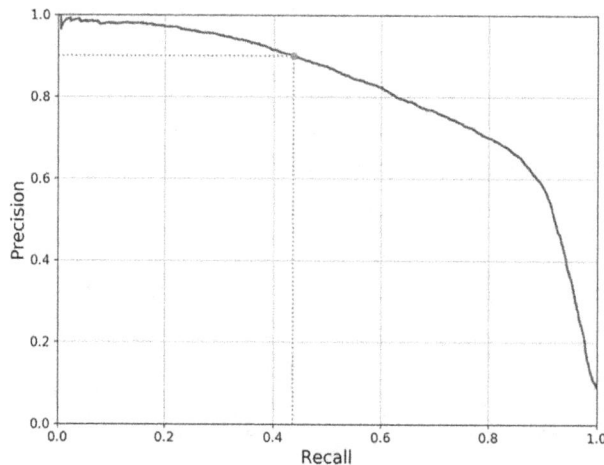

Figure 7.7: Precision vs. recall

What is the right choice for recall and precision?

Increasing recall is done by decreasing the criteria we use to identify a data point as positive. The precision is expected to decrease, but as shown in the figure above, it falls sharply at around 0.8. This is the point where we can choose the right value of recall and precision. In the above graph, if we choose 0.8 as the recall, the precision is 0.75. We can interpret it as being able to flag 80% of all the data points of interest. We flag these data points 75% accurately according to this level of precision. If there is no specific business requirement and it's for a generic use case, this may be a reasonable compromise.

Another way to show the inherent trade-off between precision and recall is by using the **Receiving Operating Curve (ROC)**. To do that, let us define two terms: **True Positive Rate (TPR)** and **False Positive Rate (FPR)**.

Let us look into the ROC curve. To calculate the TPR and FPR, we need to look at the diamonds in the pit:

$$TPR = \frac{Truly\ identified\ diamonds}{All\ diamonds\ in\ the\ pit} = \frac{TP}{TP + FN}$$

$$TNR = \frac{Truly\ identified\ stones}{All\ stones\ in\ the\ pit} = \frac{TN}{TN + FP}$$

$$FPR = \frac{Falsely\ indentified\ diamonds}{All\ stones\ in\ the\ pit} = \frac{FP}{TN + FP}$$

Note that:

- TPR is equal to the recall or hit rate.
- TNR can be thought of as the recall or hit rate of the negative event. It determines our success in correctly identifying the negative event. It is also called **specificity**.
- FPR = 1 – TNR = 1 - Specificity.

It should be obvious that TPR and FPR for these figures can be calculated as follows:

Figure number	TPR	FPR
7.4	3/5=0.6	1/3=0.33
7.5	2/5=0.4	0/3 = 0
7.6	5/5 = 1	1/3 = 0.33

Note that TPR or recall will be increased by lowering our decision threshold. In an effort to get as many diamonds as possible from the mine, we will lower our criterion for a washed stone being classified as a diamond. The result is that more stones will be incorrectly classified as diamonds, increasing FPR.

Note that a good-quality classification algorithm should be able to provide the decision score for each of the rocks in the pit, which roughly matches the likelihood of a rock being a diamond. The output of such an algorithm is shown in *Figure 7.8*. Diamonds are supposed to be on the right side and stones are supposed to be on the left side. In the figure, as we have decreased the decision threshold from 0.8 to 0.2, we expect to have a much higher increase in TRP and then FPR. In fact, the steep increase in TRP with a slight increase in FPR is one of the best indications of the quality of a binary classifier, as the classification algorithm was able to generate decision scores that directly relate with the likelihood of a rock being a diamond. If the diamonds and stones are randomly located on the decision score axis, it is equally likely that lowering the decision threshold will flag stones or diamonds. This would be the worst possible binary classifier, also called a randomizer:

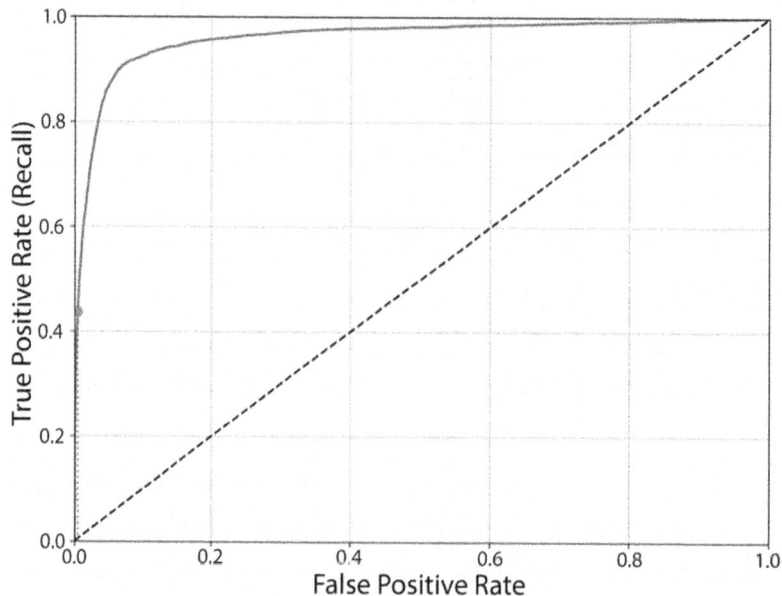

Figure 7.8: ROC curve

Understanding overfitting

If a machine learning model performs great in a development environment but degrades noticeably in a production environment, we say that the model is overfitted. This means the trained model too closely follows the training dataset. It is an indication there are too many details in the rules created by the model. The trade-off between model variance and bias best captures the idea.

When developing a machine learning model, we often make certain simplifying assumptions about the real-world phenomena that the model is supposed to capture. These assumptions are essential to make the modeling process manageable and less complex. However, the simplicity of these assumptions introduces a certain level of 'bias' in to our model.

Let's break this down further. Bias is a term that quantifies how much, on average, our predictions deviate from true values. In simple terms, if we have high bias, it means our model's predictions are far off from the actual values, which leads to a high error rate on our training data.

For instance, consider linear regression models. They assume a linear relationship between input features and output variables. However, this may not always be the case in real-world scenarios where relationships can be non-linear or more complex. This linear assumption, while simplifying our model, can lead to a high bias, as it may not fully capture the actual relationships between variables.

Now, let's also talk about 'variance.' Variance, in the context of machine learning, refers to the amount by which our model's predictions would change if we used a different training dataset. A model with high variance pays a lot of attention to training data and tends to learn from the noise and the details. As a result, it performs very well on training data but not so well on unseen or test data. This difference in performance is often referred to as overfitting.

We can visualize bias and variance using a bullseye diagram, as shown in *Figure 7.9*. Note that the center of the target is a model that perfectly predicts the correct values. Shots that are far away from the bullseye indicate high bias, while shots that are dispersed widely indicate high variance. In a perfect scenario, we would like a low bias and low variance, where all shots hit right in the bullseye. However, in real-world scenarios, there is a trade-off. Lowering bias increases variance, and lowering variance increases bias.

This is known as the bias-variance trade-off and is a fundamental aspect of machine learning model design:

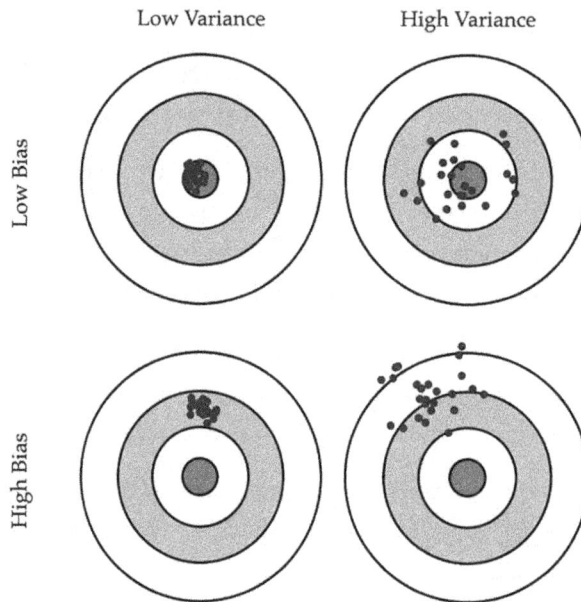

Figure 7.9: Graphical illustration of bias and variance

Balancing the right amount of generalization in a machine learning model is a delicate process. This balance, or sometimes imbalance, is described by the bias-variance trade-off. Generalization in machine learning refers to the model's ability to adapt properly to new, unseen data, drawn from the same distribution as the one used for training. In other words, a well-generalized model can effectively apply learned rules from training data to new, unseen data. A more generalized model is achieved using simpler assumptions. These simpler assumptions result in more broad rules, which in turn make the model less sensitive to fluctuations in the training data. This means that the model will have low variance, as it doesn't change much with different training sets.

However, there is a downside to this. Simpler assumptions mean the model might not fully capture all the complex relationships within the data. This results in a model that is consistently 'off-target' from the true output, leading to a higher bias.

So, in this sense, more generalization equates to lower variance but higher bias. This is the essence of the bias-variance trade-off: a model with too much generalization (high bias) might oversimplify the problem and miss important patterns, while a model with too little generalization (high variance) might overfit to the training data, capturing noise along with the signal.

Striking a balance between these two extremes is one of the central challenges in machine learning, and the ability to manage this trade-off can often make the difference between a good model and a great one. This trade-off between bias and variance is determined by the choice of algorithm, the characteristics of the data, and various hyperparameters. It is important to achieve the right compromise between bias and variance, based on the requirements of the specific problem you try to solve.

Let us now look into how we can specify different phases of a classifier.

Specifying the phases of classifiers

Once the labeled data is prepared, the development of the classifiers involves training, evaluation, and deployment. These three phases of implementing a classifier are shown in the **Cross-Industry Standard Process for Data Mining (CRISP-DM)** life cycle in the following diagram (the CRISP-DM life cycle was explained in more detail in *Chapter 5, Graph Algorithms*):

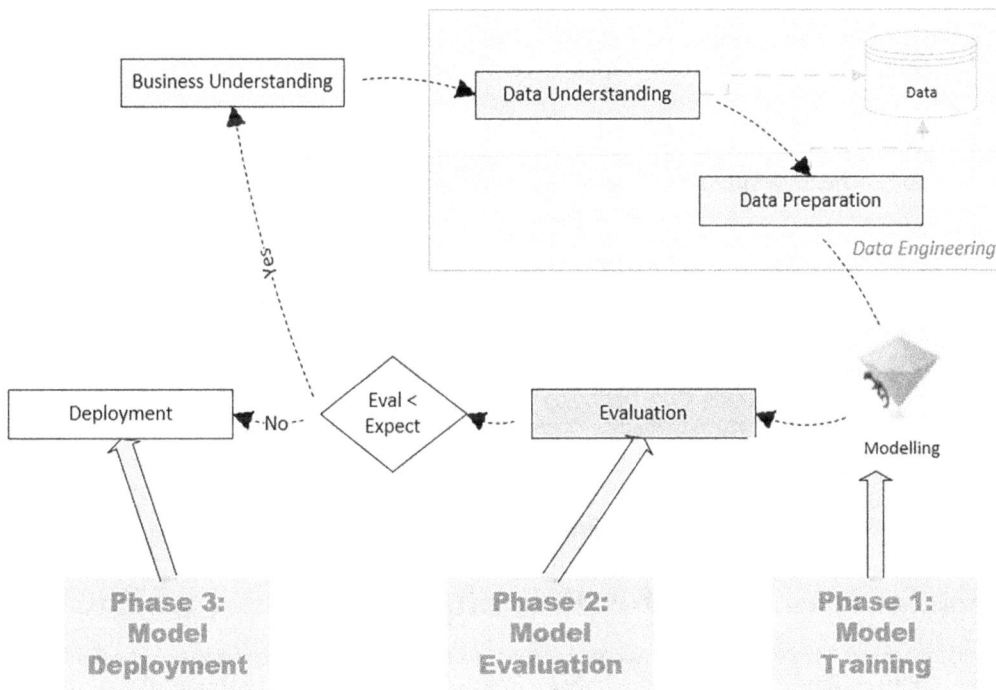

Figure 7.10: CRISP DM life cycle

When implementing a classifier model, there are several crucial phases to consider, starting with a thorough understanding of the business problem at hand. This involves identifying the data needed to solve this problem and understanding the real-world context of the data. After gathering the relevant labeled data, the next step is to split this dataset into two sections: a training set and a testing set. The training set, typically larger, is used to train the model to understand patterns and relationships within the data. The testing set, on the other hand, is used to evaluate the model's performance on unseen data.

To ensure both sets are representative of the overall data distribution, we will use a random sampling technique. This way, we can reasonably expect that patterns in the entire dataset will be reflected in both the training and testing partitions.

Note that, as shown in *Figure 7.10*, there is first a training phase, where training data is used to train a model. Once the training phase is over, the trained model is evaluated using the testing data. Different performance matrices are used to quantify the performance of the trained model. Once the model is evaluated, we have the model deployment phase, where the trained model is deployed and used for inference to solve real-world problems by labeling unlabeled data.

Now, let's look at some classification algorithms.

We will look at the following classification algorithms in the subsequent sections:

- The decision tree algorithm
- The XGBoost algorithm
- The Random Forest algorithm
- The logistic regression algorithm
- The **SVM** algorithm
- The Naive Bayes algorithm

Let's start with the decision tree algorithm.

Decision tree classification algorithm

A decision tree is based on a recursive partitioning approach (divide and conquer), which generates a set of rules that can be used to predict a label. It starts with a root node and splits it into multiple branches. Internal nodes represent a test on a certain attribute, and the result of the test is represented by a branch to the next level. The decision tree ends in leaf nodes, which contain the decisions. The process stops when partitioning no longer improves the outcome.

Let us now look into the details of the decision tree algorithm.

Understanding the decision tree classification algorithm

The distinguishing feature of decision tree classification is the generation of a human-interpretable hierarchy of rules that is used to predict the label at runtime. This model's transparency is a major advantage, as it allows us to understand the reasoning behind each prediction. This hierarchical structure is formed through a recursive algorithm, following a series of steps.

First, let's illustrate this with a simplified example. Consider a decision tree model predicting whether a person will enjoy a specific movie. The topmost decision or 'rule' in the tree might be, 'Is the movie a comedy or not?' If the answer is yes, the tree branches to the next rule, like, 'Does the movie star the person's favorite actor?' If no, it branches to another rule. Each decision point creates further subdivisions, forming a tree-like structure of rules, until we reach a final prediction.

With this process, a decision tree guides us through a series of understandable, logical steps to arrive at a prediction. This clarity is what sets decision tree classifiers apart from other machine learning models.

The algorithm is recursive in nature. Creating this hierarchy of rules involves the following steps:

1. **Find the most important feature**: Out of all of the features, the algorithm identifies the feature that best differentiates between the data points in the training dataset with respect to the label. The calculation is based on metrics such as information gain or Gini impurity.

2. **Bifurcate**: Using the most identified important feature, the algorithm creates a criterion that is used to divide the training dataset into two branches:

   - Data points that pass the criterion
   - Data points that fail the criterion

3. **Check for leaf nodes**: If any resultant branch mostly contains labels of one class, the branch is made final, resulting in a leaf node.

4. **Check the stopping conditions and repeat**: If the provided stopping conditions are not met, then the algorithm will go back to *step 1* for the next iteration. Otherwise, the model is marked as trained, and each node of the resultant decision tree at the lowest level is labeled as a leaf node. The stopping condition can be as simple as defining the number of iterations, or a default stopping condition can be used, where the algorithm stops as soon it reaches a certain homogeneity level for each of the leaf nodes.

The decision tree algorithm can be explained by the following diagram:

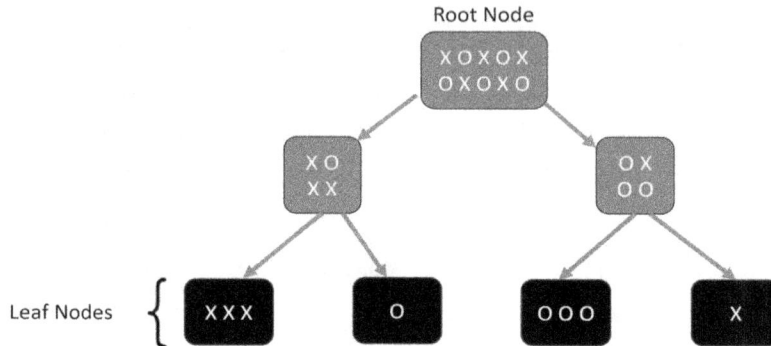

Figure 7.11: Decision Tree

In the preceding diagram, the root contains a bunch of circles and crosses. They just represent two different categories of a particular feature. The algorithm creates a criterion that tries to separate the circles from the crosses. At each level, the decision tree creates partitions of the data, which are expected to be more and more homogeneous from level 1 upward. A perfect classifier has leaf nodes that only contain circles or crosses. Training perfect classifiers is usually difficult due to the inherent unpredictability and noise in real-world datasets.

Note that the decision trees have key advantages that make them a preferred choice in many scenarios. The beauty of decision tree classifiers lies in their interpretability. Unlike many other models, they provide a clear and transparent set of 'if-then' rules, which makes the decision-making process understandable and auditable. This is particularly beneficial in fields like healthcare or finance, where comprehending the logic behind a prediction can be as important as the prediction itself.

Additionally, decision trees are less sensitive to the scale of the data and can handle a mix of categorical and numerical variables. This makes them a versatile tool in the face of diverse data types.

So, even though training a 'perfect' decision tree classifier might be difficult, the advantages they offer, including their simplicity, transparency, and flexibility, often outweigh this challenge.

We are going to use the decision tree classification algorithm for the classifiers challenge.

Now, let's use the decision tree classification algorithm for the common problem that we previously defined to predict whether a customer ends up purchasing a product:

1. First, let's instantiate the decision tree classification algorithm and train a model using the training portion of the data that we prepared for our classifiers:

```
classifier = sklearn.tree.DecisionTreeClassifier(criterion =
'entropy', random_state = 100, max_depth=2)
```

```
DecisionTreeClassifier(criterion = 'entropy', random_state = 100,
max_depth=2)
```

2. Now, let's use our trained model to predict the labels for the testing portion of our labeled data. Let's generate a confusion matrix that can summarize the performance of our trained model:

```
y_pred = classifier.predict(X_test)
cm = metrics.confusion_matrix(y_test, y_pred)
```

3. This gives the following output:

```
cm
```

```
array([[64,  4],
       [ 2, 30]])
```

4. Now, let's calculate the `accuracy`, `recall`, and `precision` values for the created classifier by using the decision tree classification algorithm:

```
accuracy= metrics.accuracy_score(y_test,y_pred)
recall = metrics.recall_score(y_test,y_pred)
precision = metrics.precision_score(y_test,y_pred)
print(accuracy,recall,precision)
```

5. Running the preceding code will produce the following output:

```
0.94 0.9375 0.8823529411764706
```

The performance measures help us compare different training modeling techniques with each other.

Let us now look into the strengths and weaknesses of decision tree classifiers.

The strengths and weaknesses of decision tree classifiers

In this section, let's look at the strengths and weaknesses of using the decision tree classification algorithm.

One of the most significant strengths of decision tree classifiers lies in their inherent transparency. The rules that govern their model formation are human-readable and interpretable, making them ideal for situations that demand a clear understanding of the decision-making process. This type of model, often referred to as a white-box model, is an essential component in scenarios where bias needs to be minimized and transparency maximized. This is particularly relevant in critical industries such as government and insurance, where accountability and traceability are paramount.

In addition, decision tree classifiers are well equipped to handle categorical variables. Their design is inherently suited to extracting information from discrete problem spaces, which makes them an excellent choice for datasets where most features fall into specific categories.

On the flip side, decision tree classifiers do exhibit certain limitations. Their biggest challenge is the tendency toward overfitting. When a decision tree delves too deep, it runs the risk of creating rules that capture an excessive amount of detail. This leads to models that overgeneralize from the training data and perform poorly on unseen data. Therefore, it's critical to implement strategies such as pruning to prevent overfitting when using decision tree classifiers.

Another limitation of decision tree classifiers is their struggle with non-linear relationships. Their rules are predominantly linear, and as such, they may not capture the nuances of relationships that aren't straight-line in nature. Therefore, while decision trees bring some impressive strengths to the table, their weaknesses warrant careful consideration when choosing the appropriate model for your data.

Use cases

Decision trees classifiers can be used in the following use cases to classify data:

- **Mortgage applications:** To train a binary classifier to determine whether an applicant is likely to default.

- **Customer segmentation:** To categorize customers into high-worth, medium-worth, and low-worth customers so that marketing strategies can be customized for each category.

- **Medical diagnosis:** To train a classifier that can categorize a benign or malignant growth.

- **Treatment-effectiveness analysis**: To train a classifier that can flag patients who have reacted positively to a particular treatment.

- **Using a decision tree for feature selection**: Another aspect worth discussing when examining decision tree classifiers is their feature selection capability. In the process of rule creation, decision trees tend to choose a subset of features from your dataset. This inherent trait of decision trees can be beneficial, especially when dealing with datasets that have a large number of features.

Why is this feature selection important, you might ask? In machine learning, dealing with numerous features can be a challenge. An excess of features can lead to models that are complex, harder to interpret, and may even result in worse performance due to the 'curse of dimensionality.'

By automatically selecting a subset of the most important features, decision trees can simplify a model and focus on the most relevant predictors.

Notably, the feature selection process within decision trees isn't confined to their own model development. The outcomes of this process can also serve as a form of preliminary feature selection for other machine learning models. This can provide an initial understanding of which features are most important and help streamline the development of other machine learning models.

Next, let us look into the ensemble methods.

Understanding the ensemble methods

In the domain of machine learning, an ensemble refers to a technique where multiple models, each with slight variations, are created and combined to form a composite or aggregate model. The variations could arise from using different model parameters, subsets of the data, or even different machine learning algorithms.

However, what does "slightly different" mean in this context? Here, each individual model in the ensemble is created to be unique, but not radically different. This can be achieved by tweaking the hyperparameters, training each model on a different subset of training data, or using diverse algorithms. The aim is to have each model capture different aspects or nuances of the data, which can help enhance the overall predictive power when they're combined.

So, how are these models combined? The ensemble technique involves a process of decision-making known as aggregation, where the predictions from individual models are consolidated. This could be a simple average, a majority vote, or a more complex approach, depending on the specific ensemble technique used.

As for when and why ensemble methods are needed, they can be particularly useful when a single model isn't sufficient to achieve a high level of accuracy. By combining multiple models, the ensemble can capture more complexity and often achieve better performance. This is because the ensemble can average out biases, reduce variance, and is less likely to overfit to the training data.

Finally, assessing the effectiveness of an ensemble is similar to evaluating a single model. Metrics such as accuracy, precision, recall, or F1-score can be used, depending on the nature of the problem. The key difference is that these metrics are applied to the aggregated predictions of the ensemble rather than the predictions of a single model.

Let's look at some ensemble algorithms, starting with XGBoost.

Implementing gradient boosting with the XGBoost algorithm

XGBoost, introduced in 2014, is an ensemble classification algorithm that's gained widespread popularity, primarily due to its foundation on the principles of gradient boosting. But what does gradient boosting entail? Essentially, it's a machine learning technique that involves building many models sequentially, with each new model attempting to correct the errors made by the previous ones. This progression continues until a significant reduction in error rate is achieved, or a pre-defined number of models has been added.

In the context of XGBoost, it employs a collection of interrelated decision trees and optimizes their predictions using gradient descent, a popular optimization algorithm that aims to find the minimum of a function – in this case, the residual error. In simpler terms, gradient descent iteratively adjusts the model to minimize the difference between its predictions and the actual values.

The design of XGBoost makes it well suited for distributed computing environments. This compatibility extends to Apache Spark – a platform for large-scale data processing, and cloud computing platforms like Google Cloud and **Amazon Web Services** (**AWS**). These platforms provide the computational resources needed to efficiently run XGBoost, especially on larger datasets.

Now, we will walk through the process of implementing gradient boosting using the XGBoost algorithm. Our journey includes preparing the data, training the model, generating predictions, and evaluating the model's performance. Firstly, data preparation is key to properly utilizing the XGBoost algorithm. Raw data often contains inconsistencies, missing values, or variable types that might not be suitable for the algorithm. Therefore, it's imperative to preprocess and clean the data, normalizing numerical fields and encoding categorical ones as needed. Once our data is appropriately formatted, we can proceed with model training. An instance of the XGBClassifier has been created, which we'll use to fit our model. Let us look at the steps:

1. This process is trained using the X_train and y_train data subsets, representing our features and labels respectively:

```
from xgboost import XGBClassifier
classifier = XGBClassifier()
classifier.fit(X_train, y_train)
```

```
XGBClassifier(base_score=None, booster=None, callbacks=None,
              colsample_bylevel=None, colsample_bynode=None,
              colsample_bytree=None, early_stopping_rounds=None,
              enable_categorical=False, eval_metric=None, feature_
types=None,
              gamma=None, gpu_id=None, grow_policy=None, importance_
type=None,
              interaction_constraints=None, learning_rate=None, max_
bin=None,
              max_cat_threshold=None, max_cat_to_onehot=None,
              max_delta_step=None, max_depth=None, max_leaves=None,
              min_child_weight=None, missing=nan, monotone_
constraints=None,
              n_estimators=100, n_jobs=None, num_parallel_tree=None,
              predictor=None, random_state=None, ...)
```

2. Then, we will generate predictions based on the newly trained model:

```
y_pred = classifier.predict(X_test)
cm = metrics.confusion_matrix(y_test, y_pred)
```

3. The produces the following output:

```
cm
```

```
array([[64, 4],
       [4, 28]])
```

4. Finally, we will quantify the performance of the model:

```
accuracy = metrics.accuracy_score(y_test,y_pred)
recall = metrics.recall_score(y_test,y_pred)
precision = metrics.precision_score(y_test,y_pred)
print(accuracy,recall,precision)
```

5. This gives us the following output:

```
0.92 0.875 0.875
```

Now, let's look at the Random Forest algorithm.

The Random Forest algorithm is an ensemble learning method that achieves its effectiveness by combining the outputs of numerous decision trees, thereby reducing both bias and variance. Here, let's dive deeper into how it's trained and how it generates predictions. In training, the Random Forest algorithm leverages a technique known as bagging, or bootstrap-aggregating. It generates N subsets from the training dataset, each created by randomly selecting some rows and columns from the input data. This selection process introduces randomness into the model, hence the name 'Random Forest.' Each subset of data is used to train an independent decision tree, resulting in a collection of trees denoted as C_1 through C_m. These trees can be of any type, but typically, they're binary trees where each node splits the data based on a single feature.

In terms of predictions, the Random Forest model employs a democratic voting system. When a new instance of data is fed into the model for prediction, each decision tree in the forest generates its own label. The final prediction is determined by majority voting, meaning the label that received the most votes from all the trees becomes the overall prediction.

It is shown in *Figure 7.12*:

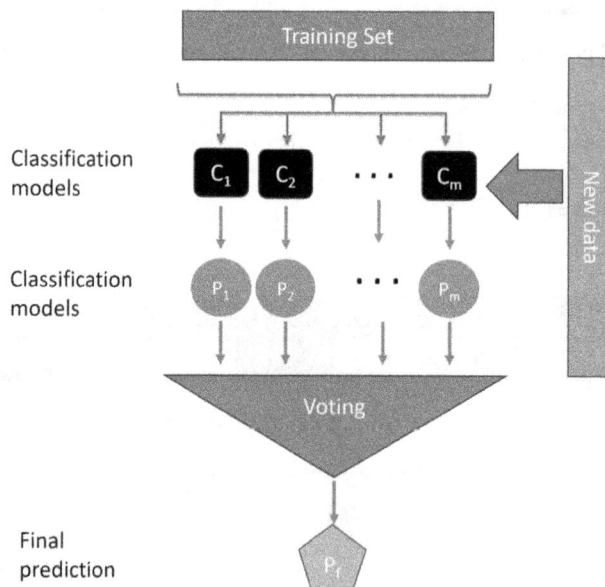

Figure 7.12: Random Forest

Note that in *Figure 7.12*, *m* trees are trained, which is represented by C_1 to C_m—that is, *Trees* = *{C₁,..,Cₘ}*.

Each of the trees generates a prediction, which is represented by a set:

Individual predictions = *P*= *{P₁,..., Pₘ}*

The final prediction is represented by `Pf`. It is determined by the majority of the individual predictions. The `mode` function can be used to find the majority decision (`mode` is the number that repeats most often and is in the majority). The individual prediction and the final prediction are linked, as follows:

```
Pf = mode (P)
```

This ensemble technique offers several benefits. Firstly, the randomness introduced into both data selection and decision tree construction reduces the risk of overfitting, increasing model robustness. Secondly, each tree in the forest operates independently, making Random Forest models highly parallelizable and, hence, suitable for large datasets. Lastly, Random Forest models are versatile, capable of handling both regression and classification tasks, and dealing effectively with missing or outlier data.

However, keep in mind that the effectiveness of a Random Forest model heavily depends on the number of trees it contains. Having too few might lead to a weak model, while too many could result in unnecessary computation. It's important to fine-tune this parameter based on the specific needs of your application.

Differentiating the Random Forest algorithm from ensemble boosting

Random Forest and ensemble boosting represent two distinct approaches to ensemble learning, a powerful method in machine learning that combines multiple models to create more robust and accurate predictions.

In the Random Forest algorithm, each decision tree operates independently, uninfluenced by the performance or structure of the other trees in the forest. Each tree is built from a different subset of the data and uses a different subset of features for its decisions, adding to the overall diversity of the ensemble. The final output is determined by aggregating the predictions from all the trees, typically through a majority vote.

Ensemble boosting, on the other hand, employs a sequential process where each model is aware of the mistakes made by its predecessors. Boosting techniques generate a sequence of models where each successive model aims to correct the errors of the previous one. This is achieved by assigning higher weights to the misclassified instances in the training set for the next model in the sequence. The final prediction is a weighted sum of the predictions made by all models in the ensemble, effectively giving more influence to more accurate models.

In essence, while Random Forest leverages the power of independence and diversity, ensemble boosting focuses on correcting mistakes and improving from past errors. Each approach has its own strengths and can be more effective, depending on the nature and structure of the data being modeled.

Using the Random Forest algorithm for the classifiers challenge

Let's instantiate the Random Forest algorithm and use it to train our model using the training data.

There are two key hyperparameters that we'll look at here:

- n_estimators
- max_depth

The n_estimators hyperparameter determines the number of individual decision trees that are constructed within the ensemble. Essentially, it dictates the size of the 'forest.' A larger number of trees generally leads to more robust predictions, as it increases the diversity of decision paths and a model's ability to generalize. However, it's important to note that adding more trees also increases the computational complexity, and beyond a certain point, the improvements in accuracy may become negligible.

On the other hand, the max_depth hyperparameter specifies the maximum depth that each individual tree can reach. In the context of a decision tree, 'depth' refers to the longest path from the root node (the starting point at the top of the tree) to a leaf node (the final decision outputs at the bottom). By limiting the maximum depth, we essentially control the complexity of the learned structures, balancing the trade-off between underfitting and overfitting. A tree that's too shallow may miss important decision rules, while a tree that's too deep may overfit to the training data, capturing noise and outliers.

Fine-tuning these two hyperparameters plays a vital role in optimizing the performance of your decision-tree-based models, striking the right balance between predictive power and computational efficiency.

To train a classifier using the Random Forest algorithm, we will do the following:

```
classifier = RandomForestClassifier(n_estimators = 10, max_depth = 4,
criterion = 'entropy', random_state = 0)
classifier.fit(X_train, y_train)
```

```
RandomForestClassifier(n_estimators = 10, max_depth = 4,criterion =
'entropy', random_state = 0)
```

Once the Random Forest model is trained, let's use it for predictions:

```
y_pred = classifier.predict(X_test)
cm = metrics.confusion_matrix(y_test, y_pred)
cm
```

Which gives the output as:

```
array ([[64, 4],
       [3, 29]])
```

Now, let's quantify how good our model is:

```
accuracy= metrics.accuracy_score(y_test,y_pred)
recall = metrics.recall_score(y_test,y_pred)
precision = metrics.precision_score(y_test,y_pred)
print(accuracy,recall,precision)
```

We will observe the following output:

```
0.93 0.90625 0.8787878787878788
```

Note that Random Forest is a popular and versatile machine learning method that can be used for both classification and regression tasks. It is renowned for its simplicity, robustness, and flexibility, making it applicable across a broad range of contexts.

Next, let's look into logistic regression.

Logistic regression

Logistic regression is a classification algorithm used for binary classification. It uses a logistic function to formulate the interaction between the input features and the label. It is one of the simplest classification techniques that is used to model a binary dependent variable.

Assumptions

Logistic regression assumes the following:

- The training dataset does not have a missing value.
- The label is a binary category variable.
- The label is ordinal—in other words, a categorical variable with ordered values.
- All features or input variables are independent of each other.

Establishing the relationship

For logistic regression, the predicted value is calculated as follows:

$$\acute{y} = \sigma\,(\omega X + j)$$

Let's suppose that:

$$z = \omega X + j$$

So now:

$$\sigma(z) = \frac{1}{1 + e^{-z}}$$

The preceding relationship can be graphically shown as follows:

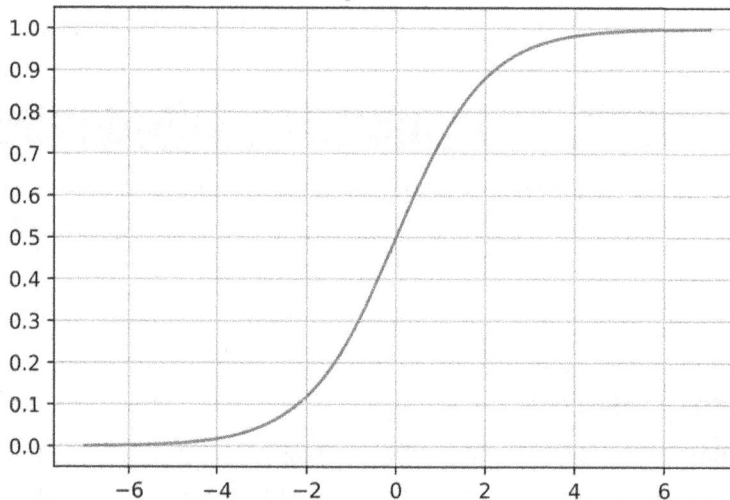

Figure 7.13: Plotting the sigmoid function

Note that if z is large, σ (z) will equal 1. If z is very small or a large negative number, σ (z) will equal 0. Also, when z is 0, then σ (z)=0.5. Sigmoid is a natural function to use to represent probabilities, as it is strictly bounded between 0 and 1. By 'natural,' we mean it is well suited or particularly effective due to its inherent properties. In this case, the sigmoid function always outputs a value between 0 and 1, which aligns with the probability range. This makes it a great tool for modeling probabilities in logistic regression. The objective of training a logistic regression model is to find the correct values for w and j.

> Logistic regression is named after the function that is used to formulate it, called the **logistic** or **sigmoid function**.

The loss and cost functions

The loss function defines how we want to quantify an error for a particular example in our training data. The cost function defines how we want to minimize an error in our entire training dataset. So, the loss function is used for one of the examples in the training dataset and the cost function is used for the overall cost that quantifies the overall deviation of the actual and predicted values. It is dependent on the choice of w and h.

The loss function used in logistic regression for a certain example i in the training set is as follows:

$$Loss\ (\acute{y}^{(i)}, y^{(i)}) = -\ (y^{(i)}\ log\ \acute{y}^{(i)} + (1-y^{(i)})\ log\ (1-\acute{y}^{(i)})$$

Note that when $y^{(i)} = 1$, $Loss(\acute{y}^{(i)}, y^{(i)}) = -\ log\acute{y}^{(i)}$. Minimizing the loss will result in a large value of $\acute{y}^{(i)}$. Being a sigmoid function, the maximum value will be 1.

If $y^{(i)} = 0$, $Loss\ (\acute{y}^{(i)}, y^{(i)}) = -\ log\ (1-\acute{y}^{(i)})$.

Minimizing the loss will result in $\acute{y}^{(i)}$ being as small as possible, which is 0.

The cost function of logistic regression is as follows:

$$Cost(\omega, b) = \frac{1}{b} \sum Loss(\acute{y}^{(i)}, y^{(i)})$$

Let us now look into the details of logistic regression.

When to use logistic regression

Logistic regression works great for binary classifiers. To clarify, binary classification refers to the process of predicting one of two possible outcomes. For example, if we try to predict whether an email is spam or not, this is a binary classification problem because there are only two possible results – 'spam' or 'not spam.'

However, there are certain limitations to logistic regression. Particularly, it may struggle when dealing with large datasets of subpar quality. For instance, consider a dataset filled with numerous missing values, outliers, or irrelevant features. The logistic regression model might find it difficult to produce accurate predictions under these circumstances.

Further, while logistic regression can handle linear relationships between features and the target variable effectively, it can fall short when dealing with complex, non-linear relationships. Picture a dataset where the relationship between the predictor variables and the target is not a straight line but a curve; a logistic regression model might struggle in such scenarios.

Despite these limitations, logistic regression can often serve as a solid starting point for classification tasks. It provides a benchmark performance that can be used to compare the effectiveness of more complex models. Even if it doesn't deliver the highest accuracy, it does offer interpretability and simplicity, which can be valuable in certain contexts.

Using the logistic regression algorithm for the classifiers challenge

In this section, we will see how we can use the logistic regression algorithm for the classifiers challenge:

1. First, let's instantiate a logistic regression model and train it using the training data:

    ```
    from sklearn.linear_model import LogisticRegression
    classifier = LogisticRegression(random_state = 0)
    classifier.fit(X_train, y_train)
    ```

2. Let's predict the values of the test data and create a confusion matrix:

    ```
    y_pred = classifier.predict(X_test)
    cm = metrics.confusion_matrix(y_test, y_pred)
    cm
    ```

3. We get the following output upon running the preceding code:

```
array ([[65, 3],
        [6, 26]])
```

4. Now, let's look at the performance metrics:

```
accuracy= metrics.accuracy_score(y_test,y_pred)
recall = metrics.recall_score(y_test,y_pred)
precision = metrics.precision_score(y_test,y_pred)
print(accuracy,recall,precision)
```

5. We get the following output upon running the preceding code:

```
0.91 0.8125 0.8996551724137931
```

Next, let's look at **SVMs**.

The SVM algorithm

The **SVM** classifier is a robust tool in the machine learning arsenal, which functions by identifying an optimal decision boundary, or hyperplane, that distinctly segregates two classes. To further clarify, think of this 'hyperplane' as a line (in two dimensions), a surface (in three dimensions), or a manifold (in higher dimensions) that best separates the different classes in the feature space.

The key characteristic that sets SVMs apart is their optimization goal – it aims to maximize the margin, which is the distance between the decision boundary and the closest data points from either class, known as the 'support vectors.' In simpler terms, the SVM algorithm doesn't just find a line to separate the classes; it also tries to find the line that's as far away as possible from the closest points of each class, thereby maximizing the separating gap.

Consider a basic two-dimensional example where we try to separate circles from crosses. Our goal with SVMs is not just to find a line that divides these two types of shapes but also to find the line that maintains the greatest distance from the circles and crosses nearest to it.

SVMs can be extremely useful when dealing with high-dimensional data, complex domains, or when the classes are not easily separable by a simple straight line. They can perform exceptionally well where logistic regression may falter, for instance, in situations with non-linearly separable data.

The margin is defined as the distance between the separating hyperplane (the decision boundary) and the training samples that are closest to this hyperplane, called the **support vectors**. So, let's start with a very basic example with only two dimensions, X_1 and X_2. We want a line to separate the circles from the crosses. This is shown in the following diagram:

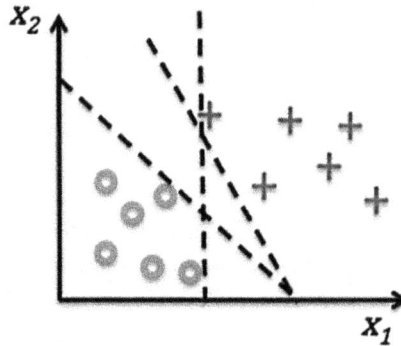

Figure 7.14: SVM algorithm

We have drawn two lines, and both perfectly separate the crosses from the circles. However, there has to be an optimal line, or decision boundary, that gives us the best chance of correctly classifying most of the additional examples. A reasonable choice may be a line that is evenly spaced between these two classes to give a little bit of a buffer for each class, as shown here:

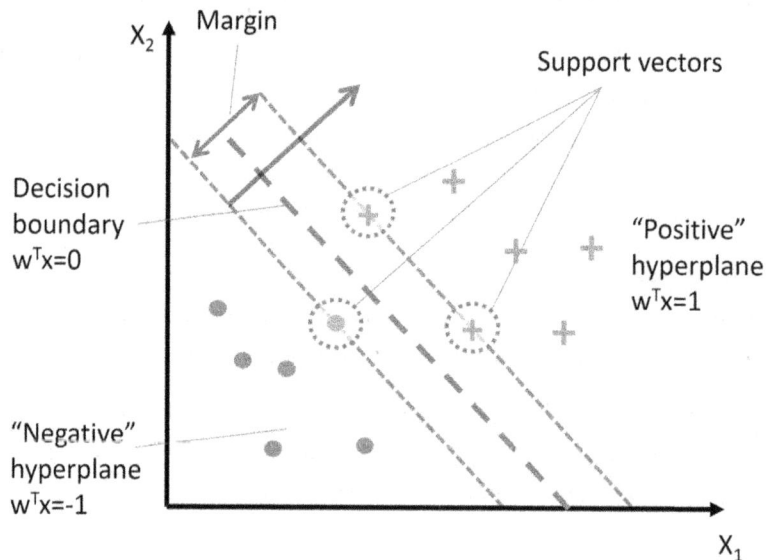

Figure 7.15: Concepts related to SVM

Moreover, unlike logistic regression, SVMs are better equipped to handle smaller, cleaner datasets, and they excel at capturing complex relationships without needing a large amount of data. However, the trade-off here is interpretability – while logistic regression provides easily understandable insights into the model's decision-making process, SVMs, being inherently more complex, are not as straightforward to interpret.

Now, let's see how we can use SVM to train a classifier for our challenge.

Using the SVM algorithm for the classifiers challenge

First, let's instantiate the SVM classifier and then use the training portion of the labeled data to train it. The kernel hyperparameter determines the type of transformation that is applied to the input data in order to make it linearly separable:

```python
from sklearn.svm import SVC
classifier = SVC(kernel = 'linear', random_state = 0)
classifier.fit(X_train, y_train)
```

1. Once trained, let's generate some predictions and look at the confusion matrix:

```python
y_pred = classifier.predict(X_test)
cm = metrics.confusion_matrix(y_test, y_pred)
cm
```

2. Observe the following output:

```
array ([[66, 2],
        [9, 23]])
```

3. Now, let's look at the various performance metrics:

```python
accuracy= metrics.accuracy_score(y_test,y_pred)
recall = metrics.recall_score(y_test,y_pred)
precision = metrics.precision_score(y_test,y_pred)
print(accuracy,recall,precision)
```

After running the preceding code, we get the following values as our output:

```
0.89 0.71875 0.92
```

Understanding the Naive Bayes algorithm

Based on probability theory, Naive Bayes is one of the simplest classification algorithms. If used properly, it can come up with accurate predictions. The Naive Bayes Algorithm is so-named for two reasons:

- It is based on a naive assumption that there is independence between the features and the input variable.

- It is based on Bayes' theorem. Note that Bayes' theorem is employed to calculate the probability of a particular class or outcome, given some observed features.

This algorithm tries to classify instances based on the probabilities of the preceding attributes/ instances, assuming complete attribute independence.

There are three types of events:

- **Independent** events do not affect the probability of another event occurring (for example, receiving an email offering you free entry to a tech event *and* a re-organization occurring in your company).

- **Dependent** events affect the probability of another event occurring; that is, they are linked in some way (for example, the probability of you getting to a conference on time could be affected by an airline staff strike or flights that may not run on time).

- **Mutually exclusive** events cannot occur simultaneously (for example, the probability of rolling a three and a six on a single dice roll is 0—these two outcomes are mutually exclusive).

Bayes' theorem

Bayes' theorem is used to calculate the conditional probability between two independent events, A and B. The probability of events A and B happening is represented by $P(A)$ and $P(B)$. The conditional probability is represented by $P(B|A)$, which is the conditional probability that event B will happen given that event A has occurred:

$$P(A|B) = \frac{P(B|A)P(A)}{P(B)}$$

When it comes to applying Naive Bayes, the algorithm is particularly effective in scenarios where the dimensionality of the inputs (number of features) is high. This makes it well suited for text classification tasks such as spam detection or sentiment analysis.

It can handle both continuous and discrete data, and it's computationally efficient, making it useful for real-time predictions. Naive Bayes is also a good choice when you have limited computational resources and need a quick and easy implementation, but it's worth noting that its "naive" assumption of feature independence can be a limitation in some cases.

Calculating probabilities

Naive Bayes is based on probability fundamentals. The probability of a single event occurring (the observational probability) is calculated by taking the number of times the event occurred and dividing it by the total number of processes that could have led to that event. For example, a call center receives over 100 support calls per day, which is 50 times over the course of a month. You want to know the probability that a call is responded to in under three minutes, based on the previous amount of time in which it was responded to. If the call center manages to match this time record on 27 occasions, then the observational probability of 100 calls being answered in under three minutes is as follows:

$$P(100 \text{ support calls in under 3 mins}) = (27/50) = 0.54 \ (54\%)$$

One hundred calls can be responded to in under three minutes in about half the time, based on the records of the 50 times it occurred in the past.

Now, let us look into the multiplication rules for AND events.

Multiplication rules for AND events

To calculate the probability of two or more events occurring simultaneously, consider whether events are independent or dependent. If they are independent, the simple multiplication rule is used:

$$P(\text{outcome 1 AND outcome 2}) = P(\text{outcome 1}) * P(\text{outcome 2})$$

For example, to calculate the probability of receiving an email with free entry to a tech event *and* re-organization occurring in your workplace, this simple multiplication rule would be used. The two events are independent, as the occurrence of one does not affect the chance of the other occurring.

If receiving the tech event email has a probability of 31% and the probability of staff re-organization is 82%, then the probability of both occurring is calculated as follows:

$$P(\text{email AND re-organization}) = P(\text{email}) * P(\text{re-organization}) = (0.31) * (0.82) = 0.2542 \ (25\%)$$

The general multiplication rule

If two or more events are dependent, the general multiplication rule is used. This formula is actually valid in both cases of independent and dependent events:

$$P(outcome\ 1\ AND\ outcome\ 2) = P(outcome\ 1) * P(outcome\ 2\ |\ outcome\ 1)$$

Note that *P(outcome 2 | outcome 1)* refers to the conditional probability of outcome 2 occurring given that outcome 1 has already occurred. The formula incorporates the dependence between the events. If the events are independent, then the conditional probability is irrelevant as one outcome does not influence the chance of the other occurring, and *P(outcome 2 | outcome 1)* is simply *P(outcome 2)*. Note that the formula in this case just becomes the simple multiplication rule.

Let's illustrate this with a simple example. Suppose you're drawing two cards from a deck, and you want to know the probability of drawing an ace first and then a king. The first event (drawing an ace) modifies the conditions for the second event (drawing a king) since we're not replacing the ace in the deck. According to the general multiplication rule, we can calculate this as *P(ace)* * *P(king | ace)*, where *P(king | ace)* is the probability of drawing a King given that we've already drawn an ace.

Addition rules for OR events

When calculating the probability of either one event or the other occurring (mutually exclusive), the following simple addition rule is used:

$$P(outcome\ 1\ OR\ outcome\ 2) = P(outcome\ 1) + P(outcome\ 2)$$

For example, what is the probability of rolling a 6 or a 3? To answer this question, first, note that both outcomes cannot occur simultaneously. The probability of rolling a 6 is (1 / 6) and the same can be said for rolling a 3:

$$P(6\ OR\ 3) = (1/6) + (1/6) = 0.33\ (33\%)$$

If the events are not mutually exclusive and can occur simultaneously, use the following general addition formula, which is always valid in both cases of mutual exclusiveness and non-mutual exclusiveness:

$$P(outcome\ 1\ OR\ outcome\ 2) = P(outcome\ 1) + P(outcome\ 2)\ P(outcome\ 1\ AND\ outcome\ 2)$$

Using the Naive Bayes algorithm for the classifiers challenge

Now, let's use the Naive Bayes algorithm to solve the classifiers challenge:

1. First, we will import the `GaussianNB()` function and use it to train the model:

```
# Fitting Decision Tree Classification to the Training set
from sklearn.naive_bayes import GaussianNB
classifier = GaussianNB()
classifier.fit(X_train, y_train)
```

```
GaussianNB()
```

2. Now, let's use the trained model to predict the results. We will use it to predict the labels for our test partition, which is `X_test`:

```
# Predicting the Test set results
y_pred = classifier.predict(X_test)
cm = metrics.confusion_matrix(y_test, y_pred)
```

3. Now, let's print the confusion matrix:

```
cm
```

```
array([[66, 2],
[6, 26]])
```

4. Now, let's print the performance matrices to quantify the quality of our trained model:

```
accuracy= metrics.accuracy_score(y_test,y_pred)
recall = metrics.recall_score(y_test,y_pred)
precision = metrics.precision_score(y_test,y_pred)
print(accuracy,recall,precision)
```

Which gives the output as:

```
0.92 0.8125 0.9285714285714286
```

For classification algorithms, the winner is...

Let's take a moment to compare the performance metrics of the various algorithms we've discussed. However, keep in mind that these metrics are highly dependent on the data we've used in these examples, and they can significantly vary for different datasets.

The performance of a model can be influenced by factors such as the nature of the data, the quality of the data, and how well the assumptions of the model align with the data.

Here's a summary of our observations:

Algorithm	Accuracy	Recall	Precision
Decision tree	0.94	0.93	0.88
XGBoost	0.93	0.90	0.87
Random Forest	0.93	0.90	0.87
Logistic regression	0.91	0.81	0.89
SVM	0.89	0.71	0.92
Naive Bayes	0.92	0.81	0.92

From the table above, the decision tree classifier exhibits the highest performance in terms of both accuracy and recall in this particular context. For precision, we see a tie between the SVM and Naive Bayes algorithms.

However, remember that these results are data-dependent. For instance, SVM might excel in scenarios where data is linearly separable or can be made so through kernel transformations. Naive Bayes, on the other hand, performs well when the features are independent. Decision trees and Random Forests might be preferred when we have complex non-linear relationships. Logistic regression is a solid choice for binary classification tasks and can serve as a good benchmark model. Lastly, XGBoost, being an ensemble technique, is powerful when dealing with a wide range of data types and often leads in terms of model performance across various tasks.

So, it's critical to understand your data and the requirements of your task before choosing a model. These results are merely a starting point, and deeper exploration and validation should be performed for each specific use case.

Understanding regression algorithms

A supervised machine learning model uses one of the regression algorithms if the label is a continuous variable. In this case, the machine learning model is called a regressor.

To provide a more concrete understanding, let's take a couple of examples. Suppose we want to predict the temperature for the next week based on historical data, or we aim to forecast sales for a retail store in the coming months.

Both temperatures and sales figures are continuous variables, which means they can take on any value within a specified range, as opposed to categorical variables, which have a fixed number of distinct categories. In such scenarios, we would use a regressor rather than a classifier.

In this section, we will present various algorithms that can be used to train a supervised machine learning regression model—or, put simply, a regressor. Before we go into the details of the algorithms, let's first create a challenge for these algorithms to test their performance, abilities, and effectiveness.

Presenting the regressors challenge

Similar to the approach that we used with the classification algorithms, we will first present a problem to be solved as a challenge for all regression algorithms. We will call this common problem the regressors challenge. Then, we will use three different regression algorithms to address the challenge. This approach of using a common challenge for different regression algorithms has two benefits:

- We can prepare the data once and use the prepared data on all three regression algorithms.
- We can compare the performance of three regression algorithms in a meaningful way, as we will use them to solve the same problem.

Let's look at the problem statement of the challenge.

The problem statement of the regressors challenge

Predicting the mileage of different vehicles is important these days. An efficient vehicle is good for the environment and is also cost-effective. The mileage can be estimated from the power of the engine and the characteristics of the vehicle. Let's create a challenge for regressors to train a model that can predict the **Miles per Gallon** (**MPG**) of a vehicle based on its characteristics.

Let's look at the historical dataset that we will use to train the regressors.

Exploring the historical dataset

The following are the features of the historical dataset data that we have:

Name	Type	Description
NAME	Category	Identifies a particular vehicle
CYLINDERS	Continuous	The number of cylinders (between four and eight)
DISPLACEMENT	Continuous	The displacement of the engine in cubic inches

| HORSEPOWER | Continuous | The horsepower of the engine |
| ACCELERATION | Continuous | The time it takes to accelerate from 0 to 60 mph (in seconds) |

The label for this problem is a continuous variable, MPG, that specifies the MPG for each of the vehicles.

Let's first design the data processing pipeline for this problem.

Feature engineering using a data processing pipeline

Let's see how we can design a reusable processing pipeline to address the regressors challenge. As mentioned, we will prepare the data once and then use it in all the regression algorithms. Let's follow these steps:

1. We will start by importing the dataset, as follows:

   ```
   dataset = pd.read_csv('https://storage.googleapis.com/neurals/data/
   data/auto.csv')
   ```

2. Let's now preview the dataset:

   ```
   dataset.head(5)
   ```

3. This is how the dataset will look:

	NAME	CYLINDERS	DISPLACEMENT	HORSEPOWER	WEIGHT	ACCELERATION	MPG
0	chevrolet chevelle malibu	8	307.0	130	3504	12.0	18.0
1	buick skylark 320	8	350.0	165	3693	11.5	15.0
2	plymouth satellite	8	318.0	150	3436	11.0	18.0
3	amc rebel sst	8	304.0	150	3433	12.0	16.0
4	ford torino	8	302.0	140	3449	10.5	17.0

Figure 7.16: Please add a caption here

4. Now, let's proceed on to feature selection. Let's drop the NAME column, as it is only an identifier that is needed for cars. Columns that are used to identify the rows in our dataset are not relevant to training the model. Let's drop this column.

5. Let's convert all of the input variables and impute all the null values:

   ```
   dataset=dataset.drop(columns=['NAME'])
   dataset.head(5)
   ```

```
dataset= dataset.apply(pd.to_numeric, errors='coerce')
dataset.fillna(0, inplace=True)
```

Imputation improves the quality of the data and prepares it to be used to train the model. Now, let's see the final step.

6. Let's divide the data into testing and training partitions:

```
y=dataset['MPG']
X=dataset.drop(columns=['MPG'])
# Splitting the dataset into the Training set and Test set
from sklearn.model_selection import train_test_split
from sklearn.cross_validation import train_test_split
X_train, X_test, y_train, y_test = train_test_split(X, y, test_size
= 0.25, random_state = 0)
```

This has created the following four data structures:

- X_train: A data structure containing the features of the training data
- X_test: A data structure containing the features of the training test
- y_train: A vector containing the values of the label in the training dataset
- y_test: A vector containing the values of the label in the testing dataset

Now, let's use the prepared data on three different regressors so that we can compare their performance.

Linear regression

Among the assortment of supervised machine learning algorithms, linear regression is often seen as the most straightforward to grasp. Initially, we will explore simple linear regression and then gradually broaden our discussion to encompass multiple linear regression.

It's important to note, however, that while linear regression is accessible and easy to implement, it is not always the 'best' choice in every circumstance. Each machine learning algorithm, including the ones we've discussed so far, comes with its unique strengths and limitations, and their effectiveness varies depending on the type and structure of the data at hand.

For instance, decision trees and Random Forests are excellent at handling categorical data and capturing complex non-linear relationships. SVMs can work well with high-dimensional data and are robust to outliers, while logistic regression is particularly effective for binary classification problems.

On the other hand, linear regression models are well suited to predicting continuous outcomes and can provide interpretability, which can be valuable in understanding the impact of individual features.

Simple linear regression

At its most basic level, linear regression establishes a relationship between two variables, usually represented as a single independent variable and a single dependent variable. Linear regression is a technique that enables us to study how changes in the dependent variable (plotted on the y-axis) are influenced by changes in the independent variable (plotted on the x-axis). It can be represented as follows:

$$\hat{y} = (X)\omega + \alpha$$

This formula can be explained as follows:

- y is the dependent variable.
- X is the independent variable.
- ω is the slope that indicates how much the line rises for each increase in X.
- α is the intercept that indicates the value of y when $X = 0$.

Linear regression operates under these assumptions:

- **Linearity**: The relationship between independent and dependent variables is linear.
- **Independence**: The observations are independent of each other.
- **No multicollinearity**: The independent variables are not too highly correlated with each other.

Some examples of relationships between a single continuous dependent variable and a single continuous independent variable are as follows:

- A person's weight and their calorie intake
- The price of a house and its area in square feet in a particular neighborhood
- The humidity in the air and the likelihood of rain

For linear regression, both the input (independent) variable and the target (dependent) variable must be numeric. The best relationship is found by minimizing the sum of the squares of the vertical distances of each point, from a line drawn through all the points. It is assumed that the relationship is linear between the predictor variable and the label. For example, the more money invested in research and development, the higher the sales.

Let's look at a specific example. Let's try to formulate the relationship between marketing expenditures and sales for a particular product. They are found to be directly relational to each other. The marketing expenditures and sales are drawn on a two-dimensional graph and are shown as blue diamonds. The relationship can best be approximated by drawing a straight line, as shown in the following graph:

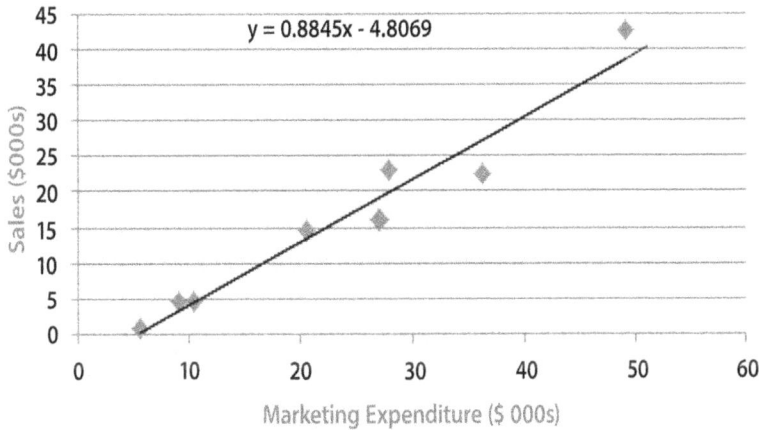

Figure 7.17: Linear regression

Once the linear line is drawn, we can see the mathematical relationship between marketing expenditure and sales.

Evaluating the regressors

The linear line that we drew is an approximation of the relationship between the dependent and independent variables. Even the best line will have some deviation from the actual values, as shown here:

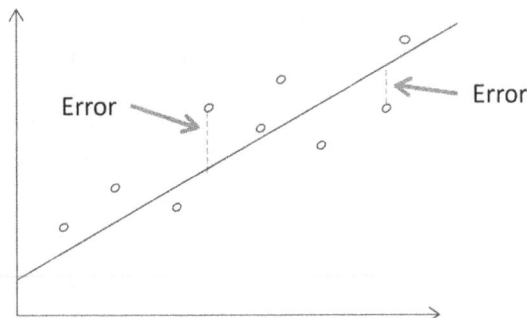

Figure 7.18: Evaluating regressors

A typical way of quantifying the performance of linear regression models is by using **Root Mean Square Error (RMSE)**. This calculates the standard deviation of the errors made by the trained model mathematically. For example, in the training dataset, the `loss` function is calculated as follows:

$$Loss\ (\acute{y}^{(i)}, y^{(i)}) = 1/2(\acute{y}^{(i)} - y^{(i)})2$$

This leads to the following cost function, which minimizes the loss of all of the examples in the training set:

$$\sqrt{\frac{1}{n}\sum_{i=1}^{n}(\acute{y}^{(i)} - y^{i})^2}$$

Let's try to interpret RMSE. If RMSE is $50 for our example model that predicts the price of a product, this means that around 68.2% of the predictions will fall within $50 of the true value (that is, α). It also means that 95% of the predictions will fall within $100 (that is, 2α) of the actual value. Finally, 99.7% of the predictions will fall within $150 of the actual value.

Let us look into multiple regression.

Multiple regression

The fact is that most real-world analyses have more than one independent variable. Multiple regression is an extension of simple linear regression. The key difference is that there are additional beta coefficients for the additional predictor variables. When training a model, the goal is to find the beta coefficients that minimize the errors of the linear equation. Let's try to mathematically formulate the relationship between the dependent variable and the set of independent variables (features).

For instance, in the housing market, the price of a house (the dependent variable) could depend on numerous factors such as its size, location, age, and more (the independent variables).

Similar to a simple linear equation, the dependent variable, y, is quantified as the sum of an intercept term, plus the product of the β coefficients multiplied by the x value for each of the i features:

$$y = \alpha + \beta_1 x_1 + \beta_2 x_2 + \cdots + \beta_i x_i + \varepsilon$$

The error is represented by ε and indicates that the predictions are not perfect.

The β coefficients allow each feature to have a separate estimated effect on the value of y because y changes by an amount of β_i for each unit increase in x_i. Moreover, the intercept (α) indicates the expected value of y when the independent variables are all 0.

Note that all the variables in the preceding equation can be represented by a bunch of vectors. The target and predictor variables are now vectors with a row, and the regression coefficients, β, and errors, ε, are also vectors.

Next, let us look into how we can use linear regression for the regressors challenge.

Using the linear regression algorithm for the regressors challenge

Now, let's train the model using the training portion of the dataset. Note that we will use the same data and data engineering logic that we discussed earlier:

1. Let's start by importing the linear regression package:

    ```
    from sklearn.linear_model import LinearRegression
    ```

2. Then, let's instantiate the linear regression model and train it using the training dataset:

    ```
    regressor = LinearRegression()
    regressor.fit(X_train, y_train)
    ```

    ```
    LinearRegression()
    ```

3. Now, let's predict the results using the test portion of the dataset:

    ```
    y_pred = regressor.predict(X_test)
    from sklearn.metrics import mean_squared_error
    sqrt(mean_squared_error(y_test, y_pred))
    ```

4. The output generated by running the preceding code will generate the following:

    ```
    19.02827669300187
    ```

As discussed in the preceding section, RMSE is the standard deviation of the error. It indicates that 68.2% of predictions will fall within 4.36 of the value of the label.

Let us look into when we can use linear regression.

When is linear regression used?

Linear regression is used to solve many real-world problems, including the following:

- Sales forecasting

- Predicting optimum product prices

- Quantifying the causal relationship between an event and the response, such as in clinical drug trials, engineering safety tests, or marketing research

- Identifying patterns that can be used to forecast future behavior, given known criteria— for example, predicting insurance claims, natural disaster damage, election results, and crime rates

Let us next look into the weaknesses of linear regression.

The weaknesses of linear regression

The weaknesses of linear regression are as follows:

- It only works with numerical features.

- Categorical data needs to be pre-processed.

- It does not cope well with missing data.

- It makes assumptions about the data.

The regression tree algorithm

Similar to classification trees used for categorical outcomes, regression trees are another subset of decision trees, but they are employed when the target, or label, is a continuous variable instead of categorical. This distinction impacts how the tree algorithm processes and learns from the data.

In the case of classification trees, the algorithm tries to identify the categories that the data points belong to. However, with regression trees, the goal is to predict a specific, continuous value. This might be something like the price of a house, a company's future stock price, or the likely temperature tomorrow.

These variations between classification and regression trees also lead to differences in the algorithms used. In a classification tree, we typically use metrics such as Gini impurity or entropy to find the best split. In contrast, regression trees utilize measures like **Mean Squared Error** (MSE) to minimize the distance between the actual and predicted continuous values.

Using the regression tree algorithm for the regressors challenge

In this section, we will see how a regression tree algorithm can be used for the regressors challenge:

1. First, we train the model using a regression tree algorithm:

    ```
    from sklearn.tree import DecisionTreeRegressor
    regressor = DecisionTreeRegressor(max_depth=3)
    regressor.fit(X_train, y_train)
    ```

    ```
    DecisionTreeRegressor(max_depth=3)
    ```

2. Once the regression tree model is trained, we use the trained model to predict the values:

    ```
    y_pred = regressor.predict(X_test)
    ```

3. Then, we calculate RMSE to quantify the performance of the model:

    ```
    from sklearn.metrics import mean_squared_error
    from math import sqrt
    sqrt(mean_squared_error(y_test, y_pred))
    ```

We get the following output:

```
4.464255966462035
```

The gradient boost regression algorithm

Now, let's shift our focus to the gradient boosting regression algorithm, which uses an ensemble of decision trees to formulate underlying patterns within a dataset.

At its core, gradient boosting regression operates by creating a 'team' of decision trees, where each member progressively learns from the mistakes of its predecessors. In essence, each subsequent decision tree in the sequence attempts to correct the prediction errors made by the tree before it, leading to an 'ensemble' that makes a final prediction based on the collective wisdom of all the individual trees. What makes this algorithm truly unique is its capability to handle a broad spectrum of data and its resistance to overfitting. This versatility allows it to perform admirably across diverse datasets and problem scenarios.

Using the gradient boost regression algorithm for the regressors challenge

In this section, we will see how we can use the gradient boost regression algorithm for the regressors challenge, predicting a car's MPG rating, which is a continuous variable and, therefore, a classic regression problem. Remember that our independent variables include features like 'CYLINDERS,' 'DISPLACEMENT,' 'HORSEPOWER,' 'WEIGHT,' and 'ACCELERATION.'

Looking closely, MPG is not as straightforward as it may seem, considering the multifaceted relationships between the influencing factors. For example, while cars with higher displacement typically consume more fuel, leading to a lower MPG, this relationship could be offset by factors like weight and horsepower. It's these nuanced interactions that may elude simpler models like linear regression or a single decision tree.

This is where the gradient boosting regression algorithm may be useful. By building an ensemble of decision trees, each learning from the errors of its predecessor, the model will aim to discern these complex patterns in the data. Each tree contributes its understanding of the data, refining the predictions to be more accurate and reliable.

For example, one decision tree might learn that cars with larger 'DISPLACEMENT' values tend to have lower MPG. The next tree might then pick up on the subtlety that lighter cars ('WEIGHT') with the same 'DISPLACEMENT' can sometimes achieve higher MPG. Through this iterative learning process, the model unveils the intricate layers of relationships between the variables:

1. The first step in our Python script is to import the necessary library:

    ```python
    from sklearn import ensemble
    ```

2. Here, we import the ensemble module from the sklearn library:

    ```python
    params = {'n_estimators': 500, 'max_depth': 4,
              'min_samples_split': 2, 'learning_rate': 0.01,
              'loss': 'squared_error'}
    regressor = ensemble.GradientBoostingRegressor(**params)
    regressor.fit(X_train, y_train)
    ```

    ```
    GradientBoostingRegressor(learning_rate=0.01, max_depth=4, n_
    estimators=500)
    ```

    ```python
    y_pred = regressor.predict(X_test)
    ```

3. Finally, we calculate RMSE to quantify the performance of the model:

```
from sklearn.metrics import mean_squared_error
from math import sqrt
sqrt(mean_squared_error(y_test, y_pred))
```

4. Running this will give us the output value, as follows:

```
4.039759805419003
```

For regression algorithms, the winner is...

Let's look at the performance of the three regression algorithms that we used on the same data and exactly the same use case:

Algorithm	RMSE
Linear regression	4.36214129677179
Regression tree	5.2771702288377
Gradient boost regression	4.034836373089085

Looking at the performance of all the regression algorithms, it is obvious that the performance of gradient boost regression is the best, as it has the lowest RMSE. This is followed by linear regression. The regression tree algorithm performed the worst for this problem.

Practical example — how to predict the weather

Now, we'll transition from theory to application, employing the concepts we've discussed in this chapter to predict tomorrow's rainfall, based on a year's worth of weather data from a specific city. This real-world scenario aims to reinforce the principles of supervised learning.

There are numerous algorithms capable of this task, but selecting the most suitable one hinges on the specific characteristics of our problem and data. Each algorithm has unique advantages and excels in specific contexts. For example, while linear regression can be ideal when there's a discernible numerical correlation, decision trees might be more effective when dealing with categorical variables or non-linear relationships.

For this prediction challenge, we have chosen logistic regression. This choice is driven by the binary nature of our prediction target (i.e., will it rain tomorrow or not?), a situation where Logistic Regression often excels. This algorithm provides a probability score between 0 and 1, allowing us to make clear yes-or-no predictions, ideal for our rainfall forecast scenario.

Remember, this practical example differs from previous ones. It's crafted to help you grasp how we select and apply a particular algorithm to specific real-world problems, offering a deeper understanding of the thought process behind algorithm selection.

The data available to train this model is in the CSV file called `weather.csv`:

1. Let's import the data as a pandas DataFrame:

```
import numpy as np
import pandas as pd
df = pd.read_csv("weather.csv")
```

2. Let's look at the columns of the DataFrame:

```
df.columns
```

```
Index(['Date', 'MinTemp', 'MaxTemp', 'Rainfall',
       'Evaporation', 'Sunshine', 'WindGustDir',
       'WindGustSpeed', 'WindDir9am', 'WindDir3pm',
       'WindSpeed9am', 'WindSpeed3pm', 'Humidity9am',
       'Humidity3pm', 'Pressure9am', 'Pressure3pm',
       'Cloud9am', 'Cloud3pm', 'Temp9am', 'Temp3pm',
       'RainToday', 'RISK_MM', 'RainTomorrow'],
      dtype='object')
```

3. Now, let's look at the header of the first 13 columns of the `weather.csv` data that show the typical weather of a city:

```
df.iloc[:,0:12].head()
```

	Date	MinTemp	MaxTemp	Rainfall	Evaporation	Sunshine	WindGustDir	WindGustSpeed	WindDir9am	WindDir3pm	WindSpeed9am	WindSpeed3pm
0	2007-11-01	8.0	24.3	0.0	3.4	6.3	7	30.0	12	7	6.0	20
1	2007-11-02	14.0	26.9	3.6	4.4	9.7	1	39.0	0	13	4.0	17
2	2007-11-03	13.7	23.4	3.6	5.8	3.3	7	85.0	3	5	6.0	6
3	2007-11-04	13.3	15.5	39.8	7.2	9.1	7	54.0	14	13	30.0	24
4	2007-11-05	7.6	16.1	2.8	5.6	10.6	10	50.0	10	2	20.0	28

Figure 7.19: Data showing typical weather of a city

4. Now, let's look at the last 10 columns of the `weather.csv` data:

```
df.iloc[:,12:25].head()
```

	Humidity9am	Humidity3pm	Pressure9am	Pressure3pm	Cloud9am	Cloud3pm	Temp9am	Temp3pm	RainToday	RISK_MM	RainTomorrow
0	68	29	1019.7	1015.0	7	7	14.4	23.6	0	3.6	1
1	80	36	1012.4	1008.4	5	3	17.5	25.7	1	3.6	1
2	82	69	1009.5	1007.2	8	7	15.4	20.2	1	39.8	1
3	62	56	1005.5	1007.0	2	7	13.5	14.1	1	2.8	1
4	68	49	1018.3	1018.5	7	7	11.1	15.4	1	0.0	0

Figure 7.20: Last 10 columns of the weather.csv data

5. Let's use x to represent the input features. We will drop the Date field for the feature list, as it is not useful in the context of predictions. We will also drop the RainTomorrow label:

```
x = df.drop(['Date','RainTomorrow'],axis=1)
```

6. Let's use y to represent the label:

```
y = df['RainTomorrow']
```

7. Now, let's divide the data into train_test_split:

```
from sklearn.model_selection import train_test_split
train_x , train_y ,test_x , test_y = train_test_split(x,y,
test_size = 0.2,random_state = 2)
```

8. As the label is a binary variable, we will train a classifier. So, logistic regression will be a good choice here. First, let's instantiate the logistic regression model:

```
model = LogisticRegression()
```

9. Now, we can use train_x and test_x to train the model:

```
model.fit(train_x , test_x)
```

10. Once the model is trained, let's use it for predictions:

```
predict = model.predict(train_y)
```

11. Now, let's find the accuracy of our trained model:

```
predict = model.predict(train_y)
from sklearn.metrics import accuracy_score
accuracy_score(predict , test_y)
```

```
0.9696969696969697
```

Now, this binary classifier can be used to predict whether it will rain tomorrow.

Summary

Wrapping up, this chapter served as a comprehensive expedition into the multifaceted landscape of supervised machine learning. We spotlighted the primary components of classification and regression algorithms, dissecting their mechanics and applications.

The chapter demonstrated a broad spectrum of algorithms through practical examples, providing an opportunity to understand the functionality of these tools in real-world contexts. This journey underscored the adaptability of supervised learning techniques and their ability to tackle varied problems.

By juxtaposing the performance of different algorithms, we emphasized the crucial role of context when selecting an optimal machine learning strategy. Factors such as data size, feature complexity, and prediction requirements play significant roles in this selection process.

As we transition to the upcoming chapters, the knowledge gleaned from this exploration serves as a robust foundation. This understanding of how to apply supervised learning techniques in practical scenarios is a critical skill set in the vast realm of machine learning. Keep these insights at your fingertips as we journey further into the compelling world of AI, preparing for an even deeper dive into the complex universe of neural networks.

Learn more on Discord

To join the Discord community for this book – where you can share feedback, ask questions to the author, and learn about new releases – follow the QR code below:

`https://packt.link/WHLel`

8

Neural Network Algorithms

Neural networks have been a topic of investigation for over seven decades, but their adoption was restricted due to constraints in computational capabilities and the dearth of digitized data. Today's environment is significantly altered due to our growing need to solve complex challenges, the explosive growth in data production, and advancements such as cloud computing, which provide us with impressive computational abilities. These enhancements have opened up the potential for us to develop and apply these sophisticated algorithms to solve complex problems that were previously deemed impractical. In fact, this is the research area that is rapidly evolving and is responsible for most of the major advances claimed by leading-edge tech fields such as robotics, edge computing, natural language processing, and self-driving cars.

This chapter first introduces the main concepts and components of a typical neural network. Then, it presents the various types of neural networks and explains the different kinds of activation functions used in these neural networks. Then, the backpropagation algorithm is discussed in detail, which is the most widely used algorithm for training a neural network. Next, the transfer learning technique is explained, which can be used to greatly simplify and partially automate the training of models. Finally, how to use deep learning to flag fraudulent documents by way of a real-world example application.

The following are the main concepts discussed in this chapter:

- Understanding neural networks
- The evolution of neural networks
- Training a neural network
- Tools and frameworks
- Transfer learning
- Case study: using deep learning for fraud detection

Let's start by looking at the basics of neural networks.

The evolution of neural networks

A neural network, at its most fundamental level, is composed of individual units known as neurons. These neurons serve as the cornerstone of the neural network, with each neuron performing its own specific task. The true power of a neural network unfolds when these individual neurons are organized into structured layers, facilitating complex processing. Each neural network is composed of an intricate web of these layers, connected to create an interconnected network.

The information or signal is processed step by step as it travels through these layers. Each layer modifies the signal, contributing to the overall output. To explain, the initial layer receives the input signal, processes it, and then passes it to the next layer. This subsequent layer further processes the received signal and transfers it onward. This relay continues until the signal reaches the final layer, which generates the desired output.

It's these hidden layers, or intermediate layers, that give neural networks their ability to perform deep learning. These layers create a hierarchy of abstract representations by transforming the raw input data progressively into a form that is more useful. This facilitates the extraction of higher-level features from the raw data.

This deep learning capability has a vast array of practical applications, from enabling Amazon's Alexa to understand voice commands to powering Google's Images and organizing Google Photos.

Historical background

Inspired by the workings of neurons in the human brain, the concept of neural networks was proposed by Frank Rosenblatt in 1957. To understand the architecture fully, it is helpful to briefly look at the layered structure of neurons in the human brain. (Refer to *Figure 8.1* to get an idea of how the neurons in the human brain are linked together.)

In the human brain, **dendrites** act as sensors that detect a signal. Dendrites are integral components of a neuron, serving as the primary sensory apparatus. They are responsible for detecting incoming signals. The signal is then passed on to an **axon**, which is a long, slender projection of a nerve cell. The function of the axon is to transmit this signal to muscles, glands, and other neurons. As shown in the following diagram, the signal travels through interconnecting tissue called a **synapse** before being passed on to other neurons. Note that through this organic pipeline, the signal keeps traveling until it reaches the target muscle or gland, where it causes the required action. It typically takes seven to eight milliseconds for the signal to pass through the chain of neurons and reach its destination:

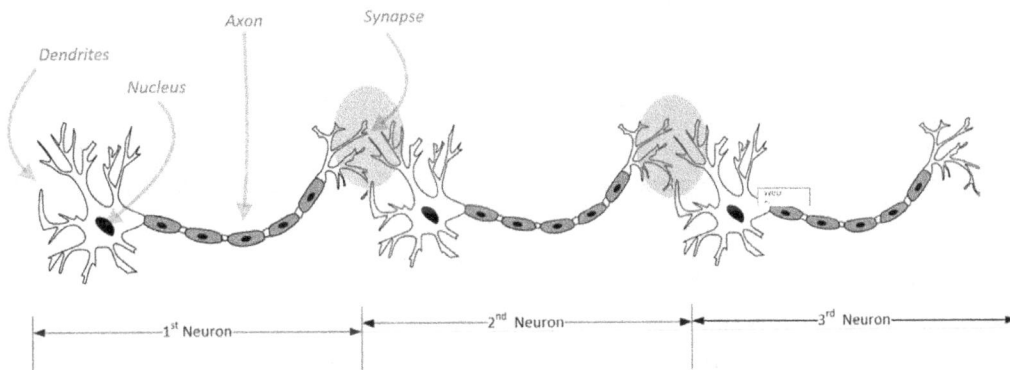

Figure 8.1: Neuron chained together in the human brain

Inspired by this natural architectural masterpiece of signal processing, Frank Rosenblatt devised a technique that would mean digital information could be processed in layers to solve a complex mathematical problem. His initial attempt at designing a neural network was quite simple and looked like a linear regression model. This simple neural network did not have any hidden layers and was named a *perceptron*. This simple neural network without any layers, the perceptron, became the basic unit for neural networks. Essentially, a perceptron is the mathematical analog of a biological neuron and hence, serves as the fundamental building block for more complex neural networks.

Now, let us delve into a concise historical account of the evolutionary journey of **Artificial Intelligence (AI)**.

AI winter and the dawn of AI spring

The initial enthusiasm toward the groundbreaking concept of the perceptron soon faded when its significant limitations were discovered. In 1969, Marvin Minsky and Seymour Papert conducted an in-depth study that led to the revelation that the perceptron was restricted in its learning capabilities. They found that a perceptron was incapable of learning and processing complex logical functions, even struggling with simple logic functions such as XOR.

This discovery triggered a significant decline in interest in **Machine Learning** (**ML**) and neural networks, commencing an era often referred to as the "AI winter." This was a period when the global research community largely dismissed the potential of AI, viewing it as inadequate for tackling complex problems.

On reflection, the "AI winter" was in part a consequence of the restrictive hardware capabilities of the time. The hardware either lacked the necessary computing power or was prohibitively expensive, which severely hampered advancements in AI. This limitation stymied the progress and application of AI, leading to widespread disillusionment in its potential.

Toward the end of the 1990s, there was a tidal shift regarding the image of AI and its perceived potential. The catalyst for this change was the advances in distributed computing, which provided easily available and affordable infrastructure. Seeing the potential, the newly crowned IT giants of that time (like Google) made AI the focus of their R&D efforts. The renewed interest in AI resulted in the thaw of the so-called AI winter. The thaw reinvigorated research in AI. This eventually resulted in turning the current era into an era that can be called the **AI spring**, where there is so much interest in AI and neural networks. Also, the digitized data was not available.

Understanding neural networks

First, let us start with the heart of the neural network, the perceptron. You can think of a single perceptron as the simplest possible neural network, and it forms the basic building block of modern complex multi-layered architectures. Let us start by understanding the working of a perceptron.

Understanding perceptrons

A single perceptron has several inputs and a single output that is controlled or activated by an activation function. This is shown in *Figure 8.2*:

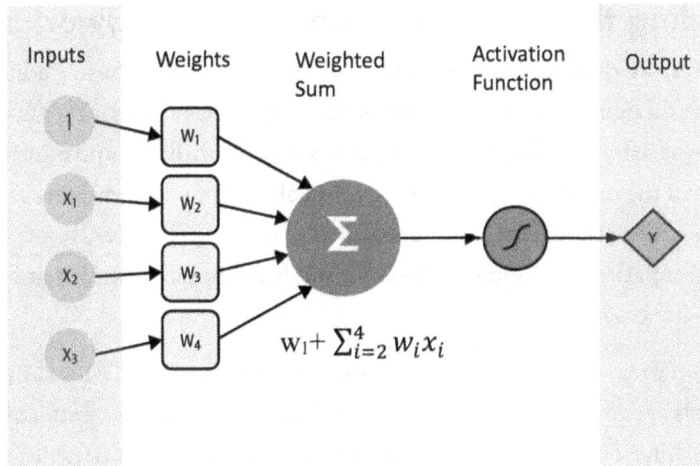

Figure 8.2: A simple perceptron

The perceptron shown in *Figure 8.2* has three input features; x_1, x_2, and x_3. We also add a constant signal called bias. The bias plays a critical role in our neural network model, as it allows for flexibility in fitting the data. It operates similarly to an intercept added in a linear equation—acting as a sort of "shift" of the activation function—thereby allowing us to fit the data better when our inputs are equal to zero. The input features and the bias get multiplied by weights and are summed up as a weighted sum ($w_1 + \sum_{i=2}^{4} w_i x_i$) This weighted sum is passed on to the activation function, which generates the output y. The ability to use a wide variety of activation functions to formulate complex relationships between features and labels is one of the strengths of neural networks. A variety of activation functions is selectable through the hyperparameters. Some common examples include the sigmoid function, which squashes values between 0 and 1, making it a good choice for binary classification problems; the tanh function, which scales values between -1 and 1, providing a zero-centered output; and the **Rectified Linear Unit (ReLU)** function, which sets all negative values in the vector to zero, effectively removing any negative influence, and is commonly used in convolutional neural networks. These activation functions are discussed in detail later in the chapter.

Let us now look into the intuition behind neural networks.

Understanding the intuition behind neural networks

In the last chapter, we discussed some traditional ML algorithms. These traditional ML algorithms work great for many important use cases. But they do have limitations as well. When the underlying patterns in the training dataset begin to become non-linear and multidimensional, it starts to go beyond the capabilities of traditional ML algorithms to accurately capture the complex relationships between features and labels. These incomprehensive, somewhat simplistic mathematical formulations of complex patterns result in suboptimal performance of the trained models for these use cases.

In real-world scenarios, we often encounter situations where the relationships between our features and labels are not linear or straightforward but present complex patterns. This is where neural networks shine, offering us a powerful tool for modeling such intricacies.

Neural networks are particularly effective when dealing with high-dimensional data or when the relationships between features and the outcome are non-linear. For instance, they excel in applications like image and speech recognition, where the input data (pixels or sound waves) has complex, hierarchical structures. Traditional ML algorithms might struggle in these instances, given the high degree of complexity and the non-linear relationships between features.

While neural networks are incredibly powerful tools, it's crucial to acknowledge that they aren't without their limitations. These restrictions, explored in detail later in this chapter, are critical to grasp for the practical and effective use of neural networks in tackling real-world dilemmas.

Now, let's illustrate some common patterns and their associated challenges when simpler ML algorithms like linear regression are employed. Picture this – we're trying to predict a data scientist's salary based on the "years spent in education." We have collected two different datasets from two separate organizations.

First, let's introduce you to Dataset 1, illustrated in *Figure 8.3(a)*. It depicts a relatively straightforward relationship between the feature (years spent in education) and the label (salary), which appears to be linear. However, even this simple pattern throws a couple of challenges when we attempt to mathematically model it using a linear algorithm:

- We know that a salary cannot be negative, meaning that regardless of the years spent in education, the salary (y) should never be less than zero.
- There's at least one junior data scientist who may have just graduated, thus spending "x_1" years in education, but currently earns zero salary, perhaps as an intern. Hence, for the "x" values ranging from zero to "x_1," the salary "y" remains zero, as depicted in *Figure 8.3(a)*.

Interestingly, we can capture such intricate relationships between the feature and label using the Rectified Linear activation function available in neural networks, a concept we will explore later.

Next, we have Dataset 2, showcased in *Figure 8.3(b)*. This dataset represents a non-linear relationship between the feature and the label. Here's how it works:

1. The salary "y" remains at zero while "x" (years spent in education) varies from zero to "x_1."

2. The salary increases sharply as "x" nears "x_2."

3. But once "y" exceeds "x_2," the salary plateaus and flattens out.

As we will see later in this book, we can model such relationships using the sigmoid activation function within a neural network framework. Understanding these patterns and knowing which tools to apply is essential to effectively leverage the power of neural networks:

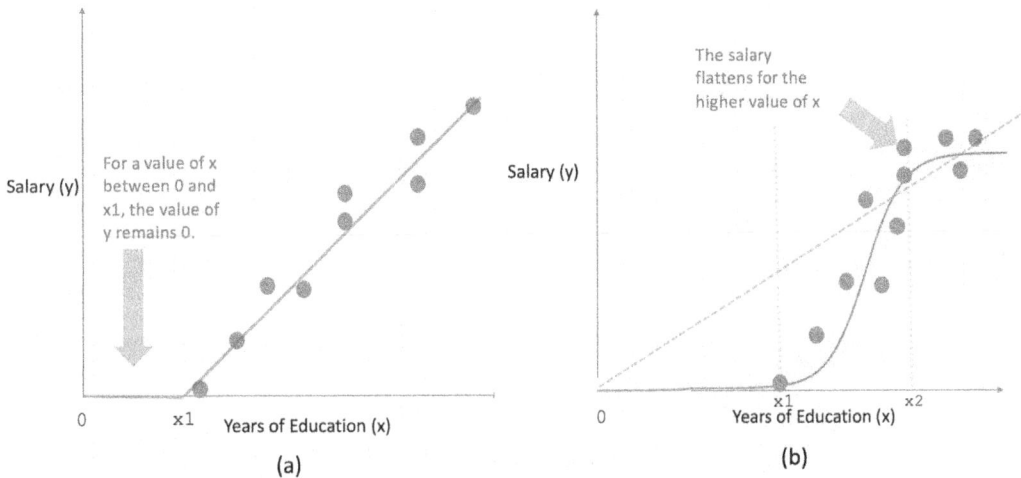

Figure 8.3: Salary and years of education

(a) Dataset 1: Linear patterns (b) Dataset 2: Non-linear patterns

Understanding layered deep learning architectures

For more complex problems, researchers have developed a multilayer neural network called a **multilayer perceptron**. A multilayer neural network has a few different layers, as shown in the following diagram. These layers are as follows:

- **Input layer:** The first layer is the input layer. At the input layer, the feature values are fed as input to the network.

- **Hidden layer(s):** The input layer is followed by one or more hidden layers. Each hidden layers are the arrays of similar activation functions.
- **Output layer:** The final layer is called the output layer.

A simple neural network will have one hidden layer. A deep neural network is a neural network with two or more hidden layers. See *Figure 8.4*.

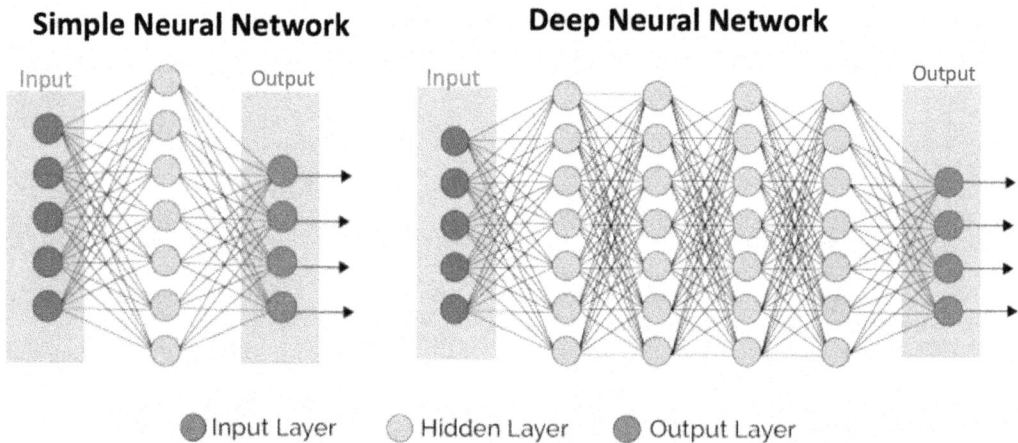

Simple Neural Network   **Deep Neural Network**

● Input Layer   ◌ Hidden Layer   ● Output Layer

Figure 8.4: Simple neural network and deep neural network

Next, let us try to understand the function of hidden layers.

Developing an intuition for hidden layers

In a neural network, hidden layers play a key role in interpreting the input data. Hidden layers are methodically organized in a hierarchical structure within the neural network, where each layer performs a distinct non-linear transformation on its input data. This design allows for the extraction of progressively more abstract and nuanced features from the input.

Consider the example of convolutional neural networks, a subtype of neural networks specifically engineered for image-processing tasks. In this context, the lower hidden layers focus on discerning simple, local features such as edges and corners within an image. These features, while fundamental, don't carry much meaning on their own.

As we move deeper into the hidden layers, these layers start to connect the dots, so to speak. They integrate the basic patterns detected by the lower layers, assembling them into more complex, meaningful structures. As a result, an originally incoherent scatter of edges and corners transforms into recognizable shapes and patterns, granting the network a level of "vision."

This progressive transformation process turns unprocessed pixel values into an elaborate mapping of features and patterns, enabling advanced applications such as fingerprint recognition. Here, the network can pick out the unique arrangement of ridges and valleys in a fingerprint, converting this raw visual data into a unique identifier. Hence, hidden layers convert raw data and refined it into valuable insights.

How many hidden layers should be used?

Note that the optimal number of hidden layers will vary from problem to problem. For some problems, single-layer neural networks should be used. These problems typically exhibit straightforward patterns that can be easily captured and formulated by a minimalist network design. For others, we should add multiple layers for the best performance. For example, if you're dealing with a complex problem, such as image recognition or natural language processing, a neural network with multiple hidden layers and a greater number of nodes in each layer might be necessary.

The complexity of your data's underlying patterns will largely influence your network design. For instance, using an excessively complex neural network for a simple problem might lead to overfitting, where your model becomes too tailored to the training data and performs poorly on new, unseen data. On the other hand, a model that's too simple for a complex problem might result in underfitting, where the model fails to capture essential patterns in the data.

Additionally, the choice of activation function plays a critical role. For example, if your output needs to be binary (like in a yes/no problem), a sigmoid function could be suitable. For multi-class classification problems, a softmax function might be better.

Ultimately, the process of selecting your neural network's architecture requires careful analysis of your problem, coupled with experimentation and fine-tuning. This is where developing a baseline experimental model can be beneficial, allowing you to iteratively adjust and enhance your network's design for optimal performance.

Let us next look into the mathematical basis of a neural network.

Mathematical basis of neural network

Understanding the mathematical foundation of neural networks is key to leveraging their power. While they may seem complex, the principles are based on familiar mathematical concepts such as linear algebra, calculus, and probability. The beauty of neural networks lies in their ability to learn from data and improve over time, attributes that are rooted in their mathematical structure:

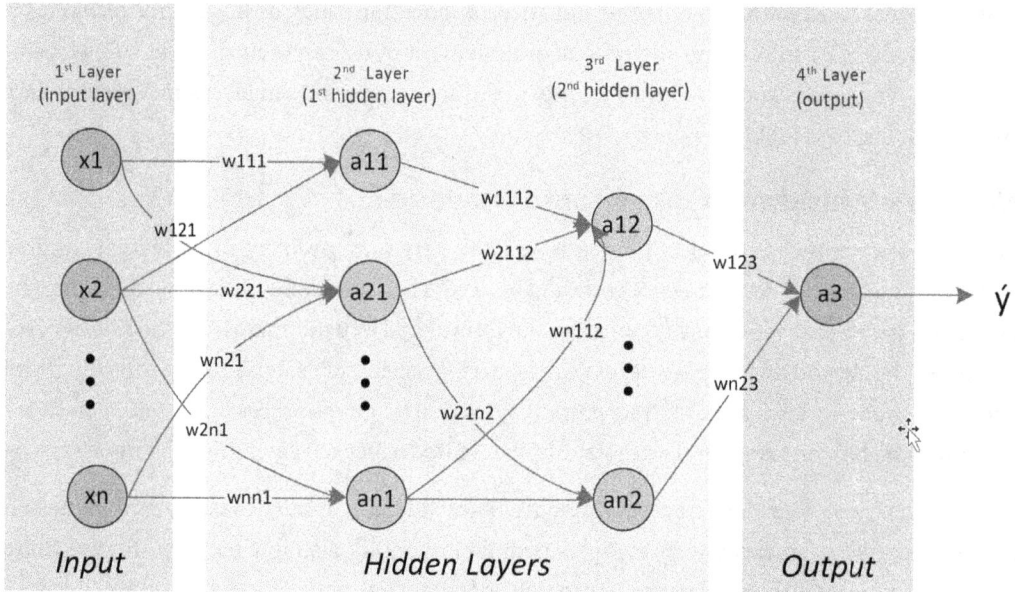

Figure 8.5: A multi-layer perceptron

Figure 8.5 shows a 4-layer neural network. In this neural network, an important thing to note is that the neuron is the basic unit of this network, and each neuron of a layer is connected to all neurons of the next layer. For complex networks, the number of these interconnections explodes, and we will explore different ways of reducing these interconnections without sacrificing too much quality.

First, let's try to formulate the problem we are trying to solve.

The input is a feature vector, x, of dimensions n.

We want the neural network to predict values. The predicted values are represented by $\acute{y}$.

Mathematically, we want to determine, given a particular input, the probability that a transaction is fraudulent. In other words, given a particular value of x, what is the probability that $y = 1$? Mathematically, we can represent this as follows:

$$\acute{y} = P(y = 1|x) : where; \; x \in \mathfrak{R}^{n_x}$$

Note that x is an n_x-dimensional vector, where n_x is the number of input variables.

The neural network shown in *Figure 8.6* has four layers. The layers between the input and the output are the hidden layers. The number of neurons in the first hidden layer is denoted by $n_h^{[l]}$. The links between various nodes are multiplied by parameters called *weights*. The process of training a neural network is fundamentally centered around determining the optimal values for the weights associated with the various connections between the network's neurons. By adjusting these weights, the network can fine-tune its calculations and improve its performance over time.

Let's see how we can train a neural network.

Training a neural network

The process of building a neural network using a given dataset is called training a neural network. Let's look into the anatomy of a typical neural network. When we talk about training a neural network, we are talking about calculating the best values for the weights. The training is done iteratively by using a set of examples in the form of training data. The examples in the training data have the expected values of the output for different combinations of input values. The training process for neural networks is different from the way traditional models are trained (which was discussed in *Chapter 7, Traditional Supervised Learning Algorithms*).

Understanding the anatomy of a neural network

Let's see what a neural network consists of:

- **Layers**: Layers are the core building blocks of a neural network. Each layer is a data-processing module that acts as a filter. It takes one or more inputs, processes them in a certain way, and then produces one or more outputs. Every time data passes through a layer, it goes through a processing phase and shows patterns that are relevant to the business question we are trying to answer.

- **Loss function**: The loss function provides the feedback signal that is used in the various iterations of the learning process. The loss function provides the deviation for a single example.

- **Cost function**: The cost function is the loss function on a complete set of examples.

- **Optimizer**: An optimizer determines how the feedback signal provided by the loss function will be interpreted.

- **Input data**: Input data is the data that is used to train the neural network. It specifies the target variable.

- **Weights**: The weights are calculated by training the network. Weights roughly correspond to the importance of each of the inputs. For example, if a particular input is more important than other inputs, after training, it is given a greater weight value, acting as a multiplier. Even a weak signal for that important input will gather strength from the large weight value (which acts as a multiplier). Thus weight ends up turning each of the inputs according to their importance.

- **Activation function**: The values are multiplied by different weights and then aggregated. Exactly how they will be aggregated and how their value will be interpreted will be determined by the type of the chosen activation function.

Let's now have a look at a very important aspect of neural network training.

While training neural networks, we take each of the examples one by one. For each of the examples, we generate the output using our under-training model. The term "under-training" refers to the model's learning state, where it is still adjusting and learning from data and has not reached its optimal performance yet. During this stage, the model parameters, such as weights, are constantly updated and adjusted to improve its predictive performance. We calculate the difference between the expected output and the predicted output. For each individual example, this difference is called the **loss**. Collectively, the loss across the complete training dataset is called the **cost**. As we keep on training the model, we aim to find the right values of weights that will result in the smallest loss value. Throughout the training, we keep on adjusting the values of the weights until we find the set of values for the weights that results in the minimum possible overall cost. Once we reach the minimum cost, we mark the model as trained.

Defining gradient descent

The central goal of training a neural network is to identify the correct values for the weights, which act like "dials" or "knobs" that we adjust to minimize the difference between the model's predictions and the actual values.

When training begins, we initiate these weights with random or default values. We then progressively adjust them using an optimization algorithm, a popular choice being "gradient descent," to incrementally improve our model's predictions.

Let's dive deeper into the gradient descent algorithm. The journey of gradient descent starts from the initial random values of weights that we set.

From this starting point, we iterate and, at each step, we adjust these weights to move us closer to the minimum cost.

To paint a clearer picture, imagine our data features as the input vector **X**. The true value of the target variable is **Y**, while the value our model predicts is **Y**. We measure the difference, or deviation, between these actual and predicted values. This difference gives us our loss.

We then update our weights, taking into account two key factors: the direction to move and the size of the step, also known as the learning rate.

The "direction" informs us where to move to find the minimum of the loss function. Think of this as descending a hill – we want to go "downhill" where the slope is steepest to get to the bottom (our minimum loss) the fastest.

The "learning rate" determines the size of our step in that chosen direction. It's like deciding whether to walk or run down that hill – a larger learning rate means bigger steps (like running), and a smaller one means smaller steps (like walking).

The goal of this iterative process is to reach a point from which we can't go "downhill", meaning we have found the minimum cost, indicating our weights are now optimal, and our model is well trained.

This simple iterative process is shown in the following diagram:

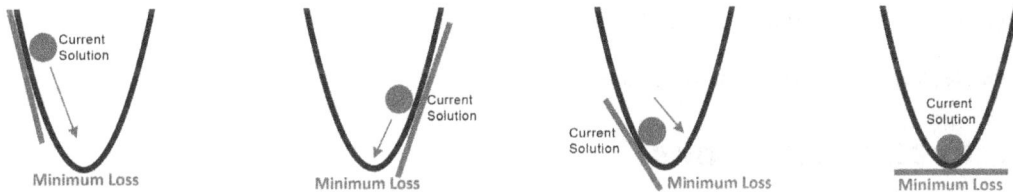

Figure 8.6: Gradient Descent Algorithm, finding the minimum

The diagram shows how, by varying the weights, gradient descent tries to find the minimum cost. The learning rate and chosen direction will determine the next point on the graph to explore.

Selecting the right value for the learning rate is important. If the learning rate is too small, the problem may take a lot of time to converge. If the learning rate is too high, the problem will not converge. In the preceding diagram, the dot representing our current solution will keep oscillating between the two opposite lines of the graph.

Now, let's see how to minimize a gradient. Consider only two variables, x and y. The gradient of x and y is calculated as follows:

$$gradient = \frac{\Delta y}{\Delta x}$$

To minimize the gradient, the following approach can be used:

```python
def adjust_position(gradient):
    while gradient != 0:
        if gradient < 0:
            print("Move right")
            # here would be your logic to move right
        elif gradient > 0:
            print("Move left")
            # here would be your logic to move left
```

This algorithm can also be used to find the optimal or near-optimal values of weights for a neural network.

Note that the calculation of gradient descent proceeds backward throughout the network. We start by calculating the gradient of the final layer first, and then the second-to-last one, and then the one before that, until we reach the first layer. This is called backpropagation, which was introduced by Hinton, Williams, and Rumelhart in 1985.

Next, let's look into activation functions.

Activation functions

An activation function formulates how the inputs to a particular neuron will be processed to generate an output.

As shown in *Figure 8.7*, each of the neurons in a neural network has an activation function that determines how inputs will be processed:

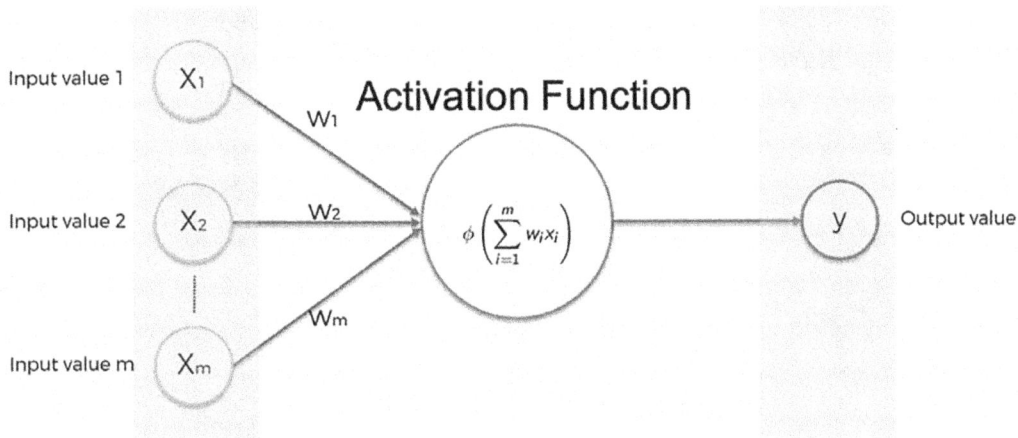

Figure 8.7: Activation function

In the preceding diagram, we can see that the results generated by an activation function are passed on to the output. The activation function sets the criteria that how the values of the inputs are supposed to be interpreted to generate an output.

For exactly the same input values, different activation functions will produce different outputs. Understanding how to select the right activation function is important when using neural networks to solve problems.

Let's now look into these activation functions one by one.

Step function

The simplest possible activation function is the threshold function. The output of the threshold function is binary: 0 or 1. It will generate 1 as the output if any of the inputs are greater than 1. This can be explained in *Figure 8.8*:

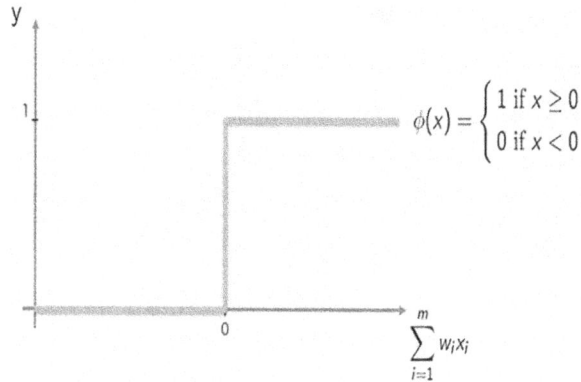

$$\phi(x) = \begin{cases} 1 \text{ if } x \geq 0 \\ 0 \text{ if } x < 0 \end{cases}$$

Figure 8.8: Step function

Despite its simplicity, the threshold activation function plays an important role, especially when we need a clear demarcation between the outputs. With this function, as soon as there's any non-zero value in the weighted sums of inputs, the output (y) turns to 1. However, its simplicity has its drawbacks – the function is exceedingly sensitive and could be erroneously triggered by the slightest signal or noise in the input.

For instance, consider a situation where a neural network uses this function to classify emails into "spam" or "not spam." Here, an output of 1 might represent "spam" and 0 might represent "not spam." The slightest presence of a characteristic (like certain key spam words) could trigger the function to classify the email as "spam." Hence, while it's a valuable tool for certain use cases, its potential for over-sensitivity should be considered, especially in applications where noise or minor variances in input data are common. Next, let us look into the sigmoid function.

Sigmoid function

The sigmoid function can be thought of as an improvement of the threshold function. Here, we have control over the sensitivity of the activation function:

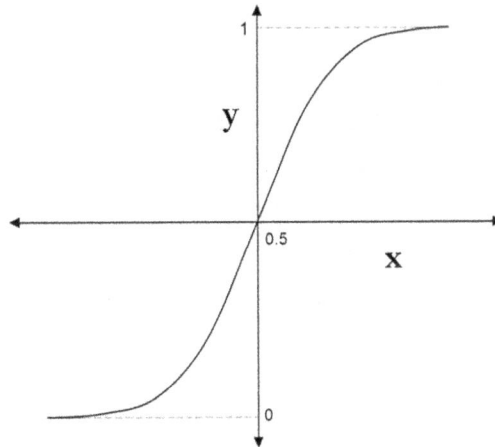

Figure 8.9: Sigmoid activation function

The sigmoid function, *y*, is defined as follows and shown in *Figure 8.9*:

$$y = f(x) = \frac{1}{1 + e^{-x}}$$

It can be implemented in Python as follows:

```
def sigmoidFunction(z):
    return 1/ (1+np.exp(-z))
```

The code above demonstrates the sigmoid function using Python. Here, `np.exp(-z)` is the exponential operation applied to `-z`, and this term is added to 1 to form the denominator of the equation, resulting in a value between 0 and 1.

The reduction in the activation function's sensitivity through the sigmoid function makes it less susceptible to sudden aberrations or "glitches" in the input. However, it's worth noting that the output remains binary, meaning it can still only be 0 or 1.

Sigmoid functions are widely used in binary classification problems where the output is expected to be either 0 or 1. For instance, if you are developing a model to predict whether an email is spam (1) or not spam (0), a sigmoid activation function would be a suitable choice.

Now, let's delve into the **ReLU** activation function.

ReLU

The output for the first two activation functions presented in this chapter was binary. That means that they will take a set of input variables and convert them into binary outputs. ReLU is an activation function that takes a set of input variables as input and converts them into a single continuous output. In neural networks, ReLU is the most popular activation function and is usually used in the hidden layers, where we do not want to convert continuous variables into category variables.

The following diagram summarizes the ReLU activation function:

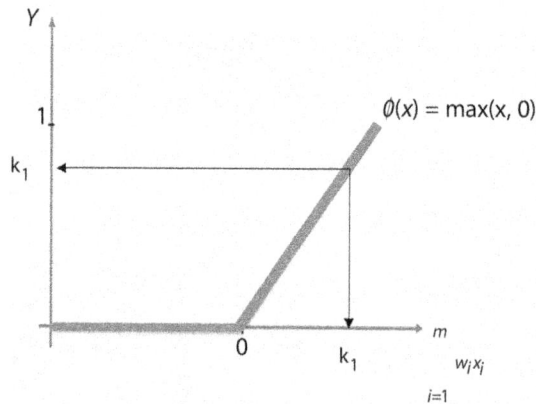

Figure 8.10: ReLU

Note that when $x \le 0$, that means $y = 0$. This means that any signal from the input that is zero or less than zero is translated into a zero output:

$$y = f(x) = 0; \quad for \ x < 0$$

$$y = f(x) = x; \quad for \ x \ge 0$$

As soon as x becomes more than zero, it is x.

The ReLU function is one of the most used activation functions in neural networks. It can be implemented in Python as follows:

```
def relu(x):
    if x < 0:
        return 0
    else:
        return x
```

Now let's look into Leaky ReLU, which is based on ReLU.

Leaky ReLU

In ReLU, a negative value for x results in a zero value for y. This means that some information is lost in the process, which makes training cycles longer, especially at the start of training. The Leaky ReLU activation function resolves this issue. The following applies to Leaky ReLu:

$$y = f(x) = \beta x; \quad for \ x < 0$$

$$y = f(x) = x; \quad for \ x \geq 0$$

This is shown in the following diagram:

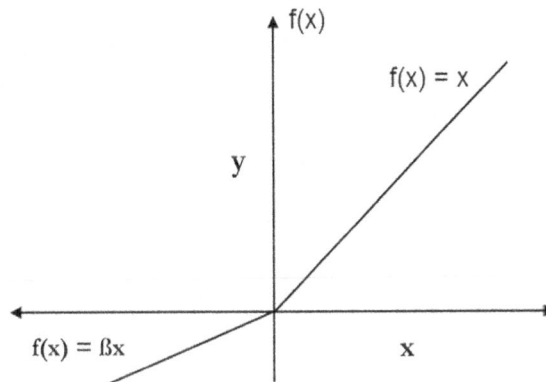

Figure 8.11: Leaky ReLU

Here, β is a parameter with a value less than one.

It can be implemented in Python as follows:

```python
def leaky_relu(x, beta=0.01):
    if x < 0:
        return beta * x
    else:
        return x
```

There are various strategies for assigning a value to β:

- **Default value:** We can assign a default value to β, typically 0.01. This is the most straight-forward approach and can be useful in scenarios where we want a quick implementation without any intricate tuning.

- **Parametric ReLU**: Another approach is to allow β to be a tunable parameter in our neural network model. In this case, the optimal value for β is learned during the training process itself. This is beneficial in scenarios where we aim to tailor our activation function to the specific patterns present in our data.

- **Randomized ReLU**: We could also choose to randomly assign a value to β. This technique, known as randomized ReLU, can act as a form of regularization and help prevent overfitting by introducing some randomness into the model. This could be helpful in scenarios where we have a large dataset with complex patterns and we want to ensure our model doesn't overfit to the training data.

Hyperbolic tangent (tanh)

The hyperbolic tangent function, or tanh, is closely related to the sigmoid function, with a key distinction: it can output negative values, thereby offering a broader output range between -1 and 1. This can be useful in situations where we want to model phenomena that contain both positive and negative influences. *Figure 8.12* illustrates this:

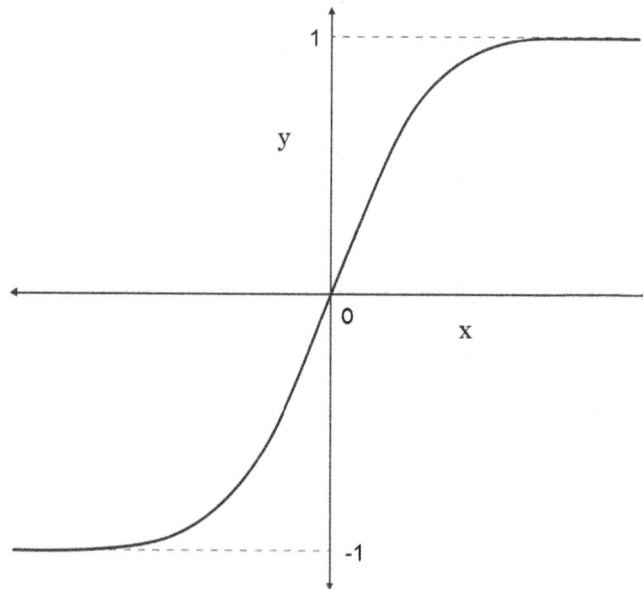

Figure 8.12: Hyperbolic tangent

The y function is as follows:

$$y = f(x) = \frac{1 + e^{-2x}}{1 + e^{-2x}}$$

It can be implemented by the following Python code:

```python
import numpy as np

def tanh(x):
    numerator = 1 - np.exp(-2 * x)
    denominator = 1 + np.exp(-2 * x)
    return numerator / denominator
```

In this Python code, we're using the numpy library, indicated by np, to handle the mathematical operations. The tanh function, like the sigmoid, is an activation function used in neural networks to add non-linearity to the model. It is often preferred over the sigmoid function in hidden layers of a neural network as it centers the data by making the output mean 0, which can make learning in the next layer easier. However, the choice between tanh, sigmoid, or any other activation function largely depends on the specific needs and complexities of the model you're working with.

Moving on, let's now delve into the softmax function.

Softmax

Sometimes, we need more than two levels for the output of the activation function. Softmax is an activation function that provides us with more than two levels for the output. It is best suited to multiclass classification problems. Let's assume that we have n classes. We have input values. The input values map the classes as follows:

$$x = \{x^{(1)}, x^{(2)}, \dots x^{(n)}\}$$

Softmax operates on probability theory. For binary classifiers, the activation function in the final layer will be sigmoid, and for multiclass classifiers, it will be softmax. To illustrate, let's say we're trying to classify an image of a fruit, where the classes are apple, banana, cherry, and date. The softmax function calculates the probabilities of the image belonging to each of these classes. The class with the highest probability is then considered as the prediction.

To break this down in terms of Python code and equations, let's look at the following:

```python
import numpy as np

def softmax(x):
    return np.exp(x) / np.sum(np.exp(x), axis=0)
```

In this code snippet, we're using the numpy library (np) to perform the mathematical operations. The softmax function takes an array of x as input, applies the exponential function to each element, and normalizes the results so that they sum up to 1, which is the total probability across all classes.

Now let us look into various tools and frameworks related to neural networks.

Tools and frameworks

In this section, we will delve into the vast array of tools and frameworks that have been developed specifically to facilitate the implementation of neural networks. Each of these frameworks has its unique advantages and possible limitations.

Among the numerous options available, we've chosen to spotlight Keras, a high-level neural network API, which is capable of running on top of TensorFlow. Why Keras and TensorFlow, you may wonder? Well, these two in combination offer several notable benefits that make them a popular choice among practitioners.

Firstly, Keras, with its user-friendly and modular nature, simplifies the process of building and designing neural network models, thereby catering to beginners as well as experienced users. Secondly, its compatibility with TensorFlow, a powerful end-to-end open-source platform for ML, ensures robustness and versatility. TensorFlow's ability to deliver high computational performance is another valuable asset. Together, they form a dynamic duo that strikes a balance between usability and functionality, making them an excellent choice for the development and deployment of neural network models.

In the following sections, we'll explore more about how to use Keras with a TensorFlow backend to construct neural networks.

Keras

Keras (`https://www.tensorflow.org/guide/keras`) is one of the most popular and easy-to-use neural network libraries and is written in Python. It was written with ease of use in mind and provides the fastest way to implement deep learning. Keras only provides high-level blocks and is considered at the model level.

Now, let's look into the various backend engines of Keras.

Backend engines of Keras

Keras needs a lower-level deep learning library to perform tensor-level manipulations. This foundational layer is referred to as the "backend engine."

In simpler terms, tensor-level manipulations involve the computations and transformations that are performed on multi-dimensional arrays of data, known as tensors, which are the primary data structure used in neural networks. This lower-level deep-learning library is called the *backend engine*. Possible backend engines for Keras include the following:

- **TensorFlow** (`www.tensorflow.org`): This is the most popular framework of its kind and is open sourced by Google.
- **Theano**: This was developed at the MILA lab at Université de Montréal.
- **Microsoft Cognitive Toolkit (CNTK)** (`https://learn.microsoft.com/en-us/cognitive-toolkit/`): This was developed by Microsoft.

The format of this modular deep learning technology stack is shown in the following diagram:

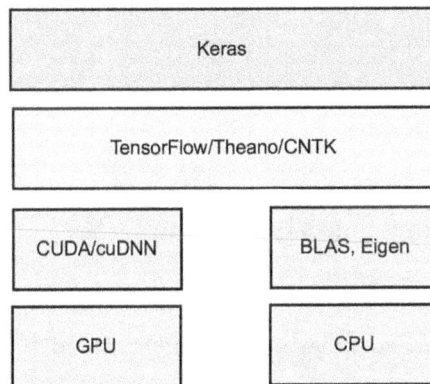

Figure 8.13: Keras architecture

The advantage of this modular deep learning architecture is that the backend of Keras can be changed without rewriting any code. For example, if we find TensorFlow better than Theona for a particular task, we can simply change the backend to TensorFlow without rewriting any code.

Next, let us look into the low-level layers of the deep learning stack.

Low-level layers of the deep learning stack

The three backend engines we just mentioned can all run both on CPUs and GPUs using the low-level layers of the stack. For CPUs, a low-level library of tensor operations called **Eigen** is used. For GPUs, TensorFlow uses NVIDIA's **CUDA Deep Neural Network (cuDNN)** library. It's noteworthy to explain why GPUs are often preferred in ML.

While CPUs are versatile and capable, GPUs are specifically designed to handle multiple operations concurrently, which is beneficial when processing large blocks of data, a common occurrence in ML tasks. This trait of GPUs, combined with their higher memory bandwidth, can significantly expedite ML computations, thereby making them a popular choice for such tasks.

Next, let us explain the hyperparameters.

Defining hyperparameters

As discussed in *Chapter 6, Unsupervised Machine Learning Algorithms*, a hyperparameter is a parameter whose value is chosen before the learning process starts. We start with common-sense values and then try to optimize them later. For neural networks, the important hyperparameters are these:

- The activation function
- The learning rate
- The number of hidden layers
- The number of neurons in each hidden layer

Let's look into how we can define a model using Keras.

Defining a Keras model

There are three steps involved in defining a complete Keras model:

1. Define the layers
2. Define the learning process
3. Test the model

We can build a model using Keras in two possible ways:

- **The Functional API**: This allows us to architect models for acyclic graphs of layers. More complex models can be created using the Functional API.
- **The Sequential API**: This allows us to architect models for a linear stack of layers. It is used for relatively simple models and is the usual choice for building models.

First, we take a look at the Sequential way of defining a Keras model:

1. Let us start with importing the tensorflow library:

   ```
   import tensorflow as tf
   ```

2. Then, load the MNIST dataset from Keras' datasets:

```
mnist = tf.keras.datasets.mnist
```

3. Next, split the dataset into training and test sets:

```
(train_images, train_labels), (test_images, test_labels) = mnist.
load_data()
```

4. We normalize the pixel values from a scale out of 255 to a scale out of 1:

```
train_images, test_images = train_images / 255.0,
                            test_images / 255.0
```

5. Next, we define the structure of the model:

```
model = tf.keras.models.Sequential([
    tf.keras.layers.Flatten(input_shape=(28, 28)),
    tf.keras.layers.Dense(128, activation='relu'),
    tf.keras.layers.Dropout(0.15),
    tf.keras.layers.Dense(128, activation='relu'),
    tf.keras.layers.Dropout(0.15),
    tf.keras.layers.Dense(10, activation='softmax'),
])
```

This script is training a model to classify images from the MNIST dataset, which is a set of 70,000 small images of digits handwritten by high school students and employees of the US Census Bureau.

The model is defined using the Sequential method in Keras, indicating that our model is organized as a linear stack of layers:

1. The first layer is a Flatten layer, which transforms the format of the images from a two-dimensional array into a one-dimensional array.

2. The next layer, a Dense layer, is a fully connected neural layer with 128 nodes (or neurons). The relu (ReLU) activation function is used here.

3. The Dropout layer randomly sets input units to 0 with a frequency of rate at each step during training time, which helps prevent overfitting.

4. Another Dense layer is included; similar to the previous one, it's also using the relu activation function.

5. We again apply a Dropout layer with the same rate as before.

6. The final layer is a 10-node softmax layer—this returns an array of 10 probability scores that sums to 1. Each node contains a score that indicates the probability that the current image belongs to one of the 10 digit classes.

Note that, here, we have created three layers – the first two layers have the relu activation function and the third layer has softmax as the activation function.

Now, let's take a look at the Functional API way of defining a Keras model:

1. First, let us import the tensorflow library:

```
# Ensure TensorFlow 2.x is being used
%tensorflow_version 2.x
import tensorflow as tf
from tensorflow.keras.datasets import mnist
```

2. To work with the MNIST dataset, we first load it into memory. The dataset is conveniently split into training and testing sets, with both images and corresponding labels:

```
# Load MNIST dataset
(train_images, train_labels), (test_images, test_labels) = mnist.
load_data()

# Normalize the pixel values to be between 0 and 1
train_images, test_images = train_images / 255.0, test_images /
255.0
```

3. The images in the MNIST dataset are 28x28 pixels in size. When setting up a neural network model using TensorFlow, you need to specify the shape of the input data, Here, we establish the input tensor for the model:

```
inputs = tf.keras.Input(shape=(28,28))
```

4. Next, the Flatten layer is a simple data preprocessing step. It transforms the two-dimensional 128x128 pixel input into a one-dimensional array by "flattening" it. This prepares the data for the following Dense layer:

```
x = tf.keras.layers.Flatten()(inputs)
```

5. Then comes the first `Dense` layer, also known as a fully connected layer, in which each input node (or neuron) is connected to each output node. The layer has 512 output nodes and uses the `relu` activation function. ReLU is a popular choice of activation function that outputs the input directly if it is positive; otherwise, it outputs zero:

```
x = tf.keras.layers.Dense(512, activation='relu', name='d1')(x)
```

6. The `Dropout` layer randomly sets a fraction (0.2, or 20% in this case) of the input nodes to 0 at each update during training, which helps prevent overfitting:

```
x = tf.keras.layers.Dropout(0.2)(x)
```

7. Finally, comes the output layer. It's another `Dense` layer with 10 output nodes (presumably for 10 classes). The `softmax` activation function is applied, which outputs a probability distribution over the 10 classes, meaning it will output 10 values that sum to 1. Each value represents the model's confidence that the input image corresponds to a particular class:

```
predictions = tf.keras.layers.Dense(10, activation=tf.nn.softmax,
name='d2')(x)

model = tf.keras.Model(inputs=inputs, outputs=predictions)
```

Note that we can define the same neural network using both the Sequential and Functional APIs. From the point of view of performance, it does not make any difference which approach you take to define the model.

Let us convert the numerical `train_labels` and `test_labels` into one-hot encoded vectors. In the following code each label becomes a binary array of size 10 with a 1 at its respective digit's index and 0s elsewhere:

```
# One-hot encode the labels
train_labels_one_hot = tf.keras.utils.to_categorical(train_labels, 10)
test_labels_one_hot = tf.keras.utils.to_categorical(test_labels, 10)
```

We should now define the learning process.

In this step, we define three things:

- The optimizer
- The `loss` function

- The metrics that will quantify the quality of the model:

```
optimizer = tf.keras.optimizers.RMSprop()
loss = 'categorical_crossentropy'
metrics = ['accuracy']


model.compile(optimizer=optimizer, loss=loss, metrics=metrics)
```

Note that we use the model.compile function to define the optimizer, loss function, and metrics.

We will now train the model.

Once the architecture is defined, it is time to train the model:

```
history = model.fit(train_images, train_labels_one_hot, epochs=10,
validation_data=(test_images, test_labels_one_hot))
```

Note that parameters such as batch_size and epochs are configurable parameters, making them hyperparameters.

Next, let us look into how we can choose the sequential or functional model.

Choosing a sequential or functional model

When deciding between using a sequential or functional model to construct a neural network, the nature of your network's architecture will guide your choice. The sequential model is suited to simple linear stacks of layers. It's uncomplicated and straightforward to implement, making it an ideal choice for beginners or for simpler tasks. However, this model comes with a key limitation: each layer can be connected to precisely one input tensor and one output tensor.

If the architecture of your network is more complex, such as having multiple inputs or outputs at any stage (input, output, or hidden layers), then the sequential model falls short. For such complex architectures, the functional model is more appropriate. This model provides a higher degree of flexibility, allowing for more complex network structures with multiple inputs and outputs at any layer. Let us now develop a deeper understanding of TensorFlow.

Understanding TensorFlow

TensorFlow is one of the most popular libraries for working with neural networks. In the preceding section, we saw how we can use it as the backend engine of Keras. It is an open-source, high-performance library that can actually be used for any numerical computation.

If we look at the stack, we can see that we can write TensorFlow code in a high-level language such as Python or C++, which gets interpreted by the TensorFlow distributed execution engine. This makes it quite useful for and popular with developers.

TensorFlow functions by using a **directed graph (DG)** to embody your computations. In this graph, nodes are mathematical operations, and the edges connecting these nodes signify the input and output of these operations. Moreover, these edges symbolize data arrays.

Apart from serving as the backend engine for Keras, TensorFlow is broadly used in various scenarios. It can help in developing complex ML models, processing large datasets, and even deploying AI applications across different platforms. Whether you're creating a recommendation system, image classification model, or natural language processing tool, TensorFlow can effectively cater to these tasks and more.

Presenting TensorFlow's basic concepts

Let's take a brief look at TensorFlow concepts such as scalars, vectors, and matrices. We know that a simple number, such as three or five, is called a **scalar** in traditional mathematics. Moreover, in physics, a **vector** is something with magnitude and direction. In terms of TensorFlow, we use a vector to mean one-dimensional arrays. Extending this concept, a two-dimensional array is a **matrix**. For a three-dimensional array, we use the term **3D tensor**. We use the term **rank** to capture the dimensionality of a data structure. As such, a **scalar** is a **rank 0** data structure, a **vector** is a **rank 1** data structure, and a **matrix** is a **rank 2** data structure. These multi-dimensional structures are known as **tensors** and are shown in the following diagram:

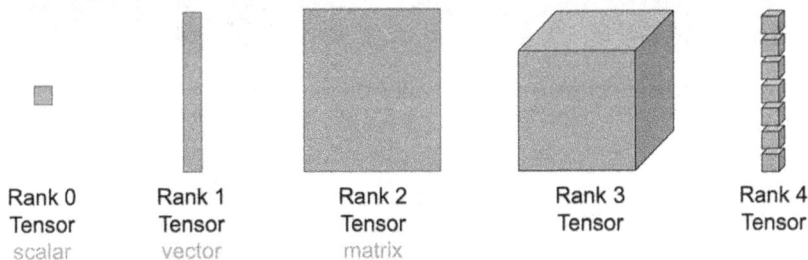

Rank 0	Rank 1	Rank 2	Rank 3	Rank 4
Tensor	Tensor	Tensor	Tensor	Tensor
scalar	vector	matrix		

Figure 8.14: Multi-dimensional structures or tensors

As we can see in the preceding diagram, the rank defines the dimensionality of a tensor.

Let's now look at another parameter, shape. shape is a tuple of integers specifying the length of an array in each dimension.

The following diagram explains the concept of shape:

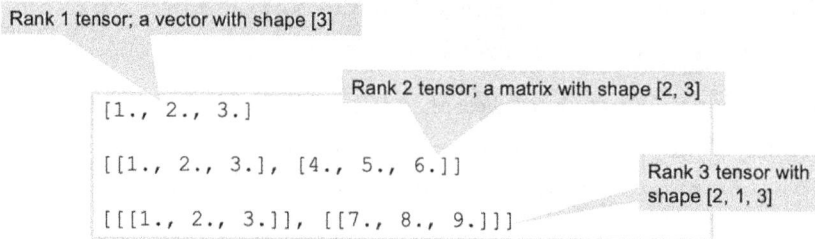

Rank 1 tensor; a vector with shape [3]

Rank 2 tensor; a matrix with shape [2, 3]

```
[1., 2., 3.]

[[1., 2., 3.], [4., 5., 6.]]

[[[1., 2., 3.]], [[7., 8., 9.]]]
```

Rank 3 tensor with shape [2, 1, 3]

Figure 8.15: Concept of a shape

Using shape and ranks, we can specify the details of tensors.

Understanding Tensor mathematics

Let's now look at different mathematical computations using tensors:

- Let's define two scalars and try to add and multiply them using TensorFlow:

```python
print("Define constant tensors")
a = tf.constant(2)
print("a = %i" % a)
b = tf.constant(3)
print("b = %i" % b)
```

```
Define constant tensors
a = 2
b = 3
```

- We can add and multiply them and display the results:

```python
print("Running operations, without tf.Session")
c = a + b
print("a + b = %i" % c)
d = a * b
print("a * b = %i" % d)
```

```
Running operations, without tf.Session
a + b = 5
a * b = 6
```

- We can also create a new scalar tensor by adding the two tensors:

```
c = a + b
print("a + b = %s" % c)
```

```
a + b = tf.Tensor(5, shape=(), dtype=int32)
```

- We can also perform complex tensor functions:

```
d = a*b
print("a * b = %s" % d)
```

```
a * b = tf.Tensor(6, shape=(), dtype=int32)
```

Understanding the types of neural networks

Neural networks can be designed in various ways, depending on how the neurons are interconnected. In a dense, or fully connected, neural network, every single neuron in a given layer is linked to each neuron in the next layer. This means each input from the preceding layer is fed into every neuron of the subsequent layer, maximizing the flow of information.

However, neural networks aren't always fully connected. Some may have specific patterns of connections based on the problem they are designed to solve. For instance, in convolutional neural networks used for image processing, each neuron in a layer may only be connected to a small region of neurons in the previous layer. This mirrors the way neurons in the human visual cortex are organized and helps the network efficiently process visual information.

Remember, the specific architecture of a neural network – how the neurons are interconnected – greatly impacts its functionality and performance.

Convolutional neural networks

Convolution neural networks (CNNs) are typically used to analyze multimedia data. In order to learn more about how a CNN is used to analyze image-based data, we need to have a grasp of the following processes:

- Convolution
- Pooling

Let's explore them one by one.

Convolution

The process of convolution emphasizes a pattern of interest in a particular image by processing it with another smaller image called a **filter** (also called a **kernel**). For example, if we want to find the edges of objects in an image, we can convolve the image with a particular filter to get them. Edge detection can help us in object detection, object classification, and other applications. So, the process of convolution is about finding characteristics and features in an image.

The approach to finding patterns is based on finding patterns that can be reused on different data. The reusable patterns are called filters or kernels.

Pooling

An important part of processing multimedia data for the purpose of ML is downsampling it. Downsampling is the practice of reducing the resolution of your data, i.e., lessening the data's complexity or dimensionality. Pooling offers two key advantages:

- By reducing the data's complexity, we significantly decrease the training time for the model, enhancing computational efficiency.

- Pooling abstracts and aggregates unnecessary details in the multimedia data, making it more generalized. This, in turn, enhances the model's ability to represent similar problems.

Downsampling is performed as follows:

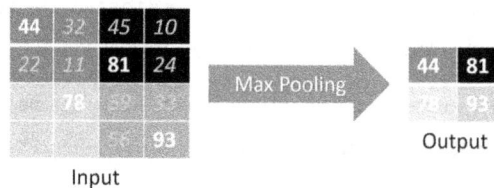

Figure 8.16: Downsampling

In the downsampling process, we essentially condense a group of pixels into a single representative pixel. For instance, let's say we condense a 2x2-pixel block into a single pixel, effectively downsampling the original data by a factor of four.

The representative value for the new pixel can be chosen in various ways. One such method is "max pooling," where we select the maximum value from the original pixel block to represent the new single pixel.

On the other hand, if we chose to take the average of the pixel block's values, the process would be termed "average pooling."

The choice between max pooling and average pooling often depends on the specific task at hand. Max pooling is particularly beneficial when we're interested in preserving the most prominent features of the image, as it retains the maximum pixel value in a block, thus capturing the most standout or noticeable aspect within that section.

In contrast, average pooling tends to be useful when we want to preserve the overall context and reduce noise, as it considers all values within a block and calculates their average, creating a more balanced representation that may be less sensitive to minor variations or noise in pixel values.

Generative Adversarial Networks

Generative Adversarial Networks, commonly referred to as GANs, represent a distinct class of neural networks capable of generating synthetic data. First introduced by Ian Goodfellow and his team in 2014, GANs have been hailed for their innovative approach to creating new data resembling the original training samples.

One notable application of GANs is their ability to produce realistic images of people who don't exist in reality, showcasing their remarkable capacity for detail generation. However, an even more crucial application lies in their potential to generate synthetic data, thereby augmenting existing training datasets, which can be extremely beneficial in scenarios where data availability is limited.

Despite their potential, GANs are not without limitations. The training process of GANs can be quite challenging, often leading to issues such as mode collapse, where the generator starts producing limited varieties of samples. Additionally, the quality of the generated data is largely dependent on the quality and diversity of the input data. Poorly representative or biased data can result in less effective, potentially skewed synthetic data.

In the upcoming section, we will see what transfer learning is.

Using transfer learning

Throughout the years, countless organizations, research entities, and contributors within the open-source community have meticulously built sophisticated models for general use cases. These models, often trained with vast amounts of data, have been optimized over years of hard work and are suited for various applications, such as:

- Detecting objects in videos or images
- Transcribing audio
- Analyzing sentiment in text

When initiating the training of a new ML model, it's worth questioning, rather than starting from a blank slate, whether we can modify an already established, pre-trained model to suit our needs. Put simply, could we leverage the learning of existing models to tailor a custom model that addresses our specific needs? Such an approach, known as transfer learning, can provide several advantages:

- It gives a head start to our model training.

- It potentially enhances the quality of our model by utilizing a pre-validated and reliable model.

- In cases where our problem lacks sufficient data, transfer learning using a pre-trained model can be of immense help.

Consider the following practical examples where transfer learning would be beneficial:

- For training a robot, a neural network model could first be trained using a simulation game. In this controlled environment, we can create rare events that are difficult to replicate in the real world. Once trained, transfer learning can then be applied to adapt the model for real-world scenarios.

- Suppose we aim to build a model that distinguishes between Apple and Windows laptops in a video feed. Existing, open-source object detection models, known for their accuracy in classifying diverse objects in video feeds, could serve as an ideal starting point. Using transfer learning, we can first leverage these models to identify objects as laptops. Subsequently, we could refine our model further to differentiate between Apple and Windows laptops.

In our next section, we will implement the principles discussed in this chapter to create a neural network for classifying fraudulent documents.

As a visual example, consider a pre-trained model as a well-established tree with many branches (layers). Some branches are already ripe with fruits (trained to identify features). When applying transfer learning, we "freeze" these fruitful branches, preserving their established learning. We then allow new branches to grow and bear fruit, which is akin to training the additional layers to understand our specific features. This process of freezing some layers and training others encapsulates the essence of transfer learning.

Case study – using deep learning for fraud detection

Using ML techniques to identify fraudulent documents is an active and challenging field of research. Researchers are investigating to what extent the pattern recognition power of neural networks can be exploited for this purpose. Instead of manual attribute extractors, raw pixels can be used for several deep learning architectural structures.

Methodology

The technique presented in this section uses a type of neural network architecture called **Siamese neural networks,** which features two branches that share identical architectures and parameters.

The use of Siamese neural networks to flag fraudulent documents is shown in the following diagram:

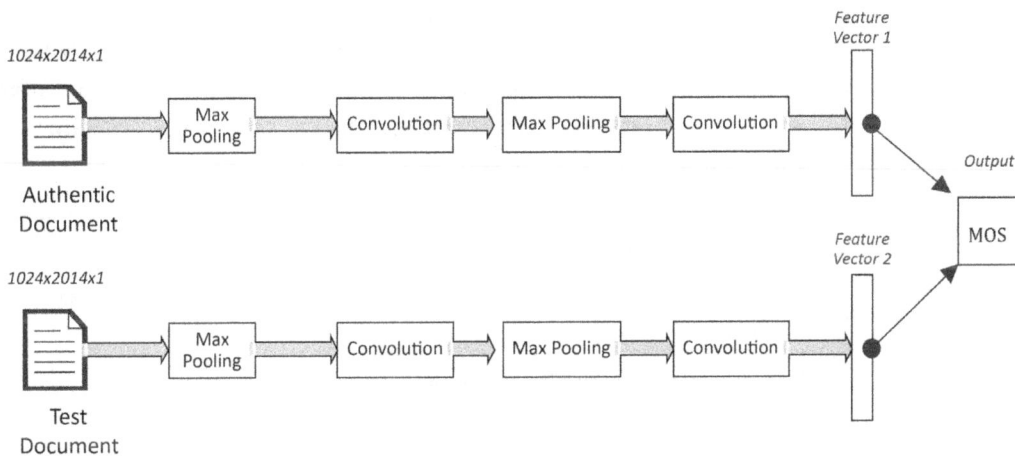

Figure 8.17: Siamese neural networks

When a particular document needs to be verified for authenticity, we first classify the document based on its layout and type, and then we compare it against its expected template and pattern. If it deviates beyond a certain threshold, it is flagged as a fake document; otherwise, it is considered an authentic or true document. For critical use cases, we can add a manual process for borderline cases where the algorithm conclusively classifies a document as authentic or fake.

To compare a document against its expected template, we use two identical CNNs in our Siamese architecture. CNNs have the advantage of learning optimal shift-invariant local feature detectors and can build representations that are robust to geometric distortions of the input image. This is well suited to our problem since we aim to pass authentic and test documents through a single network, and then compare their outcomes for similarity. To achieve this goal, we implement the following steps.

Let's assume that we want to test a document. For each class of document, we perform the following steps:

1. Get the stored image of the authentic document. We call it the **true document**. The test document should look like the true document.

2. The true document is passed through the neural network layers to create a feature vector, which is the mathematical representation of the patterns of the true document. We call it **Feature Vector 1**, as shown in the preceding diagram.

3. The document that needs to be tested is called the **test document**. We pass this document through a neural network similar to the one that was used to create the feature vector for the true document. The feature vector of the test document is called **Feature Vector 2**.

4. We use the Euclidean distance between **Feature Vector 1** and **Feature Vector 2** to calculate the similarity score between the true document and the test document. This similarity score is called the **Measure Of Similarity (MOS)**. The MOS is a number between 0 and 1. A higher number represents a lower distance between the documents and a greater likelihood that the documents are similar.

5. If the similarity score calculated by the neural network is below a pre-defined threshold, we flag the document as fraudulent.

Let's see how we can implement Siamese neural networks using Python.

To illustrate how we can implement Siamese neural networks using Python, we'll break down the process into simpler, more manageable blocks. This approach will help us follow the PEP8 style guide and keep our code readable and maintainable:

1. First, let's import the Python packages that are required:

```
import random
import numpy as np
import tensorflow as tf
```

2. Next, we define the network model that will process each branch of the Siamese network. Note that we've incorporated a dropout rate of 0.15 to mitigate overfitting:

```python
def createTemplate():
    return tf.keras.models.Sequential([
        tf.keras.layers.Flatten(),
        tf.keras.layers.Dense(128, activation='relu'),
        tf.keras.layers.Dropout(0.15),
        tf.keras.layers.Dense(128, activation='relu'),
        tf.keras.layers.Dropout(0.15),
        tf.keras.layers.Dense(64, activation='relu'),
    ])
```

3. For our Siamese networks, we'll use MNIST images. These images are excellent for testing the effectiveness of our Siamese network. We prepare the data such that each sample will contain two images and a binary similarity flag indicating whether they belong to the same class:

```python
def prepareData(inputs: np.ndarray, labels: np.ndarray):
    classesNumbers = 10
    digitalIdx = [np.where(labels == i)[0] for i in
range(classesNumbers)]
```

4. In the prepareData function, we ensure an equal number of samples across all digits. We first create an index of where in our dataset each digit appears, using the np.where function.

Then, we prepare our pairs of images and assign labels:

```python
pairs = list()
labels = list()
n = min([len(digitalIdx[d]) for d in range(classesNumbers)]) - 1
for d in range(classesNumbers):
    for i in range(n):
        z1, z2 = digitalIdx[d][i], digitalIdx[d][i + 1]
        pairs += [[inputs[z1], inputs[z2]]]
        inc = random.randrange(1, classesNumbers)
        dn = (d + inc) % classesNumbers
        z1, z2 = digitalIdx[d][i], digitalIdx[dn][i]
        pairs += [[inputs[z1], inputs[z2]]]
```

```
            labels += [1, 0]
    return np.array(pairs), np.array(labels, dtype=np.float32)
```

5. Subsequently, we'll prepare our training and testing datasets:

```
input_a = tf.keras.layers.Input(shape=input_shape)
encoder1 = base_network(input_a)
input_b = tf.keras.layers.Input(shape=input_shape)
encoder2 = base_network(input_b)
```

6. Lastly, we will implement the MOS, which quantifies the distance between two documents that we want to compare:

```
distance = tf.keras.layers.Lambda(
    lambda embeddings: tf.keras.backend.abs(
        embeddings[0] - embeddings[1]
    )
) ([encoder1, encoder2])
measureOfSimilarity = tf.keras.layers.Dense(1, activation='sigmoid')
(distance)
```

Now, let's train the model. We will use 10 epochs to train this model:

```
# Build the model
model = tf.keras.models.Model([input_a, input_b], measureOfSimilarity)
# Train
model.compile(loss='binary_crossentropy',optimizer=tf.keras.optimizers.
Adam(),metrics=['accuracy'])

model.fit([train_pairs[:, 0], train_pairs[:, 1]], tr_labels,
        batch_size=128,epochs=10,validation_data=([test_pairs[:, 0],
test_pairs[:, 1]], test_labels))
```

```
Epoch 1/10
847/847 [==============================] - 6s 7ms/step - loss: 0.3459 -
accuracy: 0.8500 - val_loss: 0.2652 - val_accuracy: 0.9105
Epoch 2/10
847/847 [==============================] - 6s 7ms/step - loss: 0.1773 -
accuracy: 0.9337 - val_loss: 0.1685 - val_accuracy: 0.9508
Epoch 3/10
```

```
847/847 [==============================] - 6s 7ms/step - loss: 0.1215 -
accuracy: 0.9563 - val_loss: 0.1301 - val_accuracy: 0.9610
Epoch 4/10
847/847 [==============================] - 6s 7ms/step - loss: 0.0956 -
accuracy: 0.9665 - val_loss: 0.1087 - val_accuracy: 0.9685
Epoch 5/10
847/847 [==============================] - 6s 7ms/step - loss: 0.0790 -
accuracy: 0.9724 - val_loss: 0.1104 - val_accuracy: 0.9669
Epoch 6/10
847/847 [==============================] - 6s 7ms/step - loss: 0.0649 -
accuracy: 0.9770 - val_loss: 0.0949 - val_accuracy: 0.9715
Epoch 7/10
847/847 [==============================] - 6s 7ms/step - loss: 0.0568 -
accuracy: 0.9803 - val_loss: 0.0895 - val_accuracy: 0.9722
Epoch 8/10
847/847 [==============================] - 6s 7ms/step - loss: 0.0513 -
accuracy: 0.9823 - val_loss: 0.0807 - val_accuracy: 0.9770
Epoch 9/10
847/847 [==============================] - 6s 7ms/step - loss: 0.0439 -
accuracy: 0.9847 - val_loss: 0.0916 - val_accuracy: 0.9737
Epoch 10/10
847/847 [==============================] - 6s 7ms/step - loss: 0.0417 -
accuracy: 0.9853 - val_loss: 0.0835 - val_accuracy: 0.9749

<tensorflow.python.keras.callbacks.History at 0x7ff1218297b8>
```

Note that we reached an accuracy of 97.49% using 10 epochs. Increasing the number of epochs will further improve the level of accuracy.

Summary

In this chapter, we journeyed through the evolution of neural networks, examining different types, key components like activation functions, and the significant gradient descent algorithm. We touched upon the concept of transfer learning and its practical application in identifying fraudulent documents.

As we proceed to the next chapter, we'll delve into natural language processing, exploring areas such as word embedding and recurrent networks. We will also learn how to implement sentiment analysis. The captivating realm of neural networks continues to unfold.

Learn more on Discord

To join the Discord community for this book – where you can share feedback, ask questions to the author, and learn about new releases – follow the QR code below:

`https://packt.link/WHLel`

9

Algorithms for Natural Language Processing

Language is the most important instrument of thought.

—Marvin Minsky

This chapter introduces algorithms for **natural language processing (NLP)**. It first introduces the fundamentals of NLP. Then it presents preparing data for NLP tasks. After that, it explains the concepts of vectorizing textual data. Next, we discuss word embeddings. Finally, we present a detailed use case.

This chapter is made up of the following sections:

- Introducing NLP
- **Bag-of-words-based (BoW-based)** NLP
- Introduction to word embedding
- Case study: Restaurant review sentiment analysis

By the end of this chapter, you will understand the basic techniques that are used for NLP. You should also understand how NLP can be used to solve some interesting real-world problems.

Let's start with the basic concepts.

Introducing NLP

NLP is a branch of machine learning algorithms that deals with the interaction between computers and human language. It involves analyzing, processing, and understanding human language to enable machines to comprehend and respond to human communication. NLP is a comprehensive subject and involves using computer linguistic algorithms and human-computer interaction technologies and methodologies to process complex unstructured data.

NLP works by processing human language and breaking it down into its constituent parts, such as words, phrases, and sentences. The goal is to enable the computer to understand the meaning of the text and respond appropriately. NLP algorithms utilize various techniques, such as statistical models, machine learning, and deep learning, to analyze and process large volumes of natural language data. For complex problems, we may need to use a combination of techniques to come up with an effective solution.

One of the most significant challenges in NLP is dealing with the complexity and ambiguity of human language. Languages are quite diverse with complex grammatical structures and idiomatic expressions. Additionally, the meaning of words and phrases can vary depending on the context in which they are used. NLP algorithms must be able to handle these complexities to achieve effective language processing.

Let's start by looking at some of the terminology that is used when discussing NLP.

Understanding NLP terminology

NLP is a vast field of study. In this section, we will investigate some of the basic terminology related to NLP:

- **Corpus**: A corpus is a large and structured collection of text or speech data that serves as a resource for NLP algorithms. It can consist of various types of textual data, such as written text, spoken language, transcribed conversations, and social media posts. A corpus is created by intentionally gathering and organizing data from various online and offline sources, including the internet. While the internet can be a rich source for acquiring data, deciding what data to include in a corpus requires a purposeful selection and alignment with the goals of the particular study or analysis being conducted.

  Corpora, the plural of corpus, can be annotated, meaning they may contain extra details about the texts, such as part-of-speech tags and named entities. These annotated corpora offer specific information that enhances the training and evaluation of NLP algorithms, making them especially valuable resources in the field.

- **Normalization:** This process involves converting text into a standard form, such as converting all characters to lowercase or removing punctuation, making it more amenable to analysis.

- **Tokenization:** Tokenization breaks down text into smaller parts called tokens, usually words or subwords, enabling a more structured analysis.

- **Named Entity Recognition (NER):** NER identifies and classifies named entities within the text, such as people's names, locations, organizations, etc.

- **Stop words:** These are commonly used words such as *and*, *the*, and *is*, which are often filtered out during text processing as they may not contribute significant meaning.

- **Stemming and lemmatization:** Stemming involves reducing words to their root form, while lemmatization involves converting words to their base or dictionary form. Both techniques help in analyzing the core meaning of words.

Next, let us study different text preprocessing techniques used in NLP:

- **Word embeddings:** This is a method used to translate words into numerical form, where each word is represented as a vector in a space that may have many dimensions. In this context, a "high-dimensional vector" refers to an array of numbers where the number of dimensions, or individual components, is quite large—often in the hundreds or even thousands. The idea behind using high-dimensional vectors is to capture the complex relationships between words, allowing words with similar meanings to be positioned closer together in this multi-dimensional space. The more dimensions the vector has, the more nuanced the relationships it can capture. Therefore, in word embeddings, semantically related words end up being closer to each other in this high-dimensional space, making it easier for algorithms to understand and process language in a way that reflects human understanding.

- **Language modeling:** Language modeling is the process of developing statistical models that can predict or generate sequences of words or characters based on the patterns and structures found in a given text corpus.

- **Machine translation:** The process of automatically translating text from one language to another using NLP techniques and models.

- **Sentiment analysis:** The process of determining the attitude or sentiment expressed in a piece of text, often by analyzing the words and phrases used and their context.

Text preprocessing in NLP

Text preprocessing is a vital stage in NLP, where raw text data undergoes a transformation to become suitable for machine learning algorithms. This transformation involves converting the unorganized and often messy text into what is known as a "structured format." A structured format means that the data is organized into a more systematic and predictable pattern, often involving techniques like tokenization, stemming, and removing unwanted characters. These steps help in cleaning the text, reducing irrelevant information or "noise," and arranging the data in a manner that makes it easier for the machine learning models to understand. By following this approach, the raw text, which may contain inconsistencies and irregularities, is molded into a form that enhances the accuracy, performance, and efficiency of subsequent NLP tasks. In this section, we will explore various techniques used in text preprocessing to achieve this structured format.

Tokenization

As a reminder, tokenization is the crucial process of dividing text into smaller units, known as tokens. These tokens can be as small as individual words or even subwords. In NLP, tokenization is often considered the first step in preparing text data for further analysis. The reason for this foundational role lies in the very nature of language, where understanding and processing text requires breaking it down into manageable parts. By transforming a continuous stream of text into individual tokens, we create a structured format that mirrors the way humans naturally read and understand language. This structuring provides the machine learning models with a clear and systematic way to analyze the text, allowing them to recognize patterns and relationships within the data. As we delve deeper into NLP techniques, this tokenized format becomes the basis upon which many other preprocessing and analysis steps are built.

The following code snippet is tokenizing the given text using the **Natural Language Toolkit** (nltk) library in Python. The nltk is a widely used library in Python, specifically designed for working with human language data. It provides easy-to-use interfaces and tools for tasks such as classification, tokenization, stemming, tagging, parsing, and more, making it a valuable asset for NLP. For those who wish to leverage these capabilities in their Python projects, the nltk library can be downloaded and installed directly from the **Python Package Index** (PyPI) by using the command pip install nltk. By incorporating the nltk library into your code, you can access a rich set of functions and resources that streamline the development and execution of various NLP tasks, making it a popular choice among researchers, educators, and developers in the field of computational linguistics. Let us start by importing relevant functions and using them:

```
from nltk.tokenize import word_tokenize
```

```
corpus = 'This is a book about algorithms.'

tokens = word_tokenize(corpus)
print(tokens)
```

The output will be a list that looks like this:

```
['This', 'is', 'a', 'book', 'about', 'algorithms', '.']
```

In this example, each token is a word. The granularity of the resulting tokens will vary based on the objective—for example, each token can consist of a word, a sentence, or a paragraph.

To tokenize text based on sentences, you can use the sent_tokenize function from the nltk. tokenize module:

```
from nltk.tokenize import sent_tokenize
corpus = 'This is a book about algorithms. It covers various topics in depth.'
```

In this example, the corpus variable contains two sentences. The sent_tokenize function takes the corpus as input and returns a list of sentences. When you run the modified code, you will get the following output:

```
sentences = sent_tokenize(corpus)
print(sentences)
```

```
['This is a book about algorithms.', 'It covers various topics in depth.']
```

Sometimes we may need to break down large texts into paragraph-level chunks. nltk can help with that task. It's a feature that could be particularly useful in applications such as document summarization, where understanding the structure at the paragraph level may be crucial. To-kenizing text into paragraphs might seem straightforward, but it can be complex depending on the structure and format of the text. A simple approach is to split the text into two newline characters, which often separate paragraphs in plain text documents.

Here's a basic example:

```
def tokenize_paragraphs(text):
    # Split by two newline characters
```

```
paragraphs = text.split('\n\n')
return [p.strip() for p in paragraphs if p]
```

Next, let us look into how we can clean the data.

Cleaning data

Cleaning data is an essential step in NLP, as raw text data often contains noise and irrelevant information that can hinder the performance of NLP models. The goal of cleaning data for NLP is to preprocess the text data to remove noise and irrelevant information, and to transform it into a format that is suitable for analysis using NLP techniques. Note that data cleaning is done after it is tokenized. The reason is that cleaning might involve operations that depend on the structure revealed by tokenization. For instance, removing specific words or altering word forms might be done more accurately after the text is tokenized into individual terms.

Let us study some techniques used to clean data and prepare it for machine learning tasks:

Case conversion

Case conversion is a technique in NLP where text is transformed from one case format to another, such as from uppercase to lowercase, or from title case to uppercase.

For example, the text "Natural Language Processing" in title case could be converted to lowercase to be "natural language processing."

This simple yet effective step helps in standardizing the text, which in turn simplifies its processing for various NLP algorithms. By ensuring that the text is in a uniform case, it aids in eliminating inconsistencies that might otherwise arise from variations in capitalization.

Punctuation removal

Punctuation removal in NLP refers to the process of removing punctuation marks from raw text data before analysis. Punctuation marks are symbols such as periods (.), commas (,), question marks (?), and exclamation marks (!) that are used in written language to indicate pauses, emphasis, or intonation. While they are essential in written language, they can add noise and complexity to raw text data, which can hinder the performance of NLP models.

It's a reasonable concern to wonder how the removal of punctuation might affect the meaning of sentences. Consider the following examples:

```
"She's a cat."
```

```
"She's a cat??"
```

Without punctuation, both lines become "She's a cat," potentially losing the distinct emphasis conveyed by the question marks.

However, it's worth noting that in many NLP tasks, such as topic classification or sentiment analysis, punctuation might not significantly impact the overall understanding. Additionally, models can rely on other cues from the text's structure, content, or context to derive meaning. In cases where the nuances of punctuation are critical, specialized models and preprocessing techniques may be employed to retain the required information.

Handling numbers in NLP

Numbers within text data can pose challenges in NLP. Here's a look at two main strategies for handling numbers in text analysis, considering both the traditional approach of removal and an alternative option of standardization.

In some NLP tasks, numbers may be considered noise, particularly when the focus is on aspects like word frequency or sentiment analysis. Here's why some analysts might choose to remove numbers:

- **Lack of relevance**: Numeric characters may not carry significant meaning in specific text analysis scenarios.
- **Skewing frequency counts**: Numbers can distort word frequency counts, especially in models like topic modeling.
- **Reducing complexity**: Removing numbers may simplify the text data, potentially enhancing the performance of NLP models.

However, an alternative approach is to convert all numbers to a standard representation rather than discarding them. This method acknowledges that numbers can carry essential information and ensures that their value is retained in a consistent format. It can be particularly useful in contexts where numerical data plays a vital role in the meaning of the text.

Deciding whether to remove or retain numbers requires an understanding of the problem being solved. An algorithm may need customization to distinguish whether a number is significant based on the context of the text and the specific NLP task. Analyzing the role of numbers within the domain of the text and the goals of the analysis can guide this decision-making process.

Handling numbers in NLP is not a one-size-fits-all approach. Whether to remove, standardize, or carefully analyze numbers depends on the unique requirements of the task at hand. Understanding these options and their implications helps in making informed decisions that align with the goals of the text analysis.

White space removal

White space removal in NLP refers to the process of removing unnecessary white spaces, such as multiple spaces and tab characters. White space in the context of text data is not merely the space between words but includes other "invisible" characters that create spacing within text. In NLP, white space removal refers to the process of eliminating these unnecessary white space characters. Removing unnecessary white spaces can reduce the size of the text data and make it easier to process and analyze.

Here's a simple example to illustrate white space removal:

- Input text: `"The quick brown fox \tjumps over the lazy dog."`
- Processed text: `"The quick brown fox jumps over the lazy dog."`

In the above example, extra spaces and a tab character (denoted by \t) are removed to create a cleaner and more standardized text string.

Stop word removal

Stop word removal is the process of eliminating common words, known as stop words, from a text corpus. stop words are words that occur frequently in a language but do not carry significant meaning or contribute to the overall understanding of the text. Examples of stop words in English include *the*, *and*, *is*, *in* and *for*. Stop word removal helps reduce the dimensionality of the data and improve the efficiency of the algorithms. By removing words that don't contribute meaningfully to the analysis, computational resources can be focused on the words that do matter, improving the efficiency of various NLP algorithms.

Note that stop word removal is more than a mere reduction in text size; it's about focusing on the words that truly matter for the analysis at hand. While stop words play a vital role in language structure, their removal in NLP can enhance the efficiency and focus of the analysis, particularly in tasks like sentiment analysis where the primary concern is understanding the underlying emotion or opinion.

Stemming and lemmatization

In textual data, most words are likely to be present in slightly different forms. Reducing each word to its origin or stem in a family of words is called **stemming**. It is used to group words based on their similar meanings to reduce the total number of words that need to be analyzed. Essentially, stemming reduces the overall conditionality of the problem. The most common algorithm for stemming English is the Porter algorithm.

For example, let us look into a couple of examples:

- Example 1: {use, used, using, uses} => use
- Example 2: {easily, easier, easiest} => easi

It's important to note that stemming can sometimes result in misspelled words, as seen in example 2 where easi was produced.

Stemming is a simple and quick process, but it may not always produce correct results. For cases where correct spelling is required, lemmatization is a more appropriate method. Lemmatization considers the context and reduces words to their base form. The base form of a word, also known as the lemma, is its most simple and meaningful version. It represents the way a word would appear in the dictionary, devoid of any inflectional endings, which will be a correct English word, resulting in more accurate and meaningful word roots.

> The process of guiding algorithms to recognize similarities is a precise and thoughtful task. Unlike humans, algorithms need explicit rules and criteria to make connections that might seem obvious to us. Understanding this distinction and knowing how to provide the necessary guidance is a vital skill in the development and tuning of algorithms for various applications.

Cleaning data using Python

Let us look into how we can clean text using Python.

First, let's import the necessary libraries:

```python
import string
import re
import nltk
from nltk.corpus import stopwords
from nltk.stem import PorterStemmer

# Make sure to download the NLTK resources
nltk.download('punkt')
nltk.download('stopwords')
```

Next, here is the main function to perform text cleaning:

```python
def clean_text(text):
```

```
"""
Cleans input text by converting case, removing punctuation, numbers,
white spaces, stop words and stemming
"""
# Convert to lowercase
text = text.lower()


# Remove punctuation
text = text.translate(str.maketrans('', '', string.punctuation))


# Remove numbers
text = re.sub(r'\d+', '', text)


# Remove white spaces
text = text.strip()


# Remove stop words
stop_words = set(stopwords.words('english'))
tokens = nltk.word_tokenize(text)
filtered_text = [word for word in tokens if word not in stop_words]
text = ' '.join(filtered_text)


# Stemming
ps = PorterStemmer()
tokens = nltk.word_tokenize(text)
stemmed_text = [ps.stem(word) for word in tokens]
text = ' '.join(stemmed_text)


return text
```

Let us test the function `clean_text()`:

```
corpus="7- Today, Ottawa is becoming cold again "
clean_text(corpus)
```

The result will be:

```
today ottawa becom cold
```

Note the word becom in the output. As we are using stemming, not all the words in the output are expected to be correct English words.

All the preceding processing steps are typically needed; the actual processing steps depend on the problem that we want to solve. They will vary from use case to use case—for example, if the numbers in the text represent something that may have some value in the context of the problem that we are trying to solve, then we may not need to remove the numbers from the text in the normalization phase.

Once the data is cleaned, we need to store the results in a data structure tailored for this purpose. This data structure is called the **Term Document Matrix (TDM)** and is explained next.

Understanding the Term Document Matrix

A TDM is a mathematical structure used in NLP. It's a table that counts the frequency of terms (words) in a collection of documents. Each row represents a unique term, and each column represents a specific document. It's an essential tool for text analysis, where you can see how often each word occurs in various texts.

For documents containing the words cat and dog:

- Document 1: cat cat dog
- Document 2: dog dog cat

	Document 1	Document 2
cat	2	1
dog	1	2

This matrix structure allows the efficient storage, organization, and analysis of large text datasets. In Python, the CountVectorizer module from the sklearn library can be used to create a TDM as follows:

```python
from sklearn.feature_extraction.text import CountVectorizer

# Define a list of documents
documents = ["Machine Learning is useful", "Machine Learning is fun",
"Machine Learning is AI"]

# Create an instance of CountVectorizer
vectorizer = CountVectorizer()
```

```
# Fit and transform the documents into a TDM
tdm = vectorizer.fit_transform(documents)

# Print the TDM
print(tdm.toarray())
```

The output looks as follows:

```
[[0 0 1 1 1 1]
 [0 1 1 1 1 0]
 [1 0 1 1 1 0]]
```

Note that corresponding to each document, there is a row, and corresponding to each distinct word, there is a column. There are three documents and there are six distinct words, resulting in a matrix with dimensions 3x6.

In this matrix, the numbers represent the frequency with which each word (column) appears in the corresponding document (row). So, for example, if the number in the first row and first column is 1, this means that the first word appears once in the first document.

TDM uses the frequency of each term by default, which is a simple way to quantify the importance of each word in the context of each individual document. A more sophisticated way to quantify the importance of each word is TF-IDF, which is explained in the next section.

Using TF-IDF

Term Frequency-Inverse Document Frequency (TF-IDF) is a method used to calculate the significance of words in a document. It considers two main components to determine the weight of each term: the **Term Frequency (TF)** and the **Inverse Document Frequency (IDF)**. The TF looks at how often a word appears in a specific document, while the IDF examines how rare the word is across a collection of documents, known as a corpus. In the context of TF-IDF, the corpus refers to the entire set of documents that you are analyzing. If we are working with a collection of book reviews, for example, the corpus would include all the reviews:

- **TF**: TF measures the number of times a term appears in a document. It is calculated as the ratio of the number of occurrences of a term in a document to the total number of terms in the document. The more frequent the term, the higher its TF value.

- **IDF:** IDF measures the importance of a term across the entire corpus of documents. It is calculated as the logarithm of the ratio of the total number of documents in the corpus to the number of documents containing the term. The rarer the term across the corpus, the higher its IDF value.

To compute TF-IDF using Python, do the following:

```python
from sklearn.feature_extraction.text import TfidfVectorizer

# Define a list of documents
documents = ["Machine Learning enables learning", "Machine Learning is
fun", "Machine Learning is useful"]

# Create an instance of TfidfVectorizer
vectorizer = TfidfVectorizer()

# Fit and transform the documents into a TF-IDF matrix
tfidf_matrix = vectorizer.fit_transform(documents)

# Get the feature names
feature_names = vectorizer.get_feature_names_out()

# Loop over the feature names and print the TF-IDF score for each term
for i, term in enumerate(feature_names):
    tfidf = tfidf_matrix[:, i].toarray().flatten()
    print(f"{term}: {tfidf}")
```

This will print:

```
enables:   [0.60366655 0.         0.          ]
fun:       [0.         0.66283998 0.          ]
is:        [0.         0.50410689 0.50410689]
learning:  [0.71307037 0.39148397 0.39148397]
machine:   [0.35653519 0.39148397 0.39148397]
useful:    [0.         0.         0.66283998]
```

Each column in the output corresponds to a document, and the rows represent the TF-IDF values for the terms across the documents. For example, the term kids has a non-zero TF-IDF value only in the second document, which is in line with our expectations.

Summary and discussion of results

The TF-IDF method provides a valuable way to weigh the importance of terms within individual documents and across an entire corpus. The resulting TF-IDF values reveal the relevance of specific terms within each document, taking into account both their frequency in a given document and their rarity across the entire collection. In the provided example, the varying TF-IDF scores for different terms demonstrate the model's ability to distinguish words that are unique to specific documents from those that are more commonly used. This ability can be leveraged in various applications, such as text classification, information retrieval, and feature selection, to enhance the understanding and processing of text data.

Introduction to word embedding

One of the major advancements in NLP is our ability to create a meaningful numeric representation of words in the form of dense vectors. This technique is called word embedding. So, what exactly is a dense vector? Imagine you have a word like apple. In word embedding, apple might be represented as a series of numbers, such as [0.5, 0.8, 0.2], where each number is a coordinate in a continuous, multi-dimensional space. The term "dense" means that most or all of these numbers are non-zero, unlike sparse vectors where many elements might be zero. In simple terms, word embedding takes each word in a text and turns it into a unique, multi-dimensional point in space. This way, words with similar meanings will end up closer to each other in this space, allowing algorithms to understand the relationships between words. Yoshua Bengio first introduced the term in his paper *A Neural Probabilistic Language Model*. Each word in an NLP problem can be thought of as a categorical object.

In word embedding, try to establish the neighborhood of each word and use it to quantify its meaning and importance. The neighborhood of a word is the set of words that surround a particular word.

To truly grasp the concept of word embedding, let's look at a tangible example involving a vocabulary of four familiar fruits: apple, banana, orange, and pear. The goal here is to represent these words as dense vectors, numerical arrays where each number captures a specific characteristic or feature of the word.

Why represent words this way? In NLP, converting words into dense vectors enables algorithms to quantify the relationships between different words. Essentially, we're turning abstract language into something that is mathematically measurable.

Consider the features of sweetness, acidity, and juiciness for our fruit words. We could rate these features on a scale from 0 to 1 for each fruit, where 0 means the feature is entirely absent, and 1 means the feature is strongly present. This rating could look like this:

```
"apple": [0.5, 0.8, 0.2] - moderately sweet, quite acidic, not very juicy
"banana": [0.2, 0.3, 0.1] - not very sweet, moderately acidic, not juicy
"orange": [0.9, 0.6, 0.9] - very sweet, somewhat acidic, very juicy
"pear": [0.4, 0.1, 0.7] - moderately sweet, barely acidic, quite juicy
```

The numbers are subjective and can be derived from taste tests, expert opinions, or other methods, but they serve to transform the words into a format that an algorithm can understand and work with.

Visualizing this, you can imagine a 3D space where each axis represents one of the features (sweetness, acidity, or juiciness), and each fruit's vector places it at a specific point in this space. Words (fruits) with similar tastes would be closer to each other in this space.

So, why the choice of dense vectors with a length of 3? This is based on the specific features we have chosen to represent. In other applications, the vector length might be different, based on the number of features you want to capture.

This example illustrates how word embedding takes a word and turns it into a numerical vector that holds real-world meaning. It's a crucial step in enabling machines to "understand" and process human language.

Implementing word embedding with Word2Vec

Word2Vec is a prominent method used for obtaining vector representations of words, commonly referred to as word embeddings. Rather than "generating words," this algorithm creates numerical vectors that represent the semantic meaning of each word in the language.

The basic idea behind Word2Vec is to use a neural network to predict the context of each word in a given text corpus. The neural network is trained by inputting the word and its surrounding context words, and the network learns to output the probability distribution of the context words given the input word. The weights of the neural network are then used as the word embeddings, which can be used for various NLP tasks:

```
import gensim

# Define a text corpus
corpus = [['apple', 'banana', 'orange', 'pear'],
```

```
        ['car', 'bus', 'train', 'plane'],
        ['dog', 'cat', 'fox', 'fish']]

# Train a word2vec model on the corpus
model = gensim.models.Word2Vec(corpus, window=5, min_count=1, workers=4)
```

Let us break down the important parameters of `Word2Vec()` function:

- **sentences**: This is the input data for the model. It should be a collection of sentences, where each sentence is a list of words. Essentially, it's a list of lists of words that represents your entire text corpus.

- **size**: This defines the dimensionality of the word embeddings. In other words, it sets the number of features or numerical values in the vectors that represent the words. A typical value might be `100` or `300`, depending on the complexity of the vocabulary.

- **window**: This parameter sets the maximum distance between the target word and the context words used for prediction within a sentence. For example, if you set the window size to 5, the algorithm will consider the five words immediately before and after the target word in the training process.

- **min_count**: Words that appear infrequently in the corpus may be excluded from the model by setting this parameter. If you set `min_count` to 2, for example, any word that appears fewer than two times across all the sentences will be ignored during training.

- **workers**: This refers to the number of processing threads used during training. Increasing this value can speed up training on multi-core machines by enabling parallel processing.

Once the Word2Vec model is trained, one of the powerful ways to use it is to measure the similarity or "distance" between words in the embedding space. This similarity score can give us insight into how the model perceives relationships between different words. Now let us check the model by looking at the distance between car and train:

```
print(model.wv.similarity('car', 'train'))
```

```
-0.057745814
```

Now let's look into the similarity of car and apple:

```
print(model.wv.similarity('car', 'apple'))
```

```
0.11117952
```

Thus, the output gives us the similarity score between individual terms based on the word embeddings learned by the model.

Interpreting similarity scores

The following details help with interpreting similarity scores:

- **Very similar**: Scores close to 1 signify strong similarity. Words with this score often share contextual or semantic meanings.

- **Moderately similar**: Scores around 0.5 indicate some level of similarity, possibly due to shared attributes or themes.

- **Weak or no similarity**: Scores close to 0 or negative imply little to no similarity or even contrast in meanings.

Thus, these similarity scores provide quantitative insights into word relationships. By understanding these scores, you can better analyze the semantic structure of your text corpus and leverage it for various NLP tasks.

Word2Vec provides a powerful and efficient way to represent textual data in a way that captures semantic relationships between words, reduces dimensionality, and improves accuracy in downstream NLP tasks. Let us look into the advantages and disadvantages of Word2Vec.

Advantages and disadvantages of Word2Vec

The following are the advantages of using Word2Vec:

- **Capturing semantic relationships**: Word2Vec's embeddings are positioned in the vector space in such a way that semantically related words are located near each other. This spatial arrangement captures syntactic and semantic relationships like synonyms, analogies, and more, enabling better performance in tasks like information retrieval and semantic analysis.

- **Reducing dimensionality**: Traditional one-hot encoding of words can create a sparse and high-dimensional space, especially with large vocabularies. Word2Vec compresses this into a denser and lower-dimensional continuous vector space (typically ranging from 100 to 300 dimensions). This condensed representation preserves essential linguistic patterns while being computationally more efficient.

- **Handling out-of-vocabulary words**: Word2Vec can infer embeddings for words that didn't appear in the training corpus by leveraging the surrounding context words. This property aids in generalizing better to unseen or new text data, enhancing robustness.

Now let us look into some of the disadvantages of using Word2Vec:

- **Training complexity**: Word2Vec models can be computationally demanding to train, particularly with vast vocabularies and higher-dimensional vectors. They require significant computing resources and may necessitate optimization techniques, such as negative sampling or hierarchical softmax, to scale efficiently.

- **Lack of interpretability**: The continuous and dense nature of Word2Vec embeddings makes them challenging to interpret by humans. Unlike carefully crafted linguistic features, the dimensions in Word2Vec don't correspond to intuitive characteristics, making it difficult to understand what specific aspects of the words are being captured.

- **Sensitive to text preprocessing**: The quality and effectiveness of Word2Vec embeddings can vary significantly based on the preprocessing steps applied to the text data. Factors such as tokenization, stemming, and lemmatization, or the removal of stopwords, must be carefully considered. The choice of preprocessing can impact the spatial relationships within the vector space, potentially affecting the model's performance on downstream tasks.

Next, let us look into a case study about restaurant reviews that combines all the concepts presented in this chapter.

Case study: Restaurant review sentiment analysis

We will use the Yelp Reviews dataset, which contains labeled reviews as positive (5 stars) or negative (1 star). We will train a model that can classify the reviews of a restaurant as negative or positive.

Let's implement this processing pipeline by going through the following steps.

Importing required libraries and loading the dataset

First, we import the packages that we need:

```python
import numpy as np
import pandas as pd
import re
from nltk.stem import PorterStemmer
from nltk.corpus import stopwords
```

Then we import the dataset from a .csv file:

```
url = 'https://storage.googleapis.com/neurals/data/2023/Restaurant_
Reviews.tsv'
dataset = pd.read_csv(url, delimiter='\t', quoting=3)
dataset.head()
```

```
                                          Review      Liked
0                         Wow... Loved this place.      1
1                            Crust is not good.        0
2             Not tasty and the texture was just nasty.   0
3        Stopped by during the late May bank holiday of...  1
4          The selection on the menu was great and so wer...  1
```

Building a clean corpus: Preprocessing text data

Next, we clean the data by performing text preprocessing on each of the reviews of the dataset using stemming and stopword removal techniques:

```
def clean_text(text):
    text = re.sub('[^a-zA-Z]', ' ', text)
    text = text.lower()
    text = text.split()
    ps = PorterStemmer()
    text = [
        ps.stem(word) for word in text
        if not word in set(stopwords.words('english'))]
    text = ' '.join(text)
    return text


corpus = [clean_text(review) for review in dataset['Review']]
```

The code iterates through each review in the dataset (in this case, the 'Review' column) and applies the clean_text function to preprocess and clean each review. The code creates a new list called corpus. The result is a list of cleaned and preprocessed reviews stored in the corpus variable.

Converting text data into numerical features

Now let's define the features (represented by y) and the label (represented by X). Remember that **features** are the independent variables or attributes that describe the characteristics of the data, used as input for predictions.

And **labels** are the dependent variables or target values that the model is trained to predict, representing the outcomes corresponding to the features:

```
vectorizer = CountVectorizer(max_features=1500)
X = vectorizer.fit_transform(corpus).toarray()
y = dataset.iloc[:, 1].values
```

Let's divide the data into testing and training data:

```
X_train, X_test, y_train, y_test = train_test_split(X, y, test_size=0.20,
random_state=0)
```

To train the model, we are using the Naive Bayes algorithm that we studied in *Chapter 7*:

```
classifier = GaussianNB()
classifier.fit(X_train, y_train)
```

Let's predict the test set results:

```
y_pred = classifier.predict(X_test)
```

Next, let us print the confusion matrix. Remember that the confusion matrix is a table that helps visualize the performance of the classification model:

```
cm = confusion_matrix(y_test, y_pred)
print(cm)
```

```
[[55 42]
 [12 91]]
```

Looking at the confusion matrix, we can estimate the misclassification.

Analyzing the results

The confusion matrix gives us a glimpse into the misclassifications made by our model. In this context, there are:

- 55 true positives (correctly predicted positive reviews)
- 42 false positives (incorrectly predicted positive reviews)
- 12 false negatives (incorrectly predicted negative reviews)
- 91 true negatives (correctly predicted negative reviews)

The 55 true positives and 91 true negatives show that our model has a reasonable ability to distinguish between positive and negative reviews. However, the 42 false positives and 12 false negatives highlight areas for potential improvement.

In the context of restaurant reviews, understanding these numbers helps business owners and customers alike gauge the general sentiment. A high rate of true positives and true negatives indicates that the model can be trusted to give an accurate sentiment overview. This information could be invaluable for restaurants aiming to improve service or for potential customers seeking honest reviews. On the other hand, the presence of false positives and negatives suggests areas where the model might need fine-tuning to avoid misclassification and provide more accurate insights.

Applications of NLP

The continued advancement of NLP technology has revolutionized the way we interact with computers and other digital devices. It has made significant progress in recent years, with impressive achievements in many tasks, including:

- **Topic identification**: To discover topics in a text repository and then classify the documents in the repository according to the topics discovered.

- **Sentiment analysis**: To classify the text according to the positive or negative sentiments that it contains.

- **Machine translation**: To translate between different languages.

- **Text to speech**: To convert spoken words into text.

- **Question answering**: This is a process of understanding and responding to a query using the information that is available. It involves intelligently interpreting the question and providing a relevant answer based on the existing knowledge or data.

- **Entity recognition**: To identify entities (such as a person, place, or thing) from text.

- **Fake news detection**: To flag fake news based on the content.

Summary

The chapter discussed the basic terminology related to NLP, such as corpus, word embeddings, language modeling, machine translation, and sentiment analysis. In addition, the chapter covered various text preprocessing techniques that are essential in NLP, including tokenization, which involves breaking down text into smaller units called tokens, and other techniques such as stemming and stop word removal.

The chapter also discussed word embeddings and then presented a use case on restaurant review sentiment analysis. Now, readers should have a better understanding of the fundamental techniques used in NLP and their potential applications to real-world problems.

In the next chapter, we will look at training neural networks for sequential data. We will also investigate how the use of deep learning can further improve NLP techniques and the methodologies discussed in this chapter.

Learn more on Discord

To join the Discord community for this book – where you can share feedback, ask questions to the author, and learn about new releases – follow the QR code below:

`https://packt.link/WHLel`

10

Understanding Sequential Models

A sequence works in a way a collection never can.

—*George Murray*

This chapter covers an important class of machine learning models, the sequential models. A defining characteristic of such models is that the processing layers are arranged in such a way that the output of one layer is the input to the other. This architecture makes them perfect to process sequential data. Sequential data is the type of data that consists of ordered series of elements such as a sentence in a document or a time series of stock market prices.

In this chapter, we will start with understanding the characteristics of sequential data. Then, we will present the working of RNNs and how they can be used to process sequential data. Next, we will learn how we can address the limitations of RNN through GRU without scarifying accuracy. Then, we will discuss the architecture of LSTM. Finally, we will compare different sequential modeling architectures with a recommendation on when to use which one.

In this chapter, we will go through the following concepts:

- Understanding sequential data
- How RNNs can process sequential data

- Addressing the limitations of RNNs through GRUs
- Understanding LSTM

Let us start by first looking into the characteristics of sequential data.

Understanding sequential data

Sequential data is a specific type of data structure where the order of the elements matters, and each element has a relational dependency on its predecessors. This "sequential behavior" is distinct because it conveys information not just in the individual elements but also in the pattern or sequence in which they occur. In sequential data, the current observation is not only influenced by external factors but also by previous observations in the sequence. This dependency forms the core characteristic of sequential data.

Understanding the different types of sequential data is essential to appreciate its broad applications. Here are the primary categories:

- **Time series data:** This is a series of data points indexed or listed in time order. The value at any point in time is dependent on the past values. Time series data is widely used in various fields, including economics, finance, and healthcare.
- **Textual data:** Text data is also sequential in nature, where the order of words, sentences, or paragraphs can convey meaning. **Natural language processing (NLP)** leverages this sequential property to analyze and interpret human languages.
- **Spatial-temporal data:** This involves data that captures both spatial and temporal relationships, such as weather patterns or traffic flow over time in a specific geographical area.

Here's how these types of sequential data manifest in real-world scenarios:

- **Time series data:** This type of data is clearly illustrated through financial market trends, where stock prices constantly vary in response to ongoing market dynamics. Similarly, sociological studies might analyze birth rates, reflecting year-to-year changes influenced by factors like economic conditions and social policies.
- **Textual data:** The sequential nature of text is paramount in literary and journalistic works. In novels, news articles, or essays, the specific ordering of words, sentences, and paragraphs constructs narratives and arguments, giving the text meaning beyond individual words.

- **Spatial-temporal data:** Areas in which this data type is vital are urban development and environmental studies. For instance, housing prices across different regions might be tracked over time to identify economic trends, while meteorological studies might monitor weather changes at specific geographical locations to forecast patterns and natural events.

These real-world examples demonstrate how the inherent sequential behavior in different types of data can be leveraged to provide insights and drive decisions across various domains.

In deep learning, handling sequential data requires specialized neural network architectures like sequential models. These models are designed to capture and exploit the temporal dependencies that inherently exist among the elements of sequential data. By recognizing these dependencies, sequential models provide a robust framework for creating more nuanced and effective machine learning models.

In summary, sequential data is a rich and complex type of data that finds applications across diverse domains. Recognizing its sequential nature, understanding its types, and leveraging specialized models enable data scientists to draw deeper insights and build more powerful predictive tools. Before we study the technical details, let us start by looking at the history of sequential modeling techniques.

Let us study different types of sequential models.

Types of sequence models

Sequential models are classified into various categories by examining the kind of data they handle, both in terms of input and output. This classification takes into account the specific nature of the data being used (like textual information, numerical data, or time-based patterns), and also how this data evolves or transforms from the beginning of the process to the end. By delving into these characteristics, we can identify three principal types of sequence models.

One-to-many

In one-to-many sequence models, a singular event or input can initiate the generation of an entire sequence. This unique attribute opens doors to a wide range of applications, but it also leads to complexities in training and implementation. The one-to-many sequence models offer exciting opportunities but come with inherent complexities in training and execution. As generative AI continues to advance, these models are likely to play a pivotal role in shaping creative and customized solutions across various domains.

The key to harnessing their potential lies in understanding their capabilities and recognizing the intricacies of training and implementation. The one-to-many sequence model is shown in *Figure 10.1*:

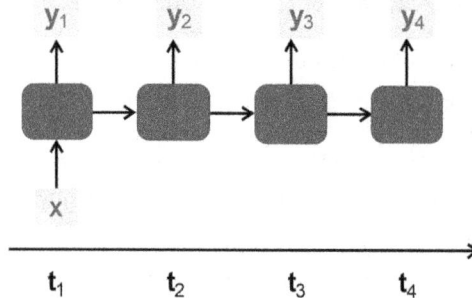

Figure 10.1: One-to-many sequential model

Let's delve into the characteristics, capabilities, and challenges of one-to-many models:

- **Wide range of applications**: The ability to translate a single input into a meaningful sequence makes one-to-many models versatile and powerful. They can be employed to write poetry, create art such as drawings and paintings, and even craft personalized cover letters for job applications.

- **Part of generative AI**: These models fall under the umbrella of generative AI, a burgeoning field that aims to create new content that is both coherent and contextually relevant. This is what allows them to perform such varied tasks as mentioned above.

- **Intensive training process**: Training one-to-many models is typically more time-consuming and computationally expensive compared to other sequence models. The reason for this lies in the complexity of translating a single input into a wide array of potential outputs. The model must learn not only the relationship between the input and the output but also the intricate patterns and structures inherent in the generated sequence.

Note that unlike one-to-one models, where a single input corresponds to a single output, or many-to-many models, where a sequence of inputs is mapped to a sequence of outputs, the one-to-many paradigm must learn to extrapolate a rich and structured sequence from a singular starting point. This requires a deeper understanding of the underlying patterns and can often necessitate more sophisticated training algorithms.

The one-to-many approach isn't without its challenges. Ensuring that the generated sequence maintains coherence, relevance, and creativity requires careful design and fine-tuning. It often demands a more extensive dataset and expert knowledge in the specific domain to guide the model's training.

Many-to-one

Many-to-one sequential models are specialized tools in data analysis that take a sequence of inputs and convert them into a single output. This process of synthesizing multiple inputs into one concise output forms the core of the many-to-one model, allowing it to distill the essential characteristics of the data.

These models have diverse applications, such as in sentiment analysis, where a sequence of words like a review or a post is analyzed to determine an overall sentiment such as positive, negative, or neutral. The many-to-one sequential model is shown in *Figure 10.2*:

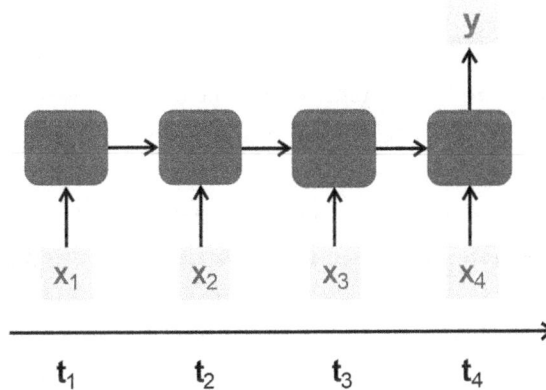

Figure 10.2: Many-to-one sequential model

The training process of many-to-one models is a complex yet integral part of their functionality. It distinguishes them from one-to-many models, whose focus is on creating a sequence from a single input. In contrast, many-to-one models must efficiently compress information, demanding careful selection of algorithms and precise tuning of parameters.

Training a many-to-one model involves teaching it to identify the vital features of the input sequence and to represent them accurately in the output. This involves discarding irrelevant information, a task that requires intricate balancing. The training process also often necessitates specialized pre-processing and feature engineering, tailored to the specific nature of the input data.

As discussed in the prior subsection, the training of many-to-one models may be more challenging than other types, requiring a deeper understanding of the underlying relationships in the data. Continuous monitoring of the model's performance during training, along with a methodical selection of data and hyperparameters, is essential for the success of the model.

Many-to-one models are noteworthy for their ability to simplify complex data into understandable insights, finding applications in various industries for tasks such as summarization, classification, and prediction. Although their design and training can be intricate, their unique ability to interpret sequential data provides inventive solutions to complex data analysis challenges.

Thus, many-to-one sequential models are vital instruments in contemporary data analysis, and understanding their particular training process is crucial for leveraging their capabilities fully. The training process, characterized by meticulous algorithm selection, parameter tuning, and domain expertise, sets these models apart. As the field progresses, many-to-one models will continue to offer valuable contributions to data interpretation and application.

Many-to-many

This is a type of sequential model that takes sequential data as the input, processes it in some way, and then generates sequential data as the output. An example of many-to-many models is machine translation, where a sequence of words in one language is translated into a corresponding sequence in another language. An illustrative example of this would be the translation of English text into French. While there are numerous machine translation models that fall into this category, a prominent approach is the use of **Sequence-to-Sequence (Seq2Seq)** models, particularly with STM networks. Seq2Seq models with LSTM have become a standard method for tasks such as English-to-French translation and have been implemented in various NLP frameworks and tools. The many-to-many sequential model is shown in *Figure 10.3*:

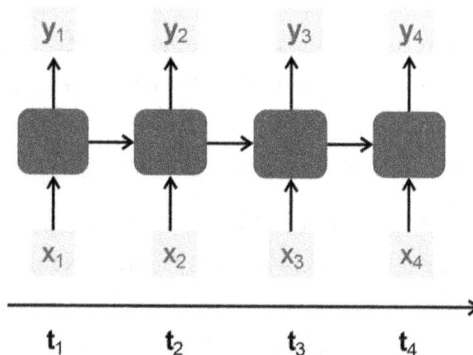

Figure 10.3: Many-to-many sequential model

Over the years, many algorithms have been developed to process and train machine learning models using sequential data. Let us start with studying how to represent sequential data with 3-dimensional data structures.

Data representation for sequential models

Timesteps add depth to the data, making it a 3D structure. In the context of sequential data, each "unit" or instance of this dimension is termed a "timestep." This is crucial to remember: while the dimension is called "timesteps," each individual data point in this dimension is a "timestep." *Figure 10.4* illustrates the three dimensions in data used for training RNNs, emphasizing the addition of timesteps:

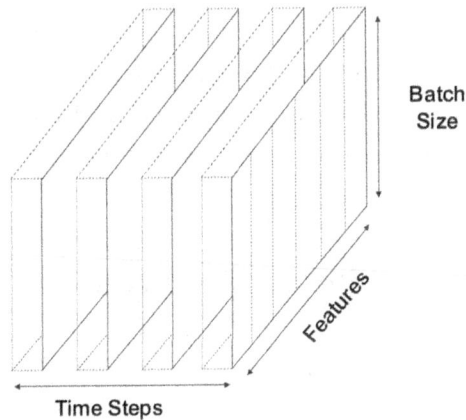

Figure 10.4: The 3D data structures used in RNN training

Given that the concept of timesteps is a new addition to our exploration, a special notation is introduced to represent it effectively. A superscript enclosing a timestep in angle brackets is paired with the variable in question. For example, using this notation, stock_price$^{<t1>}$ and stock_price$^{<t2>}$ represent the value of the variable stock_price at timestep *t1* and timestep *t2*, respectively.

The choice of dividing data into batches, essentially deciding the "length," can be both an intentional design decision and influenced by external tools and libraries. Often, machine learning frameworks provide utilities to automatically batch data, but choosing an optimal batch size can be a combination of experimentation and domain knowledge.

Let us start the discussion on sequential modeling techniques with RNNs first.

Introducing RNNs

RNNs, are a special breed of neural networks designed specifically for sequential data. Here's a breakdown of their key attributes.

The term "recurrent" stems from the unique feedback loop RNNs possess. Unlike traditional neural networks, which are essentially stateless and produce outputs solely based on the current inputs, RNNs carry forward a "state" from one step in the sequence to the next.

When we talk about a "run" in the context of RNNs, we're referring to a single pass or processing of an element in the sequence. So, as the RNN processes each element, or each "run," it retains some information from the previous steps.

The magic of RNNs lies in their ability to maintain a memory of previous runs or steps. They achieve this by incorporating an additional input, which is essentially the state or memory from the previous run. This mechanism allows RNNs to recognize and learn the dependencies between elements in a sequence, such as the relationships between consecutive words in a sentence.

Let us study the architecture of RNNs in detail.

Understanding the architecture of RNNs

First, let us define some variables:

- $x^{<t>}$: the input at timestep t
- $y^{<t>}$: actual output (ground truth) at timestep t
- $\hat{y}^{<t>}$: predicted output at timestep t

Understanding the memory cell and hidden state

RNNs stand out because of their inherent ability to remember and maintain context as they progress through different timesteps. This state at a certain timestep t is represented by $h^{<t>}$, where h stands for hidden. It is the summary of the information learned up to a particular timestep. As shown in *Figure 10.5*, the RNN keeps on learning by updating its hidden state at each timestep. The RNN uses this hidden state at each timestep to keep a context. At its core, "context" refers to the collective information or knowledge an RNN retains from previous timesteps. It allows RNNs to memorize the state at each timestep and pass this information to the next timestep as it progresses along through the sequence. This hidden state makes the RNN stateful:

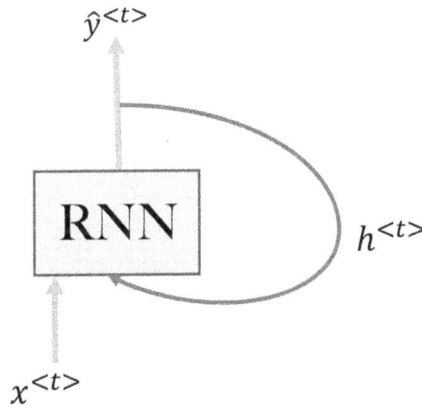

Figure 10.5: Hidden state in RNN

For example, if we use an RNN to translate a sentence from English to French, each input is a sentence that needs to be defined as sequential data. To get it right, the RNN cannot translate each word in isolation. It needs to capture the context of the words that have been translated so far, allowing the RNN to correctly translate the entire sentence. This is achieved through the hidden state that is calculated and stored at each timestep and passed on to the later ones.

> The RNN's strategy of memorizing the state with the intention of using it for future timesteps brings new research questions that need to be addressed. For example, *what* to remember and *what* to forget. And, perhaps the trickiest one, *when* to forget. The variants of RNN, like GRUs and LSTM, attempt to answer these questions in different ways.

Understanding the characteristics of the input variable

Let's get a deeper understanding of the input variable, $x^{<t>}$, and the methodology behind encoding it when working with RNNs. One of the pivotal applications for RNNs lies in the realm of NLP. Here, the sequential data we deal with comprises sentences. Think of each sentence as a sequence of words, such that a sentence can be delineated as:

$$\{x^{<1>}, x^{<2>} \ldots \ldots , x^{<T>}\}$$

In this representation, $x^{<t>}$ denotes an individual word within the sentence. To avoid confusion: each $x^{<n>}$ is not an entire sentence but rather an individual word within it.

Each word, $x^{<t>}$, is encoded using a one-hot vector. The length of this vector is defined by $|V|$, where:

- V signifies our vocabulary set, which is a collection of distinct words.
- $|V|$ quantifies the total number of entries in V.

In the context of widely-used applications, one could envision V as comprising the entire set of words found in a standard English dictionary, which may contain roughly 150,000 words. However, for specific NLP tasks, only a subset of this vast vocabulary is necessary.

Note: It's essential to differentiate between V and $|V|$. While V stands for the vocabulary itself, $|V|$ represents the size of this vocabulary.

When referring to the "dictionary," we're drawing from a general notion of standard English dictionaries. However, there are more exhaustive corpora available, like the Common Crawl, which can contain word sets stretching into the tens of millions.

For many applications, a subset of this vocabulary should be enough. Formally,

$$x^{<t>} \in R^{|V|}$$

To understand the working of RNNs, let us examine the first timestep, *t1*.

Training the RNN at the first timestep

RNNs operate by analyzing sequences one timestep at a time. Let's dive into the initial phase of this process. For the timestep *t1*, the network receives an input represented as $x^{<t1>}$. Based on this input, the RNN makes an initial prediction, which we denote as $\hat{y}^{<t1>}$. At every timestep, *tt*, the RNN leverages the hidden state from the previous timestep, $h^{<t-1>}$, to provide contextual information.

However, at *t1*, since we're just beginning, there's no prior hidden state to reference. Therefore, the hidden state $h^{<t0>}$ is initialized to zero.

The activation function in action

Referencing *Figure 10.6*, you'll notice an element marked by **A**. This represents the activation function, a crucial component in neural networks. Essentially, the activation function determines how much signal to pass onto the next layer. For this timestep, the activation function receives both the input $x^{<t1>}$ and the previous hidden state $h^{<t0>}$.

As discussed in *Chapter 8*, an activation function in neural networks is a mathematical equation that determines the output of a neuron based on its input. Its primary role is to introduce non-linearity into the network, enabling it to learn from errors and make adjustments, which is essential for learning complex patterns.

A recurring choice for the activation function in many neural networks is "tanh." But what's the reasoning behind this preference?

The world of neural networks isn't without its challenges, and one such obstacle is the vanishing gradient problem. To put it plainly, as we keep training our model, occasionally, the gradient values, which guide our weight adjustments, diminish to tiny numbers. This drop means the changes we make to our network's weights become almost negligible. Such minute tweaks result in an excruciatingly slow learning process, sometimes even coming to a standstill. Here's where the "tanh" function shines. It's chosen because it acts as a buffer against this vanishing gradient issue, steering the training process toward consistency and efficiency:

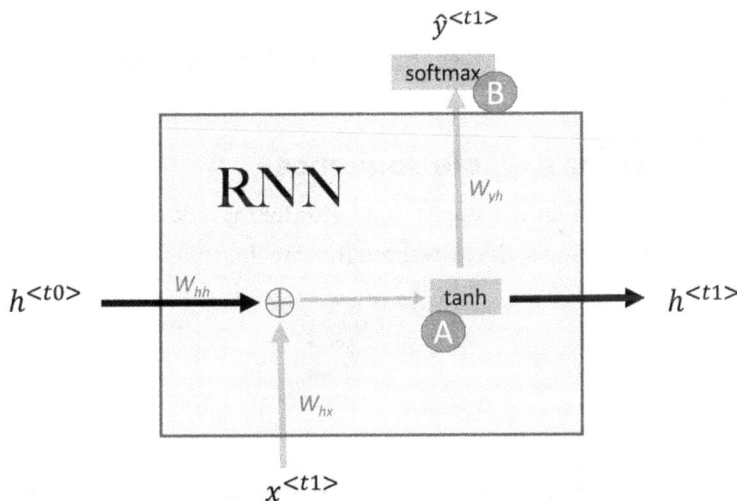

Figure 10.6: RNN training at timestep t1

As we zero in on the outcome of the activation function, we arrive at the value for the hidden state, $h^{<t1>}$. In mathematical terms, this relationship can be expressed as:

$$h^{<t1>} = \tanh(W_{hh}h^{<t0>} + W_{hx}x^{<t1>} + b_h) \qquad ...[Eq.\,10.1]$$

This hidden state is not just a passing phase. It holds value as we step into the next timestep, *t2*. Think of it as a relay racer passing on the baton, or in this case, context, from one timestep to its successor, ensuring continuity in the sequence.

The second activation function (represented by **B** in *Figure 10.7*) is used to generate the predicted output $\hat{y}^{<t1>}$ at timestep $t1$. The choice of this activation function will depend on the type of the output variable. For instance, if an RNN is employed to predict stock market prices, the ReLU function can be adopted as the output variable is continuous. On the other hand, if we are doing sentiment analysis on a bunch of posts, it can be a sigmoid activation function. In *Figure 10.7*, assuming that it is a multiclass output variable, we are using the softmax activation function. Remember that a multiclass output variable refers to a situation where the output or the prediction can fall into one of several distinct classes. In machine learning, this is common in classification problems where the aim is to categorize an input into one of several predefined categories. For example, if we are categorizing objects as a car, bike, or bus, the output variable has multiple classes, thus is termed as "multiclass." Mathematically, we can represent it as:

$$\hat{y}^{<t1>} = \text{softmax}(W_{yh}h^{<t1>} + b_y) \qquad ...[Eq.\,10.2]$$

From *Eq. 10.1* and *Eq. 10.2*, It should be obvious that the objective of training the RNN is to find the optimal values of three sets of weight matrices (W_{hx}, W_{hh}, and W_{yh}) and two sets of biases (b_h and b_y). As we progress, it becomes evident that these weights and biases maintain consistency across all timesteps.

Training the RNN for a whole sequence

Previously, we developed the mathematical formulation for the hidden state for the first timestep, $t1$. Let us now study the working of the RNN through more than one timestep to train a complete sequence, as shown in *Figure 10.7*:

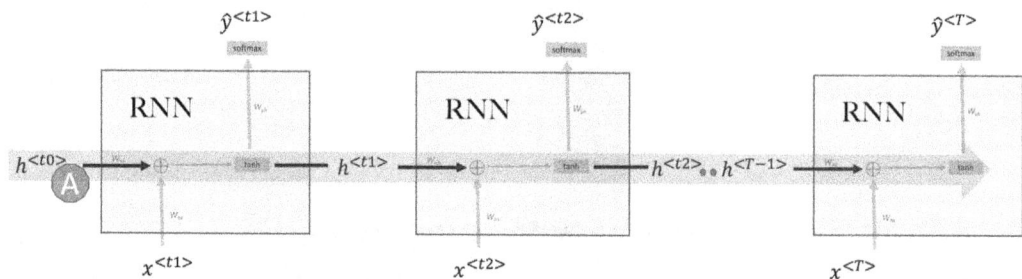

Figure 10.7: Sequential processing in RNN

> **Info:** In *Figure 10.7*, it can be observed that the hidden state travels from left to right carrying the context forward shown by the arrow **A**. The ability of RNNs and their variants to create this "information highway" propagating through time is the defining feature of RNNs.

We calculated *Eq. 10.1* for the timestep *t1*. For any timestep t, we can generalize *Eq. 10.1* as:

$$h^{<t>} = \tanh(W_{hh}h^{<t-1>} + W_{hx}x^{<t>} + b_h) \qquad ... [Eq. 10.3]$$

For NLP applications, $x^{<t>}$ is encoded as a one-hot vector. In this case, the dimension of $x^{<t>}$ will be equal to |V|, where V is the vector representing the vocabulary. The hidden variable $h^{<t>}$ will be a lower-dimensional representation of the original input, $x^{<t>}$. By lowering the dimension of the input variable $h^{<t1>}$ by many folds, we intend the hidden layer to capture only the important information of the input variable $x^{<t>}$. The dimension of $h^{<t>}$ is represented by D_h.

It is not unusual for $h^{<t>}$ to have dimensions 500 times lower than |V|.

So, typically:

$$D_h < \frac{|V|}{500}$$

Because of the lower dimensions of $h^{<t>}$, weight matrix W_{hh} is a comparatively small data structure as $W_{hh} \in R^{D_h \times D_h}$. W_{hx} on the other hand, will be as wide as $W_{hx} \in R^{D_h \times D_x}$.

Combining weight matrices

In *Eq. 10.3*, both W_{hh} and W_{hx} are used in the calculation of $h^{<t>}$. To simplify the analysis, it helps to combine W_{hh} and W_{hx} into one weight parameter matrix, W_h. This simplified representation will be quite useful for the discussion of more complex variants of RNNs that are discussed later in this chapter.

To create one combined weight matrix, W_h, we simply horizontally concatenate W_{hh} and W_{hx} horizontally to create a combined weight matrix, W_h:

$$W_h = [W_{hh} \mid W_{hx}]$$

As we are simply horizontally concatenating, the dimensions of the W_h will have the same number of rows and total number of columns, i.e.,

$$W_h \in R^{D_h \times (D_h + D_x)}$$

Using W_h in *Eq. 10.3*:

$$h^{<t>} = \tanh(W_h[h^{<t-1>}, x^{<t>}] + b_h) \qquad ... [Eq. 10.4]$$

Where $[h^{<t-1>}, x^{<t>}]$ indicates the vertical stacking of two vectors together.

$$[h^{<t-1>}, x^{<t>}] = \begin{bmatrix} h_T^{<t-1>} \\ x_T^{<t>} \end{bmatrix}$$

Where $h_T^{<t-1>}$ and $x_T^{<t>}$ are the respective transposed vectors.

Let us look at a specific example.

Let us assume that we are using RNNs for an NLP application. The size of the vocabulary is 50,000 words. It means that each input $x^{<t>}$ will be encoded as a hot vector having a dimension of 50,000. Let assume that $h^{<t>}$ has a dimension of 50. It will be the lower-dimension representation of $x^{<t>}$.

Now, it should be obvious that W_{hh} will have dimensions of (50×50). W_{hx} will have dimensions of (50×50,000).

Going back to the above example, W_h will have dimensions of (50x50,000+50) = 50×50,050, i.e.,:

$$W_h \in R^{(50 \, x \, 50,050)}$$

Calculating the output for each timestep

In our model, the output generated for a given timestep, such as *t1*, is denoted by $\hat{y}^{<t1>}$. Since we are employing the softmax function for normalization in our model, the output for any timestep, *tt*, can be generalized using the following equation:

$$\hat{y}^{<t>} = \text{softmax}(W_{yh}h^{<t>} + b_y) \qquad \text{... [Eq. 10.5]}$$

Understanding how the output is calculated at each timestep lays the foundation for the subsequent stage of training, where we need to evaluate how well the model is performing.

Now that we have a grasp of how the outputs are generated at each timestep, it becomes essential to determine the discrepancy between these predicted outputs and the actual target values. This discrepancy, referred to as "loss," gives us a measure of the model's error. In the next section, we will delve into the methods of computing RNN loss, allowing us to gauge the model's accuracy and make necessary adjustments to the weights and biases. This process is vital in training the model to make more accurate predictions, thereby enhancing its overall performance.

Computing RNN loss

As mentioned, the objective of training RNNs is to find the right values of three sets of weights (W_{hx}, W_{hh}, and W_{yh}) and two sets of biases (b_h and b_y). Initially, at timestep *t1*, these values are initialized randomly.

As the training process progresses, these values are changed as the gradient descent algorithm kicks in. We need to compute loss at each timestep of the forward propagation in RNNs. Let us break down the process of computing the loss:

1. **Compute loss for individual timestep:**

   At timestep *t1*, the predicted output is $\hat{y}^{<t1>}$. The expected output is $y^{<t1>}$. The actual loss function used will depend on the type of model we are training. For example, if we are training a classifier, then this loss at timestep *t1* will be:

$$\text{Loss}^{<t1>} = - \sum_i y_i \log{(\hat{y}_i)}^{<t1>}$$

2. **Aggregate loss for complete sequence:**

   For a complete sequence consisting of multiple timesteps, we will compute the individual losses for each of the timesteps, $\{t_1, t_2, \dots t_T\}$. The loss for one sequence with T timesteps will be the aggregate of the loss of each timestep, as calculated by the following equation:

$$\text{Loss} = \text{aggregate}\ (\text{loss}^{<t1>}, \text{loss}^{<t2>}, \dots \dots \dots, \text{loss}^{<T>}$$

3. **Compute loss for multiple sequences in a batch:**

   If there is more than one sequence in the batch, then, first, the loss is calculated for each individual sequence. We then compute the cost across all the sequences in a particular batch and use it for backpropagation.

By calculating the loss in this structured manner, we guide the model in adjusting its weights and biases to better align with the desired output. This iterative process, repeated over many batches and epochs, allows the model to learn from the data and make more accurate predictions.

Backpropagation through time

Backpropagation, as explained in *Chapter 8*, is used in neural networks to progressively learn from the examples of training datasets. RNNs add another dimension to the training data, that is, the timesteps. **Backpropagation through time (BPTT)** is designed to handle the sequential data as the training process is going through the timesteps.

Backpropagation is triggered when the forward feed process calculates the loss of the last timestep of a batch. We then apply this derivative to adjust the weights and biases for the RNN model. RNNs have three sets of weights, W_{hh}, W_{hx} and W_{hy}, and two sets of biases (b_h and b_y). Once the weights and biases are adjusted, we will continue with gradient descent for model training.

The name of this section, *Backpropagation through time*, does not hint toward any time machine that takes us back to some medieval era. Instead, it stems from the fact that once the cost has been calculated through forward-feed, it needs to run backward through each of the timesteps and update weights and biases.

The backpropagation process is crucial for tuning the model's parameters, but once the model is trained, what's next? After we've used backpropagation to minimize the loss, we have a model that's ready to make predictions. In the next section, we'll explore how to use the trained RNN model to make predictions on new data. We'll find that predicting with RNNs is similar to the process used with fully connected neural networks, where the input data is processed by the trained RNN to produce the predictions. This shift from training to prediction forms a natural progression in understanding how RNNs can be applied to real-world problems.

Predicting with RNNs

Once the model is trained, predicting with RNNs is similar to with fully connected neural networks. The input data is given as input to the trained RNN model and predictions are obtained. Here's how it functions:

1. **Input preparation:** Just like in a standard neural network, you begin by preparing the input data. In the case of an RNN, this input data is typically sequential, representing timesteps in a process or series.

2. **Model utilization:** You then feed this input data into the trained RNN model. The model's learned weights and biases, optimized during the training phase, are used to process the input through each layer of the network. In an RNN, this includes passing the data through the recurrent connections that handle the sequential aspects of the data.

3. **Activation functions:** As in other neural networks, activation functions within the RNN transform the data as it moves through the layers. Depending on the specific design of the RNN, different activation functions might be used at different stages.

4. **Generating predictions:** The penultimate step is generating the predictions. The output of the RNN is processed through a final layer, often using a softmax activation function for classification tasks, to produce the final prediction for each input sequence.

5. **Interpretation:** The predictions are then interpreted based on the specific task at hand. This could be classifying a sequence of text, predicting the next value in a time series, or any other task that relies on sequential data.

Thus, predicting with an RNN follows a process similar to that of fully connected neural networks, with the main distinction being the handling of sequential data. The RNN's ability to capture temporal relationships within the data allows it to provide unique insights and predictions that other neural network architectures might struggle with.

Limitations of basic RNNs

Earlier in the chapter, we introduced basic RNNs. Sometimes we refer to basic RNNs as "plain vanilla" RNNs. This term refers to their fundamental, unadorned structure. While they serve as a solid introduction to recurrent neural networks, these basic RNNs do have notable limitations:

1. **Vanishing gradient problem**: This issue makes it challenging for the RNN to learn and retain long-term dependencies in the data.

2. **Inability to look ahead in the sequence**: Traditional RNNs process sequences from the beginning to the end, which limits their capability to understand the future context in a sequence.

Let us investigate them one by one.

Vanishing gradient problem

RNNs iteratively process the input data one timestep at a time. This means that as the input sequences become longer, RNNs find it hard to capture long-term dependencies. Long-term dependencies refer to relationships between elements in a sequence that are far apart from each other. Imagine analyzing a lengthy piece of text, such as a novel. If a character's actions in the first chapter influence events in the last chapter, that's a long-term dependency. The information from the beginning of the text has to be "remembered" all the way to the end for full understanding.

RNNs often struggle with such long-range connections. The hidden state mechanism of RNNs, designed to retain information from previous timesteps, can be too simplistic to capture these intricate relationships. As the distance between related elements grows, the RNN may lose track of the connection. There is not much intelligence on when and what to keep in memory and when and what to forget.

For many use cases in sequential data, only the most recent information is important. For example, consider a predictive text application trying to assist a person typing an email by suggesting the next word to type.

As we know, such functionality is now standard in modern word processors. If the user is typing:

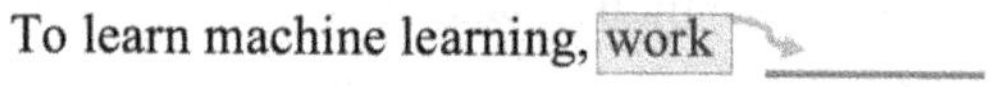

To learn machine learning, work

Figure 10.8: Predictive text example

the predictive text application can easily suggest the next word "hard". It does not need to bring the context from the prior sentences to predict the next word. For such applications, where long-term memory is not required, RNNs are the best choice. RNNs will not over-complicate the architecture without compromising on accuracy.

But for other applications, keeping the long-term dependencies is important. RNNs struggle with managing long-term dependencies. Let us look at an example:

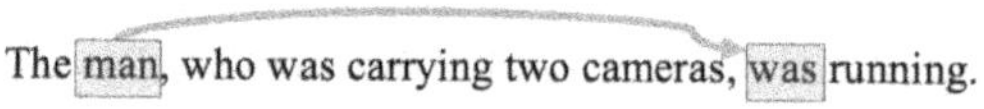

The man, who was carrying two cameras, was running.

Figure 10.9: Predictive text example with a long-term dependency

As we read this sentence from left to right, we can observe that "was" (used later in the sentence) is referring to the "man." RNNs in their original form will struggle to carry the hidden state forward for multiple timesteps. The reason is that, in RNNs, the hidden state is calculated for each timestep and carried forward.

Due to the recursive nature of this operation, we are always concerned about the signal prematurely fading while progressing from element to element in different timesteps. This behavior of RNNs is identified as the vanishing gradient problem. To combat this vanishing gradient problem, we prefer to choose tanh as the activation function. As the second derivative of tanh decays very slowly to zero, the choice of tanh helps manage the vanishing gradient problem to some extent. But we need more sophisticated architecture, like GRUs and LSTM, to better manage the vanishing gradient problem, which we will discuss in the next section.

Inability to look ahead in the sequence

RNNs can be categorized based on the direction of information flow through the sequence. The two primary types are unidirectional RNNs and bidirectional RNNs.

- **Unidirectional RNNs:** These networks process the input data in one direction, usually from the beginning of the sequence to the end. They carry the context forward, building understanding step by step as they iterate through the elements of a sequence, such as words in a sentence. Here's the limitation: unidirectional RNNs cannot "look ahead" in the sequence.

They only have access to the information they've seen so far, meaning they can't incorporate future elements to build a more accurate or nuanced context. Imagine reading a complex sentence one word at a time, without being able to glance ahead and see what's coming. You might miss subtleties or misunderstand the overall meaning.

- **Bidirectional RNNs:** In contrast, bidirectional RNNs process the sequence in both directions simultaneously. They combine insights from both the past and the future elements, allowing for a richer understanding of the context.

Let us consider the following two sentences:

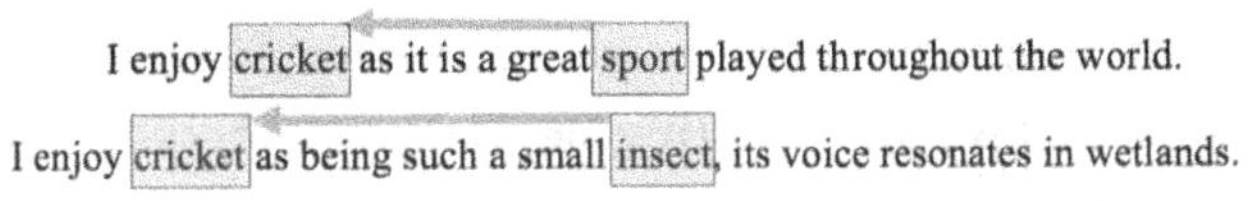

I enjoy cricket as it is a great sport played throughout the world.
I enjoy cricket as being such a small insect, its voice resonates in wetlands.

Figure 10.10: Examples where an RNN must look ahead in the sentence

Both of these sentences use the word "cricket." If the context is built only from left to right, as done in unidirectional RNNs, we cannot contextualize "cricket" properly as its relevant information will be in a future timestep. To solve this problem, we will look into bidirectional RNNs, which are discussed in *Chapter 11.11*

Now let us study GRUs and their detailed working and architecture.

GRU

GRUs represent an evolution of the basic RNN structure, specifically designed to address some of the challenges encountered with traditional RNNs, such as the vanishing gradient problem. The architecture of a GRU is illustrated in *Figure 10.8*:

y<t>
softmax
C
h<t-1>
h<t>
GRU
Γu
h̃<t>
A
B
tanh
update gate
x<t>

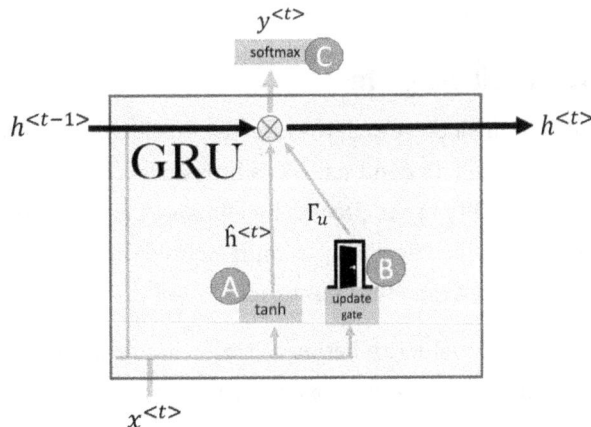

Figure 10.11: GRU

Let us start discussing GRU with the first activation function, annotated as **A**. At each timestep t, GRU first calculates the hidden state using the tanh activation function and utilizing $x^{<t>}$ and $h^{<t-1>}$ as inputs. The calculation is no different than how the hidden state is determined in the original RNNs presented in the previous section. But there is an important difference. The output is a *candidate* hidden state, which is calculated using *Eq. 10.6*:

$$\hat{h}^{<t>} = \tanh \left(W_h \left[h^{<t-1>}, x^{<t>} \right] + b_h \right) \quad \text{... [Eq. 10.6]}$$

where $\hat{h}^{<t>}$ is the candidate value of the hidden layer.

Now, instead of using the candidate hidden state straight away, the GRU takes a moment to decide whether to use it. Imagine it like someone pausing to think before making a decision. This pause-and-think step is what we call the **gating mechanism**. It checks out the information and then selects what details to remember and what to forget for the next step. It's kind of like filtering out the noise and focusing on the important stuff. By blending the old information (from the previous hidden state) and the new draft (the candidate), GRUs are better at following long stories or sequences without getting lost. By introducing a candidate hidden state, GRUs bring an added layer of flexibility. They can judiciously decide the portion of the candidate state to incorporate. This distinction equips GRUs to adeptly tackle challenges, such as the vanishing gradient, with a finesse that traditional RNNs often lack. In simpler terms, while the classic RNNs might struggle to remember long stories, GRUs, with their special features, are better listeners and retainers.

> LSTM was proposed in 1997 and GRUs in 2014. Most books on this topic prefer the chronological order and present LSTMs first. I have chosen to present these algorithms ordered by complexity. As the motivation behind GRUs was to simplify LSTMs, it may be useful to study the simpler algorithm first.

Introducing the update gate

In a standard RNN, the hidden value at each timestep is calculated and automatically becomes the new state of the memory cell. In contrast, GRUs introduce a more nuanced approach. The GRU model brings more flexibility to the process by allowing control over when to update the state of the memory cell. This added flexibility is implemented through a mechanism called the "update gate," sometimes referred to as the "reset gate."

The update gate's function is to evaluate whether the information in the candidate hidden state, $\hat{h}^{<t>}$, is significant enough to update the memory cell's hidden state or if the memory cell should retain the old hidden value from previous timesteps.

In mathematical terms, this decision-making process helps the model to manage information more selectively, determining whether to integrate new insights or continue relying on previously acquired knowledge. If the model deems that the candidate hidden state's information is not significant enough to alter the memory cell's existing state, the previous hidden value will be retained. Conversely, if the new information is considered relevant, it can overwrite the memory cell's state, thus adjusting the model's internal representation as it processes the sequence.

This unique gating mechanism sets GRUs apart from traditional RNNs and allows for more effective learning from sequential data with complex temporal relationships.

Implementing the update gate

This intelligence that we add to how the state is updated in the memory cell is the defining feature of a GRU. The decision will be taken soon of whether we should update the current hidden state with the candidate hidden state. To make this decision, we use the second activation function shown in *Figure 10.11*, annotated as **B**. This activation function is implementing the update gate.

It is implemented as a sigmoid layer that takes as input the current input and the previous hidden state. The output of the sigmoid layer is a value between 0 and 1 represented by the variable Γ_u. The output of the update gate is the variable Γ_u, which is governed by the following sigmoid function:

$$\Gamma_u = \text{sigmoid} \left(W_u \left[h^{<t-1>}, x^{<t>} \right] + b_u \right. \qquad \dots [Eq.\ 10.7]$$

As Γ_u is the output of a sigmoid function, it is close to either 1 or 0, which determines whether the update gate is open or closed. If the update gate is open, $\hat{h}^{<t>}$ will be chosen as the new hidden state. In the training process, the GRU will learn when to open the gate and when to close it.

Updating the hidden cell

For a certain timestep, the next hidden state is determined using the calculation from the following equation:

$$h^{<t>} = \Gamma_u * \hat{h}^{<t>} + (1 - \Gamma_u) * h^{<t-1>} \qquad \dots [Eq.\ 10.8]$$

Eq. 10.8 consists of two terms, annotated as **1** and **2**. Being an output of a sigmoid function, Γ_u can either be 0 or 1. It means:

$$\text{If } (\Gamma_u \approx 1): \quad h^{<t>} = \hat{h}^{<t>}$$

$$\text{If } (\Gamma_u \approx 0): \quad h^{<t>} = h^{<t-1>}$$

In other words, if the gate is open, update the value of $h^{<t>}$. Otherwise, just retain the old state.

Let us now look into how we can run GRUs for multiple timesteps.

Running GRUs for multiple timesteps

When deploying GRUs across several timesteps, we can visualize this process as depicted in *Figure 10.12*. Much like the foundational RNNs we discussed in the prior segment, GRUs create what can be thought of as an "information highway." This pathway effectively transfers context from the beginning to the end of a sequence, visualized as $\tilde{h}^{<t>}$ in *Figure 10.12* and annotated as **A**.

What differentiates GRUs from traditional RNNs is the decision-making process about how information flows on this highway. Instead of transferring information blindly at each timestep, a GRU pauses to evaluate its relevance.

Let's illustrate this with a basic example. Imagine reading a book where each sentence is a piece of information. However, instead of remembering every detail about every sentence, your mind (acting like a GRU) selectively recalls the most impactful or emotional sentences. This selective memory is akin to how the update gate in a GRU works.

The update gate serves a crucial role here. It's a mechanism that determines which portions of the prior information, or the prior "hidden state," should be retained or discarded. Essentially, the gate helps the network zoom in on and retain the most pertinent details, ensuring that the carried context remains as relevant as possible.

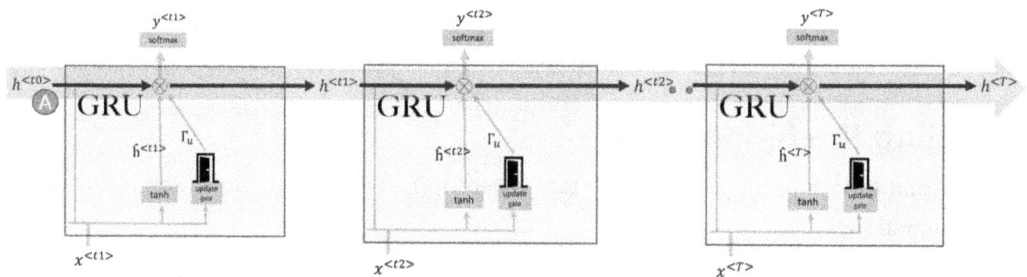

Figure 10.12: Sequential processing in RNN

Introducing LSTM

RNNs are widely used for sequence modeling tasks, but they suffer from limitations in capturing long-term dependencies in the data. An advanced version of RNNs, known as LSTM, was developed to address these limitations. Unlike simple RNNs, LSTMs have a more complex mechanism to manage context, enabling them to better capture patterns in sequences.

In the previous section, we discussed GRUs, where hidden state $h^{<t>}$ is used to carry the context from timestep to timestep. LSTM has a much more complex mechanism for managing the context. It has two variables that carry the context from timestep to timestep: the cell state and the hidden state. They are explained as follows:

1. **The cell state** (represented as $c^{<t>}$): This is responsible for maintaining the long-term dependencies of the input data. It is passed from one timestep to the next and is used to maintain information across a longer period. As we will learn later in this section, it is carefully determined by the forget gate and the update gate what should be included in the cell state. It can be considered as the "persistence layer" or "memory" of the LSTM as it maintains the information over a long period of time.

2. **The hidden state** (represented as $a^{<t>}$): This context is focused on the current timestep, which may or may not be important for the long-term dependencies. It is the output of the LSTM unit for a particular timestep and is passed as input to the next time step. As indicated in *Figure 10.23*, the hidden state, $a^{<t>}$, is used to generate the output $y^{<t>}$ at timestep t.

Let us now study these mechanisms in more detail, starting with how the current cell state is updated.

Introducing the forget gate

The forget gate in an LSTM network is responsible for determining which information to discard from the previous state, and which information to keep. It is annotated as **A** in *Figure 10.3*. It is implemented as a sigmoid layer that takes as input the current input and the previous hidden state. The output of the sigmoid layer is a vector of values between 0 and 1, where each value corresponds to a single cell in the LSTM's memory.

$$\Gamma_f = \text{sigmoid} \left(W_f \left[a^{<t-1>}, x^{<t>} \right] + b_f \right) \quad ... \text{[Eq. 10.9]}$$

As it is a sigmoid function, it means that Γ_f can be either close to 0 or 1.

If Γ_f is 1, then it means that the value from the previous state $c^{<t-1>}$ should be used to calculate $c^{<t>}$. If Γ_f is 0, then it means that the value from the previous state $c^{<t-1>}$ should be forgotten.

> **Info:** Usually, binary variables are considered active when their logic is 1. It may feel counter-intuitive that the "forget gate" forgets the previous state when $\Gamma_f = 0$, but this is how logic was presented in the original paper and is followed by the researchers for consistency.

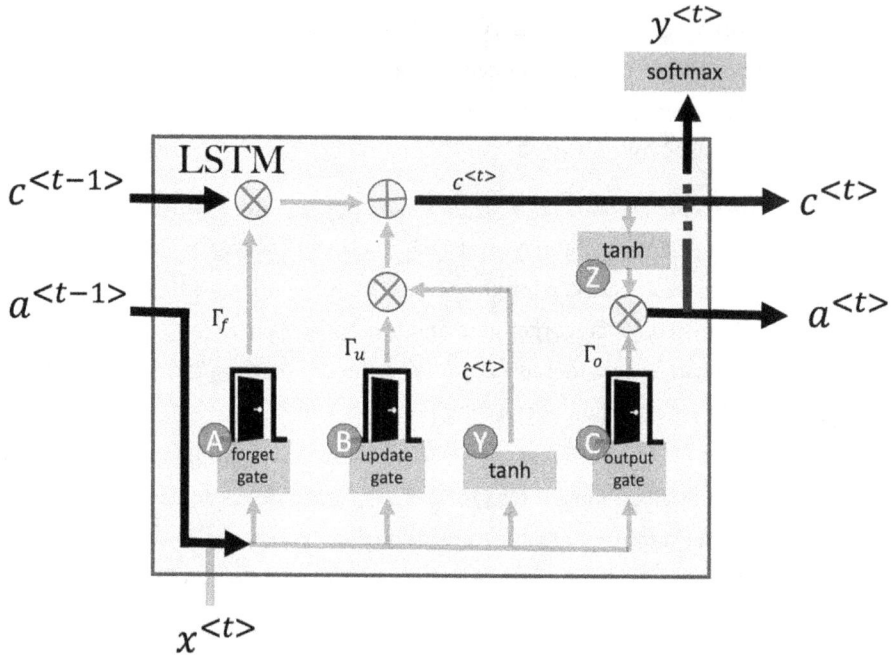

Figure 10.13: LSTM architecture

The candidate cell state

In LSTM, at each timestep, a candidate cell state, $\hat{c}^{<t>}$, is calculated, which is annotated as **Y** in *Figure 10.13*, and is the proposed new state for the memory cell. It is calculated using the current input $x^{<t>}$ and the previous hidden state $a^{<t-1>}$ as follows:

$$\hat{c}^{<t>} = \tanh(\ W_c\ [a^{<t-1>}, x^{<t>}\ ] + b_c) \qquad \text{... [Eq. 10.10]}$$

The update gate

The update gate is also called the input gate. The update gate in LSTM networks is a mechanism that allows the network to selectively incorporate new information into the current state so that the memory can focus on the most relevant information. It is annotated as **B** in *Figure 10.13*.

It is responsible for determining whether the candidate cell state $\hat{c}^{<t>}$ should be added to $c^{<t>}$. It is implemented as a sigmoid layer that takes as input the current input $x^{<t>}$ and the previous hidden state:

$$\Gamma_u = \text{sigmoid}\ (\ W_u\ [a^{<t-1>}, x^{<t>}\ ] + b_u \qquad \text{... [Eq. 10.11]}$$

The output of the sigmoid layer, Γ_u, is a vector of values between 0 and 1, where each value corresponds to a single cell in the LSTM's memory. A value of 0 indicates that the calculated $\hat{c}^{<t>}$ should be ignored, while a value of 1 indicates that $\hat{c}^{<t>}$ is significant enough to be incorporated in $c^{<t-1>}$. Being a sigmoid function, it can have any value between 0 and 1, which indicates that some of the information from $\hat{c}^{<t>}$ should be incorporated in $c^{<t>}$, but not all.

The update gate allows the LSTM to selectively incorporate new information into the current state and prevent the memory from becoming flooded with irrelevant data. By controlling the amount of new information that is added to the memory state, the update gate helps the LSTM to maintain a balance between preserving the previous state and incorporating new information.

Calculating memory state

As compared to GRU, the main difference in LSTM is that instead of having a single update gate (as we have in GRU), we have separate gates for the update and forget mechanisms for hidden state management. Each gate determines what is the right mix of various states to optimally calculate both the long-term memory $c^{<t>}$ current cell state and the current hidden state, $a^{<t>}$. The memory state is calculated by:

$$c^{<t>} = \Gamma_u * \hat{c}^{<t>} + \Gamma_f * c^{<t-1>} \quad ... [Eq.\ 10.12]$$

Eq. 10.12 consists of two terms annotated as **1** and **2**. Being an output of a sigmoid function, Γ_u and Γ_f can either be 0 or 1. It means:

$$\text{If } (\Gamma_u \approx 1): \quad h^{<t>} = \hat{h}^{<t>}$$

$$\text{If } (\Gamma_u \approx 0): \quad h^{<t>} = h^{<t-1>}$$

In other words, if the gate is open, update the value of $h^{<t>}$. Otherwise, just retain the old state.

Thus, the update gate in a GRU is a mechanism that allows the network to selectively discard information from the previous hidden state so that the hidden state can focus on the most relevant information. This is shown in *Figure 10.13*, which shows how the state travels from left to right.

The output gate

The output gate in an LSTM network is annotated as **C** in *Figure 10.13*. It is responsible for determining which information from the current memory state should be passed on as the output of the LSTM. It is implemented as a sigmoid layer that takes as input the current input and the previous hidden state. The output of the sigmoid layer is a vector of values between 0 and 1, where each value corresponds to a single cell in the LSTM's memory.

As it is a sigmoid function, it means that Γ_u can be either close to 0 or 1.

If Γ_u is 1, then it means that the value from the previous state $c^{<t-1>}$ should be used to calculate. $c^{<t>}$ If Γ_f is 0, then it means that the value from the previous state $c^{<t-1>}$ should be forgotten.

$$a^{<t>} = \Gamma_o * \tanh(c^{<t>})$$

A value of 0 indicates that the corresponding cell should not contribute to the output, while a value of 1 indicates that the cell should fully contribute to the output. Values between 0 and 1 indicate that the cell should contribute some, but not all, of its value to the output.

In LSTMs, after processing the output gate, the current state is passed through a tanh function. This function adjusts the values such that they fall within a range between -1 and 1. Why is this scaling necessary? The tanh function ensures that the LSTM's output remains normalized and prevents values from becoming too large, which can be problematic during training due to potential issues like exploding gradients.

After scaling, the result from the output gate is multiplied by this normalized state. This combined value represents the final output of the LSTM at that specific timestep.

To provide a simple analogy: imagine adjusting the volume of your music so it's neither too loud nor too soft, but just right for your environment. The tanh function acts similarly, ensuring the output is optimized and suitable for further processing.

The output gate is important because it allows the LSTM to selectively pass on relevant information from the current memory state as the output. It also helps to prevent irrelevant information from being passed on as the output.

This output gate generates the variable Γ_o, which determines that the contribution of the cell state is output to the hidden state:

$$\Gamma_o = \text{sigmoid} \left(W_o \left[a^{<t-1>}, x^{<t>} \right] + b_o \right.$$

In LSTM, ç is used as input to the gates, whereas $c^{<t>}$ is the hidden state.

In summary, the output gate in LSTM networks is a mechanism that allows the network to selectively pass on relevant information from the current memory state as the output so that the LSTM can generate appropriate output based on the relevant information it has stored in its memory.

Putting everything together

Let's delve into the workings of the LSTM across multiple timesteps, as depicted by **A** in *Figure 10.14*.

Just like GRUs, LSTMs create a conduit – often referred to as an "information highway" – which helps ferry context across successive timesteps. This is illustrated in *Figure 10.14*. What's fascinating about LSTMs is their ability to use long-term memory to transport this context.

As we traverse from one timestep to the next, the LSTM learns what should be retained in its long-term memory, denoted as $c^{<t>}$. At the start of every timestep, $c^{<t>}$ interacts with the "forget gate," allowing some pieces of information to be discarded. Subsequently, it encounters the "update gate," where new data is infused. This allows $c^{<t>}$ to transition between timesteps, continually gaining and shedding information as dictated by the two gates.

Now, here's where it gets intricate. At the close of every timestep, a copy of the long-term memory, $c^{<t>}$, undergoes transformation via the tanh function. This processed data is then sieved by the output gate, culminating in what we term short-term memory, $a^{<t>}$. This short-term memory serves a dual purpose: it determines the output at that specific timestep and lays the foundation for the subsequent timestep, as portrayed in *Figure 10.14*:

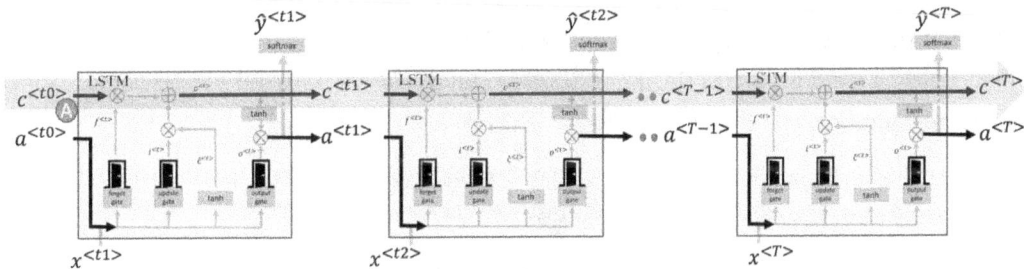

Figure 10.14: LSTM with multiple timesteps

Let us now look into how we can code RNNs.

Coding sequential models

For our exploration into LSTM, we'll be diving into sentiment analysis using the well-known IMDb movie reviews dataset. Here, every review is tagged with a sentiment, positive or negative, encoded as binary values (True for positive, and False for negative). Our aim is to craft a binary classifier capable of predicting these sentiments based solely on the text content of the review.

In total, the dataset boasts 50,000 movie reviews. For our purposes, we'll be dividing this equally: 25,000 reviews for training our model, and the remaining 25,000 for evaluating its performance.

For those seeking a deeper dive into the dataset, more information is available at Stanford's IMDB Dataset.

Loading the dataset

First, we need to load the dataset. We will import this dataset through `keras.datasets`. The advantage of importing this dataset through `keras.datasets` is that it has been processed to be used for machine learning. For example, the reviews have been individually encoded as a list of word indexes. The overall frequency of a particular word has been chosen as the index. So, if the index of the word is "7," it means that it is the 7th most frequent word. The use of pre-prepared data allows us to focus on the RNN algorithm instead of data preparation:

```python
import tensorflow as tf
from tensorflow.keras.datasets import imdb
vocab_size = 50000
(X_train,Y_train),(X_test,Y_test) = tf.keras.datasets.imdb.load_data(num_words= vocab_size)
```

Note that the argument `num_words=50000` is used to select only the top 50000 words. As the frequency of a word is used as the index, it means all the words with indexes less than 50000 are filtered out:

```
"I watched the movie in a cinema and I really like it"
[13, 296, 4, 20, 11, 6, 4435, 5, 13, 66, 447,12]
```

When working with sequences of varying lengths, it's often beneficial to ensure that they all have a uniform length. This is particularly crucial when feeding them into neural networks, which often expect consistent input sizes. To achieve this, we use padding—adding zeros at the beginning or end of sequences until they reach a specified length.

Here's how you can implement this with TensorFlow:

```python
# Pad the sequences
max_review_length = 500
x_train = tf.keras.preprocessing.sequence.pad_sequences(x_train, maxlen=max_review_length)
x_test = tf.keras.preprocessing.sequence.pad_sequences(x_test, maxlen=max_review_length)
```

Indexes are great for the consumption of algorithms. For human readability, we can convert these indexes back to words:

```
word_index = tf.keras.datasets.imdb.get_word_index()
reverse_word_index = dict([(value, key) for (key, value) in word_index.
items()])
def decode_review(padded_sequence):
    return " ".join([reverse_word_index.get(i - 3, "?") for i in padded_
sequence])
```

Note that word indexes start from 3 instead of 0 or 1. The reason is that the first three indexes are reserved.

Next, let us look into how we can prepare the data.

Preparing the data

In our example, we are considering a vocabulary of 50,000 words. This means that each word in the input sequence $x^{<t>}$ will be encoded using a one-hot vector representation, where the dimension of each vector is 50,000. A one-hot vector is a binary vector that has 0s in all positions except for the index corresponding to the word, where it has a 1. Here's we can load the IMDb dataset in TensorFlow, specifying the vocabulary size:

```
vocab_size = 50000
(x_train, y_train), (x_test, y_test) = tf.keras.datasets.imdb.load_
data(num_words=vocab_size)
```

Note that as vocab_size is set to 50,000, so the data will be loaded with the 50,000 most frequently occurring words. The remaining words will be discarded or replaced with a special token (often denoted as <UNK> for "unknown"). This ensures that our input data is manageable and only includes the most relevant information for our model. The variables x_train and x_test will contain the training and testing input data, respectively, while y_train and y_test will contain the corresponding labels.

Creating the model

We begin by defining an empty stack. We'll use this for building our network, layer by layer:

```
model = tf.keras.models.Sequential()
```

Next, we'll add an Embedding layer to our model. If you recall our discussion about word embeddings in *Chapter 9*, we used them to represent words in a continuous vector space. The Embedding layer serves a similar purpose but within the neural network. It provides a way to map each word in our vocabulary to a continuous vector. Words that are close to one another in this vector space are likely to share context or meaning.

Let us define the Embedding layer, considering the vocabulary size we chose earlier and mapping each word to a 50-dimensional vector, corresponding to the dimension of $h^{<t>}$:

```python
model.add(
    tf.keras.layers.Embedding(
        input_dim = vocab_size,
        output_dim = 50,
        input_length = review_length
    )
)
```

Dropout layers prevents overfitting and force the model to learn multiple representations of the same data by randomly disabling neurons in the learning phase. Let us randomly disable 25% of the neurons to deal with overfitting:

```python
model.add(
    tf.keras.layers.Dropout(
        rate=0.25
    )
)
```

Next, we'll add an LSTM layer, which is a specialized form of RNN. While basic RNNs have issues in learning long-term dependencies, LSTMs are designed to remember such dependencies, making them suitable for our task. This LSTM layer will analyze the sequence of words in the review along with their embeddings, using this information to determine the sentiment of a given review. We'll use 32 units in this layer:

```python
model.add(
    tf.keras.layers.LSTM(
        units=32
    )
)
```

Add a second Dropout layer to drop 25% of neurons to reduce overfitting:

```
model.add(
    tf.keras.layers.Dropout(
        rate=0.25
    )
)
```

All LSTM units are connected to a single node in the Dense layer. A sigmoid activation function determines the output from this node – a value between 0 and 1. Closer to 0 indicates a negative review. Closer to 1 indicates a positive review:

```
model.add(
    tf.keras.layers.Dense(
        units=1,
        activation='sigmoid'
    )
)
```

Now, let us compile the model. We will use binary_crossentropy as the loss function and Adam as the optimizer:

```
model.compile(
    loss=tf.keras.losses.binary_crossentropy,
    optimizer=tf.keras.optimizers.Adam(),
    metrics=['accuracy'])
```

Display a summary of the model's structure:

```
model.summary()
```

```
Layer (type)                Output Shape              Param #
=================================================================
embedding (Embedding)       (None, 500, 32)           320000
dropout (Dropout)           (None, 500, 32)           0
lstm (LSTM)                 (None, 32)                8320
dropout_1 (Dropout)         (None, 32)                0
dense (Dense)               (None, 1)                 33
=================================================================
Total params: 328,353
```

```
Trainable params: 328,353
Non-trainable params: 0
```

Training the model

We'll now train the LSTM model on our training data. Training the model involves several key components, each of which is described below:

- **Training Data**: These are the features (reviews) and labels (positive or negative sentiments) that our model will learn from.

- **Batch Size**: This determines the number of samples that will be used in each update of the model parameters. A higher batch size might require more memory.

- **Epochs**: An epoch is a complete iteration over the entire training data. The more epochs, the more times the learning algorithm will work through the entire training dataset.

- **Validation Split**: This fraction of the training data will be set aside for validation and not be used for training. It helps us evaluate how well the model is performing.

- **Verbose**: This parameter controls how much output the model will produce during training. A value of 1 means that progress bars will be displayed:

```python
history = model.fit(
    x_train, y_train,      # Training data
    batch_size=256,
    epochs=3,
    validation_split=0.2,
    verbose=1
)
```

```
Epoch 1/3
79/79 [==============================] - 75s 924ms/step - loss:
0.5757 - accuracy: 0.7060 - val_loss: 0.4365 - val_accuracy: 0.8222
Epoch 2/3
79/79 [==============================] - 79s 1s/step - loss: 0.2958
- accuracy: 0.8900 - val_loss: 0.3040 - val_accuracy: 0.8812
Epoch 3/3
79/79 [==============================] - 73s 928ms/step - loss:
0.1739 - accuracy: 0.9437 - val_loss: 0.2768 - val_accuracy: 0.8884
```

Viewing some incorrect predictions

Let's have a look at some of the incorrectly classified reviews:

```python
predicted_probs = model.predict(x_test)
predicted_classes_reshaped = (predicted_probs > 0.5).astype("int32").
reshape(-1)
incorrect = np.nonzero(predicted_classes_reshaped != y_test)[0]
```

We select the first 20 incorrectly classified reviews:

```python
class_names = ["Negative", "Positive"]
for j, incorrect_index in enumerate(incorrect[0:20]):
    predicted = class_names[predicted_classes_reshaped[incorrect_index]]
    actual = class_names[y_test[incorrect_index]]
    human_readable_review = decode_review(x_test[incorrect_index])
    print(f"Incorrectly classified Test Review [{j+1}]")
    print(f"Test Review #{incorrect_index}: Predicted [{predicted}] Actual
[{actual}]")
    print(f"Test Review Text: {human_readable_review.replace('<PAD> ',
'')}\n")
```

Summary

The foundational concepts of sequential models were explained in this chapter, which aimed to give you a basic understanding of the techniques and methodologies of such techniques. In this chapter, we presented RNNs, which are great for handling sequential data. A GRU is a type of RNN that was introduced by Cho et al. in 2014 as a simpler alternative to LSTM networks.

Like LSTMs, GRUs are designed to learn long-term dependencies in sequential data, but they do so using a different approach. GRUs use a single gating mechanism to control the flow of information into and out of the hidden state, rather than the three gates used by LSTMs. This makes them easier to train and requires fewer parameters, making them more efficient to use.

The next chapter introduces some advanced techniques related to sequential models.

Learn more on Discord

To join the Discord community for this book – where you can share feedback, ask questions to the author, and learn about new releases – follow the QR code below:

`https://packt.link/WHLel`

11

Advanced Sequential Modeling Algorithms

An algorithm is a sequence of instructions that, if followed, will solve a problem.

—Unknown

In the last chapter we looked into the core principles of sequential models. It provided an introductory overview of their techniques and methodologies. The sequential modeling algorithms discussed in the last chapter had two basic restrictions. First, the output sequence was required to have the same number of elements as the input sequence. Second, those algorithms can process only one element of an input sequence at a time. If the input sequence is a sentence, it means that the sequential algorithms discussed so far can "*attend*," or process, only one word at a time. To be able to better mimic the processing capabilities of the human brain, we need much more than that. We need complex sequential models that process an output with different lengths to the input, and which can attend to more than one word of a sentence at the same time, removing this information bottleneck.

In this chapter, we will delve deeper into the advanced aspects of sequential models to understand the creation of complex configurations. We'll start by breaking down key elements, such as autoencoders and **Sequence-to-Sequence (Seq2Seq)** models. Next, we will look at attention mechanisms and transformers, which are pivotal in the development of **Large Language Models (LLMs)**, which we will then study.

By the end of this chapter, you will have gained a comprehensive understanding of these advanced structures and their significance in the realm of machine learning. We will also provide insights into the practical applications of these models.

The following topics are covered in this chapter:

- Introduction to autoencoders
- Seq2Seq models
- Attention mechanisms
- Transformers
- LLMs
- Deep and wide architectures

First, let's explore an overview of advanced sequential models.

The evolution of advanced sequential modeling techniques

In *Chapter 10, Understanding Sequential Models*, we touched upon the foundational aspects of sequential models. While they serve numerous use cases, they face challenges in grasping and producing the complex intricacies of human language.

We'll begin our journey by discussing **autoencoders**. Introduced in the early 2010s, autoencoders provided a refreshing approach to data representation. They marked a significant evolution in **natural language processing** (**NLP**), transforming how we thought about data encoding and decoding. But the momentum in NLP didn't stop there. By the mid-2010s, **Seq2Seq** models entered the scene, bringing forth innovative methodologies for tasks such as language translation. These models could adeptly transform one sequence form into another, heralding an era of advanced sequence processing.

However, with the rise in data complexity, the NLP community felt the need for more sophisticated tools. This led to the 2015 unveiling of the **attention mechanism**. This elegant solution provided models the ability to selectively concentrate on specific portions of input data, enabling them to manage longer sequences more efficiently. Essentially, it allowed models to weigh the importance of different data segments, amplifying the relevant and diminishing the less pertinent.

Building on this foundation, 2017 saw the advent of the **transformer** architecture. Fully leveraging the capabilities of attention mechanisms, transformers set new benchmarks in NLP.

These advancements culminated in the development of **Large Language Models (LLMs)**. Trained on vast and diverse textual data, LLMs can both understand and generate nuanced human language expressions. Their unparalleled prowess is evident in their widespread applications, from healthcare diagnostics to algorithmic trading in finance.

In the sections that follow, we'll unpack the intricacies of autoencoders—from their early beginnings to their central role in today's advanced sequential models. Prepare to deep dive into the mechanisms, applications, and evolutions of these transformative tools.

Exploring autoencoders

Autoencoders occupy a unique niche in the landscape of neural network architectures, playing a pivotal role in the narrative of advanced sequential models. Essentially, an autoencoder is designed to create a network where the output mirrors its input, implying a compression of the input data into a more succinct, lower-dimensional latent representation.

The autoencoder structure can be conceptualized as a dual-phase process: the **encoding** phase and the **decoding** phase.

Consider the following diagram:

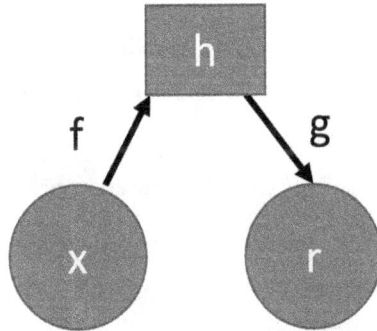

Figure 11.1: Autoencoder architecture

In this diagram we make the following assumptions:

- x corresponds to the input data
- h is the compressed form of our data
- r denotes the output, a recreation or approximation of x

We can see that the two phases are represented by f and g. Let's look at them in more detail:

- **Encoding** (f): Described mathematically as $h = f(x)$. In this stage, the input, represented as x, transforms into a condensed, hidden representation labeled h.

- **Decoding** (g): During this phase, represented as $r = g(h)$, the compacted h is unraveled, aiming to reproduce the initial input.

When training an autoencoder, the goal is to perfect h, ensuring it encapsulates the essence of the input data. In achieving a high-quality h, we ensure the recreated output r mirrors the original x with minimal loss. The objective is not just to reproduce but also to train an h that's streamlined and efficient in this reproduction task.

Coding an autoencoder

The **Modified National Institute of Standards and Technology (MNIST)** dataset is a renowned database of handwritten digits, consisting of 28x28 pixel grayscale images representing numbers from 0 to 9. It has been widely used as a benchmark for machine learning algorithms. More information and access to the dataset can be found at the official MNIST website. For those interested in accessing the dataset, it's available at the official MNIST repository hosted by Yann LeCun: yann. lecun.com/exdb/mnist/. Please note that an account may be required to download the dataset.

In this section, we'll employ an autoencoder to reproduce these handwritten digits. The unique feature of autoencoders is their training mechanism: the *input* and the *target output* are the same image. Let's break this down.

First, there is the **training phase**, where the following steps occur:

1. The MNIST images are provided to the autoencoder.

2. The encoder segment compresses these images into a condensed latent representation.

3. The decoder segment then tries to restore the original image from this representation. By iterating over this process, the autoencoder acquires the nuances of compressing and reconstructing, capturing the core patterns of the handwritten digits.

Second, there is the **reconstruction phase**:

1. With the model trained, when we feed it new images of handwritten digits, the autoencoder will first encode them into its internal representation.

2. Then, decoding this representation will yield a reconstructed image, which, if the training was successful, should closely match the original.

With the autoencoder effectively trained on the MNIST dataset, it becomes a powerful tool to process and reconstruct handwritten digit images.

Setting up the environment

Before diving into the code, essential libraries must be imported. TensorFlow will be our primary tool, but for data handling, libraries like NumPy may be pivotal:

```
import tensorflow as tf
```

Data preparation

Next, we'll segregate the dataset into training and test segments and then normalize them:

```
# Load dataset
(x_train, _), (x_test, _) = tf.keras.datasets.mnist.load_data()

# Normalize data to range [0, 1]
x_train, x_test = x_train / 255.0, x_test / 255.0
```

Note that the division by 255.0 is to normalize our grayscale image data, a step that optimizes the learning process.

Model architecture

Designing the autoencoder involves making decisions about the layers, their sizes, and activation functions. Here, the model is defined using TensorFlow's Sequential and Dense classes:

```
model = tf.keras.Sequential([
    tf.keras.layers.Flatten(input_shape=(28, 28)),
    tf.keras.layers.Dense(32, activation='relu'),
    tf.keras.layers.Dense(784, activation='sigmoid'),
    tf.keras.layers.Reshape((28, 28))
])
```

Flattening the 28x28 images gives us a 1D array of 784 elements, hence the input shape.

Compilation

After the model is defined, it's compiled with a specified loss function and optimizer. Binary cross-entropy is chosen due to the binary nature of our grayscale images:

```
model.compile(loss='binary_crossentropy', optimizer='adam')
```

Training

The training phase is initiated with the `fit` method. Here, the model learns the nuances of the MNIST handwritten digits:

```
model.fit(x_train, x_train, epochs=10, batch_size=128,
          validation_data=(x_test, x_test))
```

Prediction

With a trained model, predictions (both encoding and decoding) can be executed as follows:

```
encoded_data = model.predict(x_test)
decoded_data = model.predict(encoded_data)
```

Visualization

Let us now visually compare the original images with their reconstructed counterparts. The following script showcases a visualization procedure that displays two rows of images:

```
n = 10  # number of images to display
plt.figure(figsize=(20, 4))
for i in range(n):
    # Original images
    ax = plt.subplot(2, n, i + 1)
    plt.imshow(x_test[i].reshape(28, 28) , cmap='gray')
    ax.get_xaxis().set_visible(False)
    ax.get_yaxis().set_visible(False)

    # Reconstructed images
    ax = plt.subplot(2, n, i + 1 + n)
    plt.imshow(decoded_data[i].reshape(28, 28) , cmap='gray')
    ax.get_xaxis().set_visible(False)
    ax.get_yaxis().set_visible(False)

plt.show()
```

The following screenshot shows the outputted reconstructed images:

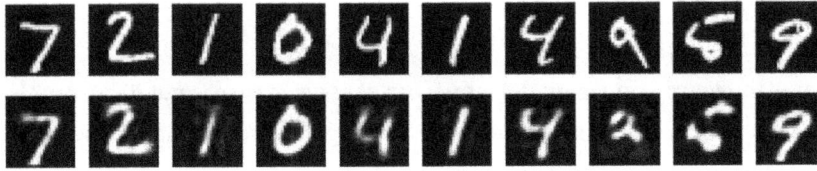

Figure 11.2: The original test images (top row) and the post-reconstruction by the autoencoder (bottom row)

The top row presents the original test images, while the bottom row exhibits the post-reconstruction images made by the autoencoder. Through this side-by-side comparison, we can discern the efficacy of our model in preserving the intrinsic features of the input.

Let us now discuss Seq2Seq models.

Understanding the Seq2Seq model

Following our exploration of autoencoders, another groundbreaking architecture in the realm of advanced sequential models is the **Seq2Seq** model. Central to many state-of-the-art natural language processing tasks, the Seq2Seq model exhibits a unique capability: transforming an input sequence into an output sequence that may differ in length. This flexibility allows it to excel in challenges like machine translation, where the source and target sentences can naturally differ in size.

Refer to *Figure 11.3*, which visualizes the core components of a Seq2Seq model:

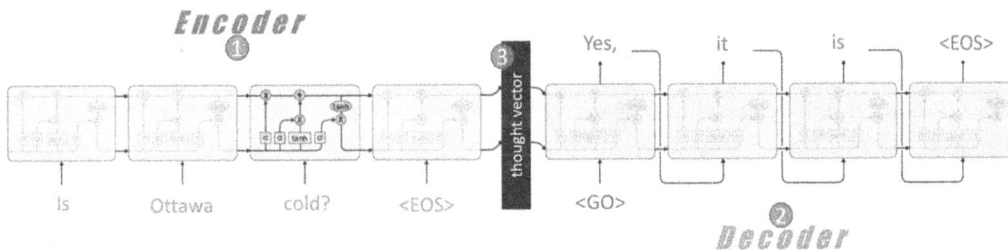

Figure 11.3: Illustration of the Seq2Seq model architecture

Broadly, there are three main elements:

- **Encoder:** Processes the input sequence
- **Thought vector:** A bridge between the encoder and decoder
- **Decoder:** Generates the output sequence

Let us explore them one by one.

Encoder

The encoder is shown as ① in *Figure 11.3*. As we can observe, it is an input **Recurrent Neural Network (RNN)** that processes the input sequence. The input sentence in this case is a three-word sentence: *Is Ottawa cold?* It can be represented as:

$$X = \{x^{<1>}, x^{<2>}, ..., x^{<L1>}\}$$

The encoder traverses through this sequence until it encounters an **End-Of-Sentence (<EOS>)** token, indicating the conclusion of the input. It will be positioned at timestep *L1*.

Thought vector

Throughout the encoding phase, the RNN updates its hidden state, denoted by $h^{<t>}$. The final hidden state, captured at the end of the sequence $h^{<L1>}$, is relayed to the decoder. This final state is termed the **thought vector**, coined by Geoffrey Hinton in 2015. This compact representation captures the essence of the input sequence. The thought vector is shown as ③ in *Figure 11.3*.

Decoder or writer

Upon completion of the encoding process, a <GO> token signals the decoder to commence. Using the encoder's final hidden state $h^{<L1>}$ as its initial input, the decoder, an output RNN, begins constructing the output sequence, $Y = \{y^{<1>}, y^{<2>}, ..., y^{<L2>}\}$. In the context of *Figure 11.3*, this output sequence translates to the sentence: *Yes, it is.*

Special tokens in Seq2Seq

While <EOS> and <GO> are essential tokens within the Seq2Seq paradigm, there are others worth noting:

- <UNK>: Standing for *unknown*, this token replaces infrequent words, ensuring the vocabulary remains manageable.
- <PAD>: Used for padding shorter sequences, this token standardizes sequence lengths during training, enhancing the model's efficacy.

A salient feature of the Seq2Seq model is its ability to handle variable sequence lengths, meaning input and output sequences can inherently differ in size. This flexibility, combined with its sequential nature, makes Seq2Seq a pivotal architecture in the advanced modeling landscape, bridging our journey from autoencoders to more complex, nuanced sequential processing systems.

Having traversed the foundational realms of autoencoders and delved deep into the Seq2Seq models, we now need to understand the limitations of the encoder-decoder framework.

The information bottleneck dilemma

As we have learned, the heart of traditional Seq2Seq models is the thought vector, $h^{<L1>}$. This is the last hidden state from the encoder, which serves as the bridge to the decoder. This vector is tasked with encapsulating the entirety of the input sequence, X. The simplicity of this mechanism is both its strength and its weakness. This weakness is highlighted when sequences grow longer; compressing vast amounts of information into a fixed-size representation becomes increasingly formidable. This is termed the **information bottleneck**. No matter the richness or complexity of the input, the fixed-length memory constraint means only so much can be relayed from the encoder to the decoder.

To learn how this problem has been addressed, we need to shift our focus from Seq2Seq models to the attention mechanism.

Understanding the attention mechanism

Following the challenges presented by the fixed-length memory in traditional Seq2Seq models, 2014 marked a revolutionary step forward. Dzmitry Bahdanau, KyungHyun Cho, and Yoshua Bengio proposed a transformative solution: the **attention mechanism**. Unlike earlier models that tried (often in vain) to condense entire sequences into limited memory spaces, attention mechanisms enabled models to hone in on specific, relevant parts of the input sequence. Picture it as a magnifying glass over only the most critical data at each decoding step.

What is attention in neural networks?

Attention, as the adage goes, is where focus goes. In the realm of NLP and particularly in the training of LLMs, attention has garnered significant emphasis. Traditionally, neural networks processed input data in a fixed sequence, potentially missing out on the relevance of context. Enter attention—a mechanism that weighs the importance of different input data, focusing more on what's relevant.

Basic idea

Just as humans pay more attention to salient parts of an image or text, attention mechanisms allow neural models to focus on more relevant parts of the input data. It effectively tells the model where to "look" next.

Example

Inspired by my recent journey to Egypt, which felt like a voyage back in time, consider the expressive and symbolic language of ancient Egypt: hieroglyphs.

Hieroglyphs were much more than mere symbols; they were an intricate fusion of art and language, representing multifaceted meanings. This system, with its vast array of symbols, exemplifies the foundational principles of attention mechanisms in neural networks.

Figure 11.4: Giza's prominent pyramids - Khufu and Khafre, accompanied by inscriptions in the age-old Egyptian script, "hieroglyphs" (photographs taken by the author)

For instance, an Egyptian scribe wishes to convey news about an anticipated grand festival by the Nile. Out of the thousands of hieroglyphs available:

- ☥ The *Ankh* hieroglyph, symbolizing life, captures the festival's vibrancy and celebratory spirit.

- ⎮ The *Was* symbol, resembling a staff, hints at authority or the Pharaoh's pivotal role in the celebrations.

- ≋ An illustration of the *Nile*, central to Egyptian culture, pinpoints the festival's venue.

However, to communicate the festival's grandeur and importance, not all symbols would hold equal weight. The scribe would have to emphasize or repeat specific hieroglyphs to draw attention to the most crucial aspects of the message.

This selective emphasis is parallel to neural network attention mechanisms.

Three key aspects of attention mechanisms

In neural networks, especially within NLP tasks, attention mechanisms play a crucial role in filtering and focusing on relevant information. Here, we'll distill the primary facets of attention into three main components: contextual relevance, symbol efficiency, and prioritized focus:

- **Contextual relevance:**

    - **Overview:** At its core, attention aims to allocate more importance to certain parts of the input data that are deemed more relevant to the task at hand.

    - **Deep dive:** Take a simple input like *"The grand Nile festival."* In this context, attention mechanisms might assign higher weights to the words *"Nile"* and *"grand."* This isn't because of their general significance but due to their task-specific importance. Instead of treating every word or input with uniform importance, attention differentiates and adjusts the model's focus based on context.

    - **In practice:** Think of this as a spotlight. Just as a spotlight on a stage illuminates specific actors during crucial moments while dimming others, attention shines a light on specific input data that holds more contextual value.

- **Symbol efficiency:**

    - **Overview:** The ability of attention to condense vast amounts of information into digestible, critical segments.

    - **Deep dive:** Hieroglyphs can encapsulate complex narratives or ideas within singular symbols. Analogously, attention mechanisms, by assigning varied weights, can determine which segments of the data contain maximal information and should be processed preferentially.

    - **In practice:** Consider compressing a large document into a succinct summary. The summary retains only the most critical information, mirroring the function of attention mechanisms that extract and prioritize the most pertinent data from a larger input.

- **Prioritized focus:**

    - **Overview:** Attention mechanisms don't distribute their focus uniformly. They are designed to prioritize segments of input data based on their perceived relevance to the task.

- **Deep dive**: Drawing inspiration from our hieroglyph example, just as an Egyptian scribe might emphasize the *"Ankh"* symbol when wanting to convey the idea of life or celebration, attention mechanisms will adjust their focus (or weights) to specific parts of the input that are more relevant.

- **In practice**: It's akin to reading a research paper. While the entire document holds value, one might focus more on the abstract, conclusion, or specific data points that align with their current research needs.

Thus, the attention mechanism in neural networks emulates the selective focus humans naturally employ when processing information. By understanding the nuances of how attention prioritizes and processes data, we can better design and interpret neural models.

A deeper dive into attention mechanisms

Attention mechanisms can be thought of as an evolved form of communication, much like hieroglyphs were in ancient times. Traditionally, an encoder sought to distill an entire input sequence into one encapsulating hidden state. This is analogous to an Egyptian scribe trying to convey an entire event using a single hieroglyph. While possible, it's challenging and may not capture the event's full essence.

Now, with the enhanced encoder-decoder approach, we have the luxury of generating a hidden state for every step, offering a richer tapestry of data for the decoder. But referencing every single hieroglyph (or state) at once would be chaotic, like a scribe using every symbol available to describe a single event by the Nile. That's where attention comes in.

Attention allows the decoder to prioritize. Just as a scribe might focus on the "Ankh" hieroglyph to signify life and vitality, or the "Was" staff to represent power, or even depict the Nile itself to pinpoint a location, the decoder assigns varying weightage to each encoder state. It decides which parts of the input sequence (or which hieroglyphs) deserve more emphasis. Using our translation example, when converting *"Transformers are great!"* to *"Transformatoren sind grossartig!"*, the mechanism emphasizes aligning *"great"* with *"grossartig,"* ensuring the core sentiment remains intact.

This selective focus, whether in neural network attention mechanisms or hieroglyphic storytelling, ensures precision and clarity in the conveyed message.

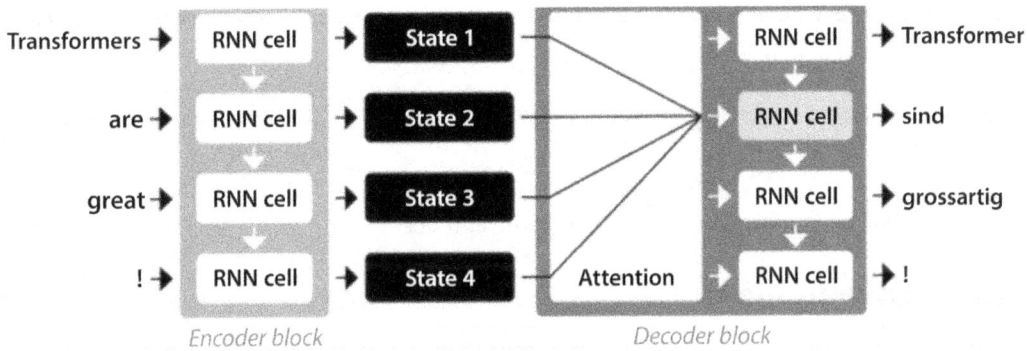

Figure 11.5: RNNs employing an encoder-decoder structure enhanced with an attention mechanism

The challenges of attention mechanisms

While incorporating attention with RNNs offers notable improvements, it's not a silver bullet. One significant hurdle is computational cost. The act of transferring multiple hidden states from encoder to decoder demands substantial processing power.

However, as with all technological progress, solutions continually emerge. One such advancement is the introduction of **self-attention**, a cornerstone of transformer architectures. This innovative variant refines the attention process, making it more efficient and scalable.

Delving into self-attention

Let's consider again the ancient art of hieroglyphs, where symbols were chosen intentionally to convey complex messages. Self-attention operates in a similar manner, determining which parts of a sequence are vital and should be emphasized.

Illustrated in *Figure 11.6* is the beauty of integrating self-attention within sequential models. Think of the bottom layer, churning with bidirectional RNNs, as the foundational stones of a pyramid. They generate what we call the **context vector (c2)**, a summary, much like a hieroglyph would for an event.

Each step or word in a sequence has its **weightage**, symbolized as α. These weights interact with the context vector, emphasizing the importance of certain elements over others.

Imagine a scenario wherein the input X_k represents a distinct sentence, denoted as k, which spans a length of *L1*. This can be mathematically articulated as:

$$X_k = \{X_k^{<1>}, X_k^{<2>}, \ldots \ldots, X_k^{<L1>}\}$$

Here, every element, $X_k^{<t>}$, represents a word or token from sentence k: the superscript <t> indicates its specific position or timestep within that sentence.

Attention weights

In the realm of self-attention, attention weights play a pivotal role, acting like a compass pointing to which words are essential. They assign an "importance score" to each word when generating the context vector.

To bring this into perspective, consider our earlier translation example: *"Transformers are great!"* translated to *"Transformatoren sind grossartig!"*. When focusing on the word *"Transformers"*, the attention weights might break down like this:

- $\alpha_{2,1}$: Measures the relationship between *"Transformers"* and the beginning of the sentence. A high value here indicates that the word *"Transformers"* significantly relies on the beginning for its context.
- $\alpha_{2,2}$: Reflects how much *"Transformers"* emphasizes its inherent meaning.
- $\alpha_{2,3}$ and $\alpha_{2,4}$: These weigh how much *"Transformers"* takes into context the words *"are"* and *"great!"*, respectively. High scores here mean that *"Transformers"* is deeply influenced by these surrounding words.

During training, these attention weights are constantly adjusted and fine-tuned. This ongoing refinement ensures our model understands the intricate dance between words in a sentence, capturing both the explicit and subtle connections.

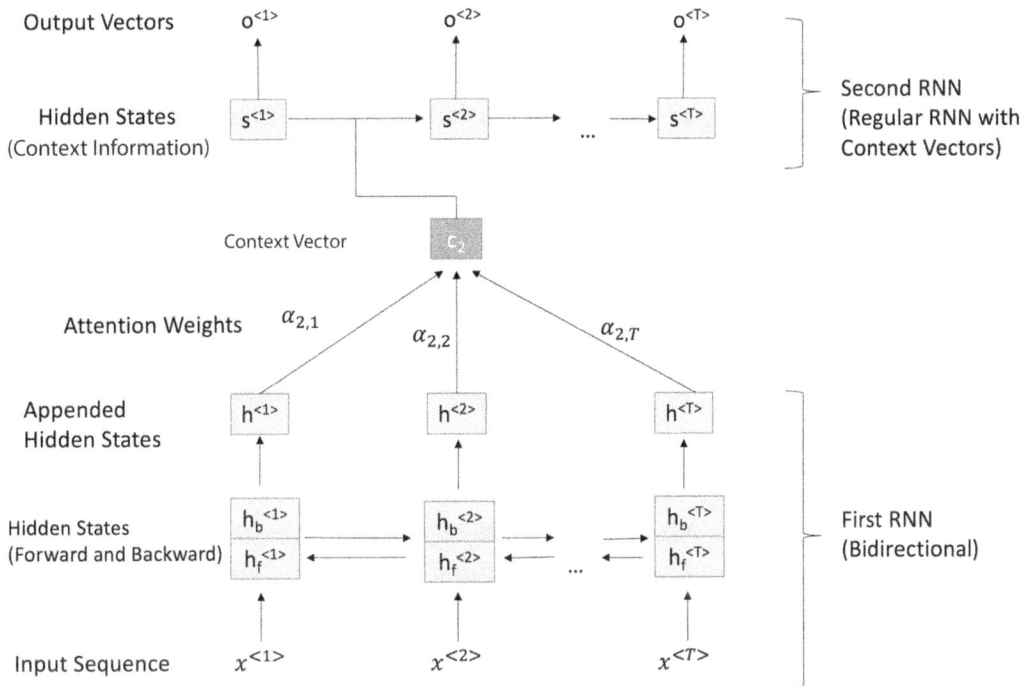

Figure 11.6: Integrating self-attention in sequential models

Before we delve deeper into the mechanisms of self-attention, it's vital to understand the key pieces that come together in *Figure 11.6*.

Encoder: bidirectional RNNs

In the last chapter we investigated the main architectural building blocks of unidirectional RNN and its variants. **Bidirectional RNNs** were invented to address that need (Schuster and Paliwal, 1997). We also identified a deficiency in unidirectional RNNs, as they are only capable of carrying the context in one direction.

For an input sequence, say *X*, the bidirectional RNN first reads it from the start to the end, and then from the end back to the start. This dual approach helps capture information based on preceding and succeeding elements. For each timestep, we get two hidden states: $h_f^{<t>}$ for the forward direction and $h_b^{<t>}$ for the backward one. These states are merged into a single one for that timestep, represented by:

$$h^{<t>} = h_f^{<t>} \mid h_b^{<t>}$$

For instance, if $h_f^{<t2>}$ and $h_b^{<t2>}$ are 64-dimensional vectors, the resulting $h^{<t2>}$ is 128-dimensional. This combined state is a detailed representation of the sequence context from both directions.

Thought vector

The thought vector, here symbolized as C_k, is a representation of the input X_k. As we have learned, its creation is an attempt to capture the sequencing patterns, context, and state of each element in X_k.

In our preceding diagram it is defined as:

$$C_k = (\alpha_k^{<1>}h^{<1>} + \alpha_k^{<2>}h^{<2>} + \cdots \alpha_k^{<L1>}h^{<L1>})$$

Where $\alpha_k^{<t>}$ are attention weights for timestep *t* that are refined during training.

Using the summation notation, it can be expressed as:

$$C_k = \sum_{t=1}^{L1} \alpha_k^{<t>}h^{<t>}$$

Decoder: regular RNNs

Figure 11.5 shows the decoder connected through the thought vector to the encoder.

The output of the decoder for a certain sentence k is represented by:

$$O_k = \{o_k^{<1>}, o_k^{<1>}, \ldots, o_k^{<L2>} \}$$

Note that the output has a length of *L2*, which is different from the length of the input sequence, which was *L1*.

Training versus inference

In the training data for a certain input sequence *k*, we have the expected output vector representing the ground truth, which is represented by a vector Y_k. This is:

$$Y_k = \{y_k^{<1>}, y_k^{<1>}, \dots, y_k^{<L2>}\ \}$$

At each timestep, the decoder's RNN gets three inputs:

- $s_k^{<t-1>}$: The previous hidden state
- C_k: The thought vector for sequence k
- $y_k^{<t-1>}$: The previous word in the ground truth vector Y_k

However, during inference, as there's no prior ground truth available, the decoder's RNN uses the prior output word, $o_k^{<t-1>}$, instead.

Now that we have learned how self-attention addresses the challenges faced by attention mechanisms and the basic operations it involves, we can move our attention to the next major advancement in sequential modeling: transformers.

Transformers: the evolution in neural networks after self-attention

Our exploration into self-attention revealed its powerful capability to reinterpret sequence data, providing each word with a contextual understanding based on its relationships with other words. This principle set the stage for an evolutionary leap in neural network designs: the **transformer** architecture.

Introduced by the Google Brain team in their 2017 paper, *Attention is All You Need* (https://arxiv.org/abs/1706.03762), the transformer architecture is built upon the very essence of self-attention. Before its advent, RNNs were the go-to. Picture RNNs as diligent librarians reading an English sentence to translate it into German, word by word, ensuring the context is relayed from one word to the next. They're reliable for short texts but can stumble when sentences get too long, misplacing the essence of earlier words.

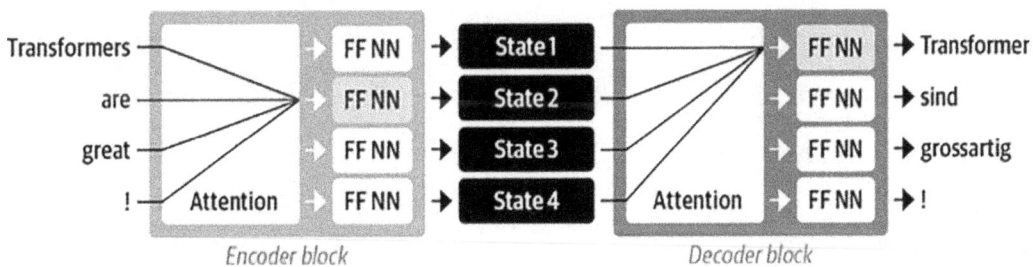

Figure 11.7: Encoder-decoder architecture of the original transformer

Transformers are a fresh approach to sequence data. Instead of a linear, word-by-word progression, transformers, armed with advanced attention mechanisms, comprehend an entire sequence in a single glance. It's like instantly grasping the sentiment of a whole paragraph rather than piecing it together word by word. This holistic view ensures a richer, all-encompassing understanding, celebrating the nuanced interplay between words.

Self-attention is central to the transformer's efficiency. While we touched upon this in the previous section, it's worth noting how pivotal it is here. Each layer of the network, through self-attention, can resonate with every other part of the input data. As depicted in *Figure 11.7*, the transformer architecture employs self-attention for both its encoder and decoder segments, which then feed into neural networks (also known as **feedforward neural networks (FFNNs)**). Beyond being more trainable, this setup has catalyzed many of the recent breakthroughs in NLP.

To illustrate, consider *Ancient Egypt: An Enthralling Overview of Egyptian History*, by Billy Wellman. Within it, the relationships between early pharaohs like Ramses and Cleopatra and pyramid construction are vast and intricate. Traditional models might stumble with such expansive content.

Why transformers shine

The transformer architecture, with its self-attention mechanism, emerges as a promising solution. When encountering a term like *"pyramids,"* the model can, using self-attention, assess its relevance to terms like *"Ramses"* or *"Cleopatra,"* irrespective of their position. This ability to attend to various input parts demonstrates why transformers are pivotal in modern NLP.

A Python code breakdown

Here's a simplified version of how the self-attention mechanism can be implemented:

```python
import numpy as np


def self_attention(Q, K, V):
    """
    Q: Query matrix
    K: Key matrix
    V: Value matrix
    """

    # Calculate the attention weights
    attention_weights = np.matmul(Q, K.T)
```

```
    # Apply the softmax to get probabilities
    attention_probs = np.exp(attention_weights) / np.sum(np.exp(attention_
weights), axis=1, keepdims=True)

    # Multiply the probabilities with the value matrix to get the output
    output = np.matmul(attention_probs, V)

    return output

# Example
Q = np.array([[1, 0, 1], [0, 2, 0], [1, 1, 0]])  # Example Query
K = np.array([[1, 0, 1], [0, 2, 0], [1, 1, 0]])  # Key matrix
V = np.array([[0, 2, 0], [1, 0, 1], [0, 1, 2]])  # Value matrix
output = self_attention(Q, K, V)
print(output)
```

Output:

```
[[0.09003057 1.57521038 0.57948752]
 [0.86681333 0.14906291 1.10143419]
 [0.4223188  0.73304361 1.26695639]]
```

This code is a basic representation, and the real transformer model uses a more optimized and detailed approach, especially when scaling for larger sequences. But the essence is the dynamic weighting of different words in the sequence, allowing the model to bring in contextual understanding.

Understanding the output

- The first row, [0.09003057 1.57521038 0.57948752], corresponds to the weighted combination of the V matrix for the first word in the query (in this case, represented by the first row of the Q matrix). This means when our model encounters the word represented by this query, it will focus 9% on the first word, 57.5% on the second word, and 57.9% on the third word from the V matrix to derive contextual understanding.

- The second row, [0.86681333 0.14906291 1.10143419], is the attention result for the second word in the query. It focuses 86.6% on the first word, 14.9% on the second, and 110.1% on the third from the V matrix.

- The third row, [0.4223188 0.73304361 1.26695639], is for the third word in the query. It has attention weights of 42.2%, 73.3%, and 126.7%, respectively, for the words in the V matrix.

Having reviewed transformers, their place in sequential modeling, their code, and their output, we can consider the next major development in NLP. Next, let us look at LLMs.

LLMs

LLMs are the next evolutionary step after transformers in the world of NLP. They're not just beefed-up older models; they represent a quantum leap. These models can handle vast amounts of text data and perform tasks previously thought to be reserved for human minds.

Simply put, LLMs can produce text, answer questions, and even code. Picture chatting with software and it replying just like a human, catching subtle hints and recalling earlier parts of the conversation. That's what LLMs offer.

Language models (LMs) have always been the backbone of NLP, helping in tasks ranging from machine translation to more modern tasks like text classification. While the early LMs relied on RNNs and **Long Short-Term Memory (LSTM)** structures, today's NLP achievements are primarily due to deep learning techniques, especially transformers.

The hallmark of LLMs? Their capacity to read and learn from vast quantities of text. Training one from scratch is a serious undertaking, requiring powerful computers and lots of time. Depending on factors like the model's size and the amount of training data—say, from giant sources like Wikipedia or the Common Crawl dataset—it could take weeks or even months to train an LLM.

Dealing with long sequences is a known challenge for LLMs. Earlier models, built on RNNs and LSTMs, faced issues with lengthy sequences, often losing vital details, which hampered their performance. This is where we start to see the role of **attention** come into play. Attention mechanisms act as a torch, illuminating essential sections of long inputs. For example, in a text about car advancements, attention makes sure the model recognizes and focuses on the major breakthroughs, no matter where they appear in the text.

Understanding attention in LLMs

Attention mechanisms have become foundational in the neural network domain, particularly evident in LLMs. Training these mammoth models, laden with millions or even billions of parameters, is not a walk in the park. At their core, attention mechanisms are like highlighters, emphasizing key details. For instance, when processing a lengthy text on NLP's evolution, LLMs can understand the overall theme, but attention ensures they don't miss the critical milestones. Transformers utilize this attention feature, aiding LLMs in handling vast text stretches and ensuring **contextual** consistency.

For LLMs, context is everything. For example, if an LLM crafts a story starting with a cat, attention ensures that as the tale unfolds, the context remains. So instead of introducing unrelated sounds like *"barking,"* the story would naturally lean toward *"purring"* or *"meowing."*

Training an LLM resembles running a supercomputer continuously for months, purely to process vast text quantities. And when the initial training is done, it's only the beginning. Think of it like owning a high-end vehicle—you'd need periodic maintenance. Similarly, LLMs need frequent updates and refinements based on new data.

Even after training an LLM, the work isn't over. For these models to remain effective, they need to keep learning. Imagine teaching someone English grammar rules and then throwing in slang or idioms—they need to adapt to these irregularities for a complete understanding.

Highlighting a historical shift, between 2017 and 2018, there was a notable change in the LLM landscape. Firms, including OpenAI, began leveraging unsupervised pretraining, paving the way for more streamlined models for tasks, like sentiment analysis.

Exploring the powerhouses of NLP: GPT and BERT

Universal Language Model Fine-Tuning (ULMFiT) set the stage for a new era in NLP. This method pioneered the reuse of pre-trained LSTM models, adapting them to a variety of NLP tasks, which saved both computational resources and time. Let's break down its process:

1. **Pretraining**: This is akin to teaching a child the basics of a language. Using extensive datasets like Wikipedia, the model learns the foundational structures and grammar of the language. Imagine this as equipping a student with general knowledge textbooks.

2. **Domain adaptation**: The model then delves into specialized areas or genres. If the first step was about learning grammar, this step is like introducing the model to different genres of literature - from thrillers to scientific journals. It still predicts words, but now within specific contexts.

3. **Fine-tuning**: Finally, the model is honed for specific tasks, such as detecting emotions or sentiments in a given text. This is comparable to training a student to write essays or analyze texts in depth.

2018's LLM pioneers: GPT and BERT

2018 saw the rise of two standout models: GPT and BERT. Let us look into them in more detail.

Generative Pre-trained Transformer (GPT)

Inspired by ULMFiT, GPT is a model that leans on the decoder side of the transformer architecture. Visualize the vastness of human literature. If traditional models are trained with a fixed set of books, GPT is like giving a scholar access to an entire library, including the BookCorpus - a rich dataset with diverse, unpublished books. This allows GPT to draw insights from genres ranging from fiction to history.

Here's an analogy: traditional models might know the plots of Shakespeare's plays. GPT, with its extensive learning, would understand not only the plots but also the cultural context, character nuances, and the evolution of Shakespeare's writing style over time.

Its focus on the decoder makes GPT a master of generating text that's both relevant and coherent, like a seasoned author drafting a novel.

BERT (Bidirectional Encoder Representations from Transformers)

BERT revamped traditional language modeling with its "masked language modeling" technique. Unlike models that just predict the next word in a sentence, BERT fills in intentionally blanked-out or "masked" words, enhancing its contextual understanding.

Let's put this into perspective. In a sentence like *"She went to Paris to visit the __,"* conventional models might predict words that fit after *"the,"* such as *"museum."* BERT, given *"She went to Paris to visit the masked,"* would aim to deduce that *"masked"* could be replaced by *"Eiffel Tower,"* understanding the broader context of a trip to Paris.

BERT's approach offers a more rounded view of language, capturing the essence of words based on what precedes and follows them, elevating its language comprehension prowess.

The key to success when training an LLM lies in combining 'deep' and 'wide' learning architectures. Think of the 'deep' part as a specialist deeply focused on a subject, while the 'wide' approach is like a jack of all trades, understanding a bit of everything.

Using deep and wide models to create powerful LLMs

LLMs are intricately designed to excel at a rather specific task: predicting the next word in a sequence. It might seem simple at first, but to achieve this with high accuracy, models often draw inspiration from certain aspects of human learning.

The human brain, a marvel of nature, processes information by recognizing and abstracting common patterns from the surrounding environment. On top of this foundational understanding, humans then enhance their knowledge by memorizing specific instances or exceptions that don't fit the usual patterns. Think of it as understanding a rule and then learning the outliers to that rule.

To infuse machines with this dual-layered learning approach, we need thoughtful machine learning architectures. A rudimentary method might involve training models solely on generalized patterns, sidelining the exceptions. However, to truly excel, especially in tasks like predicting the next word, models must be adept at grasping both the common patterns and the unique exceptions that punctuate a language.

While LLMs are not designed to fully emulate human intelligence (which is multifaceted and not solely about predicting sequences), they do borrow from human learning strategies to become proficient at their specific tasks.

LLMs are designed to understand and generate language by detecting patterns in vast amounts of text data. Consider the following basic linguistic guidelines:

1. Ancient Egyptian hieroglyphs provide a fascinating example. In this early writing system, a symbol might represent a word, sound, or even a concept. For instance, while a single hieroglyph could denote the word *"river,"* a combination of hieroglyphs could convey a deeper meaning like *"the life-giving Nile River."*

2. Now, consider how questions are formed. Typically, they begin with auxiliary verbs. However, indirect inquiries, such as *"I wonder if the Nile will flood this year"* diverge from this conventional pattern.

To effectively predict the next word or phrase in a sequence, LLMs must master both the prevailing language norms and their occasional outliers.

Bottom of Form

Thus, combining deep and wide models (*Figure 11.8*) has been shown to improve the performance of models on a wide range of tasks. Deep models are characterized by having many hidden layers and are adept at learning complex relationships between input and output.

In contrast, wide models are designed to learn simple patterns in the data. By combining the two, it is possible to capture both the complex relationships and the simple patterns, leading to more robust and flexible models.

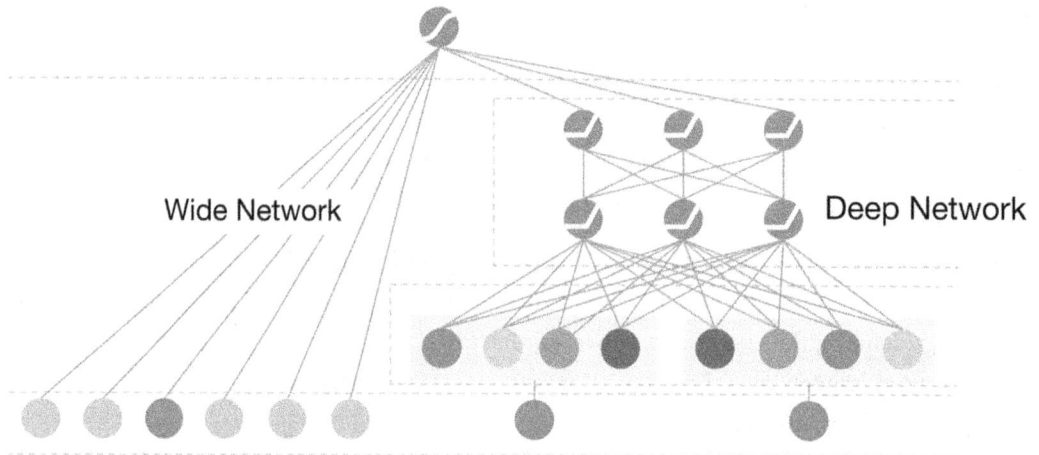

Figure 11.8: Architecture of deep and wide models

Incorporating exceptions into the training process is crucial for better generalization of models to new and unseen data. For example, a language model that is trained only on data that includes one meaning of a word may struggle to recognize other meanings when it encounters them in new data. By incorporating exceptions, the model can learn to recognize multiple meanings of a word, which can improve its performance on a variety of NLP tasks.

Deep architectures are typically used for tasks that require learning complex, hierarchical abstract representations of data. The features that exhibit generalizable patterns are called dense features. When we use deep architectures to formulate the rules, we call it learning by generalization. To build a wide and deep network, we connect the sparse features directly to the output node.

In the field of machine learning, combining deep and wide models has been identified as an important approach to building more flexible and robust models that can capture both complex relationships and simple patterns in data. Deep models excel at learning complex, hierarchical abstract representations of data, by having many hidden layers, where each layer processes the data and learns different features at different levels of abstraction. In contrast, wide models have a minimum number of hidden layers and are typically used for tasks that require learning simple, non-linear relationships in the data without creating any layer of abstraction.

Such patterns are represented through sparse features. When the wide part of the model has one or zero hidden layers, it can be used to memorize the examples and formulate exceptions. Thus, when wide architectures are used to formulate rules, we call it learning by **memorization**.

The deep and wide models can use the deep neural network to generalize patterns. Typically, this portion of the model will take lots of time to train. The wide partition and efforts to capture all the exceptions to these generalizations in real time are a part of the constant algorithmic learning process.

Summary

In this chapter we discussed advanced sequential models, which are advanced techniques designed to process input sequences, especially when the length of output sequences may differ from that of the input. Autoencoders, a type of neural network architecture, are particularly adept at compressing data. They work by encoding input data into a smaller representation and then decoding it back to resemble the original input. This process can be useful in tasks like image denoising, where noise from an image is filtered out to produce a clearer version.

Another influential model is the Seq2Seq model. It's designed to handle tasks where input and output sequences have varying lengths, making it ideal for applications like machine translation. However, traditional Seq2Seq models face the **information bottleneck** challenge, wherein the entire context of an input sequence needs to be captured in a single, fixed-size representation. Addressing this, the attention mechanism was introduced, allowing models to focus on different parts of the input sequence dynamically. The transformer architecture, introduced in the paper *Attention is All You Need*, utilizes this mechanism, revolutionizing the processing of sequence data. Transformers, unlike their predecessors, can attend to all positions in a sequence simultaneously, capturing intricate relationships within the data. This innovation paved the way for LLMs, which have gained prominence for their human-like text-generation capabilities.

In the next chapter we will look into how to use recommendation engines.

Learn more on Discord

To join the Discord community for this book – where you can share feedback, ask questions to the author, and learn about new releases – follow the QR code below:

https://packt.link/WHLel

Section 3:

Advanced Topics

As the name suggests, we will deal with some selected advanced topics related to algorithms in this section. Cryptography and large-scale algorithms are key highlights of this section. We will also look into the issues related to the large-scale infrastructure needed to train complex algorithms. The last chapter of this section explores the practical considerations one should keep in mind while implementing algorithms. The chapters included in this section are:

- *Chapter 12, Recommendation Engines*
- *Chapter 13, Algorithmic Strategies for Data Handling*
- *Chapter 14, Cryptography*
- *Chapter 15, Large-Scale Algorithms*
- *Chapter 16, Practical Considerations*

12

Recommendation Engines

The best recommendation I can have is my own talents, and the fruits of my own labors, and what others will not do for me, I will try and do for myself.

—*18–19th-century scientist John James Audubon*

Recommendation engines harness the power of available data on user preferences and item details to offer tailored suggestions. At their core, these engines aim to identify commonalities among various items and understand the dynamics of user-item interactions. Rather than just focusing on products, recommendation systems cast a wider net, considering any type of item – be it a song, a news article, or a product – and tailoring their suggestions accordingly.

This chapter starts by presenting the basics of recommendation engines. Then, it discusses various types of recommendation engines. In the subsequent sections of this chapter, we'll explore the inner workings of recommendation systems. These systems are adept at suggesting tailored items or products to users, but they're not without their challenges. We'll discuss both their strengths and the limitations they present. Finally, we will learn to use recommendation engines to solve a real-world problem.

In this chapter, we'll cover:

- An overview of recommendation engines
- Different categories of recommendation systems
- Recognizing the constraints of recommendation approaches

- Areas of practical application
- A practical example

By the end of this chapter, you should be able to understand how to use recommendation engines to suggest various items based on some preference criteria.

Let's start by looking into the background concepts of recommendation engines.

Introducing recommendation systems

Recommendation systems are powerful tools, initially crafted by researchers but now widely adopted in commercial settings, that predict items a user might find appealing. Their ability to deliver personalized item suggestions makes them an invaluable asset, especially in the digital shopping landscape.

When used in e-commerce applications, recommendation engines use sophisticated algorithms to improve the shopping experience for shoppers, allowing service providers to customize products according to the preferences of the users.

A classic example of the significance of these systems is the Netflix Prize challenge in 2009. Netflix, aiming to refine its recommendation algorithm, offered a whopping $1 million prize for any team that could enhance its current recommendation system, Cinematch, by 10%. This challenge saw participation from researchers globally, with BellKor's Pragmatic Chaos team emerging as the winner. Their achievement underlines the essential role and potential of recommendation systems in the commercial domain. More about this fascinating challenge can be explored in this chapter.

Types of recommendation engines

We can broadly classify recommendation engines into three main categories:

- **Content-based recommendation engines:** They focus on item attributes, matching the features of one product to another.
- **Collaborative filtering engines:** They predict preferences based on user behaviors.
- **Hybrid recommendation engines:** A blend of both worlds, these engines integrate the strengths of content-based and collaborative filtering methods to refine their suggestions.

Having established the categories, let's start by diving into the details of these three types of recommendation engines one by one:

Content-based recommendation engines

Content-based recommendation engines operate on a straightforward principle: they recommend items that are like ones the user has previously engaged with. The crux of these systems lies in accurately measuring the likeness between items.

To illustrate, imagine the scenario depicted in *Figure 12.1*:

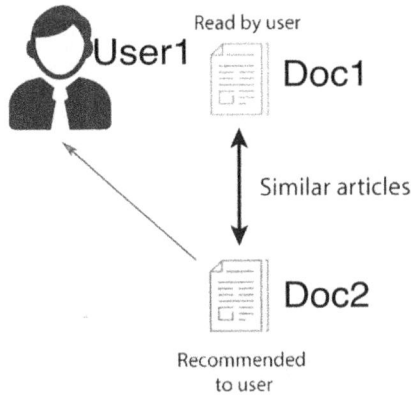

Figure 12.1: Content-based recommendation system

Let's say that *User1* has read *Doc1*. Due to the similarities between the documents, we could then recommend *Doc2* to *User1*.

This method would only be effective if we could identify and quantify these similarities. Thus, identifying similarities between items is pivotal for recommendations. Let's delve into how to quantify these similarities.

Determining similarities in unstructured documents

One way of determining the similarities between different documents is by using the co-occurrence matrix, which works on the premise that items frequently bought together likely share similarities or belong to complementary categories.

For instance, someone buying a razor might also need shaving gel. Let's decode this with data from four users' buying habits:

	Razor	Apple	Shaving cream	Bike	Hummus
Mike	1	1	1	0	1
Taylor	1	0	1	1	1

| Elena | 0 | 0 | 0 | 1 | 0 |
| Amine | 1 | 0 | 1 | 0 | 0 |

To construct the co-occurrence matrix, follow these steps:

1. Initialize an *NxN* matrix, where *N* is the number of items. This matrix will store the co-occurrence counts.

2. For each user in the user-item matrix, update the co-occurrence matrix by incrementing the cell values for pairs of items that the user has interacted with.

3. The final matrix showcases the associations between items based on user interactions.

The occurrence matrix of the above table will be as follows:

	Razor	Apple	Shaving cream	Bike	Hummus
Razor	-	1	3	1	2
Apple	1	-	1	0	1
Shaving cream	3	1	-	1	2
Bike	1	0	1	-	1
Hummus	2	1	2	1	-

This matrix, in essence, showcases the likelihood of two items being bought together. It's a valuable tool for recommendation.

Collaborative filtering recommendation engines

The recommendations from **collaborative filtering** are based on the analysis of the historical buying patterns of users. The basic assumption is that if two users show interest in mostly the same items, we can classify both users as similar. In other words, we can assume the following:

- If the overlap in the buying history of two users exceeds a threshold, we can classify them as similar users.

- Looking at the history of similar users, the items that do not overlap in the buying history become the basis of future recommendations through collaborative filtering.

For example, let's look at a specific example. We have two users, *User1* and *User2*, as shown in the following diagram:

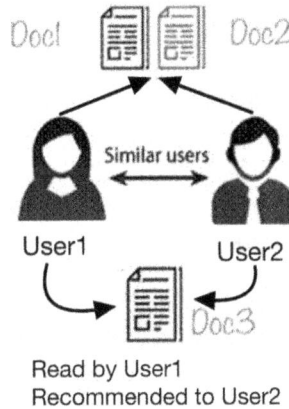

Figure 12.2: Collaborative filtering recommendation engine

Note the following:

- Both *User1* and *User2* have shown interest in exactly the same documents, *Doc1* and *Doc2*.
- Based on their similar historical patterns, we can classify both of them as similar users.
- If *User1* now reads *Doc3*, then we can suggest *Doc3* to *User2* as well.

This strategy of suggesting items to users based on their history will not always work. Let us look into the issues related to collaborative filtering in more detail.

Issues related to collaborative filtering

There are three potential issues related to collaborative filtering:

1. Inaccuracies due to a limited sample size
2. A vulnerability to **isolated analysis**
3. Over-reliance on history

Let us look into the limitations in more detail.

Inaccuracies due to a limited sample size

The accuracy and efficacy of a collaborative filtering system also hinge on the sample size. For instance, if only three documents are analyzed, the potential for accurate recommendations is limited.

However, if a system has data on hundreds or thousands of documents and interactions, its predictive capabilities become significantly more reliable. It's akin to the difference between making predictions based on a handful of data points versus having a comprehensive dataset to draw insights from.

Even when equipped with vast amounts of data, collaborative filtering isn't foolproof. The reason is that it relies purely on the historical interactions between users and items, without accounting for any external factors.

Vulnerable to isolated analysis

Collaborative filtering zeroes in on patterns formed by user behaviors and their interactions with items. This means it often misses out on external influences that might dictate a user's choice. For instance, a user might opt for a particular book not because of personal interest but because of academic needs or a friend's recommendation. The collaborative filtering model won't recognize these nuances.

Over-reliance on history

Because the system hinges on historical data, it can sometimes end up reinforcing stereotypes or not catching up with a user's evolving tastes. Imagine if a user once had a phase where they loved sci-fi movies but has since transitioned to enjoying romantic films. If they watched numerous sci-fi movies in the past, the system might still primarily recommend them, missing out on their current preferences.

In essence, while collaborative filtering is powerful, especially with more data, it's essential to understand its inherent limitations stemming from its isolated method of operation.

Next, let's look at hybrid recommendation engines.

Hybrid recommendation engines

So far, we have discussed content-based and collaborative-filtering-based recommendation engines. Both types of recommendation engines can be combined to create a **hybrid recommendation engine**. To do so, we follow these steps:

1. Generate a similarity matrix of the items.
2. Generate preference matrices of the users.
3. Generate recommendations.

Let's look into these steps one by one.

Generating a similarity matrix of the items

In hybrid recommendations, we start by creating a similarity matrix of items using content-based recommendations. This can be done by using the co-occurrence matrix or any distance measure to quantify the similarities between items.

Let's assume that we currently have five items. Using content-based recommendations, we generate a matrix that captures the similarities between items, as shown in *Figure 12.3*:

	Item1	Item2	Item3	Item4	Item5
Item1	10	5	3	2	1
Item2	5	10	6	5	3
Item3	3	6	10	1	5
Item4	2	5	1	10	3
Item5	1	3	5	3	10

Figure 12.3: Similarity matrix

Let's see how we can combine this similarity matrix with a preference matrix to generate recommendations.

Generating reference vectors of the users

Based on the history of each of the users of the system, we will produce a preference vector that captures those users' interests.

Let's assume that we want to generate recommendations for an online store named *KentStreetOnline*, which sells 100 unique items. *KentStreetOnline* is popular and has 1 million active subscribers. It is important to note that we need to generate only one similarity matrix with dimensions of 100 by 100. We also need to generate a preference vector for each of the users; this means that we need to generate 1 million preference vectors for each of the 1 million users.

Each entry of the performance vector represents a preference for an item. The value of the first row means that the preference weight for *Item 1* is 4. The preference score isn't a direct reflection of purchase counts. Instead, it's a weighted metric, potentially considering factors like browsing history, past purchases, item ratings, and more.

A score of *4* could represent a combination of interest and past interactions with *Item 1*, suggesting a strong likelihood that the user would appreciate that item.

This is graphically shown in *Figure 12.4*:

Item 1	4
Item 2	0
Item 3	0
Item 4	5
Item 5	0

Figure 12.4: User preference matrix

Now, let's look into how we can generate recommendations based on the similarity matrix, *S*, and the user preference matrix, *U*.

Generating recommendations

To make recommendations, we can multiply the matrices. Users are more likely to be interested in an item that co-occurs frequently with an item that they gave a high rating to:

$$Matrix[S] \times Matrix[U] = Matrix[R]$$

This calculation is shown graphically in *Figure 12.5*:

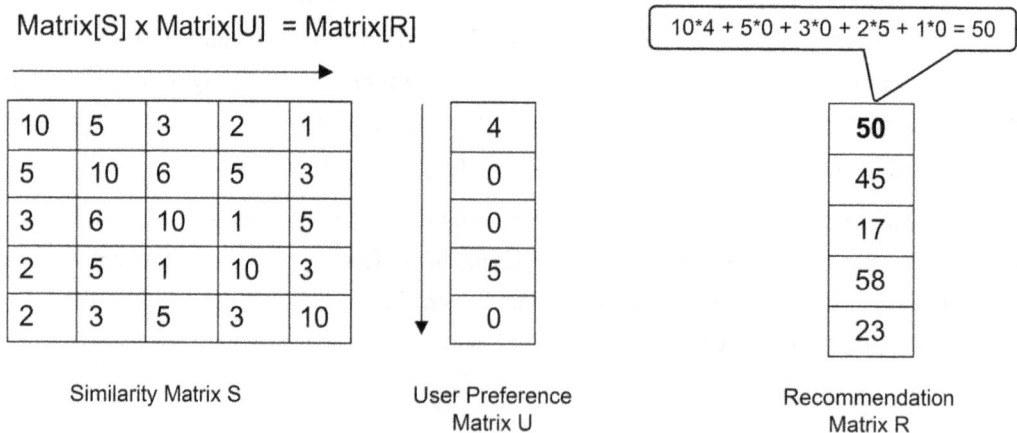

Matrix[S] x Matrix[U] = Matrix[R]

10*4 + 5*0 + 3*0 + 2*5 + 1*0 = 50

10	5	3	2	1
5	10	6	5	3
3	6	10	1	5
2	5	1	10	3
2	3	5	3	10

4
0
0
5
0

50
45
17
58
23

Similarity Matrix S   User Preference Matrix U   Recommendation Matrix R

Figure 12.5: Generation of a recommendation matrix

A separate resultant matrix is generated for each of the users. The numbers in the recommendation matrix, *Matrix[R]*, quantify the predicted interest of a user in each of the items. For example, in the resultant matrix, the fourth item has the highest number, 58. So this item is highly recommended for this particular user.

Evolving the recommendation system

Recommendation systems aren't static; they thrive on constant refinement. How does this evolution occur? By juxtaposing the recommended items (predictions) with the user's actual choices. By analyzing discrepancies, the system identifies areas to improve. Over time, by recalibrating based on user feedback and observed behaviors, the system enhances its recommendation accuracy, ensuring users always receive the most relevant suggestions.

Now, let's look into the limitations of different recommendation systems.

Understanding the limitations of recommendation systems

Recommendation engines use predictive algorithms to suggest recommendations to a bunch of users. It is a powerful technology, but we should be aware of its limitations. Let's look into the various limitations of recommendation systems.

The cold start problem

At the core of collaborative filtering lies a crucial dependency: historical user data. Without a track record of user preferences, generating accurate suggestions becomes a challenge. For a new entrant into the system, the absence of data means our algorithms largely operate on assumptive grounds, which can lead to imprecise recommendations. Similarly, in content-based recommendation systems, fresh items might lack comprehensive details, making the suggestion process less reliable. This data dependency – the need for established user and item data to produce sound recommendations – is what's termed **the cold start problem**.

There are several strategies to counterbalance the cold start challenge:

1. **Hybrid systems**: Merging collaborative and content-based filtering can offset the limitations of one system using the strengths of the other.

2. **Knowledge-based recommendations**: If historical data is scant, leaning on explicit knowledge about users and items can help bridge the gap.

3. **Onboarding questionnaires**: For new users, a brief questionnaire about preferences can seed the system with initial data, guiding early recommendations.

Understanding and countering these challenges ensures that recommendation systems remain an effective and reliable tool in user engagement strategies.

Metadata requirements

While content-based recommendation systems can function without metadata, incorporating such details can enhance their precision. It's important to note that metadata isn't confined to just textual descriptions. In our multifaceted digital ecosystem, items span various media types like images, audio, or movies. For such media, the "content" can be derived from their inherent properties. For instance, image-based metadata might be pulled from visual patterns; audio metadata from elements like waveforms or spectral features; and for movies, aspects like genre, cast, or scene structure can be considered.

Integrating these diverse content dimensions allows recommendation systems to be more adaptable, offering refined suggestions across a wide range of items.

The data sparsity problem

Across an enormous number of items, a user will have rated only a few items, resulting in a very sparse user/item rating matrix.

> Amazon has around a billion users and a billion items. Amazon's recommendation engine is said to have the sparsest data for any recommendation engine in the world.

To tackle such sparsity, various techniques are deployed. **Matrix factorization methods**, for example, can predict potential ratings in these sparse areas, providing a more complete user-item interaction landscape. Additionally, **hybrid recommendation systems**, which combine elements of content-based and collaborative filtering, can generate meaningful recommendations even when user-item interactions are limited. By integrating these and other approaches, recommendation systems can effectively navigate and mitigate the challenges posed by sparse datasets.

The double-edged sword of social influence in recommendation systems

Recommendation systems can be significantly influenced by social dynamics. Indeed, our social circles often have a marked impact on our preferences and choices. For instance, friends tend to make similar purchases and rate products or services in similar ways.

On the positive side, leveraging social connections can boost recommendation relevance. If a system observes that individuals within a particular social group enjoyed a certain movie or product, it might make sense to recommend that same item to other members of the group. This could lead to increased user satisfaction and, potentially, higher conversion rates.

However, there's a downside. Relying too heavily on social influence can introduce bias into the recommendations. It might inadvertently create echo chambers where users are only exposed to items their immediate social circle appreciate, limiting diversity and potentially missing out on products or services that could be more individually suited. Furthermore, this could lead to a self-reinforcing feedback loop, where the same items keep getting recommended, overshadowing other potentially valuable items.

Thus, while social influence is a powerful tool in shaping user preferences, it's essential for recommendation systems to balance it with individual user behavior and broader trends to ensure a diverse and personalized user experience.

Areas of practical applications

Recommendation systems play a pivotal role in our daily digital interactions. To truly understand their significance, let's delve into their applications across various industries.

Based on the comprehensive details provided about Netflix's use of data science and its recommendation system, let's look at the restructured statement addressing the points mentioned.

Netflix's mastery of data-driven recommendations

Netflix, a leader in streaming, has harnessed data analytics to fine-tune content recommendations, with 800 engineers in Silicon Valley advancing this effort. Their emphasis on data-driven strategies is evident in the Netflix Prize challenge. The winning team, BellKor's Pragmatic Chaos, used 107 diverse algorithms, from matrix factorization to restricted Boltzman machines, investing 2,000 hours in its development.

The results were a significant 10.06% improvement in their "Cinematch" system. This translated to more streaming hours, fewer subscription cancellations, and substantial savings for Netflix. Interestingly, recommendations now influence about 75% of what users watch. Töscher et al. (2009) highlighted a curious "one-day effect" suggesting shared accounts or user mood variations.

While the challenge showcased Netflix's commitment to data, it also hinted at the potential of ensemble techniques in striking a balance between recommendation diversity and accuracy.

Today, elements of the winning model remain core to Netflix's recommendation engine, but with ever-evolving technology, there's potential for further refinements, like integrating reinforcement algorithms and improved A/B testing.

Here's the source for the Netflix statistic: `https://towardsdatascience.com/netflix-recommender-system-a-big-data-case-study-19cfa6d56ff5`.

The evolution of Amazon's recommendation system

In the early 2000s, Amazon transformed its recommendation engine by shifting from user-based collaborative filtering to item-to-item collaborative filtering, as detailed in a seminal 2003 paper by Linden, Smith, and York. The strategy switched from recommending products based on similar users to suggesting products linked to individual product purchases.

The essence of this "relatedness" was deciphered from observed customer purchasing patterns. If Harry Potter book buyers often bought a Harry Potter bookmark, the items were considered related. Yet, the initial system had flaws. For high-volume buyers, the recommendations weren't as refined, leading Smith and his team to make necessary algorithmic tweaks.

Fast-forward a few years – during a 2019 re:MARS conference, Amazon highlighted its significant advancements in movie recommendations for Prime Video customers, achieving a twofold improvement.

The technique utilized for this was inspired by a matrix completion problem. This method involves representing Prime Video customers and movies in a grid and predicting the probability of a customer watching a particular movie. Amazon then applied deep neural networks to this matrix problem, leading to more accurate and personalized movie recommendations.

The future holds even more potential. With continued research and advancements, the Amazon team aims to further refine and revolutionize their recommendation algorithms, always striving to enhance the customer experience.

You can find the Amazon statistic here: `https://www.amazon.science/the-history-of-amazons-recommendation-algorithm`.

Now, let's try to use a recommendation engine to solve a real-world problem.

Practical example – creating a recommendation engine

Let's build a recommendation engine that can recommend movies to a bunch of users. We will use data put together by the GroupLens Research group at the University of Minnesota.

1. Setting up the framework

Our first task is to ensure we have the right tools for the job. In the world of Python, this means importing necessary libraries:

```
import pandas as pd
import numpy as np
```

2. Data loading: ingesting reviews and titles

Now, let's import the df_reviews and df_movie_titles datasets:

```
df_reviews = pd.read_csv('https://storage.googleapis.com/neurals/data/
data/reviews.csv')
df_reviews.head()
```

The reviews.csv dataset encompasses a rich collection of user reviews. Each entry features a user's ID, a movie ID they've reviewed, their rating, and a timestamp of when the review was made.

	userId	movieId	rating	timestamp
0	1	1	4.0	964982703
1	1	3	4.0	964981247
2	1	6	4.0	964982224
3	1	47	5.0	964983815
4	1	50	5.0	964982931

Figure 12.6: Contents of the reviews.csv dataset

The `movies.csv` dataset is a compilation of movie titles and their details. Each record usually contains a unique movie ID, the movie's title, and its associated genre or genres.

	movieId	title	genres
0	1	Toy Story (1995)	Adventure|Animation|Children|Comedy|Fantasy
1	2	Jumanji (1995)	Adventure|Children|Fantasy
2	3	Grumpier Old Men (1995)	Comedy|Romance
3	4	Waiting to Exhale (1995)	Comedy|Drama|Romance
4	5	Father of the Bride Part II (1995)	Comedy

Figure 12.7: Contents of the movies.csv dataset

3. Merging data: crafting a comprehensive view

For a holistic perspective, we need to merge these datasets. The `'movieId'` serves as our bridge between them:

```
df = pd.merge(df_reviews, df_movie_titles, on='movieId')
df.head()
```

The merged datasets should contain the following information:

	userId	movieId	rating	timestamp	title	genres
0	1	1	4.0	964982703	Toy Story (1995)	Adventure|Animation|Children|Comedy|Fantasy
1	5	1	4.0	847434962	Toy Story (1995)	Adventure|Animation|Children|Comedy|Fantasy
2	7	1	4.5	1106635946	Toy Story (1995)	Adventure|Animation|Children|Comedy|Fantasy
3	15	1	2.5	1510577970	Toy Story (1995)	Adventure|Animation|Children|Comedy|Fantasy
4	17	1	4.5	1305696483	Toy Story (1995)	Adventure|Animation|Children|Comedy|Fantasy

Figure 12.8: Merged movie data

Here's a brief on each column:

- `userId`: A unique identifier for each user.
- `movieId`: A unique identifier for each movie.
- `rating`: Represents the rating assigned by a user to a movie, ranging from 1 to 5.
- `timestamp`: Denotes when a particular movie was rated.
- `title`: The movie's title.
- `genres`: The genre(s) associated with the movie.

4. Descriptive analysis: gleaning insights from ratings

Let's dive into the heart of our data: the ratings. A good starting point is to compute the average rating for each movie. Alongside, understanding the number of users who rated a movie can provide insights into its popularity:

```
df_ratings = pd.DataFrame(df.groupby('title')['rating'].mean())
df_ratings['number_of_ratings'] = df.groupby('title')['rating'].count()
df_ratings.head()
```

The mean rating for each movie should be the following:

title	rating	number of ratings
71 (2014)	4.0	1
Hellboy : The Seeds of Creation (2004)	4.0	1
Round Midnight (1986)	3.5	2
Salem's Lot (2004)	5.0	1
Til There Was You (1997)	4.0	2

Figure 12.9: Calculating the mean rating

With these aggregated metrics, we can discern popular movies with high average ratings, potential blockbusters with numerous ratings, or hidden gems that might have fewer reviews but high averages.

This foundation will pave the way for the subsequent steps, where we'll delve into building the actual recommendation engine. As we progress, our understanding of user preferences will refine, enabling us to suggest movies that resonate with individual tastes.

5. Structuring for recommendations: crafting the matrix

The next logical step is to convert our dataset into a structure optimized for recommendations. Visualize this structure as a matrix:

- Rows represent our users (indexed by userId)
- Columns signify movie titles
- Cells within the matrix are populated with ratings, revealing what a user thought of a specific movie

The `pivot_table` function in Pandas is a versatile tool that helps reshape or pivot data in a Data-Frame to provide a summarized view. The function essentially creates a new derived table out of the original one:

```
movie_matrix = df.pivot_table(index='userId', columns='title',
values='rating')
```

Note that the preceding code will generate a very sparse matrix.

6. Putting the engine to test: recommending movies

Let's see our engine in action. Suppose a user has just watched *Avatar* (2009). How can we find other movies they might enjoy?

Our first task is to isolate all users who've rated *Avatar* (2009):

```
avatar_ratings = movie_matrix['Avatar (2009)']
avatar_ratings = avatar_ratings.dropna()
print("\nRatings for 'Avatar (2009)':")
print(avatar_ratings.head())
```

```
userId
10     2.5
15     3.0
18     4.0
21     4.0
22     3.5
Name: Avatar (2009), dtype: float64
```

From the preceding code, note the following:

- **userId**: This represents the unique identifier for each user in our dataset. The `userId` list contains 10, 15, 18, 21, and 22 – the first five users in our data snapshot who have rated *Avatar* (2009).

- **Ratings**: The numbers adjacent to each `userId` (`2.5`, `3.0`, `4.0`, `4.0`, and `3.5`) represent the ratings these users assigned to *Avatar* (2009). The ratings range between 1 and 5, where a higher value indicates a more favorable opinion about the movie. For example, *User 10* rated *Avatar* (2009) a `2.5`, suggesting they found the movie average or perhaps slightly below their expectations, and *User 22* rated it a `3.5`, expressing a slightly above-average appreciation for the movie.

Let's build a recommendation engine that can recommend movies to a bunch of users.

Finding movies correlating with Avatar (2009)

By determining how other movies correlate in rating patterns with *Avatar* (2009), we can suggest movies that might appeal to fans of *Avatar*.

To present our findings neatly:

```
similar_to_Avatar=movie_matrix.corrwith(Avatar_user_rating)
corr_Avatar = pd.DataFrame(similar_to_Avatar, columns=['correlation'])
corr_Avatar.dropna(inplace=True)
corr_Avatar = corr_Avatar.join(df_ratings['number_of_ratings'])
corr_Avatar.head()
```

	correlation	number_of_ratings
title		
'burbs, The (1989)	0.353553	17
(500) Days of Summer (2009)	0.131120	42
*batteries not included (1987)	0.785714	7
10 Things I Hate About You (1999)	0.265637	54

Understanding correlation

A higher correlation (close to 1) means a movie's rating pattern is similar to *Avatar* (2009). A negative value indicates the opposite.

However, it's crucial to approach the recommendations with caution. For instance, *batteries not included* (1987) emerged as a top recommendation for *Avatar* (2009) fans, which might not seem accurate. This could be due to the limitations of relying solely on user ratings without considering other factors, like genres or movie themes. Adjustments and refinements would be needed for a more precise recommendation system.

The resulting table showcases movies that correlate in terms of user rating behavior with *Avatar*. The table produced at the end of our analysis lists movies in terms of their correlation to *Avatar* based on user ratings. But what does this mean in simpler terms?

Correlation, in this context, refers to a statistical measure that explains how one set of data moves in relation to another set of data. Specifically, we used the Pearson correlation coefficient, which ranges from -1 to 1:

- **1**: Perfect positive correlation. This means if *Avatar* received a high rating from a user, the other movie also received a high rating from the same user.

- **-1**: Perfect negative correlation. If *Avatar* got a high rating from a user, the other movie got a low rating from the same user.

- **0**: No correlation. The ratings of *Avatar* and the other movie are independent of each other.

In our movie recommendation context, movies with a higher positive correlation value (closer to 1) to *Avatar* are deemed to be more suitable recommendations for users who liked *Avatar*. This is because these movies have shown a pattern of receiving ratings similar to *Avatar* from the users.

By inspecting the table, you can identify which movies have a rating behavior akin to *Avatar* and, thus, can be potential recommendations for its fans.

This means that we can use these movies as recommendations for the user.

Evaluating the model

Testing and evaluation are critical. One way to evaluate our model is by using methods like train-test split, where a portion of data is set aside for testing. The model's recommendations for the test set are then compared to actual user ratings. Metrics like **Mean Absolute Error (MAE)** or **Root Mean Square Error (RMSE)** can quantify the differences.

Retraining over time: incorporating user feedback

User preferences evolve. Retraining the recommendation model periodically with fresh data ensures its recommendations remain relevant. Incorporating a feedback loop where users can rate or review recommendations further refines the model's accuracy.

Summary

In this chapter, we learned about recommendation engines. We studied the selection of the right recommendation engine based on the problem that we are trying to solve. We also looked into how we can prepare data for recommendation engines to create a similarity matrix. We also learned how recommendation engines can be used to solve practical problems, such as suggesting movies to users based on their past patterns.

In the next chapter, we will focus on the algorithms that are used to understand and process data.

Learn more on Discord

To join the Discord community for this book – where you can share feedback, ask questions to the author, and learn about new releases – follow the QR code below:

```
https://packt.link/WHLel
```

13

Algorithmic Strategies for Data Handling

Data is the New Oil of the Digital Economy.

—*Wired Magazine*

In this data-driven era, the ability to extract meaningful information from large data sets is fundamentally shaping our decision-making processes. The algorithms we delve into throughout this book lean heavily on this reliance on data. Therefore, it becomes important to develop tools, methodologies, and strategic plans aimed at creating robust and efficient infrastructures for data storage.

The focus of this chapter is data-centric algorithms to efficiently manage data. Integral to these algorithms are operations such as efficient storage and data compression. By employing such methodologies, data-centric architectures enable data management and efficient resource utilization. By the end of this chapter, you should be well-equipped to understand the concepts and trade-offs involved in designing and implementing various data-centric algorithms.

This chapter discusses the following concepts:

- Introduction to data algorithms
- Classification of data

- Data storage algorithms
- Data compression algorithms

Let's first introduce the basic concepts.

Introduction to data algorithms

Data algorithms are specialized for managing and optimizing data storage. Beyond storage, they handle tasks like data compression, ensuring efficient storage space utilization, and streamline rapid data retrieval, critical in many applications.

A critical facet in understanding data algorithms, especially in distributed systems, is the CAP theorem. Here's where its significance lies: this theorem elucidates the balance among consistency, availability, and partition tolerance. In any distributed system, achieving two out of these three guarantees simultaneously is all we can hope for. Comprehending CAP's subtleties aids in discerning the challenges and design decisions in modern data algorithms.

In the scope of data governance, these algorithms are invaluable. They assure data consistency across all distributed system nodes, ensuring data integrity. They also assure efficient data availability and manage data partition tolerance, enhancing the system's resilience and security.

Significance of CAP theorem in context of data algorithms

The CAP theorem doesn't just set theoretical limits; it has practical implications in real-world scenarios where data is manipulated, stored, and retrieved. Imagine, for instance, a scenario where an algorithm must retrieve data from a distributed system. The choices made around consistency, availability, and partition tolerance directly impact the efficiency and reliability of that algorithm. If a system prioritizes availability, the data might be easily retrievable but may not be the most up-to-date version. Conversely, a system prioritizing consistency might sometimes delay data retrieval to ensure that only the most recent data is accessed.

The data-centric algorithms we discuss here are, in many ways, influenced by these CAP constraints. By intertwining our understanding of CAP theorem with data algorithms, we can make more informed decisions when dealing with data challenges.

Storage in distributed environments

Single-node architecture is effective for smaller data sets. However, with the surge in dataset sizes, distributed environment storage has become standard for large scale problems. Identifying the right strategy for data storage in such environments depends on various factors, including the nature of the data and anticipated usage patterns.

The CAP theorem provides a foundational principle for developing these storage strategies, helping us tackle challenges linked with managing expansive data sets.

Connecting CAP theorem and data compression

It might initially seem there's little overlap between the CAP theorem and data compression. But consider the practical implications. If we prioritize consistency in our system (as per CAP considerations), our data compression methods would need to ensure that data remains consistently compressed across all nodes. In a system where availability takes precedence, the compression method might be optimized for speed, even if it leads to minor inconsistencies. This interplay highlights that our choices around CAP influence even how we compress and retrieve our data, demonstrating the theorem's pervasive influence in data-centric algorithms.

Presenting the CAP theorem

In 1998, Eric Brewer proposed a theorem that later became famous as the CAP theorem. It highlights the various trade-offs involved in designing a distributed service system. To understand the CAP theorem, first, let's define the following three characteristics of distributed service systems: consistency, availability, and partition tolerance. CAP is, in fact, an acronym made up of these three characteristics:

- **Consistency** (or simply **C**): The distributed service consists of various nodes. Any of these nodes can be used to read, write, or update records in the data repository. Consistency guarantees that at a certain time, t1, independent of which node we use to read the data, we will get the same result. Every read operation either returns the latest data that is consistent across the distributed repository or gives an error message.

- **Availability** (or simply **A**): In the area of distributed systems, availability means that the system as a whole always responds to requests. This ensures that users get a reply every time they query the system, even if it might not always be the latest piece of data. So, instead of focusing on every single node being up-to-date, the emphasis is on the entire system being responsive. It's about guaranteeing that a user's request never goes unanswered, even if some parts of the system have outdated information.

- **Partition Tolerance** (or simply **P**): In a distributed system, multiple nodes are connected via a communication network. Partition tolerance guarantees that, in the event of communication failure between a small subset of nodes (one or more), the system remains operational. Note that to guarantee partition tolerance, data needs to be replicated across a sufficient number of nodes.

Using these three characteristics, the CAP theorem carefully summarizes the trade-offs involved in the architecture and design of a distributed service system. Specifically, the CAP theorem states that, in a distributed storage system, we can only have two of the following characteristics: consistency or **C**, availability or **A**, and partition tolerance or **P**.

This is shown in the following diagram:

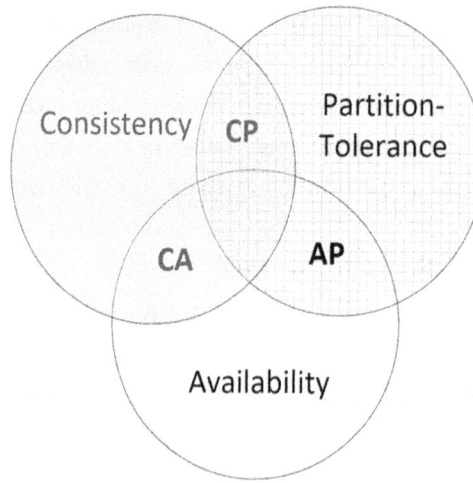

Figure 13.1: Visualizing the choices in distributed systems: the CAP theorem

Distributed data storage is increasingly becoming an essential component of modern IT infrastructure. Designing distributed data storage should be carefully considered, based on the characteristics of the data and the requirements of the problem we want to solve. When applied to distributed databases, the CAP theorem helps to guide the design and decision-making process by ensuring that developers and architects understand the fundamental trade-offs and limitations involved in creating distributed database systems. Balancing these three characteristics is crucial to achieve the desired performance, reliability, and scalability of the distributed database system. When applied to distributed databases, the CAP theorem helps to guide the design and decision-making process by ensuring that developers and architects understand the fundamental trade-offs. Balancing these three characteristics is crucial in order to achieve the desired performance, reliability, and scalability of the distributed database system. In the context of the CAP theorem, we can assume that there are three types of distributed storage systems:

- A **CA** system (implementing Consistency-Availability)
- An **AP** system (implementing Availability-Partition Tolerance)
- A **CP** system (implementing Consistency-Partition Tolerance)

Classifying data storage into **CA**, **AP**, and **CP** systems helps us to understand the various trade-offs involved when designing data storage systems.

Let's look into them, one by one.

CA systems

Traditional single-node systems are CA systems. In non-distributed systems, partition tolerance is not a concern as there is no need to manage communication between multiple nodes. As a result, these systems can focus on maintaining both consistency and availability. In other words, they are CA systems.

A system can function without partition tolerance by storing and processing data on a single node or server. While this approach may not be suitable for handling large-scale data sets or high-velocity data streams, it can be effective for smaller data sizes or applications with less demanding performance requirements.

Traditional single-node databases, such as Oracle or MySQL, are prime examples of CA systems. These systems are well-suited for use cases where data volume and velocity are relatively low, and partition tolerance is not a critical factor. Examples include small to medium-sized businesses, academic projects, or applications with a limited number of users and data sources.

AP systems

AP systems are distributed storage systems designed to prioritize availability and partition tolerance, even at the expense of consistency. These highly responsive systems can sacrifice consistency, if necessary, to accommodate high-velocity data. In doing so, these distributed storage systems can handle user requests immediately, even if it results in temporarily serving slightly outdated or inconsistent data across different nodes.

When consistency is sacrificed in AP systems, users might occasionally may get slightly outdated information. In some cases, this temporary inconsistency is an acceptable trade-off, as the ability to quickly process user requests and maintain high availability is deemed more critical than strict data consistency.

Typical AP systems are used in real-time monitoring systems, such as sensor networks. High-velocity distributed databases, like Cassandra, are prime examples of AP systems.

An AP system is recommended for implementing distributed data storage in scenarios where high availability, responsiveness, and partition tolerance are essential.

For example, if Transport Canada wants to monitor traffic on one of the highways in Ottawa through a network of sensors installed at different locations on the highway, an AP system would be the preferred choice. In this context, prioritizing real-time data processing and availability is crucial to ensuring that traffic monitoring can function effectively, even in the presence of network partitions or temporary inconsistencies. This is why an AP system is often the recommended choice for such applications, despite the potential trade-off of sacrificing consistency.

CP systems

CP systems prioritize both consistency and partition tolerance, ensuring that distributed storage systems guarantee consistency before a read process retrieves a value. These systems are specifically designed to maintain data consistency and continue operating effectively even in the presence of network partitions.

The ideal data type for CP systems is data that requires strict consistency and accuracy, even if it means sacrificing the immediate availability of the system. Examples include financial transactions, inventory management, and critical business operations data. In these cases, ensuring that the data remains consistent and accurate across the distributed environment is of paramount importance.

A typical use case for CP systems is when we want to store document files in JSON format. Document datastores, such as MongoDB, are CP systems tuned for consistency in a distributed environment.

With an understanding of the different types of distributed storage systems, we can now move on to exploring data compression algorithms.

Decoding data compression algorithms

Data compression is an essential methodology used for data storage. It not only enhances storage efficiency and minimizes data transmission times, but it also has significant implications for cost savings and performance improvements, particularly in the realm of big data and cloud computing. This section presents the details data compression techniques, with a special focus on the lossless algorithms Huffman and LZ77, and their influence on modern compression schemes, such as Gzip, LZO, and Snappy.

Lossless compression techniques

Lossless compression revolves around eliminating redundancy in data to minimize storage needs while ensuring perfect reversibility. Huffman and LZ77 are two foundational algorithms that have strongly influenced the field.

Huffman coding focuses on variable-length coding, representing frequent characters with fewer bits, while LZ77, a dictionary-based algorithm, exploits repeated data sequences and represents them with shorter references. Let us look into them one by one.

Huffman coding: Implementing variable-length coding

Huffman coding, a form of entropy encoding, is used widely in lossless data compression. The key principle underlying Huffman coding is to assign shorter codes to more frequently occurring characters in a dataset, thereby reducing the overall data size.

The algorithm uses a specific type of binary tree known as a Huffman tree, where each leaf node corresponds to a data element. The frequency of occurrence of the element determines the placement in the tree: more frequent elements are placed closer to the root. This strategy ensures that the most common elements have the shortest codes.

A quick example

Imagine we have data containing letters **A**, **B**, and **C** with frequencies 5, 9, and 12 respectively. In Huffman coding:

- **C**, being the most frequent, might get a short code like 0.
- **B**, the next frequent, could get 10.
- **A**, the least frequent, might have 11.

To understand it fully, let us go through an example in Python.

Implementing Huffman coding in Python

We start by creating a node for each character, where the node contains the character and its frequency. These nodes are then added to a priority queue, with the least frequent elements having the highest priority. For this, we create a Node class to represent each character in the Huffman tree. Each Node object contains the character, its frequency, and pointers to its left and right children. The __lt__ method is defined to compare two Node objects based on their frequencies.

```python
import functools

@functools.total_ordering
class Node:
    def __init__(self, char, freq):
        self.char = char
        self.freq = freq
        self.left = None
```

```
        self.right = None
    def __lt__(self, other):
        return self.freq < other.freq
    def __eq__(self, other):
        return self.freq == other.freq
```

Next, we build the Huffman tree. The construction of a Huffman tree involves a series of insertions and deletions in a priority queue, typically implemented as a binary heap. To build the Huffman tree, we create a min-heap of Node objects. A min-heap is a specialized tree-based structure that satisfies a simple but important condition: the parent node has a value less than or equal to its children. This property ensures that the smallest element is always at the root, making it efficient for priority operations. We repeatedly pop the two nodes with the lowest frequencies, merge them, and push the merged node back into the heap. This process continues until there is only one node left, which becomes the root of the Huffman tree. The tree can be built by build_tree function, which is defined as follows:

```
import heapq
def build_tree(frequencies):
    heap = [Node(char, freq) for char, freq in frequencies.items()]
    heapq.heapify(heap)
    while len(heap) > 1:
        node1 = heapq.heappop(heap)
        node2 = heapq.heappop(heap)
        merged = Node(None, node1.freq + node2.freq)
        merged.left = node1
        merged.right = node2
        heapq.heappush(heap, merged)
    return heap[0]  # the root node
```

Once the Huffman tree is constructed, we can generate the Huffman codes by traversing the tree. Starting from the root, we append a 0 for every left branch we follow and a 1 for every right branch. When we reach a leaf node, the sequence of 0s and 1s accumulated along the path from the root forms the Huffman code for the character at that leaf node. This functionality is achieved by creating generate_codes function as follows.

```
def generate_codes(node, code='', codes=None):
    if codes is None:
        codes = {}
    if node is None:
```

```
        return {}
    if node.char is not None:
        codes[node.char] = code
        return codes
    generate_codes(node.left, code + '0', codes)
    generate_codes(node.right, code + '1', codes)
    return codes
```

Now let us use the Huffman tree. Let us first define data that we will use for Huffman's encoding.

```
data = {
    'L': 0.45,
    'M': 0.13,
    'N': 0.12,
    'X': 0.16,
    'Y': 0.09,
    'Z': 0.05
}
```

Then, we print out the Huffman codes for each character.

```
# Build the Huffman tree and generate the Huffman codes
root = build_tree(data)
codes = generate_codes(root)
# Print the root of the Huffman tree
print(f'Root of the Huffman tree: {root}')
# Print out the Huffman codes
for char, code in codes.items():
    print(f'{char}: {code}')
```

```
Root of the Huffman tree: <__main__.Node object at 0x7a537d66d240>
L: 0
M: 101
N: 100
X: 111
Y: 1101
Z: 1100
```

Now, we can infer the following:

- **Fixed length code**: The fixed-length code for this table is 3. This is because, with six characters, a fixed-length binary representation would need a maximum of three bits ($2^3 = 8$ possible combinations, which can cover our 6 characters).

- **Variable length code**: The variable-length code for this table is
  `45(1) + .13(3) + .12(3) + .16(3) + .09(4) + .05(4) = 2.24`.

The following diagram shows the Huffman tree created from the preceding example:

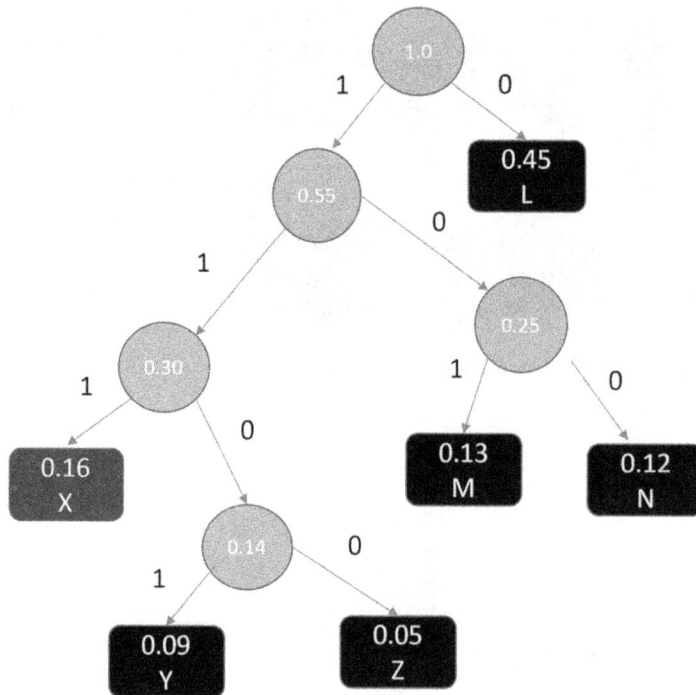

Figure 13.2: The Huffman tree: visualizing the vompression process

Note that Huffman encoding is about converting data into a Huffman tree that enables compression. Decoding or decompression brings the data back to the original format.

Having looked at Huffman's encoding, let us now explore another lossless compression technique based on dictionary-based compression.

Next, let us discuss dictionary-based compression.

Understanding dictionary-based compression LZ77

LZ77 belongs to a family of compression algorithms known as dictionary coders. Rather than maintaining a static dictionary of code words, as in Huffman coding, LZ77 dynamically builds a dictionary of substrings seen in the input data. This dictionary isn't stored separately but is implicitly referred to as a sliding window over the already-encoded input, facilitating an elegant and efficient method of representing repeating sequences.

The LZ77 algorithm operates on the principle of replacing repeated occurrences of data with references to a single copy. It maintains a "sliding window" of recently processed data. When it encounters a substring that has occurred before, it doesn't store the actual substring; instead, it stores a pair of values – the distance to the start of the repeated substring in the sliding window, and the length of the repeated substring.

Understanding with an example

Imagine a scenario where you're reading the string:

data_string = "ABABCABABD"

Now, as you process this string left to right, when you encounter the substring "CABAB", you'll notice that "ABAB" has appeared before, right after the initial "AB". LZ77 takes advantage of such repetitions.

Instead of writing "ABAB" again, LZ77 would suggest: "Hey, look back two characters and copy the next two characters!" In technical terms, this is a reference back of two characters with a length of two characters.

So, compressing our data_string using LZ77, it might look something like:

ABABC<2,2>D

Here, <2,2> is the LZ77 notation, indicating "go back by two characters and copy the next two."

Comparison with Huffman

To appreciate the power and differences between LZ77 and Huffman, it's helpful to use the same data. Let's stick with our data_string = "ABABCABABD".

While LZ77 identifies repeated sequences in data and references them, Huffman encoding is more about representing frequent characters with shorter codes.

For instance, if you were to compress our data_string using Huffman, you might see certain characters, say 'A' and 'B', that are more frequent, represented with shorter binary codes than the less frequent 'C' and 'D'.

This comparison showcases that while Huffman is all about frequency-based representation, LZ77 is about spotting and referencing patterns. Depending on the data type and structure, one might be more efficient than the other.

Advanced lossless compression formats

The principles laid out by Huffman and LZ77 have given rise to advanced compression formats. We will look into three advanced formats in this chapter.

1. LZO

2. Snappy

3. gzip

Let us look into them one by one.

LZO compression: Prioritizing speed

LZO is a lossless data compression algorithm that emphasizes rapid compression and decompression. It replaces repeated occurrences of data with references to a single copy. After this initial pass of LZ77 compression, the data is then passed through a Huffman coding stage.

While its compression ratio might not be the highest, its processing speed is significantly faster than many other algorithms. This makes LZO an excellent choice for situations where quick data access is a priority, such as real-time data processing and streaming applications.

Snappy compression: Striking a balance

Snappy is another fast compression and decompression library originally developed by Google. The primary focus of Snappy is to achieve high speeds and reasonable compression, but not necessarily the maximum compression.

Snappy's compression method is based on LZ77 but with a focus on speed and without an additional entropy encoding step like Huffman coding. Instead, Snappy utilizes a much simpler encoding algorithm that ensures speedy compressions and decompressions. The algorithm uses a copy-based strategy where it searches for repeated sequences in the data and then encodes them as a length and a reference to the previous location.

It should be noted that due to this tradeoff for speed, Snappy does not compress data as efficiently as algorithms that use Huffman coding or other forms of entropy encoding. However, in use-cases where speed is more critical than the compression ratio, Snappy can be a very effective choice.

GZIP compression: Maximizing storage efficiency

GZIP is a file format and a software application used for file compression and decompression. The GZIP data format uses a combination of the LZ77 algorithm and Huffman coding.

Practical example: Data management in AWS: A focus on CAP theorem and compression algorithms

Let us consider an example of a global e-commerce platform that runs on multiple cloud servers across the world. This platform handles thousands of transactions every second, and the data generated from these transactions needs to be stored and processed efficiently. We'll see how the CAP theorem and compression algorithms can guide the design of the platform's data management system.

1. Applying the CAP theorem

The CAP theorem states that a distributed data store cannot simultaneously provide more than two out of the following three guarantees: consistency, availability, and partition tolerance.

In our e-commerce platform scenario, availability and partition tolerance might be prioritized. High availability ensures that the system can continue processing transactions even if a few servers fail. Partition tolerance means the system can still function even if network failures cause some of the servers to be isolated.

While this means the system may not always provide strong consistency (every read receives the most recent write), it could use eventual consistency (updates propagate through the system and eventually all replicas show the same value) to ensure a good user experience. In practice, slight inconsistencies might be acceptable, for example, when it takes a few seconds for a user's shopping cart to update across all devices.

In the AWS ecosystem, we have a variety of data storage services that can be chosen based on the needs defined by the CAP theorem. For our e-commerce platform, we would prefer availability and partition tolerance over consistency. Amazon DynamoDB, a key-value NoSQL database, would be an excellent fit. It offers built-in support for multi-region replication and automatic sharding, ensuring high availability and partition tolerance.

For consistency, DynamoDB offers "eventual consistency" and "strong consistency" options. In our case, we would opt for eventual consistency to prioritize availability and performance.

2. Using compression algorithms

The platform would generate vast amounts of data, including transaction details, user behavior logs, and product information. Storing and transferring this data could be costly and time-consuming.

Here, compression algorithms like gzip, Snappy, or LZO can help. For instance, the platform might use gzip to compress transaction logs that are archived for long-term storage. Given that gzip can typically compress text files to about 30% of their original size, this could reduce storage costs significantly.

On the other hand, for real-time analytics on user behavior data, the platform might use Snappy or LZO. While these algorithms may not compress data as much as gzip, they are faster and would allow the analytics system to process data more quickly.

AWS provides various ways to implement compression depending on the type and use of data. For compressing transaction logs for long-term storage, we could use Amazon S3 (Simple Storage Service) coupled with gzip compression. S3 supports automatic gzip compression for files being uploaded, which can significantly reduce storage costs. For real-time analytics on user behavior data, we could use Amazon Kinesis Data Streams with Snappy or LZO compression. Kinesis can capture, process, and store data streams for real-time analytics, and supports compression to handle high-volume data.

3. Quantifying the benefits

The benefits can be quantified similarly as described earlier.

Let's take a practical example to demonstrate potential cost savings. Imagine our platform produces 1 TB of transaction logs daily. By leveraging gzip compression with S3, we can potentially shrink the storage requirement to roughly 300 GB. As of August 2023, S3 charges around $0.023 for every GB up to the initial 50 TB monthly. Doing the math, this equates to a saving of about $485 each month, or a significant $5,820 annually, just from the log storage. It's worth noting that the cited AWS pricing is illustrative and specific to August 2023; be sure to check current rates as they might vary.

Using Snappy or LZO with Kinesis for real-time analytics could improve data processing speed. This could lead to more timely and personalized user recommendations, potentially increasing sales. The financial gain could be calculated based on the increase in conversion rate attributed to improved recommendation speed.

Lastly, by using DynamoDB and adhering to the CAP theorem, we ensure a smooth shopping experience for our users even in the event of network partitions or individual server failures. The value of this choice could be reflected in the platform's user retention rate and overall customer satisfaction.

Summary

In this chapter, we examined the design of data-centric algorithms, concentrating on three key components: data storage, data governance and data compression. We investigated the various issues related to data governance. We analyzed how the distinct attributes of data influence the architectural decisions for data storage. We investigated different data compression algorithms, each providing specific advantages in terms of efficiency and performance. In the next chapter, we will look at cryptographic algorithms. We will learn how we can use the power of these algorithms to secure exchanged and stored messages.

Learn more on Discord

To join the Discord community for this book – where you can share feedback, ask questions to the author, and learn about new releases – follow the QR code below:

```
https://packt.link/WHLel
```

14

Cryptography

I carry my unwritten poems in cipher on my face!

—*George Eliot*

This chapter introduces you to algorithms related to cryptography. We will start by presenting the background, then we will discuss symmetric encryption algorithms. We will then explain the **Message-Digest 5 (MD5)** algorithm and the **Secure Hash Algorithm (SHA)** and present the limitations and weaknesses of symmetric algorithms. Next, we will discuss asymmetric encryption algorithms and how they are used to create digital certificates. Finally, we will present a practical example that summarizes all of these techniques.

By the end of this chapter, you will have a basic understanding of various issues related to cryptography.

The following topics are discussed in this chapter:

- Introduction to cryptography
- Understanding the types of cryptography techniques
- Example – security concerns when deploying a machine learning model

Let's start by looking at the basic concepts.

Introduction to cryptography

Techniques to protect secrets have been around for centuries. The earliest attempts to secure and hide data from adversaries date back to ancient inscriptions discovered on monuments in Egypt, where a special alphabet that was known by only a few trusted people was used. This early form of security is called obscurity and is still used in different forms today. In order for this method to work, it is critical to protect the secret, which would be the secret meaning of the alphabet in the above example. Later in time, finding foolproof ways of protecting important messages was important in both World War One and World War Two. In the late 20th century, with the introduction of electronics and computers, sophisticated algorithms were developed to secure data, giving rise to a whole new field called cryptography. This chapter discusses the algorithmic aspects of cryptography. One of the uses of these algorithms is to allow secure data exchange between two processes or users. Cryptographic algorithms find strategies for using mathematical functions to ensure the stated security goals.

First, we will look at the importance of "the weakest link" in the infrastructure.

Understanding the importance of the weakest link

Sometimes, when architecting the security of digital infrastructure, we put too much emphasis on the security of individual entities and don't pay the necessary attention to end-to-end security. This can result in us overlooking some loopholes and vulnerabilities in the system, which can later be exploited by hackers to access sensitive data. The important point to remember is that a digital infrastructure, as a whole, is only as strong as its weakest link. For a hacker, this weakest link can provide backdoor access to sensitive data in the digital infrastructure. Beyond a certain point, there is not much benefit in fortifying the front door without closing all the back doors.

As the algorithms and techniques for keeping digital infrastructure become more and more sophisticated, attackers keep upgrading their techniques as well. It is always important to remember that one of the easiest ways for attackers to hack digital infrastructure is by exploiting these vulnerabilities to access sensitive information.

In 2014, a cyber attack on a Canadian federal research institute—the **National Research Council (NRC)**—is estimated to have cost hundreds of millions of dollars. The attackers were able to steal decades of research data and intellectual property material. They used a loophole in the Apache software that was used on the web servers to gain access to the sensitive data.

In this chapter, we will highlight the vulnerabilities of various encryption algorithms.

Let's first look at the basic terminology used.

The basic terminology

Let's look at the basic terminology related to cryptography:

- **Cipher**: An algorithm that performs a particular cryptographic function.
- **Plain text**: The plain data, which can be a text file, a video, a bitmap, or a digitized voice. In this chapter, we will represent plain text as *P*.
- **Cipher text**: The scrambled text that is obtained after applying cryptography to the plain text. In this chapter, we will represent this as *C*.
- **Cipher suite**: A set or suite of cryptographic software components. When two separate nodes want to exchange messages using cryptography, they first need to agree on a cipher suite. This is important in ensuring that they use exactly the same implementation of the cryptographic functions.
- **Encryption**: The process of converting plain text, *P*, into cipher text, *C*, is called encryption. Mathematically, it is represented by *encrypt(P) = C*.
- **Decryption**: The process of converting cipher text back into plain text. Mathematically, it is represented by *decrypt(C) = P*.
- **Cryptanalysis**: The methods used to analyze the strength of cryptographic algorithms. The analyst tries to recover the plain text without access to the secret.
- **Personally Identifiable Information (PII)**: PII is information that can be used to trace an individual's identity when used alone or with other relevant data. Some examples include protected information, such as a social security number, date of birth, or mother's maiden name.

Let us first understand the security needs of a system.

Understanding the security requirements

It is important to first understand the exact security needs of a system. Understanding this will help us use the correct cryptographic technique and discover the potential loopholes in a system.

One way of developing a better understanding of the security needs of a system is by answering the following four questions:

- Which individuals or processes need to be protected?

- Who are we protecting the individuals and processes from?
- Where should we protect them?
- Why are we protecting them?

Let us take the example of a **Virtual Private Cloud** (**VPC**) in the AWS cloud. A VPC allows us to create a logical isolation network where resources like virtual machines are added to it. In order to understand the security requirements of a VPC, it is important to first identify the identities by answering those four questions:

- How many individuals are planning to use this system?
- What sort of information needs to be protected?
- Should we protect the VPC only, or we are passing a message to the system that needs to be encrypted and communicated to the VPC?
- What is the security classification of the data? What are the potential risks? Why would anyone have an incentive to try to hack the system?

Most of the answers to these questions will come by performing the following three steps:

1. Identify the entities.
2. Establish the security goals.
3. Understand the sensitivity of the data.

Let's look at these steps one by one.

Step 1: Identifying the entities

An entity can be defined as an individual, a process, or a resource that is part of an information system. We first need to identify how users, resources, and processes are present at runtime. Then, we will quantify the security needs of these identified entities, either individually or as a group.

Once we better understand these requirements, we can establish the security goals of our digital system.

Step 2: Establishing the security goals

The goal of designing a security system is to protect information from being stolen, compromised, or attacked. Cryptographic algorithms are typically used to meet one or more security goals:

- **Authentication**: Authentication is a mechanism by which we ascertain the identity of a user, device, or system, confirming that they are indeed what or who they claim to be.

- **Authorization**: Authorization is the process of giving the user permission to access a specific resource or function.

- **Confidentiality**: Data that needs to be protected is called **sensitive data**. Confidentiality is the concept of restricting sensitive data to authorized users only. To protect the confidentiality of sensitive data during its transit or in storage, you need to render the data so that it is unreadable except by authorized users. This is accomplished by using encryption algorithms, which we will discuss later on in this chapter.

- **Integrity**: Integrity is the process of establishing that data has not been altered in any way during its transit or storage. For example, **TCP/IP (Transmission Control Protocol/ Internet Protocol)** uses checksum or **Cyclic Redundancy Check (CRC)** algorithms to verify data integrity.

- **Non-repudiation**: Non-repudiation is the ability to produce unforgeable and irrefutable evidence that a message was sent or received. This evidence can be used later to prove the receipt of data.

Step 3: Understanding the sensitivity of the data

It is important to understand the classified nature of data. Data is categorized by regulatory authorities such as governments, agencies, or organizations based on how serious the consequence will be if it is compromised. The categorization of the data helps us choose the correct cryptographic algorithm. There is more than one way to categorize data, based on the sensitivity of the information it contains. Let's look at the typical ways of classifying data:

- **Public data or unclassified data**: Anything that is available for consumption to the public, for example, information found on a company's website or a government's info portal.

- **Internal data or confidential data**: Although not for public consumption, exposing this data to the public may not have damaging consequences. For example, if an employee's emails complaining about their manager are exposed, it may be embarrassing for the company but this may not have damaging consequences.

- **Sensitive data or secret data**: Data that is not supposed to be for public consumption and exposing it to the public could have damaging consequences for an individual or an organization. For example, leaking the details of a future iPhone may harm Apple's business goals and could give an advantage to rivals, such as Samsung.

- **Highly sensitive data**: Also called **top-secret data**. This is information that, if disclosed, would be extremely damaging to the organization. Examples of highly sensitive data include proprietary research, strategic business plans, or internal financial data.

Top-secret data is protected through multiple layers of security and requires special permission to access it.

> In general, more sophisticated security designs are much slower than simple algorithms. It is important to strike the right balance between the security and the performance of the system.

Understanding the basic design of ciphers

Designing ciphers is about coming up with an algorithm that can scramble sensitive data so that a malicious process or an unauthorized user cannot access it. Although, over time, ciphers have become more and more sophisticated, the underlying principles that ciphers are based on remain unchanged.

Let's start by looking at some relatively simple ciphers that will help us understand the underlying principles that are used in the design of cryptographic algorithms.

Presenting substitution ciphers

Substitution ciphers have been in use for hundreds of years in various forms. As the name indicates, substitution ciphers are based on a simple concept—substituting characters in plain text with other characters in a predetermined, organized way.

Let's look at the exact steps involved in this:

1. First, we map each character to a substitute character.
2. Then, we encode and convert the plain text into cipher text by replacing each character in the plain text with another character in the cipher text using substitution mapping.
3. To decode, we bring back the plaintext by using substitution mapping.

The following are examples of substitution-based ciphers:

- Caesar cipher
- Rotation 13

Let us look into them in more detail.

Caesar cipher

Caesar ciphers are based on substitution mapping. Substitution mapping changes the actual string in a deterministic way by applying a simple formula that is kept secret.

The substitution mapping is created by replacing each character with the third character to the right of it. This mapping is described in the following diagram:

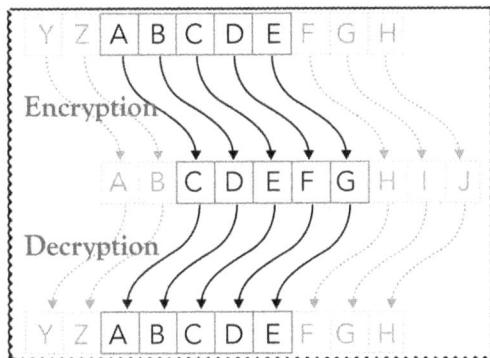

Figure 13.1: The substitution mapping of Caesar ciphers

Let's see how we can implement a Caesar cipher using Python:

```python
rotation = 3
P = 'CALM'; C=''
for letter in P:
    C = C+ (chr(ord(letter) + rotation))
```

We can see that we applied a Caesar cipher to the plaintext CALM.

Let's print the cipher text after encrypting it with the Caesar cipher:

```python
print(C)
```

```
FDOP
```

> Caesar ciphers are said to have been used by Julius Caesar to communicate with his advisers.

A Caesar cipher is a simple cipher and is easy to implement. The downside is that it is not too difficult to crack as a hacker could simply iterate through all the possible shifts of the alphabet (all 2626 of them) and see if any coherent message appears. Given the current processing abilities of computers, this is a relatively small number of combinations to do. It should not be used to protect highly sensitive data.

Rotation 13 (ROT13)

ROT13 is a special case of the Caesar cipher where the substitution mapping is created by replacing each character with the 13th character to the right of it. The following diagram illustrates this:

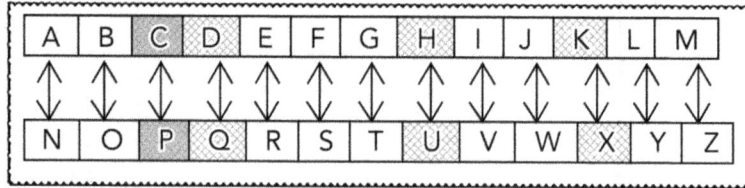

Figure 14.2: Workings of ROT13

This means that if `ROT13()` is the function that implements ROT13, then the following applies:

```
rotation = 13
P = 'CALM'; C=''
for letter in P:
    C = C+ (chr(ord(letter) + rotation))
```

Now, let's print the encoded value of C:

```
print(c)
```

```
PNYZ
```

ROT13 is actually not used to accomplish data confidentiality. It is used more to mask text, for example, to hide potentially offensive text. It can also be used to avoid giving away the answer to a puzzle, and in other similar use-cases.

Cryptanalysis of substitution ciphers

Substitution ciphers are simple to implement and understand. Unfortunately, they are also easy to crack. Simple cryptanalysis of substitution ciphers shows that if we use the English language alphabet, then all we need to determine to crack the cipher is how much we are rotating by. We can try each letter of the English alphabet one by one until we are able to decrypt the text. This means that it will take around 25 attempts to reconstruct the plain text.

Now, let's look at another type of simple cipher—transposition ciphers.

Understanding transposition ciphers

In transposition ciphers, the characters of the plain text are encrypted using transposition. Transposition is a method of encryption where we scramble the position of the characters using deterministic logic. A transposition cipher writes characters into rows in a matrix and then reads the columns as output. Let's look at an example.

Let's take the Ottawa Rocks plain text (*P*).

First, let's encode *P*. For that, we will use a 3 x 4 matrix and write in the plaintext horizontally:

O	t	t	a
w	a	R	o
c	k	s	

The read process will read the string vertically, which will generate the cipher text—OwctaktRsao. The key would be {1,2,3,4}, which is the order in which the columns are read. Encrypting with a different key, say, {2,4,3,1}, would result in a different cipher text, in this case, takaotRsOwc.

> The Germans used a cipher named ADFGVX in the First World War, which used both transposition and substitution ciphers. Years later, it was cracked by George Painvin.

So, these are some of the types of ciphers. In general, ciphers use a key to code plain text. Now, let's look at some of the cryptographic techniques that are currently used. Cryptography protects a message using encryption and decryption processes, as discussed in the next section.

Understanding the types of cryptographic techniques

Different types of cryptographic techniques use different types of algorithms and are used under different sets of circumstances. As different situations and use-cases have different requirements of security based on the business requirements and the data classification, the selection of the right technique is important for a well-designed architecture.

Broadly, cryptographic techniques can be divided into the following three types:

- Hashing
- Symmetric
- Asymmetric

Let's look at them one by one.

Using the cryptographic hash function

The cryptographic hash function is a mathematical algorithm that can be used to create a unique fingerprint of a message. It creates an output, called a hash, from plain text. The size of the output is usually fixed but can vary for some specialized algorithms.

Mathematically, this looks as follows:

$$C_1 = hashFunction(P_1)$$

This is explained as follows:

- P_1 is the plain text representing the input data
- C_1 is a fixed-length hash that is generated by the cryptographic hash function

This is shown in the following diagram. The variable-length data is converted into a fixed-length hash through a one-way hash function:

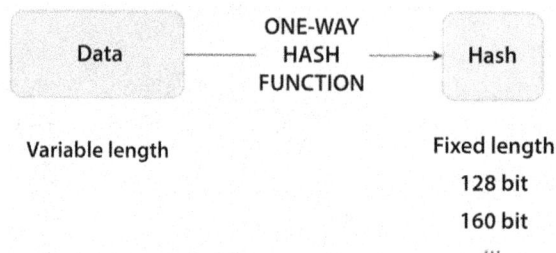

Figure 14.3: One-way hash functions

A hash function is a mathematical algorithm that transforms an arbitrary amount of data into a fixed-size string of bytes. It plays a vital role in ensuring the integrity and authenticity of data. Below are the key characteristics that define a cryptographic hash function:

- **Deterministic**: A hash function is deterministic, meaning that the same input (or "plaintext") will always produce the same output (or "hash"). No matter how many times you hash a particular piece of data, the result will remain consistent.
- **Uniqueness**: Ideally, different inputs should always produce unique hash outputs. If two distinct inputs produce the same hash, this is known as a collision. Quality hash functions are designed to minimize the likelihood of collisions.

- **Fixed length**: The output of a hash function has a fixed length, regardless of the size of the input data. Whether you're hashing a single character or an entire novel, the resulting hash will be of the same size, specific to the hash algorithm used (e.g., 128 bits for MD5, 256 bits for SHA-256).

- **Sensitive to input changes**: Even a minor alteration in the plaintext leads to a significant and unpredictable change in the resulting hash value. This property ensures that it is not feasible to derive the original input or find a different input that produces the same hash, enhancing the security of the hash function. The effect is such that even changing a single letter in a large document will result in a hash that appears entirely different from the original.

- **One-way function**: Hash functions are one-way, meaning that it is computationally infeasible to reverse the process and generate the original plaintext (P_i) from the hash (C_i). This ensures that even if an unauthorized party obtains the hash, they cannot use it to determine the original data.

If we have a situation where each unique message does not have a unique hash, we call it a collision. In other words, a collision is when the hash algorithm produces the same hash value for two different input values. For security applications, a collision is a potential vulnerability and its probability should be very low. That is, if we have two texts, P1 and P2, in the case of collision, it means $hashFunction(P_1) = hashFunction(P_2)$.

Regardless of the hashing algorithm used, collisions are rare. Otherwise, hashing wouldn't be useful. However, for some applications, collisions cannot be tolerated. In those cases, we need to use a hashing algorithm that is more complex but much less likely to generate hash values that collide.

Implementing cryptographic hash functions

Cryptographic hash functions can be implemented by using various algorithms. Let's take a deeper look at two of them:

1. MD5
2. **Secure Hashing Algorithm (SHA)**

Understanding MD5-tolerated

MD5 was developed by Poul-Henning Kamp in 1994 to replace MD4. It generates a 128-bit hash. Generating a 128-bit hash means that the resulting hash value is made up of 128 binary digits (bits).

This translates to a fixed length of 16 bytes or 32 hexadecimal characters. The fixed length ensures that no matter the size of the original data, the hash will always be 128 bits long. The purpose of this fixed-length output is to create a "fingerprint" or "digest" of the original data. MD5 is a relatively simple algorithm that is vulnerable to collision. In applications where a collision cannot be tolerated, MD5 should not be used. For example, it can be used to check the integrity of files downloaded from the internet.

Let's look at an example. In order to generate an MD5 hash in Python, we will start by using the `hashlib` module, which is part of the Python Standard Library and provides a range of different cryptographic hashing algorithms:

```
import hashlib
```

Next, we define a utility function called `generate_md5_hash()`, which takes `input_string` as a parameter. This string will be hashed by the function:

```
def generate_md5_hash(input_string):
    # Create a new md5 hash object
    md5_hash = hashlib.md5()

    # Encode the input string to bytes and hash it
    md5_hash.update(input_string.encode())

    # Return the hexadecimal representation of the hash
    return md5_hash.hexdigest()
```

Note that `hashlib.md5()` creates a new hash object. This object uses the MD5 algorithm and `md5_hash.update(input_string.encode())` updates the hash object with the bytes of the input string. The string is encoded to bytes using the default UTF-8 encoding. After all data has been updated in the hash object, we can call the `hexdigest()` method to return the hexadecimal representation of the digest. This is the MD5 hash of the input string.

Here we use the `generate_md5_hash()` function to get the MD5 hash of the string `"Hello, World!"`, and print the result to the console:

```
def verify_md5_hash(input_string, correct_hash):
    # Generate md5 hash for the input_string
    computed_hash = generate_md5_hash(input_string)

    # Compare the computed hash with the provided hash
```

```
        return computed_hash == correct_hash

# Test
input_string = "Hello, World!"
hash_value = generate_md5_hash(input_string)
print(f"Generated hash: {hash_value}")

correct_hash = hash_value
print(verify_md5_hash(input_string, correct_hash))# This should return True
```

```
Generated hash: 65a8e27d8879283831b664bd8b7f0ad4
True
```

In the `verify_md5_hash` function, we take an input string and a known correct MD5 hash. We generate the MD5 hash of the input string using our `generate_md5_hash` function and then compare it to the known correct hash.

When to use MD5

Looking back at history, weaknesses with MD5 were discovered in the late 1990s. Despite several issues, MD5 usage is still popular. It is ideal to be used for integrity checks for data. Note that the MD5 message digest does not uniquely associate the hash with its owner as the MD5 digest is not a signed hash. MD5 is used to prove that a file has not been changed since the hash was computed. It is not used to prove the authenticity of a file. Now, let's look at another hashing algorithm—SHA.

Understanding Secure Hashing Algorithm (SHA)

SHA was developed by the **National Institute of Standards and Technology (NIST)**. It's widely used to verify the integrity of data. Among its variations, SHA-512 is a popular hash function, and Python's `hashlib` library includes it. Let's see how we can use Python to create a hash using the SHA algorithm. For that, let us first import the `hashlib` library:

```
import hashlib
```

Then we will define the salt and the message. Salting is the practice of adding random characters to a password before hashing. It enhances security by making hash collisions more challenging:

```
salt = "qIo0foX5"
password = "myPassword"
```

Next, we will combine the salt with the password to apply the salting procedure:

```
salted_password = salt + password
```

Then, we will use the sha512 function to create a hash of the salted password:

```
sha512_hash = hashlib.sha512()
sha512_hash.update(salted_password.encode())
myHash = sha512_hash.hexdigest()
```

Let us print myHash:

```
myHash
```

```
2e367911b87b12f73b135b1a4af9fac193a8064d3c0a52e34b3a52a5422beed2b6276eabf9
5abe728f91ba61ef93175e5bac9a643b54967363ffab0b35133563
```

Note that when we use the SHA algorithm, the hash generated is 512 bytes. This specific size isn't arbitrary, but rather a key component of the algorithm's security features. A larger hash size corresponds to an increased number of potential combinations, thereby reducing the chances of "collisions"—instances where two different inputs produce the same hash output. Collisions compromise the reliability of a hashing algorithm, and SHA-512's 512-byte output significantly reduces this risk.

An application of the cryptographic hash function

Hash functions are used to check the integrity of a file after making a copy of it. To achieve this, when a file is copied from a source to a destination (for example, when downloaded from a web server), a corresponding hash is also copied with it. This original hash, *horiginal*, acts as a fingerprint of the original file. After copying the file, we generate the hash again from the copied version of the file—that is, *hcopied*. If *horiginal* = *hcopied*—that is, the generated hash matches the original hash—this verifies that the file has not changed and none of the data was lost during the download process. We can use any cryptographic hash function, such as MD5 or SHA, to generate a hash for this purpose.

Choosing between MD5 and SHA

Both MD5 and SHA are hashing algorithms. MD5 is simple and fast, but it does not provide good security. SHA is complex compared to MD5 and it provides a greater level of security.

Now, let's look at symmetric encryption.

Using symmetric encryption

In cryptography, a key is a combination of numbers that is used to encode plain text using an algorithm of our choice. In symmetric encryption, we use the same key for encryption and decryption. If the key used for symmetric encryption is K, then for symmetric encryption, the following equation holds:

$$EK(P) = C$$

Here, P is the plain text and C is the cipher text.

For decryption, we use the same key, K, to convert it back to P:

$$DK(C) = P$$

This process is shown in the following diagram:

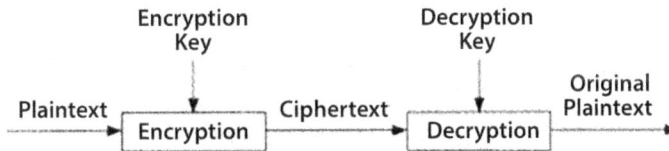

Figure 14.4: Symmetric encryption

Now, let's look at how we can use symmetric encryption with Python.

Coding symmetric encryption

In this section, we'll explore how to work with hash functions using Python's built-in `hashlib` library. `hashlib` comes pre-installed with Python and provides a wide array of hashing algorithms. First, let us import the `hashlib` library:

```
import hashlib
```

We'll use the SHA-256 algorithm to create our hash. Other algorithms like MD5, SHA-1, etc., can also be used:

```
sha256_hash = hashlib.sha256()
```

Let's create a hash for the message `"Ottawa is really cold"`:

```
message = "Ottawa is really cold".encode()
sha256_hash.update(message)
```

The hexadecimal representation of the hash can be printed with:

```
print(sha256_hash.hexdigest())
```

```
b6ee63a201c4505f1f50ff92b7fe9d9e881b57292c00a3244008b76d0e026161
```

Let's look at some of the advantages of symmetric encryption.

The advantages of symmetric encryption

The following are the advantages of symmetric encryption:

- **Simple**: Encryption and decryption using symmetric encryption are simpler to implement.
- **Fast**: Symmetric encryption is faster than asymmetric encryption.
- **Secure**: One of the most widely used symmetric key encryption systems is the U.S. government-designated **Advanced Encryption Standard (AES)**. When using a secure algorithm such as AES, symmetric encryption is at least as secure as asymmetric encryption.

The problems with symmetric encryption

When two users or processes plan to use symmetric encryption to communicate, they need to exchange keys using a secure channel. This gives rise to the following two problems:

- **Key protection**: How to protect the symmetric encryption key
- **Key distribution**: How to share the symmetric encryption key from the source to the destination

Now, let's look at asymmetric encryption.

Asymmetric encryption

In the 1970s, asymmetric encryption was devised to address some of the weaknesses of symmetric encryption that we discussed in the previous section.

The first step in asymmetric encryption is to generate two different keys that look totally different but are algorithmically related. One of them is chosen as the private key, *Kpr*, and the other one is chosen as the public key, *Kpu*. The choice of which one of the two keys is public or private is arbitrary. Mathematically, we can represent this as follows:

$$EKpr(P) = C$$

Here, *P* is the plain text and *C* is the cipher text.

We can decrypt it as follows:

$$DKpu(C) = P$$

Public keys are supposed to be freely distributed and private keys are kept secret by the owner of the key pair. For instance, in AWS, key pairs are used to secure connections to virtual instances and manage encrypted resources. The public key is used by others to encrypt data or verify signatures, while the private key, securely stored by the owner, is used to decrypt data or sign digital content. By adhering to the principle of keeping the private key secret and the public key accessible, AWS users can ensure secure communication and data integrity within their cloud environment. This separation between public and private keys is a cornerstone in the security and trust mechanisms within AWS and other cloud services.

The fundamental principle is that if you encrypt with one of the keys, the only way to decrypt it is by using the other key. For example, if we encrypt the data using the public key, we will need to decrypt it using the other key—that is, the private key.

Now, let's look at one of the fundamental protocols of asymmetric encryption—the **Secure Sockets Layer (SSL)/Transport Layer Security (TLS)** handshake—which is responsible for establishing a connection between two nodes using asymmetric encryption.

The SSL/TLS handshaking algorithm

SSL was originally developed to add security to HTTP. Over time, SSL was replaced with a more efficient and more secure protocol, called TLS. TLS handshakes are the basis of how HTTP creates a secure communication session. A TLS handshake occurs between the two participating entities—the client and the server. This process is shown in the following diagram:

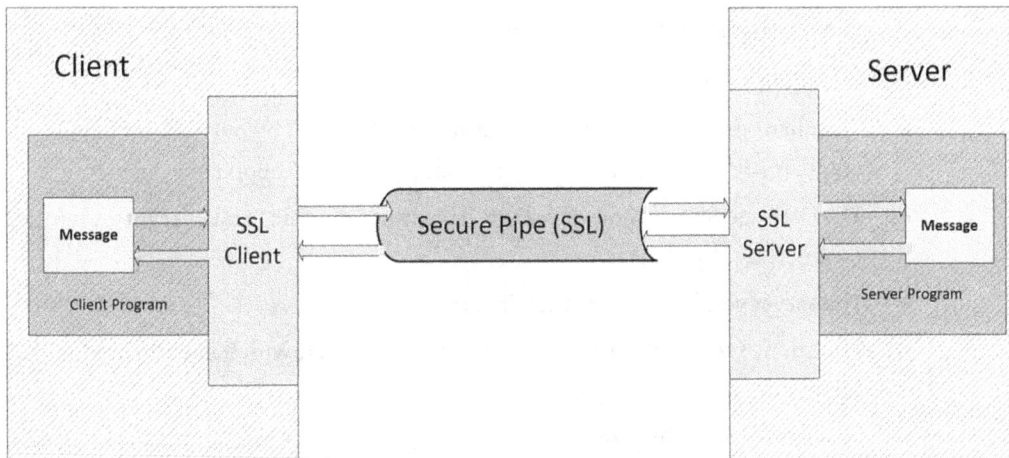

Figure 14.5: Secure session between the client and the server

A TLS handshake establishes a secure connection between the participating nodes. The following are the steps that are involved in this process:

1. The client sends a `client hello` message to the server. The message also contains the following:

   - The version of TLS that is used
   - The list of cipher suites supported by the client
   - A compression algorithm
   - A random byte string, identified by `byte_client`

2. The server sends a `server hello` message back to the client. The message also contains the following:

   - A cipher suite selected by the server from the list provided by the client.
   - A session ID.
   - A random byte string, identified by `byte_server`.
   - A server digital certificate, identified by `cert_server`, containing the public key of the server.
   - If the server requires a digital certificate for client authentication or a client certificate request, the client-server request also includes the following:

     - The distinguished names of the acceptable CAs
     - The types of certificates supported

   - The client verifies `cert_server`.
   - The client generates a random byte string, identified by `byte_client2`, and encrypts it with the public key of the server provided through `cert_server`.
   - The client generates a random byte string and identifies and encrypts it with its own private key.
   - The server verifies the client certificate.
   - The client sends a `finished` message to the server, which is encrypted with a secret key.
   - To acknowledge this from the server side, the server sends a `finished` message to the client, which is encrypted with a secret key.

- The server and client have now established a secure channel. They can now exchange messages that are symmetrically encrypted with the shared secret key. The entire methodology is shown as follows:

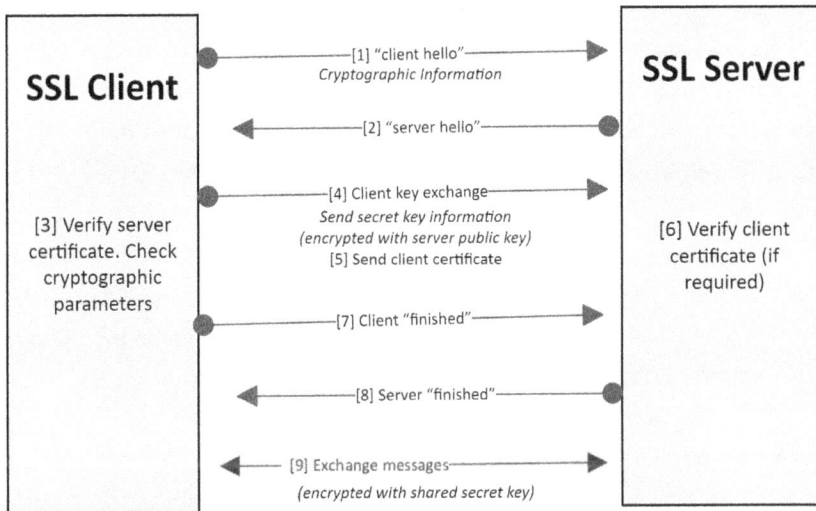

Figure 14.6: Secure session between the client and the server

Now, let's discuss how we can use asymmetric encryption to create **Public Key Infrastructure** (**PKI**), which is created to meet one or more security goals for an organization.

Public key infrastructure

Asymmetric encryption is used to implement PKI. PKI is one of the most popular and reliable ways to manage encryption keys for an organization. All the participants trust a central trusting authority called a **Certification Authority** (**CA**). CAs verify the identity of individuals and organizations and then issue them digital certificates (a digital certificate contains a copy of a person or organization's public key and its identity), verifying that the public key associated with that individual or organization actually belongs to that individual or organization.

The way it works is that the CA asks a user to prove their identity. The basic validation is called domain validation, which could involve simply verifying ownership of a domain name. The extended validation, if needed, involves a more rigorous process that involves physical proof of identity, depending on the type of digital certificate that a user is trying to obtain. If the CA is satisfied that the user is indeed who they claim to be, the user then provides the CA with their public encryption key over a secure channel.

The CA uses this information to create a digital certificate that contains information about the user's identity and their public key. This certificate is digitally signed by the CA. The certificate is a public entity as the user can then show their certificate to anyone who wants to verify their identity, without having to send it through a secure channel, as the certificate doesn't contain any sensitive information itself. The person receiving the certificate does not have to verify the user's identity directly. That person can simply verify that the certificate is valid by verifying the CA's digital signature, which validates that the public key contained in the certificate does, in fact, belong to the individual or organization named on the certificate.

> The private key of the CA of an organization is the weakest link in the PKI chain of trust. If an impersonator got hold of Microsoft's private key, for example, they could install malicious software on millions of computers around the world by impersonating a Windows update.

Blockchain and cryptography

There is no doubt that in recent years there has been a lot of excitement around blockchain and cryptocurrency. Blockchain is said to be one of the most secure technologies ever invented. The excitement about blockchain started with Bitcoin and digital currencies. Digital currencies were first developed in 1980, but with Bitcoin, they became mainstream. The rise of Bitcoin was due to the widespread availability of distributed systems. It has two important characteristics that made it a game-changer:

1. It is decentralized by design. It uses a network of miners and a distributed algorithm called blockchain.

2. Bitcoin is based on inherent incentives for miners to compete to add a block to the blockchain by attempting to answer a very complex computational puzzle. The winning miner is eligible to claim different bitcoins as a reward for their effort.

Although blockchain was developed for Bitcoin, it has found broader use and applications. Blockchain is based on a distributed consensus algorithm, using **Distributed Ledger Technology (DLT)**. It has the following characteristics:

- **Decentralization**: It is based on distributed not centralized architecture. There is no central authority. Each node in a blockchain system is involved in maintaining the integrity of the DLT. There is a consensus among all the participating nodes. In this distributed architecture, the transactions are stored on the nodes of the constituent nodes, forming a P2P network.

Note that the term "P2P" stands for "Peer-to-Peer," which means that each node, or "peer," in the network communicates directly with the others without needing to go through a central server or authority.

- **Chain-like formations**: All transactions of blockchain are accumulated in a list of blocks. When several blocks are added, it creates a chain-like formation, which is the reason for its name, blockchain.
- **Immutability**: The data is secure, replicated, and stored in immutable blocks.
- **Reliability**: A lineage or history is maintained for each transaction. Each transaction is verified and recorded using cryptographic techniques.

Under the hood, blockchain transactions use cryptographic hashes from each of the previous blocks in the chain. Hash functions are used to create a one-way fingerprint of an arbitrary chunk of data. A Merkle tree or hash tree is used to verify data stored, handled, and transferred between different participating nodes. It uses SHA-2 for hashing. A diagram of a particular transaction is shown below:

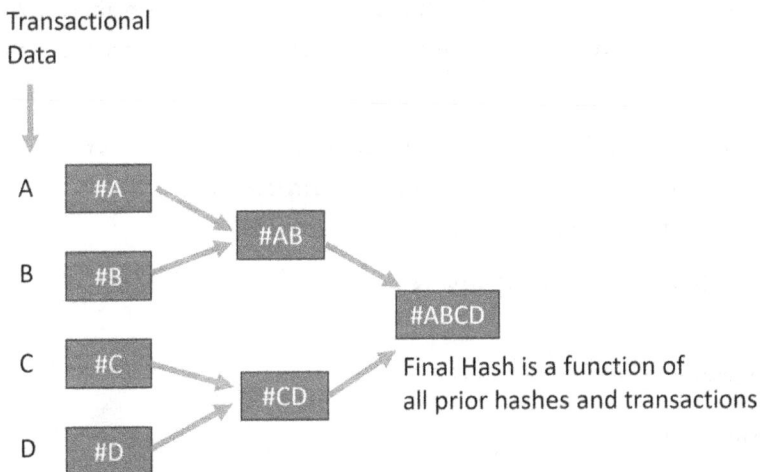

Figure 14.7: The Merkle tree of blockchain

Figure 13.7 summarizes the workings of blockchain. It shows how transactions get converted into blocks, which are, in turn, converted into chains. On the left-hand side, four transactions, A, B, C, and D, are shown. Next, the Merkle root is created by applying a hash function. The Merkle root can be considered a data structure that forms part of the block header. As transactions are immutable, the previously recorded transactions cannot be changed.

Note that the hash value of the previous block header also becomes part of the block, thus incorporating transaction records. This creates chain-like processing structures and is the reason for the name blockchain.

Each blockchain user is authenticated and authorized using cryptography, eliminating the need for third-party authentication and authorization. Digital signatures are used to secure transactions as well. The receiver of a transaction has a public key. Blockchain technology eliminates the involvement of third parties for transaction validation and relies on cryptographic proof for this. Transactions are secured using a digital signature. Each user has a unique private key that establishes their digital identity in the system.

Example: security concerns when deploying a machine learning model

In *Chapter 6, Unsupervised Machine Learning Algorithms*, we looked at the **Cross-Industry Standard Process for Data Mining** (**CRISP-DM**) life cycle, which specifies the different phases of training and deploying a machine learning model. Once a model is trained and evaluated, the final phase is deployment. If it is a critical machine learning model, then we want to make sure that all of its security goals are met.

Let's analyze the common challenges faced in deploying a model such as this and how we can address those challenges using the concepts discussed in this chapter. We will discuss strategies to protect our trained model against the following three challenges:

- **Man-in-the-Middle** (**MITM**) attacks
- Masquerading
- Data tempering

Let's look at them one by one.

MITM attacks

One of the possible attacks that we would want to protect our model against is MITM attacks. A MITM attack occurs when an intruder tries to eavesdrop on a supposedly private communication.

Let's try to understand MITM attacks sequentially using an example scenario.

Let's assume that Bob and Alice want to exchange messages using PKI:

1. Bob is using $\{Pr_{Bob}, Pu_{Bob}\}$ and Alice is using $\{Pr_{Alice}, Pu_{Alice}\}$. Bob has created a message, M_{Bob}, and Alice has created a message, M_{Alice}. They want to exchange these messages with each other in a secure way.

2. Initially, they need to exchange their public keys to establish a secure connection with each other. This means that Bob uses Pu_{Alice} to encrypt M_{Bob} before sending the message to Alice.

3. Let's assume that we have an eavesdropper, commonly referred to as Eve X, who is using $\{Pr_X, Pu_X\}$. The attacker is able to intercept the public key exchanges between Bob and Alice and replace them with its own public certificate.

4. Bob sends M_{Bob} to Alice, encrypting it with Pu_X instead of Pu_{Alice}, wrongfully thinking that this is Alice's public certificate. Eavesdropper X intercepts the communication. It intercepts the M_{Bob} message and decrypts it using Pr_{Bob}.

This MITM attack is shown in the following diagram:

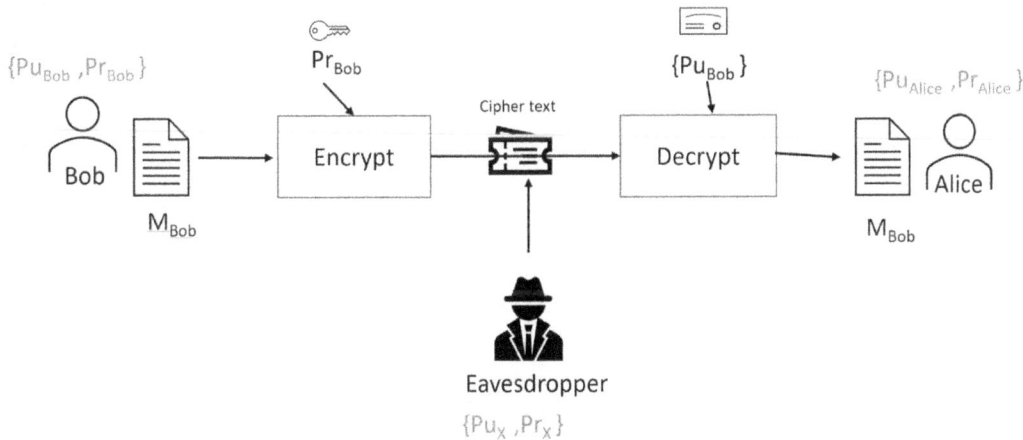

Figure 14.8: MITM attack

Now, let's look at how we can prevent MITM attacks.

How to prevent MITM attacks

Let's explore how we can prevent MITM attacks by introducing a CA to the organization. Let's say the name of this CA is myTrustCA. The digital certificate has its public key, named `PumyTrustCA`, embedded in it. myTrustCA is responsible for signing the certificates for all of the people in the organization, including Alice and Bob. This means that both Bob and Alice have their certificates signed by myTrustCA. When signing their certificates, myTrustCA verifies that they are indeed who they claim to be.

Now, with this new arrangement in place, let's revisit the sequential interaction between Bob and Alice:

1. Bob is using $\{Pr_{Bob}, Pu_{Bob}\}$ and Alice is using $\{Pr_{Alice}, Pu_{Alice}\}$. Both of their public keys are embedded into their digital certificates, signed by myTrustCA. Bob has created a message, M_{Bob}, and Alice has created a message, M_{Alice}. They want to exchange these messages with each other in a secure way.

2. They exchange their digital certificates, which contain their public keys. They will only accept the public keys if they are embedded in the certificates signed by the CA they trust. They need to exchange their public keys to establish a secure connection with each other. This means that Bob will use Pu_{Alice} to encrypt M_{Bob} before sending the message to Alice.

3. Let's assume that we have an eavesdropper, X, who is using $\{Pr_X, Pu_X\}$. The attacker is able to intercept the public key exchanges between Bob and Alice and replace them with its own public certificate, Pu_X.

4. Bob rejects X's attempt, as the bad guy's digital certificate is not signed by the CA that Bob trusts. The secure handshake is aborted, the attempted attack is logged with a timestamp and all details, and a security exception is raised.

When deploying a trained machine learning model, instead of Alice, there is a deployment server. Bob only deploys the model after establishing a secure channel, using the previously mentioned steps.

Avoiding masquerading

Attacker X pretends to be an authorized user, Bob, and gains access to sensitive data, which is the trained model, in this case. We need to protect the model against any unauthorized changes.

One way of protecting our trained model against masquerading is by encrypting the model with an authorized user's private key. Once encrypted, anyone can read and utilize the model by decrypting it through the public key of the authorized user, which is found in their digital certificate. No one can make any unauthorized changes to the model.

Data and model encryption

Once the model is deployed, the real-time unlabeled data that is provided as input to the model can also be tampered with. The trained model is used for inference and provides a label for this data. To protect data against tampering, we need to protect the data at rest and in communication. To protect the data at rest, symmetric encryption can be used to encode it.

To transfer the data, SSL-/TLS-based secure channels can be established to provide a secure tunnel. This secure tunnel can be used to transfer the symmetric key and the data can be decrypted on the server before it is provided to the trained model.

This is one of the more efficient and foolproof ways to protect data against tampering.

Symmetric encryption can also be used to encrypt a model when it has been trained, before deploying it to a server. This will prevent any unauthorized access to the model before it is deployed.

Let's see how we can encrypt a trained model at the source, using symmetric encryption with the help of the following steps, and then decrypt it at the destination before using it:

1. Let's first train a simple model using the Iris dataset:

```python
import pickle
from joblib import dump, load
from sklearn.linear_model import LogisticRegression
from sklearn.model_selection import train_test_split
from sklearn.datasets import load_iris
from cryptography.fernet import Fernet


iris = load_iris()
X = iris.data
y = iris.target
X_train, X_test, y_train, y_test = train_test_split(X, y)
model = LogisticRegression(max_iter=1000)  # Increase max_iter for
convergence
model.fit(X_train, y_train)
```

2. Now, let's define the names of the files that will store the model:

```python
filename_source = "unencrypted_model.pkl"
filename_destination = "decrypted_model.pkl"
filename_sec = "encrypted_model.pkl"
```

3. Note that `filename_source` is the file that will store the trained unencrypted model at the source. `filename_destination` is the file that will store the trained unencrypted model at the destination, and `filename_sec` is the encrypted trained model.

4. We will use `pickle` to store the trained model in a file:

```
from joblib import dump
dump(model, filename_source)
```

5. Let's define a function named `write_key()` that will generate a symmetric key and store it in a file named `key.key`:

```
def write_key():
    key = Fernet.generate_key()
    with open("key.key", "wb") as key_file:
        key_file.write(key)
```

6. Now, let's define a function named `load_key()` that can read the stored key from the `key.key` file:

```
def load_key():
    return open("key.key", "rb").read()
```

7. Next, let's define an `encrypt()` function that can encrypt and train the model, and store it in a file named `filename_sec`:

```
def encrypt(filename, key):
    f = Fernet(key)
    with open(filename,"rb") as file:
        file_data = file.read()
    encrypted_data = f.encrypt(file_data)
    with open(filename_sec,"wb") as file:
        file.write(encrypted_data)
```

8. We will use these functions to generate a symmetric key and store it in a file. Then, we will read this key and use it to store our trained model in a file named `filename_sec`:

```
write_key()
key = load_key()
encrypt(filename_source, key)
```

Now the model is encrypted. It will be transferred to the destination where it will be used for prediction:

1. First, we will define a function named decrypt() that we can use to decrypt the model from filename_sec to filename_destination using the key stored in the key.key file:

```python
def decrypt(filename, key):
    f = Fernet(key)
    with open(filename, "rb") as file:
        encrypted_data = file.read()
    decrypted_data = f.decrypt(encrypted_data)
    with open(filename_destination, "wb") as file:
        file.write(decrypted_data)
```

2. Now let's use this function to decrypt the model and store it in a file named filename_destination:

```python
decrypt(filename_sec, key)
```

3. Now let's use this unencrypted file to load the model and use it for predictions:

```python
loaded model = load(filename_destination)
result = loaded_model.score(X_test, y_test)
print(result)
```

```
0.9473684210526315
```

Note that we have used symmetric encryption to encode the model. The same technique can be used to encrypt data as well, if needed.

Summary

In this chapter, we learned about cryptographic algorithms. We started by identifying the security goals of a problem. We then discussed various cryptographic techniques and also looked at the details of the PKI. Finally, we looked at the different ways of protecting a trained machine learning model against common attacks. Now, you should be able to understand the fundamentals of security algorithms used to protect modern IT infrastructures.

In the next chapter, we will look at designing large-scale algorithms. We will study the challenges and trade-offs involved in designing and selecting large algorithms. We will also look at the use of a GPU and clusters to solve complex problems.

Learn more on Discord

To join the Discord community for this book – where you can share feedback, ask questions to the author, and learn about new releases – follow the QR code below:

`https://packt.link/WHLel`

15

Large-Scale Algorithms

Large-scale algorithms are specifically designed to tackle sizable and intricate problems. They distinguish themselves by their demand for multiple execution engines due to the sheer volume of data and processing requirements. Examples of such algorithms include **Large Language Models (LLMs)** like ChatGPT, which require distributed model training to manage the extensive computational demands inherent to deep learning. The resource-intensive nature of such complex algorithms highlights the requirement for robust, parallel processing techniques critical for training the model.

In this chapter, we will start by introducing the concept of large-scale algorithms and then proceed to discuss the efficient infrastructure required to support them. Additionally, we will explore various strategies for managing multi-resource processing. Within this chapter, we will examine the limitations of parallel processing, as outlined by Amdahl's law, and investigate the use of **Graphics Processing Units (GPUs)**. Upon completing this chapter, you will have gained a solid foundation in the fundamental strategies essential for designing large-scale algorithms.

The topics covered in this chapter include:

- Introduction to large-scale algorithms
- Efficient infrastructure for large-scale algorithms
- Strategizing multi-resource processing
- Using the power of clusters/cloud to run large-scale algorithms

Let's start with the introduction.

Introduction to large-scale algorithms

Throughout history, humans have tackled complex problems, from predicting locust swarm locations to discovering the largest prime numbers. Our curiosity and determination have led to continuous innovation in problem-solving methods. The invention of computers was a pivotal moment in this journey, giving us the ability to handle intricate algorithms and calculations. Nowadays, computers enable us to process massive datasets, execute complex computations, and simulate various scenarios with remarkable speed and accuracy.

However, as we encounter increasingly complex challenges, the resources of a single computer often prove insufficient. This is where large-scale algorithms come into play, harnessing the combined power of multiple computers working together. Large-scale algorithm design constitutes a dynamic and extensive field within computer science, focusing on creating and analyzing algorithms that efficiently utilize the computational resources of numerous machines. These large-scale algorithms allow two types of computing – distributed and parallel. In distributed computing, we divide a single task between multiple computers. They each work on a segment of the task and combine their results at the end. Think of it like assembling a car: different workers handle different parts, but together, they build the entire vehicle. Parallel computing, conversely, involves multiple processors performing multiple tasks simultaneously, similar to an assembly line where every worker does a different job at the same time.

LLMs, such as OpenAI's GPT-4, hold a crucial position in this vast domain, as they represent a form of large-scale algorithms. LLMs are designed to comprehend and generate human-like text by processing extensive amounts of data and identifying patterns within languages. However, training these models is a heavy-duty task. It involves working with billions, sometimes trillions, of data units, known as tokens. This training includes steps that need to be done one by one, like getting the data ready. There are also steps that can be done at the same time, like figuring out the changes needed across different layers of the model.

It's not an understatement to say that this is a massive job. Because of this scale, it's a common practice to train LLMs using multiple computers at once. We call these "distributed systems." These systems use several GPUs – these are the parts of computers that do the heavy lifting for creating images or processing data. It's more accurate to say that LLMs are almost always trained on many machines working together to teach a single model.

In this context, let us first characterize a well-designed large-scale algorithm, one that can fully harness the potential of modern computing infrastructure, such as cloud computing, clusters, and GPUs/TPUs.

Characterizing performant infrastructure for large-scale algorithms

To efficiently run large-scale algorithms, we want performant systems as they are designed to handle increased workloads by adding more computing resources to distribute the processing. Horizontal scaling is a key technique for achieving scalability in distributed systems, enabling the system to expand its capacity by allocating tasks to multiple resources. These resources are typically hardware (like **Central Processing Units** (**CPUs**) or GPUs) or software elements (like memory, disk space, or network bandwidth) that the system can utilize to perform tasks. For a scalable system to efficiently address computational requirements, it should exhibit elasticity and load balancing, as discussed in the following section.

Elasticity

Elasticity refers to the capacity of infrastructure to dynamically scale resources according to changing requirements. One common method of implementing this feature is autoscaling, a prevalent strategy in cloud computing platforms such as **Amazon Web Services** (**AWS**). In the context of cloud computing, a server group is a collection of virtual servers or instances that are orchestrated to work together to handle specific workloads. These server groups can be organized into clusters to provide high availability, fault tolerance, and load balancing. Each server within a group can be configured with specific resources, such as CPU, memory, and storage, to perform optimally for the intended tasks. Autoscaling allows the server group to adapt to fluctuating demands by modifying the number of nodes (virtual servers) in operation. In an elastic system, resources can be added (scaling out) to accommodate increased demand, and similarly, resources can be released (scaling in) when the demand decreases. This dynamic adjustment allows for efficient use of resources, helping to balance performance needs with cost-effectiveness.

AWS provides an autoscaling service, which integrates with other AWS services like **EC2** (**Elastic Compute Cloud**) and **ELB** (**Elastic Load Balancing**), to automatically adjust the number of server instances in the group. This ensures optimal resource allocation and consistent performance, even during periods of heavy traffic or system failures.

Characterizing a well-designed, large-scale algorithm

A well-designed, large-scale algorithm is capable of processing vast amounts of information and is designed to be adaptable, resilient, and efficient. It is resilient and adaptable to accommodate the fluctuating dynamics of a large-scale environment.

A well-designed, large-scale algorithm has the following two characteristics:

- **Parallelism**: Parallelism is a feature that lets an algorithm do several things at once. For big computing jobs, an algorithm should be able to divide tasks between many computers. This speeds up calculations because they are happening all at the same time. In the context of large-scale computing, an algorithm should be capable of splitting tasks across multiple machines, thereby expediting computations through simultaneous processing.
- **Fault tolerance**: Given the increased risk of system failures in large-scale environments due to the sheer number of components, it's essential that algorithms are built to withstand these faults. They should be able to recover from failures without substantial loss of data or inaccuracies in output.

> The three cloud computing giants, Google, Amazon, and Microsoft, provide highly elastic infrastructures. Due to the gigantic size of their shared resource pools, there are very few companies that have the potential to match the elasticity of the infrastructure of these three companies.

The performance of a large-scale algorithm is intricately linked to the quality of the underlying infrastructure. This foundation should provide adequate computational resources, extensive storage capacity, high-speed network connectivity, and reliable performance to ensure the algorithm's optimal operation. Let us characterize a suitable infrastructure for a large-scale algorithm.

Load balancing

Load balancing is an essential practice in large-scale distributed computing algorithms. By evenly managing and distributing the workload, it prevents resource overload and maintains high system performance. It plays a significant role in ensuring efficient operations, optimal resource usage, and high throughput in the realm of distributed deep learning.

Figure 15.1 illustrates this concept visually. It shows a user interacting with a load balancer, which in turn manages the load on multiple nodes. In this case, there are four nodes, **Node 1**, **Node 2**, **Node 3**, and **Node 4**. The load balancer continually monitors the state of all nodes, distributing incoming user requests between them. The decision to assign a task to a specific node depends on the node's current load and the load balancer's algorithm. By preventing any single node from being overwhelmed while others remain underutilized, the load balancer ensures optimal system performance:

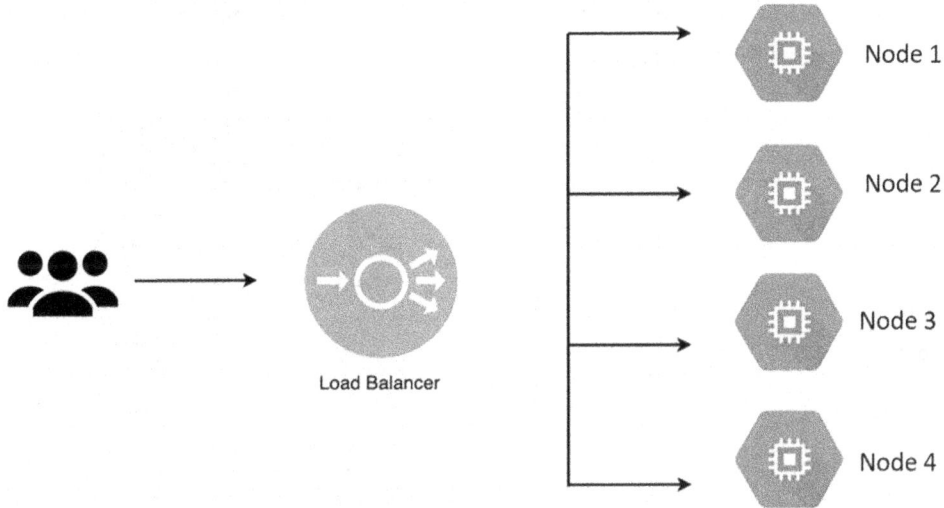

Figure 15.1: Load balancing

In the broader context of cloud computing, AWS offers a feature called **Elastic Load Balancing** (**ELB**). ELB automatically distributes incoming application traffic across multiple targets within the AWS ecosystem, such as Amazon EC2 instances, IP addresses, or Lambda functions. By doing this, ELB prevents resource overload and maintains high application availability and performance.

ELB: Combining elasticity and load balancing

ELB represents an advanced technique that combines the elements of elasticity and load balancing into a single solution. It utilizes clusters of server groups to augment the responsiveness, efficiency, and scalability of computing infrastructure. The objective is to maintain a uniform distribution of workloads across all available resources, while simultaneously enabling the infrastructure to dynamically adjust its size in response to demand fluctuations.

Figure 15.2 shows a load balancer managing four server groups. Note that a server group is a collection of nodes tasked with specific computational functions. A server group here refers to an assembly of nodes, each given a unique computational role to fulfill.

One of the key features of a server group is its elasticity – its ability to flexibly add or remove nodes depending on the situation:

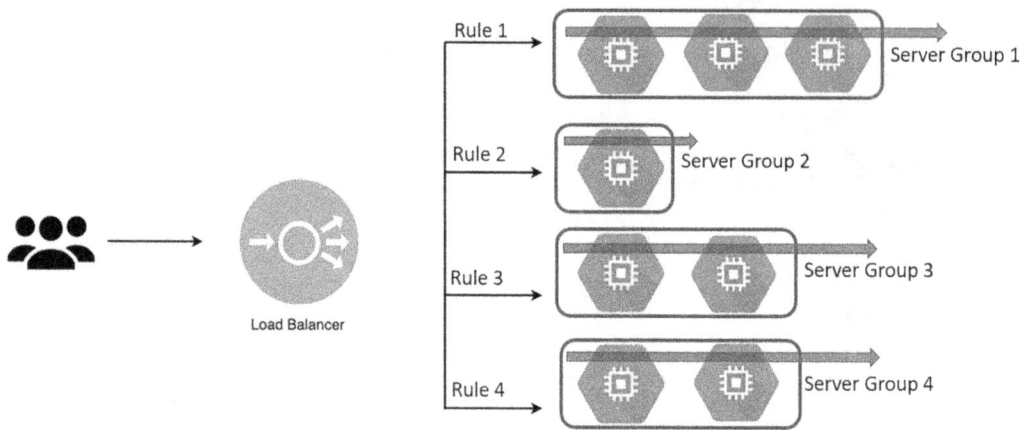

Figure 15.2: Intelligent load balancing server autoscaling

Load balancers operate by continuously monitoring workload metrics in real time. When computational tasks become increasingly complex, the requirement for processing power correspondingly increases. To address this spike in demand, the system triggers a "scale-up" operation, integrating additional nodes into the existing server groups. In this context, "scaling up" is the process of increasing the computational capacity to accommodate the expanded workload. Conversely, when the demand decreases, the infrastructure can initiate a "scale-down" operation, in which some nodes are deallocated. This dynamic reallocation of nodes across server groups ensures an optimal resource utilization ratio. By adapting resource allocation to match the prevailing workload, the system prevents resource over-provisioning or under-provisioning. This dynamic resource management strategy results in an enhancement of operational efficiency and cost-effectiveness, while maintaining high-caliber performance.

Strategizing multi-resource processing

In the early days of strategizing multi-resource processing, large-scale algorithms were executed on powerful machines called supercomputers. These monolithic machines had a shared memory space, enabling quick communication between different processors and allowing them to access common variables through the same memory. As the demand for running large-scale algorithms grew, supercomputers transformed into **Distributed Shared Memory (DSM)** systems, where each processing node owned a segment of the physical memory. Subsequently, clusters emerged, constituting loosely connected systems that depend on message passing between processing nodes.

Effectively running large-scale algorithms requires multiple execution engines operating in parallel to tackle intricate challenges. Three primary strategies can be utilized to achieve this:

- **Look within**: Exploit the existing resources on a computer by using the hundreds of cores available on a GPU to execute large-scale algorithms. For instance, a data scientist aiming to train an intricate deep learning model could harness the GPU's power to augment computing capabilities.

- **Look outside**: Implement distributed computing to access supplementary computing resources that can collaboratively address large-scale issues. Examples include cluster computing and cloud computing, which enable running complex, resource-demanding algorithms by leveraging distributed resources.

- **Hybrid strategy**: Merge distributed computing with GPU acceleration on each node to expedite algorithm execution. A scientific research organization processing vast amounts of data and conducting sophisticated simulations might adopt this approach. As illustrated in *Figure 15.3*, the computational workload is distributed across multiple nodes (**Node 1**, **Node 2**, and **Node 3**), each equipped with its own GPU. This figure effectively demonstrates the hybrid strategy, showcasing how simulations and computations are accelerated by capitalizing on the advantages of both distributed computing and GPU acceleration within each node:

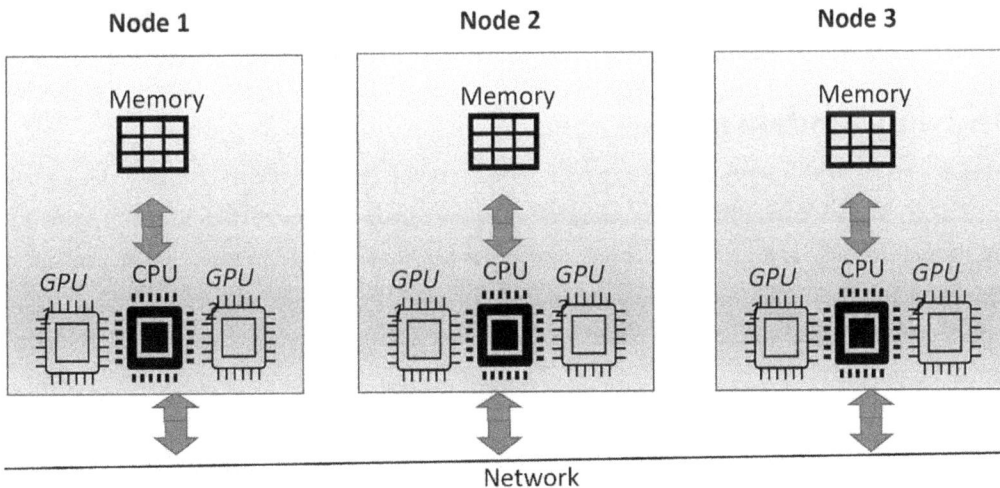

Figure 15.3: Hybrid strategy for multi-resource processing

As we explore the potential of parallel computing in running large-scale algorithms, it is equally important to understand the theoretical limitations that govern its efficiency.

In the following section, we will delve into the fundamental constraints of parallel computing, shedding light on the factors that influence its performance and the extent to which it can be optimized.

Understanding theoretical limitations of parallel computing

It is important to note that parallel algorithms are not a silver bullet. Even the best-designed parallel architectures may not give the performance that we may expect. The complexities of parallel computing, such as communication overhead and synchronization, make it challenging to achieve optimal efficiency. One law that has been developed to help navigate these complexities and better understand the potential gains and limitations of parallel algorithms is Amdahl's law.

Amdahl's law

Gene Amdahl was one of the first people to study parallel processing in the 1960s. He proposed Amdahl's law, which is still applicable today and is a basis on which to understand the various trade-offs involved when designing a parallel computing solution. Amdahl's law provides a theoretical limit on the maximum improvement in execution time that can be achieved with a parallelized version of an algorithm, given the proportion of the algorithm that can be parallelized.

It is based on the concept that in any computing process, not all processes can be executed in parallel. There will be a sequential portion of the process that cannot be parallelized.

Deriving Amdahl's law

Consider an algorithm or task that can be divided into a parallelizable fraction (f) and a serial fraction ($1 - f$). The parallelizable fraction refers to the portion of the task that can be executed simultaneously across multiple resources or processors. These tasks don't depend on each other and can be run in parallel, hence the term "parallelizable." On the other hand, the serial fraction is part of the task that cannot be divided and must be executed in sequence, one after the other, hence "serial."

Let $Tp(1)$ represent the time required to process this task on a single processor. This can be expressed as:

$$T_p(1) = N(1 - f)\tau_p + N(f)\tau_p = N\tau_p$$

In these equations, N and τp denote:

- N: The total number of tasks or iterations that the algorithm or task must perform, consistent across both single and parallel processors.

- τ_p: The time taken by a processor to complete a single unit of work, task, or iteration, which remains constant regardless of the number of processors used.

The preceding equation calculates the total time taken to process all tasks on a single processor. Now, let's examine a scenario where the task is executed on N parallel processors.

The time taken for this execution can be represented as $T_p(N)$. In the following diagram, on the X-axis, we have **Number of processors**. This represents the number of computing units or cores used to execute our program. As we move right along the X-axis, we are increasing the number of processors used. The Y-axis represents **Speedup**. This is a measure of how much faster our program runs with multiple processors compared to using just one. As we move up the Y-axis, the speed of our program increases proportionally, resulting in more efficient task execution.

The graph in *Figure 15.4* and Amdahl's law show us that more processors can improve performance, but there's a limit due to the sequential part of our code. This principle is a classic example of diminishing returns in parallel computing.

$$N = N(1 - f)\tau_p + (f)\tau_p$$

Here, the first term on the **RHS (Right Hand Side)** represents the time taken to process the serial part of the task, while the second term denotes the time taken to process the parallel part.

The speedup in this case is due to the distribution of the parallel part of the task over N processors. Amdahl's law defines the speedup $S(N)$ achieved by using N processors as:

$$S(N) = \frac{T_p(1)}{T_p(N)} = \frac{N}{N(1 - f) + (f)}$$

For significant speedup, the following condition must be satisfied:

$$1 - f << f/N \ (4.4)$$

This inequality indicates that the parallel portion (f) must be very close to unity, especially when N is large.

Now, let's look at a typical graph that explains Amdahl's law:

Amdahl's Law

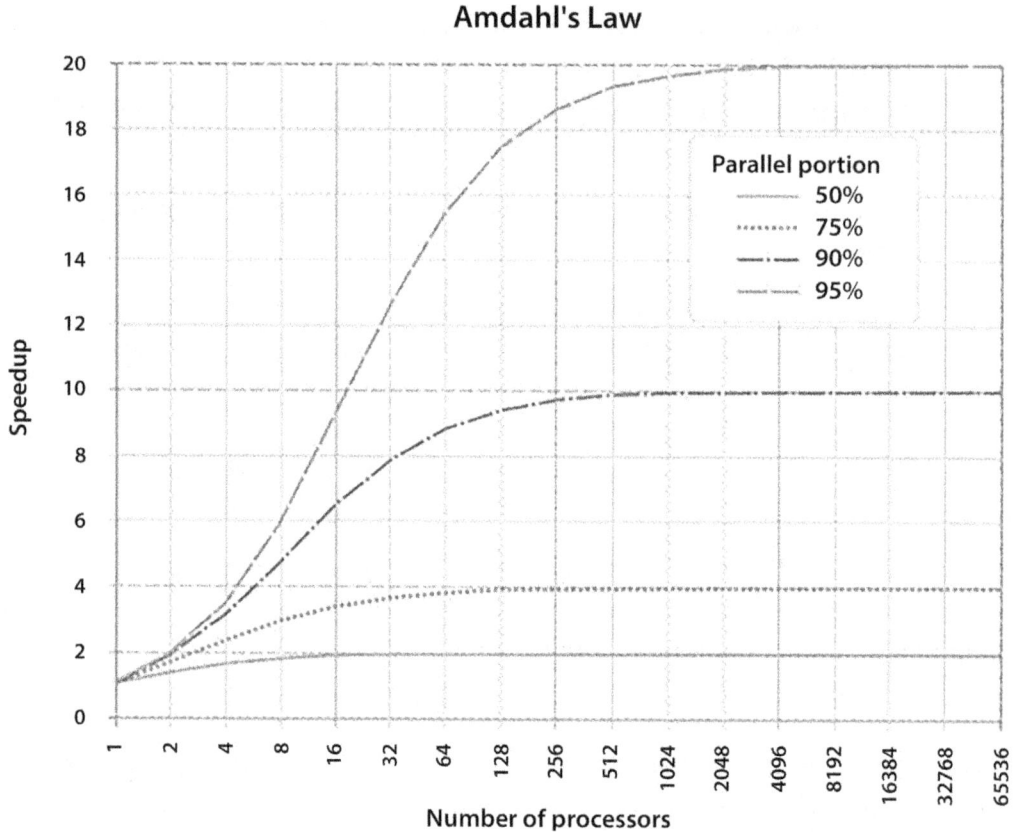

Figure 15.4: Diminishing returns in parallel processing: visualizing Amdahl's law

In *Figure 15.4*, the X-axis represents the number of processors (N), corresponding to the computing units or cores used to execute the program. As we move to the right along the X-axis, N increases. The Y-axis denotes the speedup (S), a measure of the improvement in the program's execution time T_p with multiple processors compared to using just one. Moving up the Y-axis indicates an increase in the program's execution speed.

The graph features four lines, each representing the speedup S obtained from parallel processing for different percentages of the parallelizable fraction (f): 50%, 75%, 90%, and 95%:

- 50% parallel ($f = 0.5$): This line exhibits the smallest speedup S. Although more processors (N) are added, half of the program runs sequentially, limiting the speedup to a maximum of 2.

- 75% parallel ($f = 0.75$): The speedup S is higher compared to the 50% case. However, 25% of the program still runs sequentially, constraining the overall speedup.

- 90% parallel ($f = 0.9$): In this case, a significant speedup S is observed. Nevertheless, the sequential 10% of the program imposes a limit on the speedup.

- 95% parallel ($f = 0.95$): This line demonstrates the highest speedup S. Yet, the sequential 5% still imposes an upper limit on the speedup.

The graph, in conjunction with Amdahl's law, highlights that while increasing the number of processors (N) can enhance performance, there exists an inherent limit due to the sequential part of the code ($1 - f$). This principle serves as a classic illustration of diminishing returns in parallel computing.

Amdahl's law provides valuable insights into the potential performance gains achievable in multi-processor systems and the importance of the parallelizable fraction (f) in determining the system's overall speedup. After discussing the theoretical limitations of parallel computing, it is crucial to introduce and explore another powerful and widely-used parallel processing technology: the GPU and its associated programming framework, CUDA.

CUDA: Unleashing the potential of GPU architectures in parallel computing

GPUs were originally designed for graphics processing but have since evolved, exhibiting distinct characteristics that set them apart from CPUs and resulting in an entirely different computation paradigm.

Unlike CPUs, which have a limited number of cores, GPUs are composed of thousands of cores. It's essential to recognize, however, that these cores, in isolation, are not as individually powerful as a CPU core. But, GPUs are quite efficient at executing numerous relatively simple computations in parallel.

As GPUs were originally designed for graphic processing, GPU architecture is ideal for graphic processing where multiple operations can be executed independently. For example, rendering an image involves the computation of color and brightness for each pixel in the image. These calculations are largely independent of each other and hence can be conducted simultaneously, leveraging the multi-core architecture of the GPU.

Bottom of form

This design choice allows GPUs to be extremely efficient at tasks they're designed for, like rendering graphics and processing large datasets. Here is the architecture of GPUs shown in *Figure 15.5*:

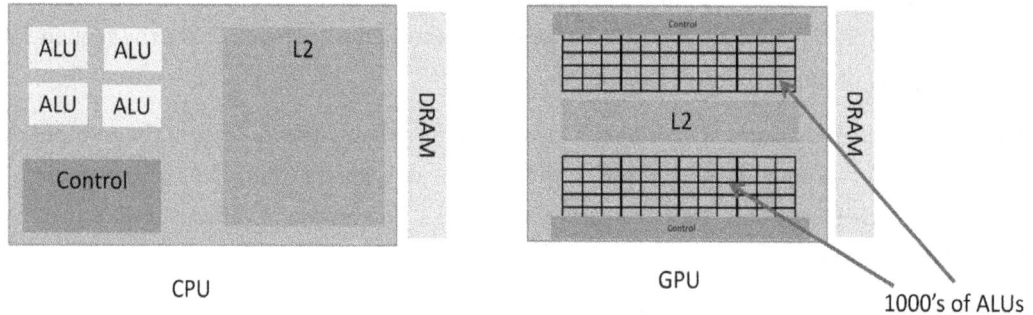

Figure 15.5: Architecture of GPUs

This unique architecture is not only beneficial for graphics processing but also significantly advantageous for other types of computational problems. Any problem that can be segmented into smaller, independent tasks can exploit this architecture for faster processing. This includes domains like scientific computing, machine learning, and even cryptocurrency mining, where massive datasets and complex computations are the norm.

Soon after GPUs became mainstream, data scientists started exploring them for their potential to efficiently perform parallel operations. As a typical GPU has thousands of **Arithmetic Logic Units (ALUs)**, it has the potential to spawn thousands of concurrent processes. Note that the ALU is the workhorse of the core that performs most of the actual computations. This large number of ALUs makes GPUs well suited to tasks where the same operation needs to be performed on many data points simultaneously, such as vector and matrix operations common in data science and machine learning. Hence, algorithms that can perform parallel computations are best suited to GPUs. For example, an object search in a video is known to be at least 20 times faster in GPUs, compared to CPUs. Graph algorithms, which were discussed in *Chapter 5*, *Graph Algorithms*, are known to run much faster on GPUs than on CPUs.

In 2007, NVIDIA developed the open-source framework called **Compute Unified Device Architecture (CUDA)** to enable data scientists to harness the power of GPUs for their algorithms. CUDA abstracts the CPU and GPU as the host and the device, respectively.

Host refers to the CPU and main memory, responsible for executing the main program and offloading data-parallel computations to the GPU.

Device refers to the GPU and its memory (VRAM), responsible for executing kernels that perform data-parallel computations.

In a typical CUDA program, the host allocates memory on the device, transfers input data, and invokes a kernel. The device performs the computation, and the results are stored back in its memory. The host then retrieves the results. This division of labor leverages the strengths of each component, with the CPU handling complex logic and the GPU managing large-scale, data-parallel computations.

CUDA runs on NVIDIA GPUs and requires OS kernel support, initially starting with Linux and later extending to Windows. The CUDA Driver API bridges the programming language API and the CUDA driver, with support for C, C++, and Python.

Parallel processing in LLMs: A case study in Amdahl's law and diminishing returns

LLMs, like ChatGPT, are intricate systems that generate text remarkably similar to human-written prose, given an initial prompt. This task involves a series of complex operations, which can be broadly divided into sequential and parallelizable tasks.

Sequential tasks are those that must occur in a specific order, one after the other. These tasks may include preprocessing steps like tokenizing, where the input text is broken down into smaller pieces, often words or phrases, which the model can understand. It may also encompass post-processing tasks like decoding, where the model's output, often in the form of token probabilities, is translated back into human-readable text. These sequential tasks are critical to the function of the model, but by nature, they cannot be split up and run concurrently.

On the other hand, parallelizable tasks are those that can be broken down and run simultaneously. A key example of this is the forward propagation stage in the model's neural network. Here, computations for each layer in the network can be performed concurrently. This operation constitutes the vast majority of the model's computation time, and it is here where the power of parallel processing can be harnessed.

Now, assume that we're working with a GPU that has 1,000 cores. In the context of language models, the parallelizable portion of the task might involve the forward propagation stage, where computations for each layer in the neural network can be performed concurrently. Let's posit that this constitutes 95% of the total computation time. The remaining 5% of the task, which could involve operations like tokenizing and decoding, is sequential and cannot be parallelized.

Applying Amdahl's law to this scenario gives us:

$$Speedup = 1 / ((1 - 0.95) + 0.95/1000) = 1 / (0.05 + 0.00095) = 19.61$$

Under ideal circumstances, this indicates that our language processing task could be completed about 19.61 times faster on a 1,000-core GPU than on a single-core CPU.

To further illustrate the diminishing returns of parallel computing, let's adjust the number of cores to 2, 50, and 100:

- For 2 cores: $Speedup = 1 / ((1 - 0.95) + 0.95/2) = 1.67$
- For 50 cores: $Speedup = 1 / ((1 - 0.95) + 0.95/50) = 14.71$
- For 100 cores: $Speedup = 1 / ((1 - 0.95) + 0.95/100) = 16.81$

As seen from our calculations, adding more cores to a parallel computing setup doesn't lead to an equivalent increase in speedup. This is a prime example of the concept of diminishing returns in parallel computing. Despite doubling the number of cores from 2 to 4, or increasing them 50-fold from 2 to 100, the speedup doesn't double or increase 50 times. Instead, the speedup hits a theoretical limit as per Amdahl's law.

The primary factor behind this diminishing return is the existence of a non-parallelizable portion in the task. In our case, operations like tokenizing and decoding form this sequential part, accounting for 5% of the total computation time. No matter how many cores we add to the system or how efficiently we can carry out the parallelizable part, this sequential portion places an upper limit on the achievable speedup. It will always be there, demanding its share of the computation time.

Amdahl's law elegantly captures this characteristic of parallel computing. It states that the maximum potential speedup using parallel processing is dictated by the non-parallelizable part of the task. The law serves as a reminder to algorithm designers and system architects that while parallelism can dramatically speed up computation, it is not an infinite resource to be tapped for speed. It underscores the importance of identifying and optimizing the sequential components of an algorithm in order to maximize the benefits of parallel processing.

This understanding is particularly important in the context of LLMs, where the sheer scale of computations makes efficient resource utilization a key concern. It underlines the need for a balanced approach that combines parallel computing strategies with efforts to optimize the performance of the sequential parts of the task.

Rethinking data locality

Traditionally, in parallel and distributed processing, the data locality principle is pivotal in deciding the optimal resource allocation. It fundamentally suggests that the movement of data should be discouraged in distributed infrastructures. Whenever possible, instead of moving data, it should be processed locally on the node where it resides; otherwise, it reduces the benefit of parallelization and horizontal scaling, where horizontal scaling is the process of increasing a system's capacity by adding more machines or nodes to distribute the workload, enabling it to handle higher amounts of traffic or data.

As networking bandwidth has improved over the years, the limitations imposed by data locality have become less significant. The increased data transfer speeds enable efficient communication between nodes in a distributed computing environment, reducing the reliance on data locality for performance optimization. The network bandwidth can be quantified by the network bisection bandwidth, which is the bandwidth between two equal parts of a network. This is important in distributed computing with resources that are physically distributed. If we draw a line somewhere between two sets of resources in a distributed network, the bisectional bandwidth is the rate of communication at which servers on one side of the line can communicate with servers on the other side, as shown in *Figure 15.6*. For distributed computing to work efficiently, this is the most important parameter to consider. If we do not have enough network bisection bandwidth, the benefits gained by the availability of multiple execution engines in distributed computing will be overshadowed by slow communication links.

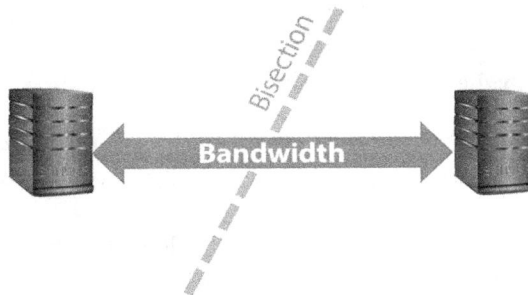

Figure 15.6: Bisection bandwidth

A high bisectional bandwidth enables us to process the data where it is without copying it. These days, major cloud computing providers offer exceptional bisection bandwidth. For example, within a Google data center, the bisection bandwidth is as high as 1 petabyte per second. Other major Cloud vendors offer similar bandwidth. In contrast, a typical enterprise network might only provide bisection bandwidth in the range of 1 to 10 gigabytes per second.

This vast difference in speed demonstrates the remarkable capabilities of modern Cloud infrastructure, making it well suited to large-scale data processing tasks.

The increased petabit bisectional bandwidth has opened up new options and design patterns for efficiently storing and processing big data. These new options include alternative methods and design patterns that have become viable due to the increased network capacity, enabling faster and more efficient data processing.

Benefiting from cluster computing using Apache Spark

Apache Spark is a widely used platform for managing and leveraging cluster computing. In this context, "cluster computing" involves grouping together several machines and making them work together as a single system to solve a problem. Spark doesn't merely implement this; it creates and controls these clusters to achieve high-speed data processing.

Within Apache Spark, data undergoes a transformation into what's known as **Resilient Distributed Datasets (RDDs)**. These are effectively the backbone of Apache Spark's data abstraction.

RDDs are immutable, meaning they can't be altered once created, and are collections of elements that can be processed in parallel. In other words, different pieces of these datasets can be worked on at the same time, thereby accelerating data processing.

When we say "fault-tolerant," we mean that RDDs have the ability to recover from potential failures or errors during execution. This makes them robust and reliable for big data processing tasks. They're split into smaller chunks known as "partitions," which are then distributed across various nodes or individual computers in the cluster. The size of these partitions can vary and is primarily determined by the nature of the task and the configuration of the Spark application.

Spark's distributed computing framework allows the tasks to be distributed across multiple nodes, which can significantly improve processing speed and efficiency.

The Spark architecture is composed of several main components, including the driver program, executor, worker node, and cluster manager.

- **Driver program:** The driver program is a key component in a Spark application, functioning much like the control center of operations. It resides in its own separate process, often located on a machine known as the driver machine. The driver program's role is like that of a conductor of an orchestra; it runs the primary Spark program and oversees the many tasks within it.

Among the main tasks of the driver program are handling and running the SparkSession. The SparkSession is crucial to the Spark application as it wraps around the SparkContext. The SparkContext is like the central nervous system of the Spark application – it's the gateway for the application to interact with the Spark computational ecosystem.

To simplify, imagine the Spark application as an office building. The driver program is like the building manager, responsible for overall operation and maintenance. Within this building, the SparkSession represents an individual office, and the SparkContext is the main entrance to that office. The essence is that these components – the driver program, SparkSession, and SparkContext – work together to coordinate tasks and manage resources within a Spark application. The SparkContext is packed with fundamental functions and context information that is pre-loaded at the start time of the application. Moreover, it carries vital details about the cluster, such as its configuration and status, which are crucial for the application to run and execute tasks effectively.

- **Cluster manager:** The driver program interacts seamlessly with the cluster manager. The cluster manager is an external service that provides and manages resources across the cluster, such as computing power and memory. The driver program and the cluster manager work hand in hand to identify available resources in the cluster, allocate them effectively, and manage their usage throughout the life cycle of the Spark application.

- **Executors:** An executor refers to a dedicated computational process that is spawned specifically for an individual Spark application running on a node within a cluster. Each of these executor processes operates on a worker node, effectively acting as the computational "muscle" behind your Spark application.

- The sharing of both memory and global parameters in this way can significantly enhance the speed and efficiency of task execution, making Spark a highly performant framework for big data processing.

- **Worker node:** A worker node, true to its name, is charged with carrying out the actual execution of tasks within the distributed Spark system.

Each worker node is capable of hosting multiple executors, which in turn can serve numerous Spark applications:

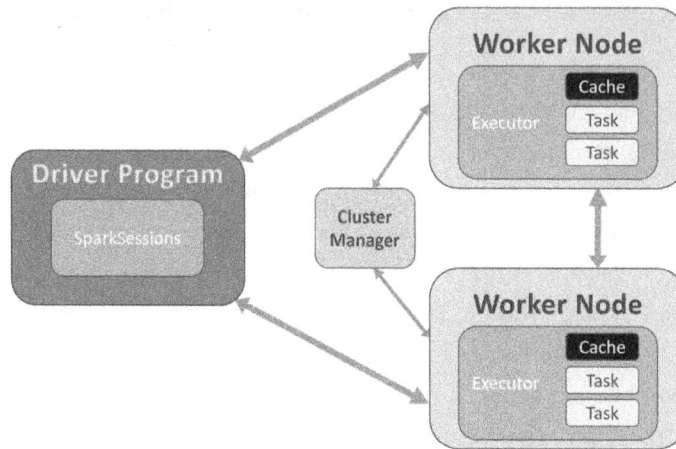

Figure 15.7: Spark's distributed architecture

How Apache Spark empowers large-scale algorithm processing

Apache Spark has emerged as a leading platform for processing and analyzing big data, thanks to its powerful distributed computing capabilities, fault-tolerant nature, and ease of use. In this section, we will explore how Apache Spark empowers large-scale algorithm processing, making it an ideal choice for complex, resource-intensive tasks.

Distributed computing

At the core of Apache Spark's architecture is the concept of data partitioning, which allows data to be divided across multiple nodes in a cluster. This feature enables parallel processing and efficient resource utilization, both of which are crucial for running large-scale algorithms. Spark's architecture comprises a driver program and multiple executor processes distributed across worker nodes. The driver program is responsible for managing and distributing tasks across the executors, while each executor runs multiple tasks concurrently in separate threads, allowing for high throughput.

In-memory processing

One of Spark's standout features is its in-memory processing capability. Unlike traditional disk-based systems, Spark can cache intermediate data in memory, significantly speeding up iterative algorithms that require multiple passes over the data.

- This in-memory processing capability is particularly beneficial for large-scale algorithms, as it minimizes the time spent on disk I/O, leading to faster computation times and more efficient use of resources.

Using large-scale algorithms in cloud computing

The rapid growth of data and the increasing complexity of machine learning models have made distributed model training an essential component of modern deep learning pipelines. Large-scale algorithms demand vast amounts of computational resources and necessitate efficient parallelism to optimize their training times. Cloud computing offers an array of services and tools that facilitate distributed model training, allowing you to harness the full potential of resource-hungry, large-scale algorithms.

Some of the key advantages of using the Cloud for distributed model training include:

- **Scalability**: The Cloud provides virtually unlimited resources, allowing you to scale your model training workloads to meet the demands of large-scale algorithms.

- **Flexibility**: The Cloud supports a wide range of machine learning frameworks and libraries, enabling you to choose the most suitable tools for your specific needs.

- **Cost-effectiveness**: With the Cloud, you can optimize your training costs by selecting the right instance types and leveraging spot instances to reduce expenses.

Example

As we delve deeper into machine learning models, especially those dealing with **Natural Language Processing (NLP)** tasks, we notice an increasing need for computational resources. For instance, transformers like GPT-3 for large-scale language modeling tasks can have billions of parameters, demanding substantial processing power and memory. Training such models on colossal datasets, such as Common Crawl, which contains billions of web pages, further escalates these requirements.

Cloud computing emerges as a potent solution here. It offers services and tools for distributed model training, enabling us to access an almost infinite pool of resources, scale our workloads, and select the most suitable machine learning frameworks. What's more, cloud computing facilitates cost optimization by providing flexible instance types and spot instances – essentially bidding for spare computing capacity. By delegating these resource-heavy tasks to the cloud, we can concentrate more on innovative work, speeding up the training process, and developing more powerful models.

Summary

In this chapter, we examined the concepts and principles of large-scale and parallel algorithm design. The pivotal role of parallel computing was analyzed, with particular emphasis on its capacity to effectively distribute computational tasks across multiple processing units. The extraordinary capabilities of GPUs were studied in detail, illustrating their utility in executing numerous threads concurrently. Moreover, we discussed distributed computing platforms, specifically Apache Spark and cloud computing environments. Their importance in facilitating the development and deployment of large-scale algorithms was underscored, providing a robust, scalable, and cost-effective infrastructure for high-performance computations.

Learn more on Discord

To join the Discord community for this book – where you can share feedback, ask questions to the author, and learn about new releases – follow the QR code below:

https://packt.link/WHLel

16

Practical Considerations

There are a bunch of algorithms presented in this book that can be used to solve real-world problems. In this chapter, we'll examine the practicality of the algorithms presented in this book. Our focus will be on their real-world applicability, potential challenges, and overarching themes, including utility and ethical implications.

This chapter is organized as follows. We will start with an introduction. Then, we will present the issues around the explainability of an algorithm, which is the degree to which the internal mechanics of an algorithm can be explained in understandable terms. Then, we will present the ethics of using an algorithm and the possibility of creating biases when implementing them. Next, the techniques for handling NP-hard problems will be discussed. Finally, we will investigate factors that should be considered before choosing an algorithm.

By the end of this chapter, you will have learned about the practical considerations that are important to keep in mind when using algorithms to solve real-world problems.

In this chapter, we will cover the following topics:

- Introducing practical considerations
- The explainability of an algorithm
- Understanding ethics and algorithms
- Reducing bias in models
- When to use algorithms

Let's start with some of the challenges facing algorithmic solutions.

Challenges facing algorithmic solutions

In addition to designing, developing, and testing an algorithm, in many cases, it is important to consider certain practical aspects of starting to rely on a machine to solve a real-world problem. For certain algorithms, we may need to consider ways to reliably incorporate new, important information that is expected to keep changing even after we have deployed our algorithm. For example, the unexpected disruption of global supply chains may negate some of the assumptions we used to train a model predicting the profit margins for a product. We need to carefully consider whether incorporating this new information will change the quality of our well-tested algorithm in any way. If so, how is our design going to handle it?

Expecting the unexpected

Most solutions to real-world problems developed using algorithms are based on some assumptions. These assumptions may unexpectedly change after the model has been deployed. Some algorithms use assumptions that may be affected by changing global geo-political situations. For example, consider a trained model that predicts the financial profit for an international company with offices all over the world. An unexpected disruptive event like a war or the spread of a sudden deadly virus may result in fundamentally changing the assumptions for this model and the quality of predictions. For such use cases, the advice is to "expect the unexpected" and strategize for surprises. For certain data-driven models, the surprise may come from changes in the regulatory policies after the solution has been deployed.

> When we are using algorithms to solve a real-world problem, we are, in a way, relying on machines for problem-solving. Even the most sophisticated algorithms are based on simplification and assumptions and cannot handle surprises. We are still not even close to fully handing over critical decision-making to algorithms we've designed ourselves.

For example, Google's recommendation engine algorithms have recently faced the European Union's regulatory restrictions due to privacy concerns. These algorithms may be some of the most advanced in their field but if banned, these algorithms may turn out to be useless as they won't be used to solve the problems they were supposed to tackle.

But, the truth of the matter is that, unfortunately, the practical considerations of an algorithm are still after-thoughts that are not usually considered at the initial design phase.

For many use cases, once an algorithm is deployed and the short-term excitement of providing the solution is over, the practical aspects and implications of using an algorithm will be discovered over time and will define the success or failure of the project.

Let's look into a practical example where not paying attention to the practical considerations failed a high-profile project designed by one of the best IT companies in the world.

Failure of Tay, the Twitter AI bot

Let's present the classical example of Tay, which was presented as the first-ever AI Twitter bot created by Microsoft in 2016. Using an AI algorithm, Tay was trained as an automated Twitter bot capable of responding to tweets about a particular topic. To achieve that, it had the capability of constructing simple messages using its existing vocabulary by sensing the context of the conversation. Once deployed, it was supposed to keep learning from real-time online conversations and by augmenting its vocabulary of the words used often in important conversations. After living in cyberspace for a couple of days, Tay started learning new words. In addition to some new words, unfortunately, Tay picked up some words from the racism and rudeness of ongoing tweets. It soon started using newly learned words to generate tweets of its own. A tiny minority of these tweets were offensive enough to raise a red flag. Although it exhibited intelligence and quickly learned how to create customized tweets based on real-time events, as designed, at the same time, it seriously offended people. Microsoft took it offline and tried to re-tool it, but that did not work. Microsoft had to eventually kill the project. That was the sad end of an ambitious project.

Note that although the intelligence built into it by Microsoft was impressive, the company ignored the practical implications of deploying a self-learning Twitter bot. The NLP and machine learning algorithms may have been best in class, but due to the obvious shortcomings, it was practically a useless project. Today, Tay has become a textbook example of a failure due to ignoring the practical implications of allowing algorithms to learn on the fly. The lessons learned by the failure of Tay definitely influenced the AI projects of later years. Data scientists also started paying more attention to the transparency of algorithms.

> To delve deeper, here's a comprehensive study on Tay: https://spectrum.ieee.
> org/in-2016-microsofts-racist-chatbot-revealed-the-dangers-of
> -online-conversation.

That brings us to the next topic, which explores the need for and ways to make algorithms transparent.

The explainability of an algorithm

First, let us differentiate between a black box and a white box algorithm:

- A black box algorithm is one whose logic is not interpretable by humans either due to its complexity or due to its logic being represented in a convoluted manner.

- A white box algorithm is one whose logic is visible and understandable to a human.

Explainability in the context of machine learning refers to our capacity to grasp and articulate the reasons behind an algorithm's specific outputs. In essence, it gauges how comprehensible an algorithm's inner workings and decision pathways are to human cognition.

Many algorithms, especially within the machine learning sphere, are often termed "black box" due to their opaque nature. For instance, consider neural networks, which we delve into in *Chapter 8, Neural Network Algorithms.* These algorithms, which underpin many deep learning applications, are quintessential examples of black box models. Their complexity and multi-layered structures make them inherently non-intuitive, rendering their inner decision-making processes enigmatic to human understanding.

However, it's crucial to note that the terms "black box" and "white box" are definitive categorizations, indicating either complete opacity or transparency, respectively. It's not a gradient or spectrum where an algorithm can be somewhat black or somewhat white. Current research is fervently aimed at rendering these black box algorithms, like neural networks, more transparent and explainable. Yet, due to their intricate architecture, they remain predominantly in the black box category.

If algorithms are used for critical decision-making, it may be important to understand the reasons behind the results generated by the algorithm. Avoiding black box algorithms and using white box ones instead also provides better insights into the inner workings of the model. The decision tree algorithm discussed in *Chapter 7, Traditional Supervised Learning Algorithms,* is an example of such white box algorithms. For example, an explainable algorithm will guide doctors as to which features were actually used to classify patients as sick or not. If the doctor has any doubts about the results, they can go back and double-check those particular features for accuracy.

Machine learning algorithms and explainability

In the realm of machine learning, the concept of explainability is paramount. But what exactly do we mean by explainability? At its core, explainability refers to the clarity with which we can understand and interpret a machine learning model's decisions.

It's about pulling back the curtain on a model's predictions and understanding the "why" behind them.

When leveraging machine learning, especially in decision-making scenarios, individuals often need to place trust in a model's output. This trust can be significantly amplified if the model's processes and decisions are transparent and justifiable. To illustrate the significance of explainability, let's consider a real-world scenario.

Let's assume that we want to use machine learning to predict the prices of houses in the Boston area based on their characteristics. Let's also assume that local city regulations will allow us to use machine learning algorithms only if we can provide detailed information for the justification of any predictions whenever needed. This information is needed for audit purposes to make sure that certain segments of the housing market are not artificially manipulated. Making our trained model explainable will provide this additional information.

Let's look into different options that are available for implementing the explainability of our trained model.

Presenting strategies for explainability

For machine learning, there are fundamentally two strategies to provide explainability to algorithms:

- **A global explainability strategy**: This is to provide the details of the formulation of a model as a whole. For example, let us consider the case of a machine learning model used to approve or refuse loans for individuals for a major bank. A global explainability strategy can be used to quantify the transparency of the decisions of this model. The global explainability strategy is not about the transparency of individual decisions but about the transparency of aggregated trends. Let us say that if there is speculation in the press about gender bias in this model, a global explainability strategy will provide the necessary information to validate or negate the speculation.

- **A local explainability strategy**: This is to provide the rationale for a single individual prediction made by our trained model. The aim is to provide transparency for each individual decision. For instance, consider our earlier example of predicting house prices in the Boston area. If a homeowner questions why their house was valued at a specific price by the model, a local explainability strategy would provide the detailed reasoning behind that specific valuation, offering clarity on the various factors and weights that contributed to the estimate.

For global explainability, we have techniques such as **Testing with Concept Activation Vectors (TCAV)**, which is used to provide explainability for image classification models. TCAV depends on calculating directional derivatives to quantify the degree of the relationship between a user-defined concept and the classification of pictures. For example, it will quantify how sensitive a prediction of classifying a person as male is to the presence of facial hair in the picture. There are other global explainability strategies, such as partial dependence plots and calculating the permutation importance, which can help explain the formulations in our trained model. Both global and local explainability strategies can either be model-specific or model-agnostic. Model-specific strategies apply to certain types of models, whereas model-agnostic strategies can be applied to a wide variety of models.

The following diagram summarizes the different strategies available for machine learning explainability:

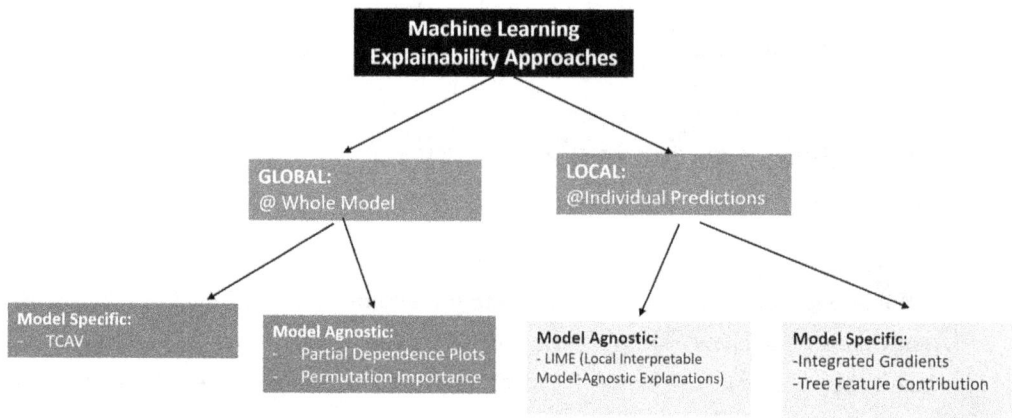

Figure 16.1: Machine learning explainability approaches

Now, let's look at how we can implement explainability using one of these strategies.

Implementing explainability

Local Interpretable Model-Agnostic Explanations (LIME) is a model-agnostic approach that can explain individual predictions made by a trained model. Being model-agnostic, it can explain the predictions of most types of trained machine learning models.

LIME explains decisions by inducing small changes to the input for each instance. It can gather the effects on the local decision boundary for that instance. It iterates over the loop to provide details for each variable. Looking at the output, we can see which variable has the most influence on that instance.

Let's see how we can use LIME to make the individual predictions of our house price model explainable:

1. If you have never used `LIME` before, you need to install the package using `pip`:

   ```
   !pip install lime
   ```

2. Then, let's import the Python packages that we need:

   ```
   import sklearn
   import requests
   import pickle
   import numpy as np
   from lime.lime_tabular import LimeTabularExplainer as ex
   ```

3. We will train a model that can predict housing prices in a particular city. For that, we will first import the dataset that is stored in the `housing.pkl` file. Then, we will explore the features it has:

   ```
   # Define the URL
   url = "https://storage.googleapis.com/neurals/data/data/housing.pkl"

   # Fetch the data from the URL
   response = requests.get(url)
   data = response.content

   # Load the data using pickle
   housing = pickle.loads(data)
   housing['feature_names']
   ```

   ```
   array(['crime_per_capita', 'zoning_prop', 'industrial_prop',
          'nitrogen oxide', 'number_of_rooms', 'old_home_prop',
          'distance_from_city_center', 'high_way_access',
          'property_tax_rate', 'pupil_teacher_ratio',
          'low_income_prop', 'lower_status_prop',
          'median_price_in_area'], dtype='<U25')
   ```

Based on these features, we need to predict the price of a home.

4. Now, let's train the model. We will be using a random forest regressor to train the model. First, we divide the data into testing and training partitions and then we use it to train the model:

```
from sklearn.ensemble import RandomForestRegressor
X_train, X_test, y_train, y_test = sklearn.model_selection.train_
test_split(housing.data, housing.target)


regressor = RandomForestRegressor()
regressor.fit(X_train, y_train)
```

```
RandomForestRegressor()
```

5. Next, let us identify the category columns:

```
cat_col = [i for i, col in enumerate(housing.data.T)
                        if np.unique(col).size < 10]
```

6. Now, let's instantiate the LIME explainer with the required configuration parameters. Note that we are specifying that our label is 'price', representing the prices of houses in Boston:

```
myexplainer = ex(X_train,
    feature_names=housing.feature_names,
    class_names=['price'],
    categorical_features=cat_col,
    mode='regression')
```

7. Let us try to look into the details of predictions. For that, first, let us import pyplot as the plotter from matplotlib:

```
exp = myexplainer.explain_instance(X_test[25], regressor.predict,
        num_features=10)


exp.as_pyplot_figure()
from matplotlib import pyplot as plt
plt.tight_layout()
```

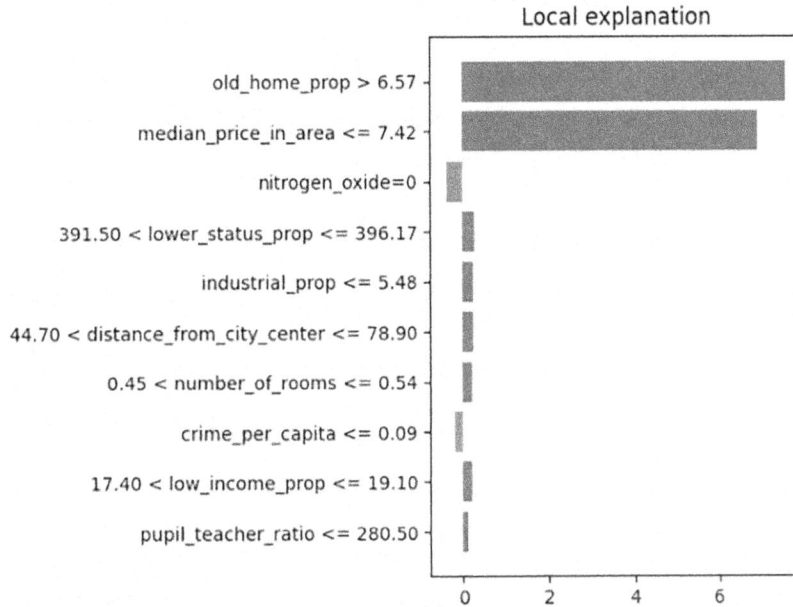

Figure 16.2: Feature-wise explanation of a Housing Price Prediction

8. As the LIME explainer works on individual predictions, we need to choose the predictions we want to analyze. We have asked the explainer for its justification of the predictions indexed as 1 and 35:

```
for i in [1, 35]:
    exp = myexplainer.explain_instance(X_test[i], regressor.predict,
            num_features=10)
exp.as_pyplot_figure()
plt.tight_layout()
```

Local explanation

old_home_prop > 6.61
median_price_in_area > 16.70
crime_per_capita > 2.87
330.00 < pupil_teacher_ratio <= 666.00
18.90 < low_income_prop <= 20.20
lower_status_prop <= 375.69
distance_from_city_center > 93.90
high_way_access <= 2.08
0.53 < number_of_rooms <= 0.62
9.69 < industrial_prop <= 18.10

Local explanation

old_home_prop <= 5.90
11.38 < median_price_in_area <= 16.70
pupil_teacher_ratio <= 277.00
nitrogen_oxide=1
17.00 < low_income_prop <= 18.90
0.08 < crime_per_capita <= 0.22
property_tax_rate=4
0.45 < number_of_rooms <= 0.53
9.69 < industrial_prop <= 18.10
3.13 < high_way_access <= 5.25

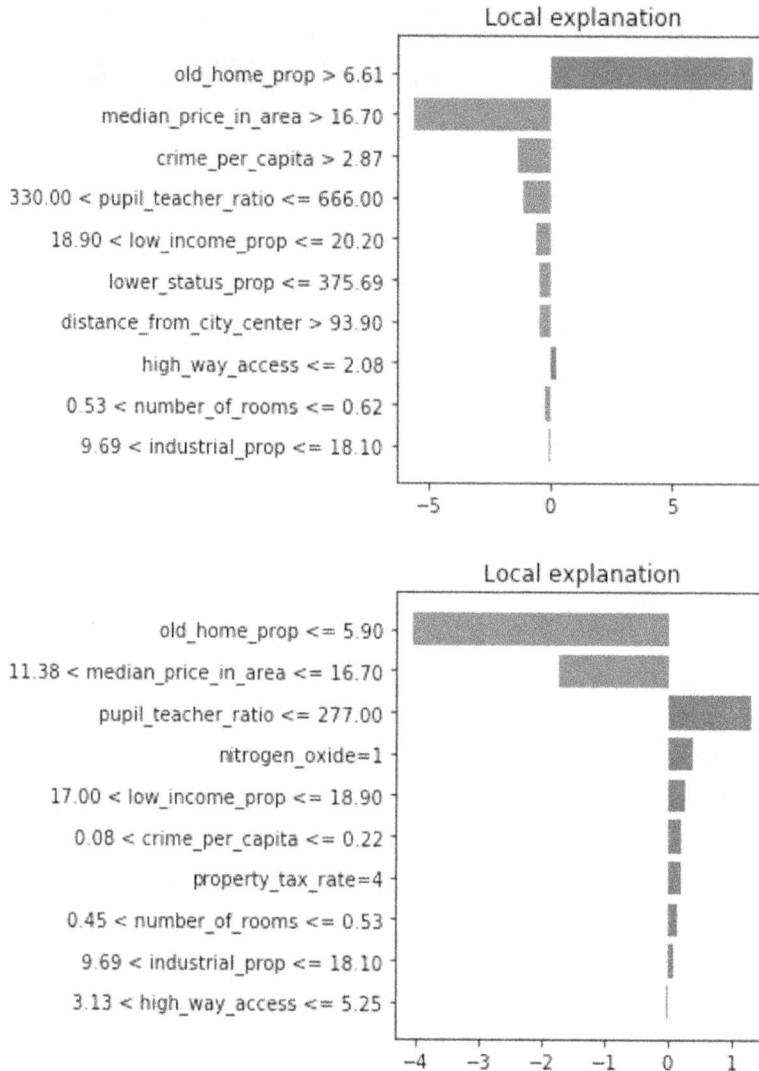

Figure 16.3: Highlighting key features: Dissecting predictions for test instances 1 and 35

Let's try to analyze the preceding explanation by LIME, which tells us the following:

- **The list of features used in the individual predictions**: They are indicated on the y-axis in the preceding screenshot.

- **The relative importance of the features in determining the decision**: The larger the bar line, the greater the importance is. The value of the number is on the x-axis.

- **The positive or negative influence of each of the input features on the label**: Red bars show a negative influence and green bars show the positive influence of a particular feature.

Understanding ethics and algorithms

Algorithmic ethics, also known as computational ethics, delves into the moral dimensions of algorithms. This crucial domain aims to ensure that machines operating on these algorithms uphold ethical standards. The development and deployment of algorithms may inadvertently foster unethical outcomes or biases. Crafting algorithms poses a challenge in anticipating their full range of ethical repercussions. When we discuss large-scale algorithms in this context, we refer to those processing vast volumes of data. However, the complexity is magnified when multiple users or designers contribute to an algorithm, introducing varied human biases. The overarching goal of algorithmic ethics is to spotlight and address concerns arising in these areas:

- **Bias and discrimination**: There are many factors that can affect the quality of the solutions created by algorithms. One of the major concerns is unintentional and algorithmic bias. The reason may be the design of the algorithm resulting in giving some data more importance than other data. Or, the reason may be in the data collection and selection of data. It may result in data points that should be computed by the algorithm being omitted, or data that shouldn't be involved being included. An example is the use of an algorithm by an insurance company to calculate risk. It may be using data about car accidents that includes the gender of drivers involved. Based on the data available, the algorithm might decide that women are involved in more crashes and therefore women drivers automatically receive higher-cost insurance quotes.

- **Privacy**: The data used by algorithms may have personal information and may be used in ways that could intrude on the privacy of individuals. For example, the algorithms that enable facial recognition are one example of the privacy issues that are caused by the use of algorithms. Currently, many cities and airports are using facial recognition systems around the world. The challenge is to use these algorithms in a way that protects individuals against any privacy breaches.

> More and more companies are making the ethical analysis of an algorithm part of its design. But the truth is that problems may not become apparent until we find a problematic use case.

Problems with learning algorithms

Algorithms capable of fine-tuning themselves according to changing data patterns are called learning algorithms. They are in learning mode in real time, but this real-time learning capability may have ethical implications. This creates the possibility that their learning could result in decisions that may have problems from an ethical point of view. As they are created to be in a continuous evolutionary phase, it is almost impossible to continuously perform an ethical analysis of them.

For example, let us study the problem that Amazon discovered in the learning algorithm they designed to hire people. Amazon started using an AI algorithm for hiring employees in 2015. Before it was deployed, it went through stringent testing to make sure that it met both functional and non-functional requirements and had no bias or any other ethical issue. As it was designed as a learning algorithm, it was constantly fine-tuning itself with new data as it became available. A couple of weeks after it was deployed, Amazon discovered that the AI algorithm had surprisingly developed a gender bias. Amazon took the algorithm offline and investigated. It was found that gender bias was introduced due to some specific patterns in the new data. Specifically, in recent data, there were far more men than women. And the men in the recent data happened to have a more relevant background for the job posted. The real-time fine-tuning learning had some unintentional consequences and resulted in the algorithm starting to favor men over women, thus introducing bias. The algorithm started using gender as one of the deciding factors for hiring. The model was re-trained and necessary safety guardrails were added to make sure that gender bias was not re-introduced.

> As the complexity of algorithms grows, it is becoming more and more difficult to fully understand their long-term implications for individuals and groups within society.

Understanding ethical considerations

Algorithmic solutions are mathematical formulations. It is the responsibility of the people responsible for developing algorithms to ensure that they conform to ethical sensitivities around the problem we are trying to solve. Once the solutions are deployed, they may need to be periodically monitored to make sure that they do not start creating ethical issues as new data becomes available and underlying assumptions shift.

These ethical considerations of algorithms depend on the type of the algorithm. For example, let's look into the following algorithms and their ethical considerations. Some examples of powerful algorithms for which careful ethical considerations are needed are as follows:

- Both classification and regression algorithms serve distinct purposes in machine learning. Classification algorithms categorize data into predefined classes and can be directly instrumental in decision-making processes. For instance, they might determine visa approvals or identify specific demographics in a city. On the other hand, regression algorithms predict numerical values based on input data, and these predictions can indeed be utilized in decision-making. For example, a regression model might predict the optimal price for listing a house on the market. In essence, while classification offers categorical outcomes, regression provides quantitative predictions; both are valuable for informed decision-making in varied scenarios.

- Algorithms, when used in recommendation engines, can match resumes to job seekers, both for individuals and groups. For such use cases, the algorithms should implement the explainability at both a local and global level. Local-level explainability will provide traceability for a particular individual resume when matched to available jobs. Global-level explainability will provide transparency of the overall logic being used to match resumes to jobs.

- Data mining algorithms can be used to mine information about individuals from various data sources that may be used by governments for decision-making. For example, the Chicago police department uses data mining algorithms to identify criminal hotspots and high-risk individuals in the city. Making sure these data mining algorithms are designed and used in a way that satisfies all requirements related to ethics is done through careful design and constant monitoring.

Hence, the ethical consideration of algorithms will depend on the particular use case they are used in and the entities they directly or indirectly affect. Careful analysis is needed from an ethical point of view before starting to use an algorithm for critical decision-making. These ethical considerations should be part of the design process.

Factors affecting algorithmic solutions

The following are the factors that we should keep in mind while performing an analysis of how good algorithmic solutions are.

Considering inconclusive evidence

In machine learning, the quality and breadth of your dataset play crucial roles in the accuracy and reliability of your model's outcomes. Often, data might appear limited or may lack the comprehensive depth required to provide a conclusive result.

For instance, let's consider clinical trials: if a new drug is tested on a small group of people, the results might not comprehensively reflect its efficacy. Similarly, if we examine patterns of fraud in a particular postal code of a city, limited data might suggest a trend that isn't necessarily accurate on a broader scale.

It's essential to differentiate between "limited data" and "inconclusive evidence." While most datasets are inherently limited (no dataset can capture every single possibility), the term 'inconclusive evidence' refers to data that doesn't provide a clear or definitive trend or outcome. This distinction is vital as basing decisions on inconclusive patterns could lead to errors in judgment. Always approach decision-making with a critical eye, especially when working with algorithms trained on such data.

> Decisions that are based on inconclusive evidence are prone to lead to unjustified actions.

Traceability

Machine learning algorithms typically have separate development and production environments. This can potentially create a disconnection between the training phase and the inference phase. It means that if there is some harm caused by an algorithm, it is very hard to trace and debug. Also, when a problem is found in an algorithm, it is difficult to actually determine the people who were affected by it.

Misguided evidence

Algorithms are data-driven formulations. The **Garbage-in, Garbage-out (GIGO)** principle means that results from algorithms can only be as reliable as the data on which they are based. If there are biases in the data, they will be reflected in the algorithms as well.

Unfair outcomes

The use of algorithms may result in harming vulnerable communities and groups that are already at a disadvantage.

Additionally, the use of algorithms to distribute research funding has been proven on more than one occasion to be biased toward the male population. Algorithms used for granting immigration are sometimes unintentionally biased toward vulnerable population groups.

Despite using high-quality data and complex mathematical formulations, if the result is an unfair outcome, the whole effort may bring more harm than benefit.

Let us look into how we can reduce the bias in models.

Reducing bias in models

As we have discussed, the bias in a model is about certain attributes of a particular algorithm that cause it to create unfair outcomes. In the current world, there are known, well-documented general biases based on gender, race, and sexual orientation. It means that the data we collect is expected to exhibit those biases unless we are dealing with an environment where an effort has been made to remove them before collecting the data.

Most of the time, bias in algorithms is directly or indirectly introduced by humans. Humans introduce bias either unintentionally through negligence or intentionally through subjectivity. One of the reasons for human bias is the fact that the human brain is vulnerable to cognitive bias, which reflects a person's own subjectivity, beliefs, and ideology in both the data process and logic creation process of an algorithm. Human bias can be reflected either in data used by the algorithm or in the formulation of the algorithm itself. For a typical machine learning project following the **CRISP-DM** (short for **Cross-Industry Standard Process**) lifecycle, which was explained in *Chapter 5, Graph Algorithms*, the bias looks like the following:

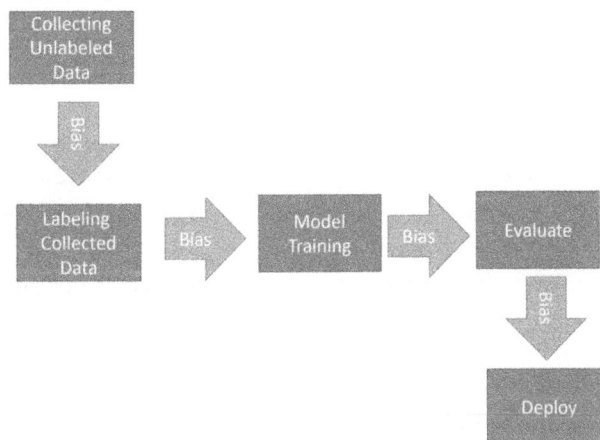

Figure 16.4: Bias can be introduced in different phases of the CRISP-DM lifecycle

The trickiest part of reducing bias is to first identify and locate unconscious bias.

Let us look into when to use algorithms.

When to use algorithms

Algorithms are like tools in a practitioner's toolbox. First, we need to understand which tool is the best one to use under the given circumstances. Sometimes, we need to ask ourselves whether we even have a solution for the problem we are trying to solve and when the right time to deploy our solution is. We need to determine whether the use of an algorithm can provide a solution to a real problem that is actually useful, rather than the alternative. We need to analyze the effect of using the algorithm in terms of three aspects:

- **Cost:** Can use justify the cost related to the effort of implementing the algorithm?
- **Time:** Does our solution make the overall process more efficient than simpler alternatives?
- **Accuracy:** Does our solution produce more accurate results than simpler alternatives?

To choose the right algorithm, we need to find the answers to the following questions:

- Can we simplify the problem by making assumptions?
- How will we evaluate our algorithm?
- What are the key metrics?
- How will it be deployed and used?
- Does it need to be explainable?
- Do we understand the three important non-functional requirements—security, performance, and availability?
- Is there any expected deadline?

Upon selecting an algorithm based on the above-mentioned criteria, it's worth considering that while most events or challenges can be anticipated and addressed, there are exceptions that defy our traditional understanding and predictive capabilities. Let us look into this in more detail.

Understanding black swan events and their implications on algorithms

In the realm of data science and algorithmic solutions, certain unpredictable and rare events can present unique challenges. Coined by Nassim Taleb in "Fooled by Randomness" (2001), the term "black swan event" metaphorically represents such rare and unpredictable occurrences.

To qualify as a black swan event, it must satisfy the following criteria:

- **Unexpectedness**: The event surprises most observers, like the atomic bomb drop on Hiroshima.
- **Magnitude**: The event is disruptive and significant, akin to the Spanish flu outbreak.
- **Post-event predictability**: After the event, it becomes apparent that if clues had been noted, the event could've been anticipated, like overlooked signs before the Spanish flu became a pandemic.
- **Not a surprise to all**: Some individuals might've anticipated the event, as the scientists involved in the Manhattan Project did with the atomic bomb.

> Before black swans were first discovered in the wild, for centuries, they were used to represent something that could not happen. After their discovery, the term remained popular but there was a change in what it represented. It now represents something so rare that it cannot be predicted.

Challenges and opportunities for algorithms with black swan events:

- **Forecasting dilemmas**: While there are numerous forecasting algorithms, from ARIMA to deep learning methodologies, predicting a black swan event remains elusive. Using standard techniques might provide a false sense of security. Predicting the exact timing of another event, like COVID-19, for example, is fraught with challenges due to insufficient historical data.
- **Predicting implications**: Once a black swan event occurs, foreseeing its broad societal impacts is complex. We may lack both the relevant data for the algorithms and an understanding of societal interrelations affected by the event.
- **Predictive potential**: While black swan events appear random, they result from overlooked complex precursors. Herein lies an opportunity for algorithms: devising strategies to predict and detect these precursors might help anticipate a potential black swan event.

The relevance of a practical application:

Let's consider the recent COVID-19 pandemic, a prime black swan event. A potential practical application might involve leveraging data on prior pandemics, global travel patterns, and local health metrics. An algorithm could then monitor for unusual spikes in illness or other potential early indicators, signaling a potential global health threat. However, the uniqueness of black swan events makes this challenging.

Summary

In this chapter, we learned about the practical aspects that should be considered while designing algorithms. We looked into the concept of algorithmic explainability and the various ways we can provide it at different levels. We also looked into the potential ethical issues in algorithms. Finally, we described which factors to consider while choosing an algorithm.

Algorithms are engines in the new automated world that we are witnessing today. It is important to learn about, experiment with, and understand the implications of using algorithms. Understanding their strengths and limitations and the ethical implications of using algorithms will go a long way in making this world a better place to live in, and this book is an effort to achieve this important goal in this ever-changing and evolving world.

Learn more on Discord

To join the Discord community for this book – where you can share feedback, ask questions to the author, and learn about new releases – follow the QR code below:

```
https://packt.link/WHLel
```

‹packt›

packt.com

Subscribe to our online digital library for full access to over 7,000 books and videos, as well as industry leading tools to help you plan your personal development and advance your career. For more information, please visit our website.

Why subscribe?

- Spend less time learning and more time coding with practical eBooks and Videos from over 4,000 industry professionals
- Improve your learning with Skill Plans built especially for you
- Get a free eBook or video every month
- Fully searchable for easy access to vital information
- Copy and paste, print, and bookmark content

At www.packt.com, you can also read a collection of free technical articles, sign up for a range of free newsletters, and receive exclusive discounts and offers on Packt books and eBooks.

Other Books You May Enjoy

If you enjoyed this book, you may be interested in these other books by Packt:

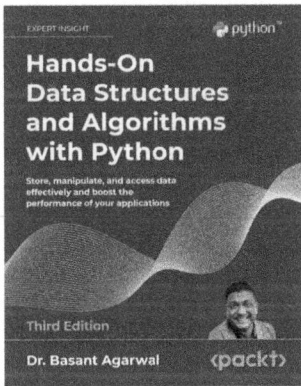

Hands-On Data Structures and Algorithms with Python – Third Edition

Dr. Basant Agarwal

ISBN: 9781801073448

- Understand common data structures and algorithms using examples, diagrams, and exercises
- Explore how more complex structures, such as priority queues and heaps, can benefit your code
- Implement searching, sorting, and selection algorithms on number and string sequences
- Become confident with key string-matching algorithms

- Understand algorithmic paradigms and apply dynamic programming techniques
- Use asymptotic notation to analyze algorithm performance with regard to time and space complexities
- Write powerful, robust code using the latest features of Python

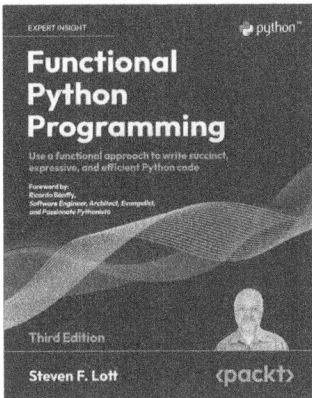

Functional Python Programming – Third Edition

Steven F. Lott

ISBN: 9781803232577

- Use Python's libraries to avoid the complexities of state-changing classes
- Leverage built-in higher-order functions to avoid rewriting common algorithms
- Write generator functions to create lazy processing
- Design and implement decorators for functional composition
- Make use of Python type annotations to describe parameters and results of functions
- Apply functional programming to concurrency and web services
- Explore the PyMonad library for stateful simulations

Packt is searching for authors like you

If you're interested in becoming an author for Packt, please visit authors.packtpub.com and apply today. We have worked with thousands of developers and tech professionals, just like you, to help them share their insight with the global tech community. You can make a general application, apply for a specific hot topic that we are recruiting an author for, or submit your own idea.

Share your thoughts

Now you've finished *50 Algorithms Every Programmer Should Know - Second Edition*, we'd love to hear your thoughts! Scan the QR code below to go straight to the Amazon review page for this book and share your feedback or leave a review on the site that you purchased it from.

https://packt.link/r/1803247762

Your review is important to us and the tech community and will help us make sure we're delivering excellent quality content.

Index

D

Download a free PDF copy of this book

Thanks for purchasing this book!

Do you like to read on the go but are unable to carry your print books everywhere? Is your eBook purchase not compatible with the device of your choice?

Don't worry, now with every Packt book you get a DRM-free PDF version of that book at no cost.

Read anywhere, any place, on any device. Search, copy, and paste code from your favorite technical books directly into your application.

The perks don't stop there, you can get exclusive access to discounts, newsletters, and great free content in your inbox daily

Follow these simple steps to get the benefits:

1. Scan the QR code or visit the link below

https://packt.link/free-ebook/9781803247762

2. Submit your proof of purchase
3. That's it! We'll send your free PDF and other benefits to your email directly